I Belonged to the 116th

A Narrative of the 116th Ohio Volunteer
Infantry during the Civil War

Gerald L. Earley

HERITAGE BOOKS
2007

HERITAGE BOOKS
AN IMPRINT OF HERITAGE BOOKS, INC.

Books, CDs, and more—Worldwide

For our listing of thousands of titles see our website
at
www.HeritageBooks.com

Published 2007 by
HERITAGE BOOKS, INC.
Publishing Division
65 East Main Street
Westminster, Maryland 21157-5026

Copyright © 2004 Gerald L. Earley

All rights reserved. No part of this book may be reproduced or transmitted in any form or by any means, electronic or mechanical, including photocopying, recording or by any information storage and retrieval system without written permission from the author, except for the inclusion of brief quotations in a review.

International Standard Book Number: 978-0-7884-2529-5

CONTENTS

Preface	v
Chapter 1 The Last True Volunteers	1
Chapter 2 Camp Putnam	5
Chapter 3 "All Agreed To Be Good Boys"	13
Chapter 4 Rumble With Grumble	21
Chapter 5 "I'll Parole Every Devil Of You!"	30
Chapter 6 Milroy's Weary Boys	39
Chapter 7 "I Would Rather Be With My Regiment"	57
Chapter 8 To Fight "Mit Sigel"	65
Chapter 9 "They Stood The Terrible Test Magnificently"	75
Chapter 10 "Black Dave's" Folly	94
Chapter 11 Somebody Else's War	109
Chapter 12 "Old Jube's" Revenge	120
Chapter 13 "Tell Colonel Wildes To Come On!"	140
Chapter 14 "Uncle George's" Splendid Day	150
Chapter 15 A Triumph Of Moral Courage	157
Chapter 16 "A Sharp Little Fight With The Johnneys"	162
Chapter 17 One Of Only Two	170
Chapter 18 Answering Grant's Call	186
Chapter 19 "A Most Murderous Fire"	195
Chapter 20 "In At The Death"	211
Epilogue	222
Appendix	228
Notes	233
Bibliography	255
Index	260

PREFACE

Anyone who has visited an old cemetery anywhere across the United States has seen them: the white granite or marble upright government headstones scattered about the cemetery grounds. Most people know that these headstones mark the graves our nation's veterans. Before World War II, depending upon the type of headstone used, the veteran's name, rank, and military organization or unit was usually inscribed. Since World War II the headstones list the veteran's name, rank, branch of service and war in which he or she served. Clearly the unit in which the veteran served was more important then than now. To the Civil War veteran the mention of his regiment was an evocation of his service record and his war experience. The state and regimental number on a Civil War veteran's headstone allows him, in effect, to speak from the grave, as each number refers to a community of men with their own unique and colorful saga.

This book is the story of the veterans with the stones inscribed 116th Ohio, one of the many hundreds of Federal regiments that served in the Civil War. Today there is an emphasis on social history, more particularly the heretofore-neglected topics, and less interest in traditional Civil War literature. Furthermore, there are a number of good regimental studies and histories presently available. Among these modern unit histories are *The Twentieth Maine*, *The Iron Brigade* and *Mother May You Never See the Sights I Have Seen*. These are excellent, informative books. So why a book about another Civil War regiment? The aforementioned books and others like them do not address the native born soldiers of the lower Midwest who fought for the Union—men with values associated with the North as well as the South.

It was not a mere coincidence that the 116th Ohio was recruited over one year into the Civil War. The population of the counties along the Ohio River in Southern Ohio consisted to a large extent of families with roots and relatives in the South. River related commerce and trade with adjoining slave states was important in these counties. The initial hesitancy to enlist was overcome by the rising threat of Southern invasion by the summer of 1862, but almost immediately after the men put on the Federal uniform, a wave of disaffection swept the region. The subordination of personal perceptions and opinions for the good of the country led this regiment to serve with distinction in the Civil War.

The 116th Ohio was recruited almost exclusively from native-born Ohioans. There was only a scattering of immigrants who served in the 116th, mostly from Germany and Switzerland. For example, of the forty-two men from Company F who transferred to the 62nd Ohio in June 1865 only one soldier was foreign born and only three were born in states other than Ohio. A good many of the soldiers in the 116th were Americans with ties to this continent predating the Revolution. The bulk of the regiment was recruited in Monroe County, Ohio, a Democratic county with a Democratic newspaper—critical of the war. These men chose to fight for an administration not necessarily popular in their own neighborhood. The composition of the 116th Ohio differs markedly from the regiments chronicled in the familiar regimental histories, yet the men from the 116th were representative of a significant portion of the men who served in blue.

The attitudes and perceptions of the men from the 116th came filtering through the pages of their accounts of the war. Their perceptions were intentionally incorporated in this version of their story. To the veterans the rebels were truly admirable for their valor, commitment, determination and fighting ability. Yet they were also traitors who fought for an odious and unjust cause. James Dalzell, a veteran of the 116th, summed up his view of those who served the Confederacy in an address years after the war. "Every rebel was wrong," he asserted. "Every pulsation of the fiendish, dastardly, cowardly, traitorous heart of Jeff. Davis, from beginning to end, was wrong, and it is wrong to-night."[1]

In order to preserve the original structure and substance of all sources, all quotations are verbatim with no attempt to correct spelling or grammar and no interpolation of *sic* anywhere in the text. Occasionally a parenthetical word or phrase is inserted in quotations but only for clarity. Some of the quotations had words deleted by the source. Others used objectionable terms and phrases, but all are used verbatim to present the story of the 116th from the perspective of the veterans themselves without interference.

Thomas F. Wildes quoted Civil War veteran and Supreme Court Justice Oliver Wendell Holmes in the preface of his book about the 116th: "I would not give a fig for a man, every one of whose geese is not better than any other man's swans."[2] Wildes had to admit that his partiality might have slightly colored his version of events. Sometimes Wildes' account of the 116th made his comrade's deeds sound as if they were on par with King David's mighty men. However, his record of the 116th bears up well under scrutiny, and it served no purpose for Wildes to mention the malingerers and bummers from his regiment. The same is true of this version of their story.

I would like to acknowledge the contributions of the following helpful and generous people and thank them for helping make this book possible:

My wife Myrna and daughters Maria and Lenora endured long trips to Virginia battlefields so that I could research and examine the places where the 116th fought. The long waits while I searched in distant libraries were accepted without complaint, and only encouragement was spoken by Myrna during the many hours spent filling the pages of this book. Maria also assisted with photograph and data entry tasks.

Gavin Thomas of the Wichita Public Library was most efficient in finding otherwise unavailable books etc.; he supplied me with much of the source material for this book.

The staff of Wilson's Creek National Battlefield provided me with an excellent list of resource material very valuable for the research and writing of this book.

Mark D. Okey provided a helpful list of resources and photographs of officers and men who belonged to the 116th.

Chris Calkins of Petersburg National Battlefield was very helpful in providing maps and troop movement information for the Battles of Fort Gregg, Rice's Station and Appomattox. He also reviewed the chapters relating to the Petersburg and Appomattox Campaigns.

Mary V. De Salvo provided me with copies of letters from her relatives who served in the Civil War and in the 116th Ohio. She also provided detailed information about Benjamin and Bazil Dye of Company A.

The staff of the Monroe County Historical Society courteously answered requests for materials regarding the 116th and suggested others who could provide helpful information.

Bill Kelble of the Cedar Creek Battlefield Center helped me locate positions where the 116th fought during the Battle of Cedar Creek. He answered numerous questions about the battle and its vicinity. He also offered suggestions for and reviewed the chapters pertaining to Cedar Creek and Stickley's Farm.

Karen Romick of the Monroe County Genealogy Society answered questions about the history of that county and provided a list of participants in the Underground Railroad operation at Stafford, Ohio. She also arranged to mention my interest in the 116th in a newsletter. As a result several people sent information about their relatives who served in the 116th.

Doug Miller has accumulated an extensive list of Civil War veterans buried in several states. He provided me with a list of burial sites, in the Midwest, of men who served in the 116th.

The staff of the Ohio Historical Society answered questions about documents from and about the 116th and provided rare and valuable resources for this book including a representation of the regimental flag.

Karl Angelo Lamberte provided computer graphics and other useful computer related assistance.

THE LAST TRUE VOLUNTEERS
1

In July of 1862, the United States was in its second year of brutal and fratricidal civil war. The Federal Government, whose avowed reason for waging war was restoration of the Union, was experiencing far greater obstacles than expected. Although the U.S. Navy under Admiral David Farragut had captured New Orleans in April, the Rebels still held sway over the Mississippi River with citadels at Vicksburg, Mississippi, and Port Hudson, Louisiana, capable of destroying any commercial shipping bound for New Orleans. With the Mississippi River blocked, the Ohio River could no longer serve as a conduit for exporting grain and farm goods from the Midwest and Ohio Valley. Also in the Western Theater, Rebel General Braxton Bragg launched an invasion of Kentucky hoping to bring Kentucky into the Confederacy. The situation in the Eastern Theater had also dramatically worsened for the Federal Government. General George B. McClellan's Peninsular Campaign intended to capture Richmond, Virginia, had ended in a repulse after a bloody series of battles. McClellan had retreated to Harrison's Landing, a supply base on the James River east of Richmond. The Rebel army near Richmond under General Robert E. Lee then marched north and routed the Federal army again at the Second Battle of Bull Run on August 30, 1862. By September Lee was ready to invade Maryland and points north with a view of gaining foreign support for the rebel cause.

President Abraham Lincoln and the government had issued calls for troops in 1861 that had raised over 700,000 men for service, 657,868 of them for three years.[1] By the following summer, battle, disease and disability had reduced the army substantially. More men were required immediately or the war to save the Union would be lost. Accordingly, the Federal Government issued a call for 300,000 more men for three years service on July 2, 1862.

The Federal Government assigned quotas to the Northern states to facilitate an equitable burden based on each state's ability to provide men. Ohio's quota was 36,858 men.[2] Ohio raised thirty-eight infantry regiments and other cavalry and artillery units for a total of 58,325 men between July and October 1862, thus exceeding the government's quota.[3] The 116th Ohio Volunteer Infantry was recruited during this period of the nation's greatest need.

On July 9, 1862, Ohio's governor called upon the district including the southeast corner of the state to provide two full regiments for the state's quota.[4] Monroe County, for instance, was to provide seven companies, or over 700 men for the quota.[5] The first regiment from the district, the 92nd Ohio Infantry, was filled two weeks after recruiting began. Monroe County provided two companies for the 92nd. With five companies yet to be furnished, officials went to work to help raise the 116th. Monroe County exhibited the greatest enthusiasm for recruiting of any county in the district. Democratic Congressman James R. Morris was prominent in the work in Monroe County; and he with William Okey, Jacob Mitchell, S. L. Mooney, J. B. Noll, William Read and others stormed the county to gather recruits. Within three weeks Monroe's five required companies were filled for the 116th Ohio Infantry. The congressman's brother, also from Monroe County, joined the regiment.

Remarkable unanimity was exhibited in Southeast Ohio during this call for men, perhaps never seen before or after. Community leaders from both the Democratic and Republican parties worked as one to fill the state's quota. In Athens County for instance, two prominent and wealthy Democrats, John Frame and Elmer Armstrong, worked relentlessly day and night to find men for the quota. Elmer Armstrong later accepted an appointment as regimental sutler. Each of these men did much for the welfare of the regiment throughout its term of service.

The ease with which Ohio exceeded its quota in the summer of 1862 was truly remarkable. News of the horror and hardship of the war had reached the home front. Casualty lists from such sanguinary battles as Shiloh had been printed in the papers. Maimed and sickly soldiers brought home woeful tales from the war. Unlike the volunteers of 1861, the men who enlisted in the summer of 1862 knew that their service would be an ordeal.

Not all of the states experienced the same success in meeting their quotas for the call of July 1862. In fact, seven states failed to furnish enough men to meet the government requirement.6 In Maine, for instance, it was harder to meet the quota of 1862 than it had been in 1861; indeed, Maine failed to meet the 1862 quota.7 This was a harbinger for the succeeding government calls for new men. By the summer of 1863, with an increasingly war-weary public, the government instituted a national draft. The state and federal governments began to pay bounties to entice men to enlist. These bounties grew to substantial amounts in some areas as the war progressed. In Massachusetts in 1864, for example, the federal, state and local bounties sometimes totaled $725, enough for a man to purchase his own property in 1864. 8

The volunteers of the 116th Ohio Infantry should be distinguished from those of 1861 as well as those recruited from 1863 to the close of the war. In the summer of 1861 thousands of men rushed to join the army without any sense of what the war would bring. Private Dalzell of the 116th explained the mystic attraction of war to the uninitiated, " What is in human nature that makes what is so repulsive and abhorrent as war, attractive to the childish fancy?"9

Why, then, did they volunteer at this crucial time? Recent studies of Civil War soldier letters give numerous indications that men enlisted for many reasons ranging from family pressure to the desire for adventure. But Colonel Thomas Wildes of the 116th observed that patriotism was the motivation; the regiment's subsequent record and the letters of the regiment's men go a long way to substantiate his view. Wildes wrote of his comrades, "War had no charms or allurements for them, else they had seized the sword at the first alarum of war. They were rather of those who suffer much before resenting insult, but who, when aroused, are the more formidable antagonists."10

There were too many men, in many instances, trying to join the army in 1861. Elisha Hunt Rhodes recorded his experience during the recruiting frenzy of 1861, and it serves as a good illustration. Rhodes was acting as a clerk during the recruitment of the 2nd Rhode Island Infantry in 1861. The colonel in charge of recruiting told Rhodes, "We want only good men." Rhodes was instructed to select only men he knew to be of good character and quality. When Rhodes asked to join as a private, the surgeon wanted to reject him. He appealed to the colonel who asked him his age, state of health, if his father was living, and if his mother was willing for him to go.11 It is very unlikely that such a dialogue would have occurred in 1862.

When the regiments raised in the summer of 1862 reached the front, the veterans from 1861 must have at least secretly respected them for joining when they did. The veterans realized that they themselves had joined with the hope of an easy victory, and they must have wondered if they would have joined under similar circumstances. Many of them certainly did not reenlist in 1864.

Because of the circumstances that occurred after 1862, that is the draft and the bounty system, the volunteers from the summer of 1862 should be recognized as the last true volunteers of the Civil War. Patriotism was without question the primary motive for the 1862 enlistments. This does not imply that patriotic men did not join thereafter. It simply means that coercion and enticement entered the picture and thus altered the conditions of volunteering. The men raised as replacements after 1862 were often viewed, fairly or unfairly, as sullen draftees, substitutes, or bounty men.

The record clearly shows that the regiments raised in 1861 and 1862 did most of the fighting in the Civil War. Many of the 1861 regiments were mustered out in 1864 after their enlistment expired, thus shifting more of the burden upon the men recruited in 1862. A study of the regiments raised in Ohio after 1862 reveals that the vast majority of them were used for garrison and guard duty. Only two regiments raised in Ohio after 1862 suffered significant combat deaths, and even those two regiments suffered only a fraction of the usual number of combat deaths of early war Ohio regiments.12 Of course the boys who went to war in 1862 could not have known this; they simply knew that they were needed immediately. It is only fair to note that there were some regiments raised in other states later in the war that endured high casualties and experienced hard fighting. However, the prevalent tendency of the government was to use the veteran regiments already placed in the armies in the field to do the heavy fighting while using the new regiments formed after 1862 for rear echelon service.

No story of these volunteers would be complete without noting the important role of the women of that time. Their support and patriotism for the cause of their country was indispensable. Thomas Wildes, the 116th's Lieutenant Colonel wrote, "Who can find words to describe the womanly fervor which counted loss, suffering, self-denial, and even life as nothing so that God might give victory to the Union arms in the battle for liberty and the right?"13 Wildes also predicted that future historians would give women "first place" in the work of defeating the rebels.14 The tangible results of their effort included "basket" meetings where women furnished excellent meals at recruiting rallies, feeding troops passing on railroads, participation in the Sanitary Commission, and efforts to raise supplies for the troops afield. The letters, encouragement and will to sacrifice of the wives, mothers, sisters and friends of the soldiers made the burden of war lighter to bear, and it was never forgotten by the boys of '62.

CAMP PUTNAM
2

On August 25, 1862, the 116th Ohio Infantry rendezvoused at Camp Putnam, Ohio, to begin the organization process. The men made their way from the various counties from which they had been recruited, some by boat down the Ohio River. Companies A, C, D, E, and F were raised in Monroe County, Companies B and G in Meigs County, Companies I and K in Athens County, and Company H in Noble County. Companies B and C were already employed in guarding the Marietta and Cincinnati Railroad against possible rebel raids from across the Ohio River.

The various military committees from the counties mentioned had met in Marietta on August 17, 1862, and had selected the following field and staff officers for recommendation to Governor Tod: James Washburn, of Monroe County, Colonel; Thomas F. Wildes, Athens County, Lieutenant Colonel; W. T. Morris, Monroe County, Major; W. R. Golden, Athens County, Adjutant; and A. W. Williams, Meigs County, Quartermaster. Governor Tod accepted and commissioned all of these men except W. R. Golden, whom the Governor declined because he was lame. Fredrick Ballard, of Athens County was later named adjutant. Later the officers held a meeting and elected Rev. E. W. Brady Chaplain and Elmer Armstrong Sutler. Armstrong, as mentioned earlier, had been very active in helping to recruit in Athens County, and he had the confidence of Thomas Wildes as to his holding the best interests of the men at heart. Doctor Walter Gilkey was assigned to the regiment as surgeon, Doctor J. Q. A. Hudson as first assistant surgeon, and Doctor James Johnson as second assistant surgeon.

Only three or four of the officers in the entire regiment had seen any military service. Captain Mathew Brown had served as a lieutenant in the 27th Ohio Infantry, and Colonel Washburn had been a captain in the 25th Ohio Infantry, both seeing some active field service. Colonel Washburn had a reputation as a brave and capable officer, but he had not yet arrived in camp. This situation greeted the men as they arrived at Camp Putnam to begin drilling and indoctrination.

These neophyte soldiers, arriving for their first taste of the soldier's life, had some adjusting ahead of them. Many of the men were natives of Southeast Ohio and had grown up in a society that had recently been part of the frontier. It had been a much more egalitarian life when they were children, as explained by Private James Dalzell of Company H:

> There was no caste. All were of one class. All were on visiting terms...Even those who owned no land of their own were held to

Colonel James Washburn, of Woodsfield, Ohio, Commanding Officer of the 116th. (Courtesy of Mark D. Okey)

Lieutenant Colonel Thomas F. Wildes, of Athens, Ohio. (Courtesy of Mark D. Okey)

be on an equal footing with the best of the land-holders. You could see no difference between the boys and girls, the young men and women, of the landlord and the free-holder. They romped together, sat on the same bench in the church and at the log school-house, courted each other, intermarried, and in all things were on an equality.1

Dalzell never did totally appreciate the military caste system. Many of the men must have found it just as odious as Dalzell did. Yet the men were soon to learn, and later accept as necessary, the army's drills and routines. It was at Camp Putnam the men were introduced to company drill, and the old "hay foot, straw foot" story. At Camp Putnam some squad and company drill was attempted, but the regiment was never formed in line there. Proficiency at marching in formation was required before the more demanding tasks such as battalion drill could be attempted. The process of training new recruits takes time, and the few experienced officers and NCOs with the 116th had to make do.

Camp Putnam was located at Marietta, Ohio, in an area that would become the Washington County Fairgrounds.2 The camp had been in use for some time as a staging and organizing place for newly formed Ohio regiments. Marietta is located on a bend of the Ohio River in the extreme southeast section of Ohio. The state of Virginia was directly across the river; that area had not yet become part of West Virginia.

Colonel Putnam, who had been stationed at the camp, came rushing in on the afternoon of September first with orders for the 116th. Governor Tod had directed Colonel Putnam to send the 116th to Parkersburg, Virginia, immediately. The governor and the residents of Parkersburg were worried that the rebel General Jenkins would move on the city, as Jenkins was active in the area. The whole section of Southeast Ohio would soon be in alarm as well.

The 116th had not yet been mustered into service. None of the officers and men had uniforms, they still were wearing farm clothes or whatever civilian attire they had come to camp in. The men had been armed with old Belgian muskets, which Colonel Wildes said were, "intended more for show than use, and they did not even make a good show, being rusty and out of order, and in a demoralized condition generally."3 No blankets, accoutrements, or even cooking utensils had yet been issued. None of the officers knew how to form the regiment in line of battle, or even how to march it out of camp.

Such was the state of affairs when the 116th was first ordered to the seat of war. The officers and men were dismayed, but the order was obeyed without question, and the regiment was ready to march for Parkersburg within an hour. Colonel Wildes described the scene:

There was no pageant in that march from Camp Putnam...No banners waved over those men, no music cheered them...The farmer, the professor, the student, the smith and the miner were in that line...Here were the sturdy yeomanry of Southeastern Ohio marching to the scenes of war. From the hills and quiet fields of Monroe, were five hundred of her hardy sons of toil; from Meigs two hundred...from little Athens, two hundred...the stoutest and hardiest of the miners of the Hocking Valley; from Noble one hundred...And these thousand true men...made of sterling stuff, were on their way to war, to actual war.4

The move to Parkersburg fortunately proved uneventful except for a humorous incident at the rail station. It was raining when the men arrived in Parkersburg, and as they had no place to camp, the men commandeered the freight station there. Grain sacks stored in the building were spread about for the men to sleep upon. When the old freight agent arrived in the morning he was furious. When some of the men laughed at his plight, the agent knocked them down in his rage. The agent was quickly tied to a post, and the men made their escape. This was the first example noted of the men's attitude towards Virginia, and the attitude of Virginia's inhabitants toward them.

Colonel Mulligan arrived at Parkersburg with his "Irish Brigade" and camped next to the 116th. These troops were the 23rd Illinois Volunteer Infantry newly arrived from the West. Mulligan's men had been surrounded and captured by Sterling Price's rebel army at the Battle of Lexington, Missouri, the previous year, but they had put up a good fight first. They were experienced soldiers, and seeing the situation of the 116th, they loaned their cooking utensils and helped teach the men about army life in general. The 116th never forgot this kindness, and afterwards they would cheer the "green flags of those gallant and whole-souled Irishmen," whenever they encountered them.5

Colonel Washburn and Major Morris arrived in camp on September fourth. Two days later the 116th was ordered to hurry to Gallipolis, Ohio, located southwest of Parkersburg. Federal General Morgan had retreated from Cumberland Gap to the Ohio River near Gallipolis, and all available force including the "Home Guard" and militia was being concentrated for the defense of Gallipolis. On the way the 116th passed through Athens County, and the people there thronged the men and brought coffee, meat, pies, etc. The men enjoyed the reception; it was a stark contrast to what they would encounter later in Virginia and may have colored their attitude toward the disloyal sections of the country. The men would find that in Virginia they would have to buy, confiscate and steal to eat, and the residents of that state were for the most part indifferent at best.

The 116th passed through Oak Hill and camped at Centerville on the seventh. The next day it arrived at Gallipolis and camped at the fairgrounds. There was a very large force of militia present, and all the Federal forces from West Virginia and Eastern Kentucky were along the Ohio River and the Baltimore and Ohio Railroad. Colonel Washburn departed on September twelfth with three companies of the 92nd Ohio Infantry to reinforce the Federal forces near Charleston, Virginia. He was gone three days.

While the 116th was at its first camp in Gallipolis it began drilling diligently. Here they had their first glimpse of the rebels who were occasionally seen on the opposite side of the river. The rebels seemed content to stay on their side of the river, and no incidents of note occurred. General Cox arrived from the recent battles of South Mountain and Antietam to take command of the Federal forces. After General Cox arrived, the 116th was moved to a camp three miles below Gallipolis.

Many of the men of the 116th had been in service for over a month by this time; however, none of them had been officially mustered into United States service. Finally on September sixteenth and seventeenth, the 116th was mustered in. That is, all of the 116th except companies F and K. These two companies had been reduced by rejections and desertions to less than the required complement for mustering in. Company K had a serious problem. Lieutenant Miers and forty men from Company K refused to be mustered and left camp. This unfortunate predicament resulted in companies F and K being set aside until more recruits could be found to bring them up to strength for muster. Consequently, at no fault of the loyal men of these companies, their time of discharge would be different from the rest of the 116th. The three-year enlistment began at muster in, not at the time of joining and state service.

Captain Frank Muhlenberg of the 13th U.S. Infantry mustered the 116th into United States service. The mustering in ceremony usually began with the company to be mustered gathering for inspection. The men then took the oath of allegiance to the United States as prescribed by the tenth Article of War. The Articles of War were then read to the men. It was a solemn occasion intended to impress the responsibilities and duties of soldiering upon those who would serve. The penalties for infractions of the Articles, including death in some cases, were stressed as a measure to ensure obedience and discipline.6 Following the ceremony the men were officially in the service of the United States Government, even though the regiment retained the title of 116th Ohio Volunteer Infantry.

At this time the regiment received uniforms, clothing, camp equipage and better arms. The old Belgian muskets were at least replaced, but the arms supplied were still not satisfactory. The 116th now began to take on the appearance and status of army troops rather than a band of armed civilians. Colonel Wildes noted, "We had now a fine looking regiment. Most of the men were very large, healthy, strong fellows..."7 He believed that the regiment was made up of the best men, and few Ohio regiments had better personnel.8 While at Gallipolis the 116th received a visit from General George B. Wright who helped substantiate Wildes' opinion. General Wright made a speech to the 116th complimenting them for the alacrity they exhibited in the movements to Parkersburg and Gallipolis and their willingness to defend the Ohio border even before they had been mustered in and properly equipped.

There was now time and opportunity for drill, and the officers and men rapidly improved in the manual of arms, squad drill and company drill. A great variety of military evolutions had to be learned. The men were taught to load their weapons, to use the bayonet, and to position their weapons for saluting and marching. They were formed by companies and taught to march in formation, to march forward, to the left or right, by the oblique, etc. 9 An officer's school was established to provide instruction for the many complex movements required for battalion drill and brigade tactics. Some battalion drill was attempted at Gallipolis, but the lack of experienced officers hampered the effort. Nevertheless, the 116th was fortunate to have two of the three essential elements required of a good civil war infantry regiment already in place. The regiment was blessed with good men in the ranks and natural leaders as officers and would in time acquire the drill and discipline needed to complete the package.

An incident at Gallipolis illustrated how seriously some of the novice soldiers took their duties. Captain Teters of Company H had the duty on the river road east of town one-day. The twenty-five year old Teters would later be promoted to commander of the regiment. A mounted man with no visible rank tried to pass the guard and refused to halt when challenged by Captain Teters. When the Captain grabbed the horse's bridle, the mounted man reached for his holster to draw his revolver. Captain Teters drew his revolver first, and he ordered the man to "dismount and surrender." The man promptly obeyed. He then identified himself as Colonel Taylor of the 40th Ohio Infantry and demanded to be allowed to pass immediately. The Captain, angered by the incident, would have none of it and was about to order the colonel taken under guard to the Provost Marshall. At this point General Cox happened to ride by with members of his staff. The general thanked Captain Teters for his diligence in enforcing orders, and corrected Colonel Taylor for his reprehensible behavior.10

The period while the 116th remained at Gallipolis was "probably the darkest and gloomiest" of the war for the Federal Army according to Colonel Wildes.11 Thomas Wildes was a politically astute observer in a position to know. Born in Racine, Canada, in 1834 of Irish descent, Wildes had moved to Ohio with his parents in 1839. He was college educated and was an articulate writer. In 1861 he moved to Athens, Ohio, to assume control of the Republican newspaper *The Athens Messenger* after owner Nelson Van Vorhes enlisted in the army. Nelson Van Vorhes was a prominent Republican who became the colonel of the 92nd Ohio Infantry. Like Van Vorhes, Thomas Wildes was an "ardent Republican."12 Wildes recognized that the despondency in the army was a direct result of President Lincoln's proclamation of September twenty-second and the Democratic Party's opposition to it.

On September 22, 1862, President Abraham Lincoln issued the Emancipation Proclamation which read in part, "all persons held as slaves within any State or designated part of a State, the people whereof shall then be in rebellion against the United States, shall be then, thenceforward, and forever free; and the Executive Government of the United States, including the military and naval authority thereof, will recognize and maintain the freedom of such persons…"13 This move by the President was a complete departure from his announced policy at the onset of war. In his Inaugural Address Lincoln declared, "I have no purpose, directly or indirectly, to interfere with the institution of slavery in the states where it exists. I believe I have no lawful right to do so, and I have no inclination to do so."14 The proclamation then reversed the Lincoln Administration's original stance toward slavery, freed the slaves, and obligated the military to guarantee the slave's freedom.

The effect of the Emancipation Proclamation was immediately demoralizing to the army and the North on the whole. Many officers resigned from the Federal Army feeling that the war was no longer about restoring the union or fighting traitors; instead, the war seemed to many to be directed against slavery. In September of 1862 it seemed the war had changed, it had become an "abolition war." The Proclamation seemed to give credence to the fears Southerners had before the war. The kind of fear Lincoln had sought to assuage in his First Inaugural. Probably less than ten percent of Northern soldiers had joined with abolition as their first priority.15 A soldier from Indiana, for example, wrote about his opinion of emancipation: "No one who has ever seen the nigger in all his glory on the southern plantations will ever vote for emancipation."16

There can be no doubt that Wildes knew that the pervasive melancholy had also struck the 116th and posed a threat. The region where the 116th had been recruited was called the "Lower North" by Kevin Phillips in his book *The Cousins Wars*.17 Phillips noted, "Ohio, Indiana, and Illinois…had the only large, concentrated, southern-sprung population within the political boundaries of the North." Monroe County, where the largest contingent of the 116th had been recruited, did not support Lincoln.18 Athens County, home of Colonel Wildes and companies I and K, had almost invariably voted a small majority to Whigs and later Republicans through the years, but the congressional district had a Democrat for Representative.19 Kevin Phillips may have best summed up the region as a whole with the following comments: "Most would probably have voted to simultaneously bar plantation owners with their wage-lowering black slaves and Yankee abolitionist…it meant 'no slavery—and no blacks—wanted here'."20

As noted, the Emancipation Proclamation resulted in a backlash, one immediately apparent at the ballot box. In the fall elections in Ohio, the Democrats won fourteen of nineteen U.S. House seats.21 Still the effect was not so strong as to topple the Federal Government. Measures were taken in the army to suppress dissent and by loyal Governors to reassure the public as to the propriety of the President's policy. The loyal people on the whole, civilians and soldiers, Republicans and Democrats, came to understand that freeing the slaves was the necessary and right thing to do. The 116th went dutifully on, much to their credit, in spite of the situation that greeted them at their time of entry into government service.

By mid October the military situation in Southern Ohio no longer required the presence of the 116th. The War Department had determined to send the 116th to active service in Western Virginia rather than in the Western Theater where the other regional regiment, the 92nd Ohio Infantry, was headed. The 116th departed Gallipolis on October 16, 1862, for Parkersburg, Virginia, and points east.

The march to Parkersburg took the regiment through Meigs and Athens Counties where some of the companies had been raised. Many of the men had one more opportunity to see friends and relatives before the long separation to come. Citizens again thronged the men as they marched through the towns and farms, and grand receptions were held with lavish attention heaped upon the men at each stop.

On October nineteenth the regiment arrived at Belpre, across the Ohio River from Parkersburg. Something had to be done about the two under-strength companies that were yet to be mustered into Federal service. Colonel Washburn gave the situation his full attention, taking companies F and K to Camp Putnam to await new recruits. The balance of the 116th, commanded by Lieutenant Colonel Wildes, crossed over the Ohio River into Parkersburg on October twenty-second and caught a train bound for Clarksburg, Virginia.

Enlistments were essential now to bring the 116th into compliance with the regulations for infantry companies. The two companies required a total of about 100 men each to conform to regulations. Without these two companies, the 116th would not meet requirements for recognition as an infantry regiment. As noted, the sentiments in Ohio had changed dramatically from July to October. Finding about a dozen men for each company this time around proved more difficult than recruiting the entire regiment in August.22 The friends and neighbors of the men already in the ranks of Company F and Company K were sought to fill the remaining vacancies.

Company F had been raised in and around the hamlet of Stafford, Ohio, in Monroe County. Interestingly, Stafford had an Underground Railroad station before the war. The people of Stafford knew about the station helping fugitive slaves in violation of Federal law. Several residents of the Stafford area and nearby Noble County took part in the operation with no interference.23 One of the young men from the Stafford area who joined Company F in October was Freeman Thompson, and he was one of the 116th Ohio's bravest. One day as a soldier in the 116th he would win his nation's highest award for valor.

"ALL AGREED TO BE GOOD BOYS"
3

While Colonel Washburn and the two companies remained in Ohio, the rest of the 116th filed into "rickety old cattle cars" at Parkersburg on October twenty-second for a train ride to Clarksburg, Virginia, about seventy miles to the east.1 It was a very cold night, and of course the cars had no heat. As the train wended its way around the mountains and through valleys, sitting in the freezing cars in the darkness became unbearable. The men held a "council of war", as they called it, and decided that something had to be done.2 Disregarding the possible disciplinary consequences, they began to tear the wooden lining away from the walls of the cars. The lining was broken into pieces for firewood. Fires were then built on the wooden benches within the cars. Men took turns watching the fires and moving the fires when the benches began to burn through. By enduring the smoke for as long as possible and then opening the car doors to vent it, the men were able to ward off the cold. Thick smoke billowed from the train appearing to envelop all the cars from the engine back. When the train reached Clarksburg in the morning, veterans of the war against the cold emerged from the cars with blackened hands and faces to match the burned condition of the old cars. The trainmen were probably not amused, but Colonel Wildes seemed to view the men's behavior as necessary, as he did not mention any incidence of punishment.

The 116th remained in Clarksburg for three days to receive an issue of tents, teams and equipage. Sibley tents were supplied to the regiment. These were large cone shaped tents that were more spacious than most tents but more cumbersome as well. They could not be carried by the men on the march and required transport by wagon or other means.

While the 116th was in Clarksburg two veteran infantry regiments from General Cox's Kanawha Division were also in town. These were the 23rd and 36th Ohio Infantries just arrived from the battlefield at Antietam. Two future Presidents, Rutherford B. Hays and William McKinley, served in the 23rd Ohio Infantry during the war. The men of the 116th took great interest in the stories of these veterans, especially details about the Battle at South Mountain where Cox's division had fought well the previous month. The men realized that now they too were soldiers who would soon experience similar trials. They felt a new kinship to other soldiers, a kinship by virtue of a common cause requiring blood sacrifice. The deeds of others mattered as never before, because each fight had an impact on the overall course of the war and how it would play out.

It was at Clarksburg that the 116th met General Robert Milroy their new commander for the first time. He would somehow prove to be popular with the men under his command, and he would earn the loyalty and respect of Colonel Wildes. Milroy had flowing locks of gray hair resembling the feathers on an eagle's head. With a hawk-like nose, piercing eyes and an upright posture, the General looked the part of the *nome de guerre* given by his men. To them he was the "Silver Eagle."3

Robert Milroy was born in Washington County, Indiana, in 1816. He was an energetic, fervent, outspoken man with extensive military experience. In 1843 he graduated from Norwich Military Academy in Vermont (then Captain Partridge's Academy), and he used this training during the Mexican War as a company commander in the 1st Indiana Volunteers. Following that war he earned a law degree from Indiana University and became a judge. In 1854 he opened a private law practice. When the Civil War erupted, Milroy quickly gave up his law practice to raise an infantry company. Soon he was promoted to colonel of the 9th Indiana Infantry. In September 1861 he was promoted to the rank of brigadier general. He served in the West Virginia Campaign during the winter of 1861 and 1862 and then was defeated by Stonewall Jackson at McDowell during Jackson's famous Valley Campaign. By the time the 116th came under his command, Milroy was on his way to an infamous reputation among Southerners for his behavior and policy in the Virginia Valley.4

On October twenty-sixth the 116th departed Clarksburg in a pouring rain on a march to Buckhannon. The roads were in terrible shape, and the men got a good lesson on the hardships of soldiering. They camped that night in their new Sibley tents; but as they had not yet been issued Sibley Stoves, the campfires inside the tents soon had the men choking from smoke.

Disregarding the miserable conditions and continual downpour, some of the men went out "foraging." This was the beginning of a long and prodigious record compiled by the 116th in this field of expertise. Foraging can mean searching for provisions, legally or sanctioned. Foraging can mean raiding for food—stealing. Foraging can mean rummaging for food, legally or otherwise. The exact assessment of the type of foraging done by these men is unclear, except they returned in the morning with roast pig and turkey for breakfast. That would beat hard crackers and salt pork, the usual fare, any time.

The 116th arrived in Buckhannon the next day followed by a train of twenty-seven loaded wagons to haul their tents and traps. Along with the wagons came a horde of angry citizens complaining of how their horses, wagons and property had been "pressed" into government service by the troops. According to Colonel Wildes, General Milroy was "hard pressed for an apology," but he soon returned the wagons and property to the rightful owners with enough "good army rations" to get them on their way in fair humor.5

General Milroy began to realize that he had a group of independent minded characters in his new regiment with what he had heard about the train ride from Parkersburg and now this. Colonel Wildes wrote of Milroy, "He thought the 116th Ohio could take care of itself. We thought so, too."6

Another new Ohio regiment came along the same route soon afterward with the same teams and circumstances. By then General Milroy was losing patience: he soon issued an order requiring that only property from disloyal residents could be "pressed," and evidence was required of said disloyalty. Such evidence seemed always available to the 116th whenever they needed transportation thereafter. From the record it appears that General Milroy seldom interfered. The general feeling among the soldiers seems to have been that if the people were loyal they wouldn't object to the army's requests and needs. The war and circumstances quickly proved that the regiment's behavior in Virginia would not be the same as it had been in Ohio.

On October 28, 1862, Companies F and K, having found the required recruits, were mustered into Federal service at Camp Putnam, Ohio. Colonel Washburn joined the regiment with these two companies on the thirty-first at Buckhannon. The 116th was now at full strength and fully equipped. A brigade was then formed from all new Ohio infantry regiments, and Colonel James Washburn of the 116th was appointed Brigade Commander. The new brigade was composed of the 116th, 122nd, and 123rd Ohio regiments. Colonel Washburn took Adjutant Ballard and Quartermaster Lee with him for his staff, and some changes were made to fill the positions within the regiment. Lieutenant Colonel Thomas Wildes assumed command of the 116th in place of Colonel Washburn.

At Buckhanon the 116th returned to intensive drilling and increased discipline. Each day seemed to bring improvement in the more advanced drilling evolutions and tactics. According to Colonel Wildes the first serious illness leading to the first death in the regiment occurred at this time when Lieutenant Robert Wilson of Company A developed a fever and then died when sent home. Colonel Wildes had the highest praise for the Lieutenant, saying that he might have been the best officer in the regiment.7 According to Private James Dalzell of Company H, the first enlisted man died at about this time. Dalzell wrote of his own friend's death: "Jim Stoneking...was striken with typhoid fever...and died within a week. He was the first man in the One Hundred and Sixteenth Ohio Volunteer Infantry to die..."8

Private Alfred E. Steele, Company A. This image of Steele in dress uniform was probably taken shortly after the regiment was mustered in. (Courtesy of USAMHI)

Grave of Private James A. Stoneking, Company H, at Antietam National Cemetery. Stoneking was the first man from the 116th to die away from home. James Dalzell wrote: "...let us never forget those humbler heroes who, like Jim Stoneking, felt death's destroying wound, not in the heat of battle, but in the quiet hospital of agony."

Lieutenant Colonel Wildes began to develop his opinion of General Milroy during the stay at Buckhannon. According to Colonel Wildes, "We found General Milroy a very kind and courteous officer, full of energy and loyalty. No slave was ever turned back from *his* lines, for he ardently supported the policy of the Administration, embodied in the emancipation proclamation."9 The "ardent Republican" Wildes would support the "Silver Eagle" ever after, despite Milroy's soon to be obvious deficiencies.

West Virginia in 1862, particularly the central and eastern half where the 116th was stationed, was an area of active guerila warfare. Soldiers had to be very careful when leaving camp to avoid capture or worse. While the guerilla bands in West Virginia would never rival those of Missouri for vicious and murderous atrocities, they were still a threat to small groups of soldiers and individuals. The soldiers considered the guerillas as bushwhackers capable of murder. Citizens who acted as peaceable farmers during the day would sometimes arm themselves and band to gather to attack Federals in the dark.

The 116th posted pickets in camp and sent patrols out on scout as measures against the guerilla menace. Officers tried to impress the importance of discipline and obedience on the men by requiring passes and authorization to leave camp. Nevertheless, the officers were hard-pressed to keep the men from wandering about from camp or during marches and patrols. Soldiers quickly became bored with camp and camp food; thus, foraging or simply diversions away from camp became a powerful temptation.

Unauthorized foraging was an inevitable occurrence that was never fully controlled wherever the 116th went on campaign. "No other regiment in Uncle Sam's service had shed more blood as the 116th, that is sheep, cattle, hogs, chickens and turkeys," and thus the regiment was called the "Bloody 116th," according to a soldier correspondent writing to the *Spirit of Democracy* newspaper in Woodsfield, Ohio. 10

One night at Buckhannon several men left camp "away in the country foraging on their own account." Their absence was discovered and a detail was sent in search of them. "They were met some distance out, loaded down with honey and fresh meat of different kinds, and marched to headquarters," according to Colonel Wildes. More men were found with plunder in camp from an earlier trip. Colonel Washburn quickly learned of this. As brigade commander he did not want his own regiment setting a bad example, so he stopped by the camp to discipline these "unruly fellows." Colonel Wildes explained, "The boys never forgot the short, sharp lecture he delivered to them, and going out of camp after plunder during the night was put a stop to for some time afterwards.

Nobody was punished and all agreed to be good boys in the future, and they kept their word."11

Private James Dalzell's account of his wartime experiences chronicled his foraging operations in considerable detail, and he wrote about some foraging on the march during this time. However, it may be true that the particular group caught in this instance did stop leaving camp to forage for some time. James Dalzell and his friends in the regiment were expert foragers, and Dalzell had a special arrangement to circumvent officers, orders and guards. He was college educated and probably should have been an officer. He was promoted to sergeant major in February of 1863, but he chose to return to his company as a private. No explanation was given for this in the regimental roster. Dalzell explained his special position, "...I was conceded to be the best penman and accountant in our company...when I was a schoolmaster, my present captain...W. B. Teters...had been a student in my school years before, and we were intimate friends."12 With this connection, Private Dalzell, as he preferred to be called, became the clerk of Company H. As company clerk he could write passes for anyone to pass through the picket lines. He could write in the style of a general and was willing to fake signatures for realism. Throughout the war Private Dalzell sent his friends out on foraging expeditions, sometimes risking their lives. When they returned with their plunder, Private Dalzell would get his share and a share to appease the officers. The drawback to this system of foraging was that it resulted in an unequal distribution of food to the rest of the regiment. There was only so much food to be foraged within an area. With a large share going to a few, many in the regiment did without when the 116th was on short rations in an area where the population had already been tapped. This situation would plague the regiment later in the war when the army was forced to live off the land. To Private Dalzell, his arrangement was just part of the fortunes of war.

The 116th broke camp and left Clarksburg taking up the march for Beverly, Virginia, on November ninth. That night they camped on the middle fork of the Tygart Valley River. Colonel Wildes mentioned yet another example of his boy's mischievous behavior occurring at this place. A mule team and wagon stampeded just as the men were stacking arms at the campsite. The wagon overturned spilling the contents and smashing the wagon while the mules continued on the run. Soldiers rushed to the wrecked wagon to help the driver and control the mules. Wildes wrote, "The wagon proved to be loaded with medical stores, among which was a large quantity of bottled wine, whisky and brandy, and observing the contents of the dilapidated wagon, the soldiers very soon captured 'the bottles with corks out,' as they afterward said, when called to account, but it was more than suspected that they also captured all the bottles whose 'corks' could be pulled out." The men blamed the 123rd Ohio for taking the unopened bottles, and said they were only trying to save the already open bottles from waste. "It was," wrote Wildes, "too intricate a question to settle off hand in the conflicting state of the proof, and was dropped as one of those things 'no fellow can find out.' Major Morris, to whom an investigation of the matter was referred, was found next morning with several bottles with 'corks out'..."13

That next morning the 116th continued the march to Beverly, passing the battlefield at Rich Mountain, one of the war's first battles. Colonel Wildes noted the scenery calling it "some of the most beautiful mountain scenery in Virginia."14

Beverly was the home of General Stonewall Jackson's only surviving sister. "She was," wrote Colonel Wildes, "a thoroughly loyal woman, and kept the stars and stripes constantly flying over her house. She was, besides, kind-hearted and attentive...to the Union soldiers, many and many an one owing his life to her care."15

Colonel Washburn left Beverly at this time on a trip to Columbus, Ohio, to seek better arms for the 116th. His mission would prove successful, as new arms would be forthcoming.

Lieutenant Colonel Wildes commanded the 116th in the Colonel's absence. On November 12, 1862, while at Beverly, Colonel Wildes wrote the following in a letter:

> We ate our supper—a good one—just before dark, after which the Major, Doctor Johnson, Lieutenant Cochran, Lieutenant Sibley and a few others came in and seated themselves around as charming a fire as you ever saw in civilization. Then we ate apples and drank cider! What do you think of that? Let me explain. The apples and cider were "foraged" to-day. Then we smoked and chatted, and finally the Major led off in a song...though it is raining quite hard, the men are running about through the camp following the 'postmaster.' Commissary Sergeant Walker has just come dancing in, exclaiming 'a letter from my wife.' Here comes the Orderly now...and a letter is announced for 'the Colonel,' another for 'the Major,' and so on until nearly all of us are supplied. Then one after another went to his own quarters to read his letters from home...Nothing does a poor, forlorn soldier so much good as a cheerful letter from home...A letter, assuring them that all is right and comfortable at home, removes many a dark cloud and heavy trouble. I can see its effect at once in their countenances and cheerful discharge of duty."16

The stay at Beverly was pleasant enough, but on November fifteenth the 116th got up early for a march to Webster, Virginia. In two days the 116th marched forty-two miles and passed through the Phillipi Battlefield of 1861. At Webster the wagon master, Hiram L. Baker, took charge of the wagon train and left for New Creek, Virginia. The 116th caught a ride on the Baltimore and Ohio Railroad to New Creek.

As part of the Railroad Division of the Eighth Army Corps, the 116th moved as needed to guard towns and bridges along the Baltimore and Ohio Railroad. The stay at New Creek would last almost one month. While there the men presented a field glass to Colonel Washburn after he returned from Ohio. Quartermaster Lee made the presentation speech for the men, and the colonel responded by thanking the men and saying that he hoped to lead the brigade in battle soon against the rebels.

Colonel Mulligan's "Irish Brigade" was stationed at New Creek, so Colonel Mulligan was asked to supply a detail of his best drill sergeants and his adjutant to drill the officers and men of the 116th. The instruction of the more experienced Irishmen proved "most satisfactory."[17] Irish soldiers earned an excellent reputation during the Civil War. A regimental historian from another Irish Brigade described the aura of the Irish soldier, "Instinctively one associates an Irishman with dash and courage, whether viewed as the presiding genius at Donnybrook Fair or as the leader of armies. The very name...was redolent of dash and gallantry of precision of evolution and promptness of action."[18] With Colonel Mulligan's help, the 116th began to acquire the final elements required of an excellent Civil War fighting regiment, drill and discipline.

Up to the point of arriving at New Creek, the 116th had been very healthy with few losses from illness. Most of the men were from farms or fairly isolated villages where contagious disease seldom manifested itself. This fact made the 116th particularly vulnerable to childhood diseases like measles. It seemed that regiments recruited from large cities had men accustomed to crowded and unsanitary conditions. These city soldiers were better adapted to camp conditions, and they seemed to have developed better immunity to the types of disease seldom seen in the countryside.[19] With November weather setting in, and camped with the Illinois veterans, measles swept the 116th like a dreadful flooding tide. Within days one-fourth of the men were bed-ridden with the disease.

Measles was one of the worst camp afflictions to be visited upon Civil War soldiers. It very often swept through new regiments during their first encampment with deadly results. Measles could be deadly in itself, but the disease often weakened its victims and brought on pneumonia and other illnesses that also brought death in large numbers.[20]

When the 116th left New Creek, 124 men were left behind in the hospital and later sent to the larger hospital at Cumberland, Maryland.

Private James Earley of Company F was one of the men sent to Cumberland on December eleventh. He was one of five sons of Alexander Earley of Monroe County serving in the Federal Army. His older brother William died of lung disease the following month while serving in Illinois. The 116th had several examples of brothers serving in the same company and many examples of relatives serving in the regiment. The Okey family, for instance, had at least five relatives serving in the 116th. Disease in a Civil War regiment was potentially devastating to families or even small communities, because in regiments like the 116th so many family members and neighbors served together. Overall during the Civil War disease killed twice as many soldiers as battle.21 The 116th, however, did not conform to the overall war average as nearly an equal number of men were killed in battle as died from disease. 22

On November twenty-eighth Captain Teters commanding Company H took his men through Tucker County for the purpose of eliminating a band of guerillas and thieves infesting that area. Colonel Wildes claimed that the captain "did the work thoroughly and returned to the regiment on the 11th of December." Unfortunately, the captain "was obliged to leave fourteen men in hospital at St. George."23 These men also had measles.

The 116th broke camp on the twelfth of December, leaving the sick temporarily behind, and marched for Burlington. The survivors of the measles epidemic would return to the regiment from Cumberland as they recovered. After only a few days in Burlington, the 116th was again on the march, this time for Petersburg where they camped in a ploughed field on the bank of the South Branch of the Potomac.

Now the 116th embarked on active combat duty that would not cease until the end of the war. Many of the regiments like the 116th that had been raised during the summer of 1862 had already experienced heavy combat in the battles at South Mountain, Antietam, and Perryville. The 116th had been fortunate to have a period of time to learn soldiering. From here on the 116th would close with the enemy, remaining on enemy soil, with only a few brief exceptions, until mustering out in the spring and summer of 1865.

RUMBLE WITH GRUMBLE
4

Hampshire and Hardy counties in the rugged northeastern section of West Virginia were " full of rebel cavalry and guerrillas," according to Colonel Wildes.1 Rebel General Thomas (Stonewall) Jackson had occupied this same region the previous winter. Jackson had conducted a winter campaign in the region with a view of cutting the flow of materials along the Chesapeake & Ohio Canal. The canal and the Baltimore and Ohio (B&O) Railroad carried thousands of tons of coal from Appalachian mines and other materials to Washington. In effect, the North "depended heavily on the canal to provide their stoves with Appalachian coal."2 The region was also important because of its proximity and access to the Shenandoah Valley. When Jackson withdrew to begin his famous Shenandoah Campaign, the region was reoccupied by Federal troops. It was no mere coincidence that Colonel Wildes observed so many rebels there in December of 1862. The Rebel Government understood the strategic value of Northeast West Virginia. If the rebels could not control the region, they wanted to deny its use to the North. So another bold rebel general was pushing into the region with a large cavalry force intent, like Jackson, on making mischief for the Federals.

While the 116th was in Petersburg, West Virginia, about ten days, an increase in rebel strength and boldness was becoming apparent to Colonel Wildes. Two incidents pointed to this fact. First, a single rebel soldier temporarily captured Lieutenant Colonel Hunter of the 123rd Ohio while on the march to Petersburg. Hunter was fortunate to be recaptured when his men appeared. The next incident involved Captain Brown and Lieutenant Cochran of the 116th. The two officers were out beyond the picket lines foraging when rebel cavalry appeared and fired at them. They were hard pressed but managed to make an escape back to camp.

On December twenty-first, Captain Teters and Lieutenant Karr with 100 men were sent out on a scout or patrol. They returned with nineteen prisoners the next day. The captain had been sent on a similar mission the previous month, and now several prisoners were under guard. Lieutenant Mallory was detailed to escort the prisoners to Wheeling where a military prison for the region had been established.

General Milroy had decided to establish his headquarters in Winchester, Virginia, so the 116th, a section of Battery D 1st West Virginia Light Artillery commanded by Lieutenant Daniel, and a cavalry company were sent to relieve Milroy at Moorefield on the twenty-eighth.

Colonel Washburn, as brigade commander, remained in Petersburg with the 123rd Ohio, two cavalry companies, and the remaining section of the artillery battery. Lieutenant Colonel Wildes was in command of the force relieving Moorefield, and he arrived there on the afternoon of the twenty-eighth to find General Milroy ready to depart.

Captain J. H. McNeill of Rebel Colonel Imboden's Cavalry had been building quite a reputation as a swashbuckling raider in the mountainous region. McNeill made one of his usual daring attacks on General Milroy's wagon train as it departed Moorefield that afternoon. Practically under the general's nose, he swooped down on the train and stole the horses and mules from thirteen wagons and made his escape. Men like McNeill had the advantage of information from rebel sympathizers in the area in much the same manner as guerillas everywhere. This would not be the last that the 116th would see of him.

After General Milroy departed, Lieutenant Colonel Wildes began to feel anxious about his isolated position at Moorefield. The area was "most thoroughly rebel" according to Wildes, with only a handful of loyal families residing there.3 Soon word of rebel plans to attack Moorefield began to filter in to Wildes from escaped slaves and Unionist. Wildes telegraphed General Milroy to inquire about the large rebel force he had heard was near Strasburg, Virginia, in preparation to attack his isolated post. The general answered back in typical Milroy fashion: "I will take care of the rebels at Strasburg soon. If you are attacked, fight till the 123rd can come to your relief. You can whip any force that comes against you."4 While this may have reassured Wildes, it did nothing to help him. The general's telegraph seems overly optimistic in light of the fact that Wildes would have to face 4,000 rebels with a garrison of 650 men and two guns. In any case, General Milroy did not take care of the "rebels at Strasburg."

Rebel General William E. (Grumble) Jones knew about the Yankees up in Petersburg and Moorefield. He also knew that Milroy had divided his force by placing troops at three different towns. On January 2, 1863, he left the Virginia Valley with a force that included the 6th, 7th, and 12th Regiments Virginia Cavalry, 17th Battalion Virginia Cavalry, 1st Battalion Maryland Cavalry, 1st Battalion Maryland Infantry, and two batteries of artillery. With this force of approximately 4,000 men and two batteries, General Jones intended to crush the 650 men of the 116th and the section of artillery holding Moorefield.5

Grumble Jones was a most formidable opponent, with a reputation as the most caustic personality in the entire Rebel Army. He had the appearance of a Biblical prophet with piercing eyes wreathed by a bushy beard and a balding head, according to one description of the general.6 Jones was born into an upper class family in 1824 and lived in

Washington County, Virginia. He was educated at Emory and Henry College before attending West Point, where he graduated twelfth in the class of 1848. After his young bride was swept from his arms and drowned during a shipwreck, Jones began to develop the traits that earned his reputation and appellation, "embittered, complaining and suspicious."[7] He resigned from the army and returned to his estate in 1856, where his reputation was impressed upon his neighbors.

At the start of the Civil War, Grumble Jones raised a company of cavalry from his home county that served under Jeb Stuart in the 1st Virginia Cavalry at First Manassas. He eventually became colonel of that regiment, but his men voted him out as colonel because of his harsh discipline and embittered personality. Jones was a valuable and talented officer whom the Confederacy could not afford to waste, so he was given command of another regiment of cavalry. Like Stonewall Jackson, Grumble Jones was careless about his personal appearance, but he was careful about drill and discipline. General Jackson recognized Jones' skills and abilities. At Stonewall Jackson's request, Grumble Jones was appointed brigadier general in September 1862.[8]

On January 2, 1863, General Jones decided to pounce on the garrison at Moorefield. He planned to and expected to capture the 116th at Moorefield, Colonel Washburn and his men at Petersburg, and the first troops sent to reinforce the two towns with this single movement. He pushed hard out of the valley and reached Moorefield by 7a.m. the next day.[9]

Lieutenant Henry Okey of Company D was posted with a picket to watch the Petersburg Road on the western outskirts of Moorefield early on the morning of the third. The Lieutenant shouldn't have been there. Okey had tendered his resignation "on account of the severe illness of two of my children and the ill health of my wife which require my imediate person at home."[10] The resignation had been accepted the previous day, but the Lieutenant's discharge had not yet arrived. Before Lieutenant Okey and his picket had time to react, part of the 7th Virginia Cavalry snatched them up and hustled them away as prisoners of war.

Nevertheless, Colonel Wildes and the 116th were not caught off guard. On the eastern approach to Moorefield, where Jones had placed a wing of his force to attack the town from the Lost River Road, the 116th occupied an excellent defensive position. The position was on rising ground protected on three sides by woods and thick underbrush. When the rebels sent a dismounted force across the open field approaching Moorefield under the cover of a battery, Companies B, G, and F opened fire from their concealed position and drove the rebels back with "some loss."[11]

One of Lieutenant Daniel's guns was brought up and placed behind the three companies in an open space to bear upon Jones' men. The dismounted rebels again advanced across the open field, this time being allowed to nearly reach the foot of the hill where the Federals were posted. The single cannon roared into action joined by the three concealed infantry companies. This hot reception was probably a little more than the dismounted rebels expected, because they quickly took to their heels.

Major Morris with Companies E, C, and K were covering the approach to Moorefield via the Winchester Road. A few minutes after the repulse of the rebels along the Lost River Road, a large force attacked Major Morris' position without success.

The mountainous terrain surrounding Moorefield limited the rebel chieftain's control of the attack and led him to divide his force. He had hoped to quickly overwhelm the 116th in much the same manner as the picket had been captured. Jones was "wholly unacquainted with the topography of the country."[12] In effect, he chose to strike the town from three separate roads using two wings of his command. While his men were trying to capture Moorefield from the East, Jones sent a large mounted force up the Petersburg Road past the captured picket position and into the town. Company H under Captain Teeters was waiting. Teeters' men "treated them to some fine, vigorous street firing, and drove them out again on the run."[13]

In preparation for the attack General Jones had relied on a native of the area, Captain Harness of the 17th Virginia Cavalry Battalion, to position his battery on the south side of Moorefield along the Petersburg Road. The section of guns under Lieutenant Daniel outclassed the rebel batteries after the initial attacks failed. "The hills selected on each side of the Petersburg road are so distant that our six pieces, with their defective ammunition, were no match for the two of the enemy," explained Jones. "Nearly all our shots fell far short, while theirs passed over or struck in our midst."[14]

At about 10 a.m., with his artillery outmatched and his initial plans thwarted, General Jones drew his cavalry off from view of the 116th, and his guns fell silent. He shifted the position of his cavalry to threaten Company H and placed one gun to support this move. Colonel Wildes responded by sending Company I down to support H. One of Lieutenant Daniel's guns was moved into a position to meet the new threat. Wildes was swiftly reacting to every move the rebels made. Jones remained cautious; he was becoming concerned that mischief could befall his divided force should Federal reinforcements suddenly arrive.

The one rebel gun that had been positioned in support of the cavalry fired a shell at about noon. Almost instantly a shot in reply from the gun supporting Company H struck and dismounted the rebel gun. The sergeant who fired the shot received a promotion to Lieutenant in the 5th West Virginia Infantry for this remarkable feat. The incident no doubt helped to reinforce Jones' belief that his own artillery was inferior.

Grumble Jones continued his efforts to surround and capture Moorefield, but he did not yet risk a direct assault. He needed to determine the size of the force defending the town. His probes thus far had been ineffective. Looking for an opening, a force was moved into position to block the Romney Road. To meet the new threat, Colonel Wildes called for Company A to cover the road and placed Company C in supporting position as a reserve. Company I was recalled from supporting H and placed along with C in reserve. The rebels did not attempt an attack along the Romney Road; Jones seemed to be seeking an opening or preparing for a general assault by both wings of his force.

Lieutenant Daniel moved his two guns to a protected spot within range to engage the rebel battery along the Petersburg Road. Daniel's guns soon engaged in a duel with the rebel battery. The results of this duel were most unsatisfactory to Jones. The Federal guns were handled with precision, and another rebel gun was disabled before long. The rebel artillery was being blasted, but an exploding shell from the rebel guns managed to wound Corporal William Scott of Company I in the shoulder. Corporal Scott was the first man from the 116th to be wounded in action.

Daniel's guns soon drove the rebel artillery from the field. Jones withdrew this battery and sent his men under cover. The Federal guns dominated the field and things grew quiet until about 3 p.m. The few times the rebels tried to gather during the afternoon, they were quickly shelled and forced to seek shelter. Jones mentioned in his report that he could not unite the two wings of his command for an assault because, "the ground between was swept" by artillery.14

Colonel Wildes remained watchful, "every moment expecting a charge from some direction," aware that he was nearly surrounded.15 Suddenly the rebel batteries opened and lines of skirmishers appeared and began to move carefully towards the town. Wildes and his men expected the rebels to make a final dash from every direction to overwhelm the 116th. The citizens of Moorefield anxiously awaited Grumble's charge, hoping the hated Yankees would be gobbled up, hoping it would be over quickly and their homes would be safe.

Soon the rebels were seen massing for an attack from several directions, as expected, from behind the lines of skirmishers. But as the skirmishers advanced, a rumble was heard in the distance over the sound of the rebel guns. Shells were seen exploding around the rebel battery that had been positioned to support the final attack, shells that were not fired from Daniel's guns. Colonel Wildes and the men in town could not see who was firing from beyond the rebel rear; only smoke from the distant guns could be seen from the heights around Moorefield. The rebel lines fell back, and Jones called in his skirmishers.

Men from the 116th looked to the south anxiously. They hoped the "Old Colonel" was coming up from Petersburg with the 123rd Ohio Infantry and the rest of the West Virginia Battery. But they could not be sure, as not even field glasses could confirm it. The colors were placed conspicuously at a commanding point to be seen by the troops approaching from the south so that the approaching relief would know the 116th was still in the fight. Daniel's section of guns was turned on the rebel battery along the Petersburg Road, and the rebel guns were soon being shelled from both directions at once. Several unsuccessful attempts were made to send a courier through to determine if Colonel Washburn was indeed approaching from the south. Finally Hiram Baker was chosen to attempt a passage under the cover of an artillery barrage. Daniel's guns concentrated their fire to open a path for Baker. Under the cover of Daniel's guns, Baker made it through to Colonel Washburn's lines.

While Hiram Baker slipped through the rebel lines, a courier, under the cover of the same artillery barrage, arrived from Colonel Washburn to confirm that his force was approaching from Petersburg and attacking the rebel rear. This encouraging news prompted an offensive move. A portion of the 116th was sent against the wing of Jones' force on the opposite side of town. At this point the Jones became concerned that he could not unite his divided force, and he was aware that more Federal reinforcements from New Creek could arrive. He probably did not know it, but his force was still strong enough to capture Moorefield. Jones decided to hold his position with his right wing while the other portion of his force retreated. Then, according to Jones, "when, my battery having expended the last of its well-husbanded, worthless ammunition, and when Colonel Dulany was so far on his way as to be out of danger, I retired up the South Fork."[16]

Jones slipped past Colonel Washburn, and the rest of his force joined him late that night about ten miles from Moorefield. Being disappointed with not capturing the town, Jones prepared for another attack to be attempted the next day. He blamed his failure to take the town on his "worthless" artillery ammunition and his "ignorance of the country," thus leading to the loss of "the rich fruits of hard labor."[17] Grumble Jones was accustomed to success. His subsequent record of success would indicate that the 116th had behaved splendidly at Moorefield.

Colonel Washburn and his force reached Moorefield before dark to save the 116th from "either a severe and bloody fight, or capture, and perhaps both."[18] Washburn's men had made the relief march without tents and blankets, so the men of the 116th did their best to provide for their comfort during the night.

The following day Colonel Mulligan marched in with his 23rd Illinois Infantry from New Creek. General Jones had been making preparations for another attempt to capture Moorefield when he learned of Mulligan's approach. Without artillery ammunition and facing more difficult odds, Jones decided to retreat back to Virginia. The combined Federal force made an attempt to follow. Finding evidence that the rebels were in full retreat, the Federals returned to Moorefield.

The outcome of the Battle of Moorefield could not have been much more satisfactory to the Federals. Only three men from the 116th were wounded, two of them slightly. The following men were captured, most probably from the picket surprised early in the morning: Lieutenant Henry Okey, of Company D; Sergeant Benjamin Sheffield; Byron Battin; William H. Brown; Abraham Butterworth; Joseph Cullison; Asa Ladd; Isaiah Matheny; William Robinett; George Sigler; Daniel Weddle; John Wilkinson; all of Company K; Corporal Harrison Cochran; Andrew Henthorn; Adam Ollam; John Walter; Robert J. Hathaway; Samuel Luthey; all of Company E. The regimental sutler, Elmer Armstrong, was caught by the rebels at the home of Major Harness, a local resident. Armstrong had gone there to hide his money and goods, as he was a friend of Major Harness. The rebels released him the following day several miles from Moorefield, and he was forced to walk through the unfamiliar mountains back to town, arriving thoroughly worn out. The fact that Armstrong was a Democrat did not seem to help much with his captors who heaped insults upon him.

Some of the captured men were exchanged within the month, but others remained captives until June and July. Lieutenant Okey was taken to Richmond as a prisoner of war. Like so many others in Libby Prison he took sick, and he seemed to have never fully recovered his health. Okey had tendered his resignation before his capture, and as soon as his discharge reached the regiment the rebel authorities were informed. Soon afterwards Okey was released from rebel prison, and in April he was released from Camp Parole and allowed to return home. His loyalty was never doubted; it was understood that his health had broken down during his time in service, and at forty-seven he was too old for active field service.

Elmer Armstrong claimed that the rebels who captured him believed that at least three regiments were defending Moorefield. He said the rebels called him a liar when he told them that only the 116th defended the town. Of course General Jones did not mention this in his report, but the rebel commander's caution may have resulted from an overestimation of Federal strength at Moorefield. Had Jones attacked Moorefield with his whole force in the morning, it is probable that the 116th and the town would have been captured.

The skirmish at Moorefield was the regiment's first combat experience, and the men had every reason to be proud of their conduct. General Milroy, Colonel Washburn, and Colonel Mulligan each highly commended the regiment for its behavior in the face of an overwhelming enemy force. The day after the battle General Milroy sent the following message:

"Lt. Col. T. F. Wildes, Moorefield, Va.:

"Accept my congratulations and thanks, yourself and your gallant command, for the courage and skill with which you defended your post against such overwhelming numbers of the enemy. I thought I was not mistaken when I told you, Dec. 30th, 'you can whip any force that comes against you.' I bespeak for you and your noble regiment a glorious record."

"R. H. Milroy, Maj. Gen'l Commanding" [18]

This was a very high complement, richly deserved. Milroy was saying that he expected great things from the 116th. They would not disappoint. However, Milroy had reason to be thankful. Had the 116th been captured, as it should have been, Milroy would have been responsible. The episode at Moorefield was only a prelude to further and greater ineptitude on the part of Milroy's generalship. Additionally, Milroy may have created some incentive for the rebels to attack Moorefield by ordering the 116th to crack down on residents who would not take an oath of allegiance. Even female residents were not exempt. At least one Moorefield woman was sent to prison in Wheeling for apparent disloyal behavior. Milroy was busy in Winchester building such a repugnant reputation that even loyal people were sometimes outraged. The Confederate Government began to take notice of Milroy's behavior and eventually asked the Federal Government to look into it.

On January sixth Grumble Jones wrote a complaining report about his attack on Moorefield that was forwarded to General Robert E. Lee. General Lee referred the report to the Confederate Secretary of War, probably because of concern for the general's complaints about his artillery ammunition. Rebel Colonel Gorgas responded, "... I am quite as much inclined to blame General Jones' artillerists, as he is to blame my ammunition. Without wishing to detract from his skill as an officer, I may be allowed to state that he is known to be very apt to find fault."[19]

Jones was building his reputation for grumbling, Milroy was building his for meanness, and the 116th was building a reputation for steadfastness in battle that would prove just as real as the others.

"I'LL PAROLE EVERY DEVIL OF YOU"
5

The 116th was ordered to occupy Romney, West Virginia, and on January 9, 1863, the regiment departed Moorefield. Four men remained in the town while the regiment took up the march. Sergeant Charles Allison and Carmi Allison, both of Company K, and Sergeant Robert Wells and D. J. Haning, of Company G, were captured in Moorefield while the town was still in sight of the rear guard. The rebels moved in to reoccupy Moorefield as soon as the 116th departed, and these men were quickly taken as prisoners. The four men were paroled; this meant that the rebels released them on a promise that the prisoners would not participate as soldiers again until properly exchanged for a rebel prisoner of war or parolee.

Somehow many of the slaves in the region had come to believe that the Emancipation Proclamation was applicable to them and that they were free. Actually the proclamation did not apply to West Virginia. Nevertheless, many escaped slaves flocked to Moorefield because slaves living in the area had spread the news that the 116th was going to move. Some of these "contrabands", as escaped slaves were called, followed the regiment on the march to Romney to escape their masters.

As it happened that day was very poor for marching. It was very cold and it was snowing hard. The roads were soon in very bad condition, making the march miserable and fatiguing. While the blacks had not been invited to accompany the regiment, they were not turned away. That afternoon the hospital steward, apparently seeing two contraband women struggling in the snow, allowed them to ride with him on the seat of the ambulance.

Someone, probably in a letter sent to Ohio, made an accusation that "Colonel Washburn and Lieutenant Colonel Wildes had turned sick men out of their ambulances and put niggers in to ride."[1] As the story reached Ohio and was told and retold, it grew in proportions and became more distorted. Lieutenant Colonel Wildes still had ties to the *Athens Messenger* newspaper in Athens County; so to quash the ugly, insidious rumor he and several officers prepared a card to be sent to that newspaper to explain the truth. Colonel Wildes wrote, "such was then the bitter prejudice against the colored people, that their action seemed not only advisable, but really necessary, in order to relieve the public mind from the impression gained that the 116th had officers who would throw their sick men out of ambulances to make room for 'niggers'." [2] The following officers attached their names to the explanation sent to the newspaper:

John Hull, Capt. Co. E; Levi Lupton, 2nd Lt. Co. C; Wilson Martin, Lt. Co. F; Jas. Mann 1st Lt. Co. C; E. Brady, Chaplain; C. Ridgeway, Capt. Co. A; H. Sibley, 2nd Lt., Co. B; Wm. Myers, Capt. Co. D; John Varley, Capt. Co. E; H. Karr, 1st Lt. Co. G; Mathew Brown, Capt. Co. F; W. Gilkey, Surgeon; T. Mallory, 1st Lt. Co. B; Edwin Keys, Capt. Co. B; A. Frame, Lt. Co. I; B. Chaney, 2nd Lt. Co. D; and F. Arckenoe, Capt. Co. C.

The snow fell hard throughout the first day of the march to Romney. That night the men made their camp in a foot of snow. Top fence rails of local farmers quickly fell prey to soldiers seeking campfire fuel. The men huddled around the fires for warmth through the night and were probably glad to be on their way early the next morning.

On January eleventh the 116th reached Romney to assume their occupation duty. For the next two months the 116th would busily engage in drilling, foraging, and picketing, ever watchful for the seemingly ubiquitous guerrillas and rebel raiders. At Moorefield the men had finally realized the value of drill and discipline, and after that battle they were much less inclined to complain about the tedium and boredom of drilling. General William Hazen, who commanded Ohio troops in the West, aptly explained why drill and discipline were so vital to the army during the war:

> Living is better than dying, health better than sickness, thrift better than squalor...discipline alone makes order possible... And just in proportion as men oppose or officers fail to enforce organization and discipline, they are enemies to humanity.3

Hazen's views on discipline may have been more intense than Colonel Washburn's; nevertheless, the men had learned that drill and discipline could help get them out of a bad spot in battle. An incident near Romney the following month involving Company F would validate Hazen's viewpoint.

Soon after the 116th arrived in Romney, a party of twenty-five guerrillas made away with a shipment of mail bound for the railroad. Carelessness on the part of the cavalry escort was blamed for the loss. The men were no doubt outraged to think their personal letters to their wives and sweethearts were in the hands of the enemy. The mail at best was lost; at worst it would serve as an amusement to the guerrillas.

A few days later a soldier, from Company I, presented himself to headquarters with a plan to help solve the mail theft problem. The soldier asked to be allowed to act as a scout to gather information about the whereabouts of the guerillas. With his help, he told the officers, the army would have advance information about guerrilla movements and thus be able to avoid another guerrilla attack on the mail. This seemed like a very brave offer considering the danger and risk involved in his plan. An officer asked if he could deceive the enemy about his true identity in the event of his capture. The soldier considered it briefly and then replied, "I guess I can, I have deceived everyone I have ever had anything to do with so far in life." Headquarters was convinced, and the soldier was sent off on his "scouting mission." A few days later, the "scout" was found at a house near the picket line where he had all the while been "sparking" a girl. According to Colonel Wildes, "His authority to scout was revoked, but his ability to 'deceive' remained unquestioned ever afterwards."4

    The most forgettable combat affair in the history of the regiment occurred on February sixteenth near Romney; it was the only truly shameful action on the regiment's record. Captain Mathew Brown had taken most of his Company F and some troopers from the Ringgold Cavalry Battalion out on a foraging mission to escort the forage train. The rebel report claimed that at least twenty-seven wagons were in the train. According to Colonel Washburn's report, and Lieutenant Colonel Wildes' account, the train and guard were captured because of negligence on the part of the escort commander Captain Brown. As Wildes told it, when the train was about seven miles from Romney on its return, the soldiers on escort duty were straggling and wandering along the road. The men were in all likelihood doing a little foraging of their own at farmsteads along the way. Captain Mathew Brown and First Lieutenant Wilson Martin were riding ahead of the train apparently unconcerned that the escort was not doing its job. Rebel Captain McNeill of Imboden's Cavalry, who as mentioned before was a daring raider, saw his opportunity to strike the train and attacked with, as he told it, twenty-four men. There was no resistance, and it seems no were shots fired at anyone. As the rebels rushed in among the wagons with pistols drawn, Captain McNeill yelled out, "I don't want to hurt you, throw down your arms and I'll parole every devil of you and you can go home."5 At least sixty men complied while the remainder fled. Captain Brown "ran off at full speed to camp, never making even the slightest attempt to join his men, or avert this disaster."6 A few of the men managed to escape with Captain Brown and Lieutenant Martin.

    Captain McNeill wisely gathered his prisoners and the wagons and prepared to make his escape. The wagon reins were cut to free the teams, and the wagons were set afire. The rebel raiders managed to gather at least fifty horses and eight mules that were taken away. As soon as news of the attack reached Romney, a large cavalry force was sent to find McNeill and his men, but the rebels had made their escape with the horses and prisoners. The following day, true to his word, McNeill paroled most of the men from the 116th, telling them to have Captain Brown send out his shoulder straps to him. Obviously, McNeill thought that after this disgraceful affair Captain Brown wouldn't need his shoulder straps.

The debacle was a great embarrassment to the 116th and especially Colonel Wildes. Captain Brown and First Lieutenant Martin were arrested, and charges were preferred against them. In the resulting court martial both men were acquitted, but they were publicly reprimanded. Colonel Wildes placed the whole blame on Captain Brown. Henceforth Brown was anathema to him. Colonel Wildes was careful not to criticize his comrades in the 116th, but he did not hesitate to criticize Captain Brown and denounce him. Conversely, he forgave Lieutenant Martin and wrote, "No braver officer belonged to the 116th than Lieutenant Martin afterwards proved himself; and no company of men did any more gallant service than company F performed throughout its term of service."7 Subsequent events showed that Wildes was not simply smoothing his comrades' feelings. Some of the bravest men in the 116th and some of the best fighting came from Company F.

It is not too surprising that Captain Brown was acquitted in the proceedings. The captain, Colonel Washburn, and Major Morris were residents of Monroe County, and more than half the men in the regiment had been recruited there. Captain Brown was in fact wealthier than the colonel and the major.8 It should be remembered that the men had only been in the army for a few months; yet they had been neighbors for years, and many would remain neighbors after the war.

At least twenty-eight men from Company F were captured in the affair near Romney. Some of the men returned to the regiment as soon as McNeill paroled them. Others seem to have followed McNeill's advice and went home. Family records indicate that Private Henry Martin went home and stayed until he was exchanged; and another seven of the parolees didn't return to the regiment until June, it is probable that they also went home. The following men were listed as captured near Romney on February 16, 1863: Sergeants Andrew Stevens and Mathias Rucker, Corporals Robert Martin and Richard Wilson, Privates William Allen, Sheppard Barnhouse, Reason Carpenter, Robert Carpenter, Henry Dillon, Jacob Dillon, John Dillon, William Fisher, Amos Jones, Henry King, William King, Morris Krouse, Henry Martin, Jacob Matz, John Morris, Thomas Peterson, George Ray, Abalard Shahan, Robert Smith, Jonas Steed, James Steen, William Sutton, Samuel Wilson, and Peter Yoho. The men who returned to the regiment within a few days were, Sergeant Rucker, Corporal Robert Martin, Privates William and Henry King, Reason and Robert Carpenter, John Morris, Jonas Steed, William Sutton, and Peter Yoho.

According to a newspaper report filed from Romney, seven men escaped with the two officers "under a heavy fire of the enemy." These "few lucky fellows that escaped" were Sergeant Leander Shahan; Privates Lewis Dearth, Stephen Hogue, Edward King, John Martin, Solomon Railing, and Thos. Simmons. Company F had eleven in the hospital, seventeen sick in quarters, and only seventeen remaining on duty after the debacle. "So wags Company F," quipped the correspondent.9

While the 116th idled at Romney in the winter of 1863, the nation was in the throes of dissatisfaction and despair. A combination of military disappointments and political disaffection brought the lowest morale of the war to the army and the nation. The United States never came closer to "the brink of ruin" than during the winter of 1863.10

On the military front, the Federal Armies had turned back the rebel efforts to invade northern territory in September 1862. General George B. McClellan's Army of the Potomac had stopped General Robert E. Lee's attempt to invade Pennsylvania at the terribly bloody Battle of Antietam, Maryland. The Federal Army in the West had also defeated rebel General Braxton Bragg's plans to control Kentucky at the Battle of Perryville, Kentucky. McClellan had a rare opportunity at Antietam to destroy Lee's army and possibly end the war, but his excessive caution allowed the rebels to escape. President Lincoln permanently removed McClellan from command. His successor General Ambrose E. Burnside was soundly defeated with heavy losses by Lee's army at Fredericksburg, Virginia, in December. Burnside's subsequent attempt at a campaign, the infamous "Mud March," was another dismal failure. The army and the nation were thoroughly disgusted with the overall inept military leadership.

Following Burnside's bungling failures in Virginia, the forlorn Lincoln Administration couldn't explain the seemingly endless string of military disappointments. Federal General William S. Rosecrans saved the Administration with his narrow victory near Murfreesboro, Tennessee. On December 31, 1862, through January 2, 1863, the Federals under Rosecrans barely held off repeated rebel attacks to defeat General Braggs' army at Stones River. President Lincoln acknowledged the magnitude of the battle in a message to Rosecrans, "I can never forget, whilst I remember anything, that you gave us a hard-earned victory, which, if there had been a defeat instead, the nation could scarcely have lived over."11

The string of military disappointments followed Lincoln's Emancipation Proclamation and coincided with its implementation. The Proclamation was easily "the most explosive and unpopular act of Lincoln's presidency."12 To many of the Ohio soldiers the Proclamation was a betrayal. They had joined the army to preserve the Union and the Constitution. Many soldiers believed that "emancipation was an unconstitutional and illegitimate war aim," and by January 1863 "a bitter and explicit disagreement about emancipation divided northern soldiers."13 Emancipation divided Northerners to such an extent that, according to Colonel Wildes, "it was feared that the North itself might become the scene of civil strife."14

In the midst of this pervasive despondency, the rebels attempted a "trial balloon" parole policy. Federal soldiers from the Romney area were going home or returning to camp and refusing to do duty on the grounds that they had been captured and paroled by the rebels. An investigation revealed that local rebel sympathizers kept fake parole forms signed by guerrilla chiefs to offer to homesick and disaffected soldiers. As more soldiers became aware of this opportunity, they would go out to get a "parole," sometimes paying for it with coffee and sugar. According to Colonel Wildes, "Paroles became as common, at one time, as sutler's checks…It was determined to put a stop to it at all hazards, for it was simply another way of deserting."15 It can be substantiated that this local parole policy had its equivalent in the regular rebel command structure. Rebel General William Jones in a report to General Robert E. Lee wrote: "A lieutenant who deserted from the One Hundred and Tenth Ohio represents much dissatisfaction among the troops on account of the emancipation proclamation." (The 110th was one of the regiments in Colonel Washburn's Brigade.) Jones continued, " He represents many would follow his example if insured kind treatment by our Government." General Lee replied in a letter dated February 3, 1863, "You are authorized to offer kind treatment to all who come into your lines."16

A plan was devised to check the loss of men from gratuitous paroles. The authorities in Southeast Ohio were told to arrest all soldiers at home without furloughs. These soldiers were returned to camp, and the soldiers with fake paroles in camp were armed and returned to duty. It was soon obvious that the fake parole excuse would no longer serve as a pass for homesick soldiers to return home. Paroles became a symbol of cowardice that the more dedicated soldiers viewed with disgust. After the army took action to arrest parolees and the men in the ranks realized the shame of paroles the problem quickly faded away.

Colonel Wildes was very concerned with the regiment's morale during the stay in Romney. The 116th was recruited in a region with a Democratic Party voting majority. Many Democrats in Ohio were vehemently opposed to emancipation, and the soldiers were receiving letters encouraging them to desert. Some newspapers were so critical of the administration that General Milroy took action to suppress them, most notably the *Wheeling Register*. The men were told that if disloyal letters and newspapers continued to show up in camp the mail would also be suppressed. This undemocratic measure was viewed as necessary to prevent an even more serious collapse of discipline, but something more effective was needed.

In February the officers and men of the 116th gathered for a patriotic meeting. The officers made resolutions designed to encourage the troops and to send a message to the home front in no uncertain terms that the 116th Ohio Infantry intended to see the war through. The resolutions were written in emphatic Victorian language and published the counties in Ohio where the 116th had been raised. The following is an example of the text of the resolutions:

> Resolve, That nothing but *"unconditional surrender"* will answer the demands of the true soldier and patriot.
>
> Resolved, That we, as a loyal soldiery, acknowledge the Administration the medium through which the destruction of the rebellion is to be made effectual; and that we owe it to all we hold sacred in our blood bought, free institutions, to give it such support as will enable us to hand down to generations to come, intact, this glorious Union of ours.
>
> Resolved, That any party, or set of men who, by fractious opposition to the Administration, the Government, or the prosecution of the war, injure our noble cause, *will meet with overwhelming and popular indignation from the soldiery both now and* HEREAFTER.17

The resolutions condemned "copperheads" and those sending disloyal letters to the camp, and served to make clear that the 116th was loyal to the Administration. Colonel Wildes noted that a similar meeting on a much greater scale was held at Murfreesboro, Tennessee, by the Army of the Cumberland to impress upon the Northern people the need to stay the course and accept nothing short of the surrender of the rebels.

It was a gradual process, but slowly the North came to accept emancipation. The soldiers and the people understood that the wealthy Southern planter class had brought on the war for the sake of slavery, and the threat of war would always exist until slavery was forever swept away. With each month after January of 1863 the army's morale improved. Patriotic sentiment waxed stronger by the day. Resentment of the "Southern traitors" and love of country, the main motives for volunteering in the first place, overcame fears of governmental infringement of personal liberties.

Of all the explanations of how the country overcame the governmental crisis during the winter of 1863, that of Colonel Wildes came as close as any. Wildes wrote that the "conversion was doubtless attributable to the patriotic notion of checking the rising anarchy by a sacrifice of personal opinion to the general welfare."18 It was certainly true of the soldiers of the 116th, the Democrats in particular.

Colonel Wildes gave the impression that this sentiment was unanimous in the 116th. According his version no soldier dissented. Doubtless this was simply not the case. There were clearly many soldiers who did not want to stay. However, there can be no doubt that the overwhelming majority of the rank and file of the 116th did want to fight on. Letters and statements during and after the war by soldiers such as James Dalzell, Benjamin Dye, Henry Johnson and others are filled with resentment toward the rebellion. A letter from Camp Marietta dated August 23, 1862, by one of the Dye brothers of Monore County who served in the army gives an excellent example of how the Ohio soldiers felt about the war and why they were in it. The letter began with the preamble, "The Union now, henceforth, and forever! Amen!" Half way into the letter Dye wrote, "It is true that I won't make much money by going to war. I did not volunteer for that purpose. I could have made more money by staying at home. But I think it my duty to fight for my country, liberty, the Union, and the Constitution. That is what I am fighting for...I am willing to face the cannonballs for 13 dollars a month for my country and liberty."19

The 116th, like the rest of the country, weathered the trial of that winter and forged ahead. The two months at Romney were put to good use for drilling, officer and NCO schools, and attention to discipline. An unfortunate accident on February seventeenth marred an otherwise productive stay at Romney. Private Amos S. Beyers, of Company C, was killed when a musket was fired accidentally. Beyers was said to be an excellent soldier, and his death, though tragic and mourned, impressed upon the regiment the danger of carelessness in the handling of arms.

As any veteran knows, service in wartime is not all horror and drudgery. Colonel Wildes seemed to enjoy his stay at Romney. His letter from Romney serves as a reminder that some of the best memories of a man's lifetime are made in the service. Here he mentions some of the "genuine fun and amusement" he experienced at Romney:

> In the Adjutant's office just now is heard the sweet sounds of the violin and the Major's strong bass voice with the Sergeant Major's fine tenor, while, overhead, in the Quartermaster's room, is heard the fun and frolic of Lee, Walker and Campbell, and the useless protests of the matter-of-fact old Quartermaster. I would like to take this whole headquarters crew home with me and show them to you. You would think us wild barbarians no doubt, and it

is more than likely we have all forgotten the ways of civilized life, but we are all apt scholars, and with good teachers would soon learn them again.20

In March, with the onset of the season for active campaigning, General Milroy consolidated his division at Winchester, Virginia. On March 15, 1863, the 116th left Romney and their duty in that sector behind for good. They reached Winchester on March seventeenth. It was here in the Shenandoah Valley that the 116th would render its most important service to the Union and experience the bulk of its fighting and dying.

MILROY'S WEARY BOYS
6

When the 116th reached Winchester, it was reassigned to a new brigade commanded by Brigadier General Washington L. Elliott, as Milroy's Division was undergoing reorganization. The brigade was known as Elliott's Brigade or the First Brigade of Milroy's Second Division and was composed the 110th, 116th, 122nd and 123rd Ohio Infantry Regiments, the 12th and 13th Pennsylvania Cavalry Regiments, and Battery L, 5th U. S. Artillery. All of the units in the new brigade were relatively inexperienced; none of the units had yet participated in a major battle or seen heavy combat. Colonel James Washburn, his brigade now incorporated into Elliott's Brigade, returned as colonel of the 116th. Some of the officers Washburn had taken with him for his brigade staff returned to the regiment; these officers included Adjutant Ballard, Quartermaster Williams, Lieutenant Sibley, Lieutenant Cochran, and some enlisted men who had also been on brigade staff duty.

The 116th now embarked on a new and more active phase in the war. After arriving at Winchester, the 116th was almost constantly engaged in foraging and scouting operations. There were several hard fatiguing marches, the only useful purpose of which was to toughen the men for what lay ahead. One such march, to Capon Springs and Lost River, was memorable only for the beautiful scenery encountered along the way. Private James Dalzell of Company H remembered that very fatiguing march with great disgust, noting that General Elliott had not properly prepared for a washed out bridge the regiment encountered, forcing the men to back-track many miles. During two of their forays up the valley the 116th made contact with the enemy near Strasburg. While other units suffered casualties during the spring on these scouting and reconnaissance missions, the 116th, fortunately, did not. On April twenty-eighth near Strasburg, the 13th Pennsylvania Cavalry was ambushed and the 116th came up in support. The cavalry lost six men killed and several wounded.

In the first week of May the 116th again marched up the valley as far as New Market on a reconnaissance. No important rebel force was encountered, and the 116th returned to Winchester by the ninth. The regiment's next duty assignment was macadamizing (paving with broken stone) on the Martinsburg Road north of Winchester.

As previously mentioned, Colonel Washburn had traveled to Columbus in an effort to secure better arms for the 116th and had met with success. On April 3, 1863, the 116th was issued new Springfield Rife Muskets. Designed at the famous Springfield Armory in Springfield,

Massachusetts, Springfield Rifle Muskets were by far the most popular muzzle loading infantry arms of the Civil War, and regiments receiving them felt fortunate. Lieutenant Colonel Wildes was pleased with the new arms as he wrote, "now we felt, for the first time, that we had a serviceable and respectable arm."1 The men were probably just as pleased with their new Springfields as another Yankee who wrote about his regiment receiving them, "Our guns were issued to us, beautiful pieces, walnut stock, well oiled, the spring of the lock just stiff and just limber enough; barrel, long and glistening."2 Along with the new muskets the 116th would be issued matching accouterments and bayonets.

While the 116th was stationed at Winchester, the rebel war effort reached the pinnacle of its power and success. Following General Lee's punishing victory at Fredericksburg in December, President Lincoln had again looked to a new man to lead the Army of the Potomac. Major General Ambrose Burnside was replaced by Major General Joseph "Fighting Joe" Hooker in late January. After assuming command General Hooker devised a brilliant plan to outflank the rebels at Fredericksburg. With the coming of spring, Hooker put his plan into action and succeeded in placing his army across the Rappahannock River and past Lee's army at Fredericksburg. When General Lee responded, a fierce battle erupted in the forested region near Fredericksburg at a crossroads called Chancellorsville. General Lee, in his typical high-risk style, divided his army and surprised General Hooker with a flank attack. "Fighting Joe" Hooker, in effect, lost his nerve, and Lee won his greatest victory of the war over the Army of the Potomac at Chancellorsville. Hooker's offensive had been thwarted. The Army of the Potomac began retreating back across the Rappahannock River on May 4, 1863.

The victory at Chancellorsville had proved costly to the rebels. General Thomas "Stonewall" Jackson had been accidentally wounded and subsequently died; thus, Lee lost his best subordinate. General Lee was above all a Virginian, and he longed to rid his state of the scourge of war. After Chancellorsville Lee was highly confident, and he believed that a decisive victory in the North could shorten or even effectively win the war for the rebels. Accustomed to winning by taking long chances, Lee made plans for his greatest gamble of the war. Lee decided to attempt a second invasion of the North. If his plan succeeded, the rebels could hope for foreign recognition, or, even better, force the Federal Government to seek peace on rebel terms.

Lee's invasion plans held substantial drawbacks for the rebels. While Lee was winning at Chancellorsville, Federal General Ulysses S. Grant was laying siege to the rebel citadel at Vicksburg, Mississippi. Rebel President Jefferson Davis wanted to send some of Lee's troops to help defend Vicksburg. Davis knew that holding Vicksburg was vital to the

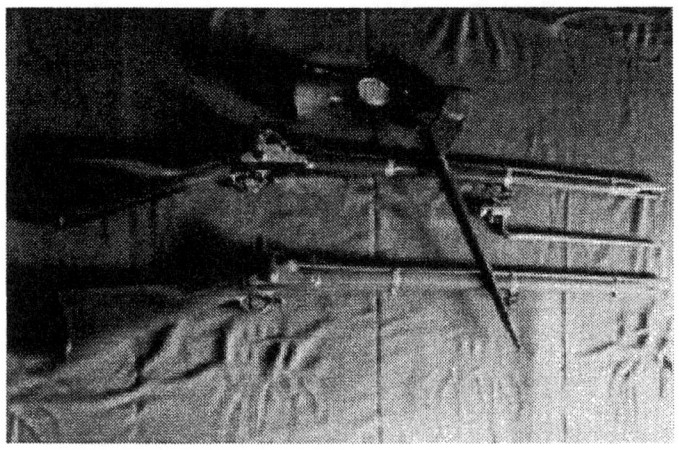

Arms of the 116th: Top to bottom: Waistbelt with cap box and bayonet scabbard, Model 1861 Springfield Rifle Musket and bayonet, Model 1863 Rifle Musket. The 116th was armed with new Springfields on April 3, 1863.

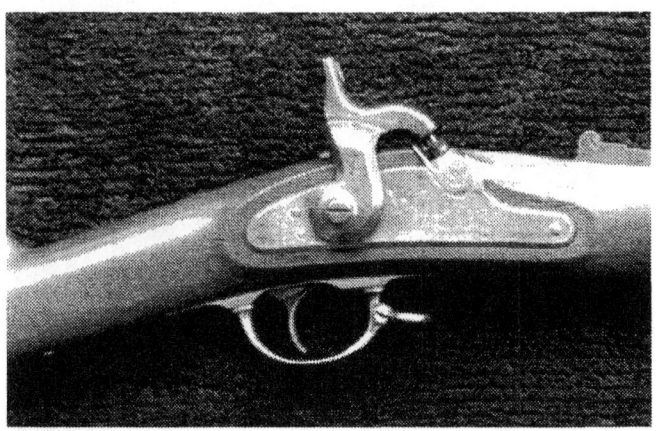

Model 1863 Springfield Rifle Musket lock and hammer.

rebel war effort. In essence it was a question of whether Davis was willing to risk the capture of Vicksburg on General Lee's invasion plan. Davis understood that Lee had to win decisively in the North. Ultimately he placed the fate of his cause in the hands of General Lee and approved his plan of invasion. Lee's invasion plan for the summer of 1863 has become known to history as the Gettysburg Campaign, and when Lee launched this campaign, he knew that failure was not an option.

The 116th and Milroy's command at Winchester lay directly in the path of General Lee's invasion route. Lee planned to march his army into the Shenandoah Valley north of Strasburg and proceed north toward Chambersburg, Pennsylvania. Before embarking on the campaign, Lee had reorganized his Army of Northern Virginia into three corps rather than two. Replacing General Jackson in command of the II Corps was Lieutenant General Richard S. Ewell. Following the battle between Lee's cavalry and the Army of the Potomac's cavalry at Brandy Station, Lee launched Ewell's II Corps on June tenth. Ewell was given the assignment of destroying Milroy's force at Winchester.

In early June the 116th was suffering from an outbreak of serious illness. Several men had contracted typhoid fever and were incapacitated. Only one physician remained on duty with the 116th during this period, as the other two had resigned. Doctor W. R. Gilkey, the remaining surgeon, died on June fourth from the fever. Doctor Gilkey was overworked tending the sick, and he "fell a sacrifice to his extraordinary devotion to duty."3 Private Jacob Butts of Company G also died on the fourth in the hospital. Butts was reportedly one of the physically strongest men in the regiment. Fortunately for the 116th three replacement doctors were appointed to fill the vacancies of surgeon and assistant surgeons. Doctor Thomas Shannon was appointed surgeon and Doctors Brown and Smith filled the other two positions.

As Ewell's Corps moved into the Shenandoah Valley south of Winchester, General Milroy remained determined to hold his position at Winchester. As late as June fourth Milroy held a business-as-usual grand review of his division. The Federal High Command was unsure of the location of Lee's army, and General in Chief Henry Halleck began suggesting that Milroy withdraw from Winchester to Harper's Ferry, some thirty miles to the northeast. Just as he had encouraged Lieutenant Colonel Wildes to hold Moorefield against General Jones the previous January, Milroy fatuously decided to hold Winchester for no explainable reason. Milroy insisted that he could defend Winchester "against any force the Rebels could afford to bring against it."4

Milroy's reasoning for attempting to hold Winchester is difficult to assess. Milroy perhaps believed that a series of earthworks constructed on a line of low hills or ridges west of Winchester would enable him to defend the town. This line of earthworks consisted of three forts known as the Star Fort, West Fort, and Flag Fort (also called Fort Milroy). All of the earthworks except the Flag Fort were commanded by higher ground to the west; and the rebels could easily approach the West Fort unseen within two hundred yards, because the woods to the west of the fort had not been sufficiently cleared. Milroy overestimated the strength of the defenses at Winchester. An example of his over confidence showed in February when he wrote: "They may come in sufficient numbers to surround me, but they will never capture me."5

Colonel Wildes in his account of Winchester mentioned that by June twelfth the troops in Winchester were on alert expecting the appearance of a rebel force. On the twelfth the 116th, 123rd Ohio, 12th West Virginia and some cavalry were deployed south of town near Kernstown and met a rebel force that had appeared near the picket lines. After some skirmishing, at one point the 116th managed to enfilade the rebel line, a much larger rebel force was seen approaching from the south. Several rebels were captured in the skirmishing. General Milroy was informed, and he rode out to reconnoiter. The force with the 116th remained in line of battle until dusk, when they were withdrawn into Winchester.

On Saturday, June thirteenth Ewell was within striking distance of Winchester. General Lee had been planning to destroy Milroy and his force for several months; now Ewell assigned Major General Jubal A. Early and his division to do the job. General Early approached Winchester from the south on the Valley Pike. As the rebels neared Kernstown, a hamlet just south of Winchester, General Early deployed his division and commenced probing the Federal positions there. Little more than some skirmishing was needed for Early's Division to push beyond Kernstown, but the rebels were checked before reaching Winchester by a strong Federal force on Bower's Hill. Milroy had posted artillery and infantry there. General Early later wrote, "the enemy shelled my brigades heavily from his guns on Bower's Hill; and by the time they were made it became too dark to proceed farther."6 Milroy then ordered his troops under the cover of his forts. Early's rebels remained on the field through "the night in a drenching rain."7

General Ewell had arrived in the vicinity with Major General Edward Johnson's Division while Early probed the southern approach to Winchester. Johnson's Division would be employed the following day on the eastern edge of Winchester as a diversion to distract attention from Early's main attack.

The 116th had been split up and assigned separate details preceding the rebel attack. Companies A and I had been placed with Colonel Andrew McReynold's command and were at Bunker Hill, West Virginia, on the thirteenth. Company C was sent to the West Fort to support

Battery L, 5th U.S. Artillery positioned there, and another company was sent to the Star Fort. The rest of the regiment was assigned to work on the fortifications.

Major Morris with Companies A and I had been left in Bunker Hill when a strong rebel cavalry force appeared on the afternoon of the thirteenth. Morris and his men occupied a fortified church with loopholes and barricades for protection. Morris, thinking that only a small rebel force was present, emerged from the brick church with his two companies to confront the enemy. To his surprise a force of about 2,000 rebels suddenly attacked. Nearly half of Morris' force were shot or captured as they retreated to the relative safety of the church. The rebels surrounded the church but could not force its surrender. They were obliged to keep a respectful distance from its protective walls. Captain Cochran of Company I was severely wounded in front of the church when the rebels attacked, and Lieutenant A. B. Frame assumed command of the company. He was mentioned for conspicuous bravery for his coolness and leadership while covering the retreat to the church under heavy enemy fire. The Lieutenant was one of the last men to enter the church.

Morris and his two companies spent several anxious hours after dark surrounded by the vastly superior rebel force. The rebels once approached the church under a flag of truce to negotiate the surrender of Morris' force. Morris promptly refused saying, "We are not doing that kind of business."[8] At about 2 a.m. the rebels let down their guard enough for Morris and his men to find a gap. They managed to steal away and reached Winchester about 7 a.m. on the fourteenth.

As the rebels closed in on Winchester on the morning of Sunday, June 14, 1863, even President Lincoln was anxious and worried about Milroy's command. The President wired General Schenck, the department commander, hoping that it was not too late. He ordered Schenck to "Get Milroy from Winchester to Harper's Ferry if possible. He will be gobbled up, if he remains, if he is not already past salvation."[9]

The morning of June 14, 1863, opened with General Early sending two regiments forward to occupy Bowers Hill, still held by a thin line of Federal skirmishers. Soon afterwards Early and General Ewell met on the high ground to assess the Federal positions and determine their plan of attack. The two generals could see that higher ground to the west commanded the forts near Winchester. Ewell ordered Early to take part of his division around to the west of town and then reconnoiter in preparation for an assault on the Federal forts. In the meantime, Ewell assigned General Johnson's Division the task of probing the southeastern and eastern approaches to Winchester to distract Milroy's attention from Early's main attack. The rebel commander also directed Johnson to be prepared to march north of Winchester in the event that Early's attack was successful; Ewell intended for Johnson's Division to be in place to block Milroy's escape route on the Martinsburg Pike near Stephenson's Depot.

Early left Brigadier General John B. Gordon's Brigade in place at Bower's Hill and took the rest of his division on a circuitous route to his objective near the West Fort. Even though the "Silver Eagle" spent most of the day perched "in a lookout, high up on the flag-staff in the center of the main fort, coolly directing every movement," he failed to detect Early's movemenets.[10] As Ewell had hoped, Milroy was distracted by the skirmishing of Gordon's Brigade to the south and Johnson's men to the east.

While on his route Early managed to find a skillful guide, a Mr. James Baker, who "had been made to feel the tyranny of Milroy." [11] The guide directed Early to a wooded ridge facing the West Fort. Milroy had ordered the wooded ridge cleared for a field of fire from the forts near the town, but only about 150 yards in front of the West Fort had been cut. The wooded ridge provided a perfect opportunity for the rebels to get their artillery in place to bombard the forts without being detected. The general dismissed his guide and reconnoitered the area facing the West Fort in preparation for his assault. By one account Early drew fire from the fort; and as the bullets buzzed around him, he cursed the Yankees and made a quick escape.[12] Early made no mention of it in his account; however, if he did draw fire it was quite possibly from members of the 116th Ohio's Company C who were in the West Fort.

The rebel artillery was placed in two concealed positions, one on the ridge and the other in a cornfield to the north. The guns could be quickly pushed into the clearing to subject the West Fort to artillery crossfire. Early left two of his brigades to the northwest of this position near the Pughtown Road and chose Brigadier General Harry Hays and his Louisiana Brigade to charge the West Fort. These troops were placed on the wooded ridge and aligned in attack formation. They were prepared to emerge from the woods and rush across the 150 yards of cleared ground in front of the West Fort.

It took Early most of the day to reach the attack point, reconnoiter, and get set for the attack. Yet Milroy failed to detect Early's movements; Milroy's only cavalry patrol, sent west on the Pughtown Road, failed to detect Early's force. He did send Colonel J. W. Keifer and his 110th Ohio Infantry into the West Fort and adjacent works to reinforce Company C. The rest of the 116th was scattered throughout Milroy's fortifications, mainly in the Star Fort and Flag Fort. A large part of Milroy's force was positioned to watch the southern approaches to Winchester, but with three cavalry regiments Milroy should have had better reconnaissance patrols on the western approaches.

Late in the afternoon all of the rebel preparations were completed, and Early ordered the artillery bombardment to commence. The cannon were quickly rolled out from concealment and twenty guns "opened almost simultaneously" upon the unprepared West Fort.13 Snow falling from the June skies would not have been a much greater surprise to the fort's defenders than the artillery shells that came raining down on them. The rebels kept pounding the fort for approximately forty-five minutes.

Inside the West Fort the soldiers scrambled for cover. Shells were bursting overhead and into the parapets opening large holes and sending showers of dirt into the air. An artillery caisson and a limber chest were knocked to pieces. The artillery horses from Battery L were killed by the dozens. By the time the artillery fire slackened, only two guns were still in operation to meet the attack.

At about 6 p.m. Early sent the nervous Louisiana Tigers out from the woods intent on reaching the fort in one brief rush across the narrow field of fire. The rebels sent two lines forward with the 6th, 7th and 9th Louisiana Infantry in the first line and the 5th and 8th Louisiana Infantry in the second. At first the Tigers moved forward deliberately, still under the cover of their artillery. When they came within sight of the rebel batteries, the guns ceased fire to keep from hitting their own men. At this point, about 150 yards from the fort, the charge was sounded, and the Tigers rushed the fort.

Inside the fort the dazed defenders rose as the artillery fire slackened to the sight an entire rebel brigade swarming across the short distance separating them and immediately opened fire. Several rebels tumbled down, including the color bearer of the 9th Louisiana. The two operational Federal guns blasted gaps in the rebel lines, and some rebels stumbled and fell, giving the defenders the impression that they were inflicting heavy casualties. The rebels only briefly recoiled and soon forged ahead to reach the parapet, yelling and cursing as they struggled to get into the fort. Several of the defenders broke for the rear as the rebels topped the parapet, but Captain Frederick Arckenoe stood his ground with Company C to protect the nearby artillery gunners. Arckenoe, holding his men in place, was firing his pistol into the onrushing rebels when a bullet ripped through his head and killed him. Sergeant Oswald Heck was also reported killed in the melee. Most of the 110th Ohio managed to escape, but Lieutenant Levi Lupton and almost a third of Company C of the 116th were captured during their stand.

The colonels in their battle reports offered differing versions of the fight at the West Fort. Hays wrote that the defenders in the fort had time for only a few volleys and the Federal guns fired only a few canister

Grave of Captain Frederick Arckenoe, Company C, at Winchester National Cemetery. Captain Arckenoe, a German immigrant, was killed in action at the West Fort near Winchester on June 14, 1863.

Hill at the site of the West Fort at Winchester, VA.

rounds. The defenders had few losses, he wrote, because of the difficulty his troops experienced in reaching and entering the fort, and the "precipitate flight of the enemy" once his troops swarmed over the parapet.14 Once inside the fort his men captured the guns, caissons and artillery horses of Battery L except for the ones shot to prevent removal of the guns. Hays listed his losses on the day as two officers and ten men killed, eight officers and fifty-nine men wounded, for a total of seventy-nine killed and wounded.

Colonel Keifer's report differed markedly from the rebel report. He wrote that about fifty artillery horses were killed and the artillery caissons were destroyed by the rebel bombardment. General Elliott also reported that nearly all of the artillery horses were killed in the fort. Although Keifer reported that the lead rebel regiment carried the U.S. flag, there was no indication that the fort's defenders were fooled by it. He also thought that many more rebels were shot down than the rebel casualty report indicated, and, unlike Hays, that the fort was "of such a character as to afford no obstruction to the entrance of the enemy."15 According to Keifer the 110th fought within the fort until outnumbered and withdrew under the cover of the guns in the main fort. His report also did mention that Captain Arckenoe "was killed while nobly urging on his men, his face to the foe."16

Early's attack and capture of the West Fort was the main action of the day; the rest of the fighting around Winchester was only a rebel diversion. Once the fort was captured, a furious artillery battle commenced and continued until dark. Early ordered up the two other brigades he had on hand. According to Colonel Wildes, "charge after charge was made by their infantry...they charged in heavy masses right up to the ditch surrounding the forts..."17 Actually, these efforts by the rebels were not full scale attacks. By the time Early had brought up his other troops and probed the Federal lines it was nearly dark; consequently, the rebels pulled back under cover for the night.

The fighting on June 13 and 14, 1863, had nearly used up three companies from the 116th. The regiment had been assigned to different positions and marched to and fro during the fighting at the West Fort; still, the bulk of the regiment had been gathered in the main forts by nightfall. The survivors of Company C had retreated to the main fort where Lieutenant Mann gathered them and reported to Colonel Horn of the 6th Maryland. They remained with the 6th on the Federal left for the rest of the day.

The capture of the West Fort gave the rebels a position to batter most of the remaining Federal works with their artillery. General Milroy finally realized that he must evacuate Winchester or eventually surrender if he remained. He held a council of war with his senior officers and determined to try an escape along the Martinsburg Pike during the night. In order to mislead the rebels, he decided to abandon all of his artillery in place to give the impression that his men still manned the forts. Accordingly he ordered all of the guns to be spiked and left behind.

Although the Federals had no other choice except surrender, the decision to withdraw from the forts in the darkness was an invitation to disaster. Somehow Milroy succeeded in pulling his entire division out of Winchester and onto the Martinsburg Pike without being attacked. The sick and wounded were left behind, as were the wagons and supplies. The 116th quietly left the forts around 2 a.m. on June fifteenth, and the situation soon began to unravel. In the confusion and darkness the 116th did not join in marching order with the rest of Elliott's Brigade; instead, it fell in with the Second Brigade.

As previously mentioned, General Ewell had planned to cut off Milroy's escape route with General Johnson's Division. Johnson was in position to block the Martinsburg Pike by 3:30 a.m. with about 3,500 men and some artillery. Colonel Wildes indicated that Milroy and his army were aware of the rebels on the pike before reaching the blockade point near Stephenson's Depot at the junction of the Martinsburg Pike and Charlestown Road. When his force reached the point about four miles north of Winchester, Milroy discovered that both roads were blocked. He had no alternative except to attack Johnson's blocking force and create a breach.

Milroy had no way of knowing the strength of the rebel force confronting him at the junction. The rebels occupied a strong position covering a bridge over a railroad cut along the main road. Milroy put his force in a line of battle spread out over a large area and attacked piecemeal in the pre-dawn darkness. The 116th occupied a position on the left to the west of the Martinsburg Pike. "Here we remained under fire for some minutes," reported Colonel Washburn, before orders were received to "attack the enemy in the rear of the woods on the left of the pike."[18]

Fortunately for the 116th, a staff officer found Colonel Washburn and ordered him to break off the attack and make his retreat the best way possible. A guide from General Milroy arrived to lead the troops on the Federal left in their retreat. Making the escape along with the 116th were the 12th West Virginia Infantry, the 1st New York Cavalry and part of the 12th Pennsylvania Cavalry. Company C remained with the 6th Maryland and escaped with them to Harper's Ferry.

Most of Milroy's infantry fared worse than the 116th at Stephenson's Depot. The regiments attacking along the Charlestown Road suffered the most in the confused and poorly directed fight. The 123rd Ohio and 18th Connecticut charged the center of the rebel lines and were repulsed.

When Brigadier General James Walker's Brigade arrived to reinforce the rebels, the 123rd Ohio and 18th Connecticut surrendered almost en masse. As the fighting sputtered out, "The 13th Pennsylvania Cavalry staged a valiant last charge, but its ranks were shattered by Confederate artillery fire; 300 of the 600 troopers went down."19 (These figures differ from the official casualty report.) The units on the right, including the 110th and 122nd Ohio Infantries, broke through and reached Harper's Ferry, although they lost hundreds captured by the rebels.

The 116th skirmished with the edge of the rebel line until gaining some separation. When the 116th reached a clearing beyond the battlefield, it joined the other regiments that had escaped on the left and the shattered remnants of other regiments. Colonel Washburn took command of the battered survivors and organized a retreat with the infantry in the lead and the cavalry covering the rear.

After some maneuvering through the fields, Washburn's column retreated in the direction of Berkley Springs, West Virginia. Eventually a rebel force found the column and took up the chase. Although Colonel Wildes didn't mention it in his description of the retreat, the men were thoroughly demoralized and only intent on escape. The only real threat posed by the rebels during retreat occurred as the column approached the initial mountain pass. The 12th Pennsylvania galloped ahead to hold the pass before the enemy could block it, and Washburn's column passed through safely. Washburn pushed on to Berkley Springs before resting. At the springs the men washed away the battle grime and briefly rested before resuming the march to St. John's Run. The rebels were still in the vicinity seeking to cut off the retreat; hence, the column was hurried across the ford of the Potomac at St. John's Run. Just as the column completed the crossing, a rebel force appeared on the south side of the river. Washburn moved the column on to Hancock and posted a strong guard at the ford there. The men were allowed to rest at Hancock until 10 p.m.

Washburn's retreating column was much more fortunate than most of Milroy's Division; nevertheless, the 116th lost heavily in captured and missing. The disjointed and uncoordinated fight in the darkness north of Winchester had resulted in disaster for the Federals. No one can truly say whether another commander could have kept his forces intact in that situation, but under Milroy the battle dissolved into chaos. The final tally of casualties at Winchester from June 13-15, 1863, totaled 4,443, of which 4,000 were captured.20 Nearly all of the captures, other than the sick left behind, occurred during the battle north of Winchester and along the retreat route. The rebels reported their losses at Winchester as 42 killed and 210 wounded for a total of 252.21

According to Wildes the 116th lost 7 killed, 21 wounded, and 175 captured from June 13—15, 1863, for a total of 203.22 The following is a casualty list for the 116th Ohio Infantry at Bunker Hill and Winchester:

KILLED AT BUNKER HILL.

Company A— Simpson Smith, John Welch and John A. Bowman –3.

WOUNDED AT BUNKER HILL.

Company A—Abel Hall, Henry Harman, Daniel P. Hubbard, James Lafevere, James W. Oliver, Jacob Ring, Jacob Zimmerly, Hiram Shafer, Solomon Shafer, Cyrus Spriggs, Samuel Tidd, Edward J. Tillett, Aaron Weakly, George C. Williamson, Samuel Steel, and Corporal Newton Meek—16.
Company I –Captain Alexander Cochran, Caleb I. Baker and George W. Burch –3.

CAPTURED AT BUNKER HILL

Company A –Lieutenant John S. Manning, Sergeants Mann Smith, James H. Worder, Daniel C. Hurd, Corporals Benjamin F. Dye, Jesse Keyser, William Brock, Newton Meek, Privates John D. Brown, Albert Gates, Joseph R. Brock, John C. Bean, William Bonam, Jesse Coulter, Abraham Coulter, William Danford, William Dyer, Frederick Edge, Samuel Gates, Jefferson Gratton, Abel Hall, Henry Harman, Daniel P. Hubbard, Joseph Paith, Jacob Ring, Cyrus Spriggs, Samuel Tidd, Edward J. Tillet, Samuel Zimmerly, James Lafevere, Samuel H. McHugh, George C. Williamson, Benjamin Ring –33.

Company I—Captain Alexander Cochran, Sergeant George Bean, Privates William Scott, John O. Athey, Jacob E. Athey, John C. Balley, Caleb I. Baker, Elias Baker, Bradley F. Barrows, Jesse Burton, George W. Burch, James A. Campbell, Samuel H. Cramblett, John A. Dennis, Samuel P. Fleak, (escaped June 16th) Ephraim W. Frost, James H. Gilchrist, Samuel McCulloch, William McMillan, Leonard S. Mickle, Joseph Morrison, John Norris, Sheldon Parker, Hopson L. Sherman, George Tucker—25.

KILLED AT WINCHESTER.

Captain Frederick H. Arckenoe, Co. C; Sergeant Oswald Heck, Co. C; Samuel Luthey, Co. E; Theodore Mathias, Co. E—4.

WOUNDED AT WINCHESTER

John H. Lang, Co. C, in arm; Charles D. Watson, Co. C, in right shoulder—2.

CAPTURED AT WINCHESTER.

Assistant Surgeon Thomas C. Smith, Assistant Surgeon Josiah L. Brown, Chaplin E. W. Brady, Q. M. Sergeant William J. Lee, Sutler Elmer Armstrong—5.

Company B—Lieutenant Hiram L. Sibley, Sergeant Edmond Tiffany, Privates, Henry Jennings, Leonard J. Cooley, Benjamin McLane, John Campbell, Daniel Rose, Aurellius P. Wiley—8.

Company C—Lieutenant Levi Lupton, Corporal Oliver A. Hardesty, Privates Wilson A. Mann, David A. Mann, John Mahoney, Miller Booth, Jacob Butt, Eli Evans, Robert Chambers, George W. Gannon, William Montgomery, Reinhard Straub, Jacob Walton, John Latchaw, George W. Matchett, George W. Sampson, John Egger, William Bush, Clarkson W. Adams, William W. Wheaton, Citizen H. Henderson, Samuel Dobbins, Emon H. Beardmore, James A. Preshaw, Henry Fleishman, Lewis Steuber, Charles I. Eberle, Alexander Robbins—28.

Company D—Corporal William A. Ferrell, Privates Isaac Price, Jackson Cox, Leander A. Eddy, John Gowdy, Henry Mowder, Thomas Rawley, Sampson Patterson, Robert Armstrong, Hugh Thompson, James Simmons—10.

Company E—Corporal John J. Walter, Privates Robert S. Hutchison, John Smith, John Morrow, Benjamin J. Ridgeway, Jacob Fisher, Jacob S. Hurd, Jacob Walter—8.

Company F—Privates William H. Bell, James Earley, Charles Latch, James Marsh, Christian Rhmer— 5.

Company G—Lieutenant J. C. S. Cobb, Privates Ira Wood, James Davis, William Davies, Jacob Fisher, George W. Hysell, Eben Hysell, Samuel L. Smith, Isaac C. Swett, William J. Chase—10.

Company H—Privates Daniel Bock, Joseph Gerlds, Mathew Grandon, E. J. Mathews, Lafayette Moore, Michael J. Moore, Hugh Shafer, Joseph Dudley, James Smith, Stephen C. McCoy, Jacob Wannhas, Samuel B. Mathews—12.

Company I—Lieutenant Richmond O. Knowles, Sergeant John B. Humphrey, Corporal Wisley Mickle, Corporal Joseph P. Parrish, Privates George Bates, Asher Buckley, Alvah D. Carlton, Luther H. Clayton, James W. Glasier, Morris Humphrey, William S. Parrott, Rufus B. Stanley, Enoch Taylor, Chares W. Waterman—14.

Company K—Corporals Carmi Allison and Jesse Allen, Drummer Boy Lucius Hull, Privates John Koons, Reason Risley, Hiram Pitcock, William Rutter, Abraham Butterworth, John Hartley, S. Fenton, George Mcdonald, Harley Gilbert, Craven Ayers, Emory Newton, William Robinett, Asa Ladd—16.

Many of the men from the 116th who were captured on the fifteenth were either in the hospital at Winchester or too sick to escape with the rest of the regiment. Colonel Wildes mentioned Lieutenant Hiram Sibley as an example. The lieutenant had been bedfast for a week when the rebels attacked Winchester. According to Wildes, on the night of the retreat Sibley was riding Surgeon Smith's horse, "and was finally captured in Colonel Ely's surrender (18th Connecticut) in the morning attack. Many of the prisoners at Winchester were sick in the hospital, but it is impossible to distinguish, from any records...who were captured in hospital, or who in action."23 John Gowdy of Company D (who was captured at Winchester but is not on Wildes' list) was said to have been captured in the hospital while suffering from fever on the fifteenth. The pension file of James Earley of Company F who was captured on the fifteenth states that following his exchange from the rebel POW camp he was diagnosed with "Typhoid Debilitar." In June the 116th had an outbreak of typhoid fever that claimed the life of the regiment's Doctor Gilkey. These three documented fever cases support Wildes' explanation that many of the captured men were too ill to escape during the retreat.

For those fortunate enough to escape, the retreat was a trial by ordeal. Sergeant George Way explained: "...(the 116th) passed through what no one but a soldier could endure, hunger, thirst, lack of sleep and numerous other privations only known to that army which has retreated in an

Corporal Jesse Hill Allen, Company K., was captured at the Battle of Winchester on June 15, 1863. He died at Andersonville prison. (Courtesy of Richard Kehl)

Second Lieutenant John S. Manning, Company A. Lt. Manning was captured at the Battle of Bunker Hill, W. Va. on June 13, 1863. (Courtesy of Mark D.Okey)

enemy's country without supplies." When the regiment reached "glorious Old Pennsylvania...a happier set of boys...considering the circumstances, were never heard of."24

Following the retreat to Hancock, the 116th assumed an adjunctive role in the Gettysburg Campaign on the periphery of the war's greatest battle. After resting at Hancock until 10p.m., the 116th marched all night and until the afternoon of the sixteenth to reach Orleans Station on the B&O Railroad. Rations were issued at the station. Colonel Washburn also received orders from General Milroy to meet him at Bloody Run, Pennsylvania, to cooperate with the Army of the Potomac against Lee's invasion. The 116th reached Bloody Run on June nineteenth.

General Milroy arrived at Bloody Run on June twentieth from Harper's Ferry, where he had been relieved of command. Colonel Wildes described his appearance, "The 'Old Grey Eagle' looked gloomy and broken-hearted, we drew up in line to receive him, and, as he approached, presented arms, and cheered him loud and long."25 As always, Wildes was loyal and did not mention that Milroy had been relieved of his command at Harper's Ferry.

While the 116th remained at Bloody Run, General Ewell sent Major General Robert Rhodes and his division up the Cumberland Valley into Pennsylvania. Within days most of Lee's army had crossed the Potomac and was advancing into Pennsylvania. General Hooker's Army of the Potomac remained in Virginia until June twenty-fifth and then took up the chase.

The residents of Bloody Run were thankful to have the 116th around with the invading rebels so nearby. They prepared a wonderful feast for the 116th that was never forgotten by the soldiers. According to Colonel Wildes, "Long tables were placed in the middle of the principal street, which were loaded with warm and cold meats, potatoes, bread, pickles, splendid hot coffee, and great bowls and pails of milk. We were nearly starved, and no meal we ever ate was so heartily relished."26

General Milroy was ordered to report to Baltimore where General Schenck placed him in arrest on June twenty-seventh. Colonel Wildes mentioned Milroy's departure by noting simply that the general "left us to await further orders."27 General in Chief Halleck placed the onus for the debacle at Winchester firmly on Milroy's shoulders; Milroy would later request a court of inquiry to clear his name. Meanwhile the discredited General Joseph Hooker resigned the day after Milroy's arrest, and Major General George G. Meade was assigned as commander of the Army of the Potomac.

On June thirtieth the 116th moved to Bedford, Pennsylvania. During the next three days fighting raged around the village of Gettsburg several miles to the east. At Gettysburg General Meade's Army of the Potomac defeated the rebel army and thwarted General Lee's invasion plans. In what was the all too common Federal practice during the Civil War, the outlying troops not assigned to the army in battle were not concentrated at the scene of the fighting; so the 116th remained idle during the greatest battle of the Civil War. The 116th returned to Bloody Run on July third, and the following morning at 4 a.m. took up the march to be in position to harass the rebels preparing to retreat from Gettysburg.

The rains, which General Lee feared would raise the Potomac and prevent his army's escape, began on the morning of the fourth as the 116th marched east toward McConnellsburg. On the fifth the 116th reached Loudon by 2 p.m. and went into camp. That night the 116th was ordered to immediately march to Mercersburg, Pennsylvania, to guard wagons captured by the cavalry from Lee's retreating column. The men were ordered out of camp and into formation, and quickly the 116th was on the march again. Mercersburg was reached at about 1 a.m.

Early on the morning of July sixth, the 116th departed Mercersburg with the captured wagons and about 1,000 captured rebels under guard for a trip back to Loudon, Pennsylvania. From Loudon the 116th operated against Lee's trains passing in front of his retreating army. The cavalry attacked Lee's train, and with assistance from the 116th nearly 400 rebel wagons were captured, many loaded with rebel wounded. In a letter dated July 6, 1863, from Loudon, Colonel Wildes wrote the following account of Lee's retreat:

> We are doing good work here, harassing the rebels on their flank, cutting up their trains, and picking up their stragglers. There probably never was so complete a rout as Lee's army sustained. A train six miles long passed by on the Cumberland pike yesterday. It was terribly cut up by our cavalry and Plesanton's. It will probably all be captured, or destroyed. Providence is favoring us with such copious rains. The Potomac has risen several feet... The demoralization of Lee's army is something awful to witness, and if General Meade would press it hard, fully half of it would certainly be destroyed, or captured. Why he does not press forward is a mystery to us, who can see its hopeless condition here, as it passes by.28

President Lincoln was nearly beside himself with frustration during this period. The President wrote a letter to General Meade venting his anger, but he never sent the letter. The following is a paragraph from that letter:

Again, my dear general, I do not believe you appreciate the magnitude of the misfortune involved in Lee's escape. He was within your easy grasp, and to have closed upon him would, in connection with our other late successes, have ended the war. As it is, the war will be prolonged indefinitely. If you could not safely attack Lee last Monday, how can you possibly do so south of the river, when you take with you very few more than two-thirds of the force you then had in hand? It would be unreasonable to expect, and I do not expect you can now effect much. Your golden opportunity is gone, and I am distressed immeasurably because of it. 29

While General Meade dawdled, Lee retreated to the Potomac; and when the river receded enough for his infantry to ford, Lee's army escaped. The 116th followed in the wake of Lee's army marching to Greencastle on July thirteenth. The next day the 116th marched into Hagerstown, Maryland, and met the Army of the Potomac. The great opportunity to destroy Lee's army was lost, so the 116th stacked arms and ate its first square meal since leaving Bloody Run. The men were exhausted having spent the previous four days without much sleep or food except what could be found in the fields and woods. Colonel Wildes noted that when the men finally lay down to sleep they looked like the dead.

The following day the 116th moved south again marching through the battlefield of Antietam to reach Sharpsburg, Maryland. The regiment remained at Sharpsburg until August fourth. The remnant of Company C, separated from the regiment since June fifteenth, joined the command on August fourth at Sharpsburg. The lost company had retreated to Harper's Ferry during the fight north of Winchester and had been integrated with the 110th Ohio. Following the evacuation of Harper's Ferry, the company joined with the 110th in escorting the stores shipped from Harper's Ferry to Washington. When Lee began his retreat, the 110th was reassigned to the 2nd Brigade, 3rd Division, III Corps of the Army of the Potomac, and Company C joined in the pursuit of Lee's army. Company C participated in a skirmish with Lee's army at Manassas Gap and then was ordered to return to the 116th at Sharpsburg.

The regiment, now complete except for the 141 captured officers and men, departed Sharpsburg on the fourth bound for Martinsburg, West Virginia. Martinsburg would be the headquarters for the 116th for the next nine months. Following the Federal victory at Gettysburg, there was a hiatus in the Eastern Theater of the war. No further major large-scale battles were fought in the east until May 1864. The 116th assumed a new role at Martinsburg, the role of guarding railroads, a role the regiment did not relish but performed well.

Thomas Wildes covered the subject of General Milroy's troubles resulting from the disaster at Winchester in detail in his book about the 116th. He took the task of Milroy's defense to heart, assuming the role of Milroy's apologist. Perhaps Wildes' affection for the "Gray Eagle" colored his perception of the facts. His analysis of the causes for the defeat at Winchester reads like a defense attorney's presentation, complete with evidence supporting Milroy and the omission of any damaging evidence against Milroy.

According to Thomas Wildes the disaster north of Winchester was the result of Colonel McReynolds' disobedience of Milroy's orders at a crucial moment in that battle. He did not specify which orders were disobeyed. Wildes also wrote, "There was never any division of opinion among Milroy's army, but that he did the best that bravery and skill could do, under the circumstances."30 Wildes also believed that Halleck used Milroy to distract attention from his own failure to keep track of Lee's army. Wildes wrote that Halleck's attempt to shift the blame was "a heartless and cruel injustice, exceeding anything to be found in the ignoble career of that incompetent and malevolent chief."31

The facts indicate that General in Chief Halleck wanted Milroy to evacuate Winchester before Ewell's Corps was in position to attack. Halleck felt that Winchester was only useful as an outpost and was not worth the risk of continued occupation while Lee's army was loose. Milroy simply did not want to abandon Winchester and did not believe he was in any serious danger.

When Halleck removed Milroy from command, Milroy appealed to President Lincoln. He accused Halleck of prejudice against him because he was not a West Point graduate. Lincoln's letter of reply got to the heart of the matter in a way only Lincoln's genius could. The following is from the first paragraph of that letter:

> I have never doubted your courage and devotion to the cause. But you have just lost a division, and *Prima facie* the fault is upon you; and while that remains unchanged, for me to put you in command again, is to justly subject me to the charge of having put you there on purpose to have you lose another. If I knew facts sufficient to satisfy me that you were not in fault, or error, the case would be different. But the facts I do know, while they are not at all conclusive, and I hope they may never prove so, tend the other way.32

The only possible good coming from the debacle at Winchester was that the three-day battle delayed Lee's invasion of Pennsylvania. General Hooker, General Milroy and Colonel Wildes, all of whom had reason to give meaning to the battle, each stated that the Battle of Winchester saved Harrisburg and possibly other cities in Pennsylvania from destruction.

While Milroy never was charged or censured during his court of inquiry, the men who served under him were covered by a cloud of disrepute that was difficult to expurgate. In his telegram to General Schenck on June 15, 1863, Milroy informed his commander of his defeat and said, "We were pursued by a large cavalry force, who picked up numbers of my weary boys."33 Milroy's words caught on as a nickname for the troops transferred from Milroy's Division to the VI Corps of the Army of the Potomac after Winchester. Those troops (the 110th and 122nd Ohio Infantry and the 67th and 87th Pennsylvania Infantry) became part of two brigades of the VI Corps' Third Division; and because they "had been led to defeat so often" by Milroy, they became known as "Milroy's weary boys."34 The 116th remained attached to the VIII Corps and was not subject to the same disparagement as their former comrades transferred to the Army of the Potomac. There was nothing about the performance of the 116th at Winchester to be ashamed of. The 116th would go on to prove it was one of the most reliable and best outfits in the VIII Corps.

"I WOULD RATHER BE WITH MY REGIMENT"
7

The situation facing the Federal Government in August 1863 was significantly better than the previous August when the 116th Ohio had been recruited. From July 1863 onward the rebel cause was doomed. The only hope for the rebels at this point was to prolong the war; if the war could be prolonged indefinitely, the North might become discouraged and thus accept something less than victory. In the first week of July 1863 the rebels suffered two devastating and irreparable defeats. Rebel President Jefferson Davis and General Robert E. Lee had risked everything on a second invasion of the North. Lee's invasion had utilized the troops needed for the relief of the rebel citadel at Vicksburg, Mississippi. Without a relief force to lift a siege, Vicksburg was surrendered to Federal General Ulysses Grant on July 4, 1863; and with Lee's defeat at Gettysburg, the rebels had gained nothing to compensate for the loss of Vicksburg.

Following the surrender of Vicksburg, the remaining rebel stronghold on the Mississippi River at Port Hudson, Louisiana, also surrendered on July 9, 1863. Nearly 29,000 rebels surrendered at Vicksburg, and another 6,000 rebels surrendered at Port Hudson. Control of the entire Mississippi River was restored to the United States with the fall of Port Hudson. The rebels could no longer blockade the nation's most important shipping conduit.

As the 116th settled into a new routine at Martinsburg in August 1863, the pace of the war slowed in the East. General Mead followed the usual routine of the Federal commanders before Grant, and the Army of the Potomac followed the great battle of Gettysburg with a period of relative inactivity. The 116th remained in the VIII Corps, and its duty was to guard the northern sector of the Shenandoah Valley and the B & O Railroad.

Colonel McReynolds of the 1st New York Cavalry was initially in command at Martinsburg. Lieutenant Colonel Wildes made no secret of his contempt for McReynolds He believed that McReynolds held excessive sympathies for Southerners. When Colonel McReynolds ordered the 116th to guard the property and home of a prominent rebel named Faulkner, Wildes refused. Colonel McReynolds immediately placed Colonel Wildes in arrest. The 116th could have lost the services of perhaps its most gifted officer, but the department commander, General Kelley, instead ordered the arrest of Colonel McReynolds on charges of disobedience of orders during the Battle of Winchester. Colonel McReynolds was forwarded to Washington for trial, and Lieutenant

Colonel Wildes was released from arrest. The 116th provided no further protection for Faulkner's property.

While the 116th was stationed at Martinsburg, the men who had been captured around Winchester began returning to the regiment, and the fate of the captives became known. The officers had been placed in Libby Prison in Richmond, and most of the men had been sent to Belle Island Prison near Richmond. As noted, many of the captured men were sick and probably would not have survived a long incarceration.

Fortunately for Milroy's boys captured at Winchester nearly 40,000 rebels had surrendered or had been captured in July. The rebels captured at Vicksburg were disarmed and paroled by General Grant. Under parole stipulations the parolees could not return to battle unless exchanged for Federal POWs. There was an exchange system or cartel in place to arrange for prisoner exchanges in 1863. The Rebel Government could not afford to lose 40,000 men, so the rebels quickly acted to return nearly all of the troops captured at Winchester, excepting many officers, to be exchanged for some of the rebels captured in July. The men captured at Winchester were taken to City Point on the James River near Petersburg, Virginia, and transported by ship to Annapolis, Maryland. Annapolis was the eastern Camp Parole where parolees waited, out of the war, to be exchanged for rebel POWs or parolees. There were also hospitals in Annapolis to treat and rehabilitate the sick returning Federal POWs. Camp Parole held approximately 2,765 men from Milroy's command in August of 1863, 130 were from the 116th Ohio.1 Only approximately forty-five officers and men from the 116th had not returned to Camp Parole by the end of July 1863.

One of the men at Camp Parole from the 116th was Corporal Benjamin F. Dye. He was one of several men from Company A captured during the fighting at Bunker Hill on June 13, 1863. On July 9, 1863, Benjamin Dye wrote a letter to his wife from Annapolis. Dye's letter gives an account of his captors and gives a good representation of a literate soldier's impression of the war in July 1863.

Dear Wife,
    It is again that I take my pen in hand to let you know that I am well and hoping these few lines will find you well. This is the second letter I have written since I came here. I wrote you the particulars of my capture in the other letter that I sent you.
    I thought I would write you again for fear that you might not get it. I feel a great deal better than I did when I first got here, for I was pretty nearly starved. We have plenty to eat here and plenty to drink, but I would rather be with my regiment in the fields doing duty. I have not heard anything about the 116th yet, where it

is or how many there are left in it. I suppose you know more about that than I do by this time.

Our force was badly used up at Winchester by overwhelming numbers, but thank God, they have met with their match in Pennsylvania. That they will never forget while they live, and if they get back to Virginia, they may think themselves well off.

When they took us they were going through Pennsylvania to Pittsburg and there cross into Ohio and destroy every thing as they would go along. They seemed to be confident of success. They told us they had taken an oath to go through or die. Some of the more intelligent of the guards that were guarding us said that if they were not successful in this raid in the North, there cause was gone, and some of them told me they would desert as soon as they got into Maryland.

The news came in the paper today confirming the surrender of Vicksburg. Our cause is gaining fast. I have a strong hope that this wicked rebellion will speedily come to a close. My faith in this is stronger since I was at Richmond, that dirty, filthy hot bed of treason. When we were there five thousand men could have taken the place with all ease. The sound of Union cannon would have been pleasant music to me then. I would like to help plant the stars and stripes over that place where their secession rag with 2 bars in it hangs.

Well, Martha, I will have to close for this time. If I am not exchanged the next exchange that is made, I will try to get home. I remain as ever
    Your loving husband,
    Benjamin F. Dye
Write soon. Direct to Camp Parole
Annapolis Maryland
116 Regt OV T Co.
Fourth Battalion

Dye's service record indicates that he was released from Belle Island on July 1, 1863. The service record of James Earley of Company F indicates that he was released on July 19, 1863. The men were obviously released in groups, probably depending on documentation status and availability of transportation. Most of the POWs from the 116th were in Camp Parole by July 25, 1863. However, not all of the men were released from rebel prisons that July. Most of the officers from the 116th who were captured at Winchester were not released until much later. Lieutenant Levi Lupton of Company C, who was captured in the West

Fort at Winchester on June 14, 1863, was never released; and he died September 12, 1864, in rebel prison at Charleston, South Carolina. Likewise, Corporal Jesse Allen of Company K was never released. The corporal was eventually sent to Andersonville Prison Camp where he died of dysentery on April 15, 1864.

Benjamin Dye was exchanged and returned to the 116th on October 8, 1863. Processing the exchanges took time, and the captured men incrementally returned to the 116th through the fall and winter. Some of the men were too sick to return to the 116th immediately and remained in the hospital system at Annapolis for months. Others died shortly after leaving Camp Parole, probably unable to recover from illness made worst by their incarceration.

The men captured at Winchester were very fortunate to be released and exchanged so quickly. After General Grant assumed overall command of the Federal Army in 1864, he suspended the exchange system. The soldiers captured during the campaigns of 1864 suffered horribly in rebel prisons, some until the close of the war without exchange. Had the lenient system of paroles and exchanges broken down before the men captured at Winchester had been released, many more men from the 116th would undoubtedly have died.

Lieutenant Colonel Wildes assumed command of the post at Martinsburg after the departure of Colonel McReynolds. Soon the 116th was sent on a new and unpleasant mission. General Kelley sent orders for the 116th to collect assessments from rebel sympathizers in the vicinity of Charlestown, Kearneyville and Shepherdstown to indemnify loyal citizens whose property had been destroyed by rebel guerrillas operating in that area. According to Colonel Wildes the malicious raids against Unionists in the region decreased dramatically when it became known that disloyal residents would be held responsible for the damage. The following summer Rebel General Jubal Early pursued a similar and more drastic policy of demanding reparations of loyal towns in Maryland and Pennsylvania. It was an unfortunate fact that civilians on both sides of the war suffered reprisals for no other reason than their proximity to the war. There were many acts of reprisal directed against uninvolved civilians intended to discourage guerrilla activities throughout the war. The policy was so pervasive that many such acts are now lost to history.

The 116th was allowed to cast their votes for the fall election of 1863 at Martinsburg. The race for governor of Ohio was between John Brough and Clement L. Vallandigham. The regiment had been recruited in a region of Ohio that usually elected a Democratic Representative. However, Vallandigham, the Democrat, was a controversial critic of the Lincoln Administration and the war. He was suspected of disloyalty, and many considered him a Southern sympathizer and copperhead. In reality he was more a critic of sectional strife than a Southern sympathizer.

The vote from the 116th totaled 398 votes for Brough and 50 votes for Vallandigham. There was no attempt made to interfere with or influence the voting, but many in the regiment felt that a vote for Vallandigham was an indication of disloyalty to the Union cause. The fact that Vallandigham received 50 votes in the regimental election caused considerable curiosity and indignation in the ranks. No doubt many of the men who voted for Vallandigham did so because of party loyalty or because their homefolk expected them to vote Democratic. Indeed, Democratic Representative James Morris, who had helped recruit the 116th and hailed from Monroe County, had given support to Vallandigham. The officers found it necessary to order a halt to political arguments to prevent unrest in the camp, and afterwards the election controversy subsided.

Corporal Benjamin Dye in a letter to his wife following the election mentioned how he voted. The following is a paragraph from his letter that thoroughly explains his reasons for voting against the Democrat:

> You said some of the friends wanted to know if I voted for Brough. You can inform them that I did that very thing and am not ashamed to own it. I voted for him because I was afraid of a dangerous man being elected to the office of governor. I am for men who have no sympathy for rebels, and the destroyers of my country. I will fight them upon the field and at the ballot box. If God spares me to serve my three years out, and these rebels are not put down, I will volunteer again. The stars and stripes must float over every foot of territory wrested from our glorious Union by these ---- fiends who are starving our brave comrades in their filthy prisons, I mean the prisoners they have taken from us. I have no doubt but that this war will end before my time is out. A few more such moves as the Napoleon of the western hemisphere has made on them at Chattanooga will bring them to their understanding.[2]

Colonel Wildes mentioned that while the 116th was stationed at Martinsburg, Lieutenant William Spriggs of Company H was dismissed from the service for "using disloyal and treasonable language against the Government of the United States, disrespectful language of the President, and other conduct unbecoming an officer and a gentleman."[3] He did not mentioned whether Lieutenant Spriggs was a supporter of Clement Vallandigham or if his behavior was related to the election controversy.

During October Company E of the 116th was stationed at North Mountain along with a company from the 1st New York Cavalry and one from the 12th Pennsylvania Cavalry. These troops cooperated to surround and capture forty of the rebel Gilmore's men and about fifty horses in a ravine. The surprise was so complete that neither side fired a shot.

While at Martinsburg the 116th played host to other regiments arriving at the camp. Colonel Wildes mentioned one humorous story involving the arrival of the 18th Connecticut Infantry. Most of that regiment had just been released from Camp Parole; and when they marched into Martinsburg, they were short on rations. They quickly gathered around the sutler from the 116th, Mr. Armstrong, and clamored for "cookies." Armstrong couldn't figure what they meant by "cookies," and his confused reaction to the men from Connecticut was a sight to behold. From that day on, the 18th Connecticut was known to the 116th as the "cookie regiment."

Martinsburg was the home of a notorious and irrepressible rebel spy named Belle Boyd. She was a twenty-year-old daughter of a rebel cavalryman and was a veteran of many spy, courier and scout missions for the Confederacy and General Stonewall Jackson. General Jackson so valued her service that he authorized a commission for her and appointed her as an aide. Following the war she toured the country giving recitals of her wartime adventures as a rebel spy. Colonel Wildes noted that, "Doubtless she was often among us in disguise when we knew nothing about it...she was always the same arrant little rebel, and ready at all times for an argument against the Government, and in favor of secession."4

After November 19, 1863, the 116th left Martinsburg to be detailed at various points along the B&O Railroad. The regiment was scattered from Sleepy Creek to Kearneyville. Major Morris was in command of the companies at North Mountain and points west, and he established his headquarters there. Lieutenant Colonel Wildes was detailed as president of a court-martial at that time, and Colonel Washburn was temporarily in charge of a brigade. With the regiment so scattered and the field officers preoccupied, there was no opportunity for brigade drill and battle training.

The duty along the B&O was strenuous and demanding. The railroad had to be protected from guerrilla and rebel cavalry raids. Almost daily the companies sent out patrols and often pursued small bands of rebels intent on doing some mischief to the railroad or and its bridges. Colonel Wildes summed up the period by noting that the companies cleared the area of bushwhackers and captured an aggregate number of prisoners greater than their own. He also noted that no successful rebel raid was made and no damage done to the B&O while the 116th was guarding it.

Company F was detailed at Duffield Station west of Harper's Ferry. On November 25th, 1863, Sergeant Silas King returned to the station from a scout with a number of captured arms. Sergeant William Brister noticed one of the arms, an old flintlock musket, and seeing Private Stephen Hogue approaching, he pointed the old musket at Hogue in jest. Hogue playfully reacted by taking a nearby musket and pointing it at the sergeant. Assuming that the musket was unloaded, Hogue pulled the trigger. The musket fired into Sergeant Brister's chest, and he died in minutes. The two men were friends and had been near neighbors in Monroe County. Hogue was distraught, but he found the will to write home to Brister's friends about the dreadful accident, sorrowfully explaining how he had killed his best friend. The sergeant's body was sent back to Monroe County.

The men of the 116th were encouraged by the war's progress during the fall and winter. In the Western Theater, the Federal Army had been defeated just south of Chattanooga, Tennessee, in September. Yet it had been a Pyrrhic victory for the rebels. Rebel General Longstreet's Corps from the Army of Northern Virginia had been sent west to reinforce General Braxton Bragg's Army with a view of crushing the Federal Army of General William Rosecrans. The rebels intended to recapture Chattanooga, Tennessee, and then drive the Federal forces out of East Tennessee. The rebel victory in September at the Battle of Chickamauga resulted in heavy rebel casualties, and Chattanooga was never recaptured. General Ulysses Grant replaced General Rosecrans in command of the western forces and drove General Bragg and his army away from Chattanooga. General Longstreet had separated his Corps from Bragg's Army for the purpose of laying siege to Knoxville, Tennessee. General Ambrose Burnside with his IX Corps and troops from the Army of the Ohio held Knoxville. Longstreet's attempted siege was a miserable failure. When Federal reinforcements were sent toward Knoxville, Longstreet and his Corps retreated and eventually returned to the Army of Northern Virginia. The entire rebel campaign in Tennessee, undertaken with maximum effort made possible by the calm in the East, was a failure.

Letters written by soldiers of the 116th during this period indicate that newspaper stories about the war had reached them along the railroad. Benjamin Dye seemed encouraged in a letter to his wife from Sleepy Creek dated January 10, 1864, as he wrote, "In my mind this wicked rebellion is fast playing out. I fancy I can see old Jeff Davis's knees a trembling like Belshozzar of old. If every man in the North puts his shoulder to the wheel and works with a will, the rotten fabric of tyranny, despotism, and darkness at Richmond will fall sooner than a great many people think, for it is now reduced to the last ditch."[5] The men had shown with their votes in October the same beliefs that Dye shared with his wife in his letters, belief that victory would come by perseverance. Dye waxed poetic on the same subject in a letter to his brother: "The goddess of liberty will carry the emblem of union and liberty, independence and justice, the red, white, and blue, against anarchy, despotism, and blood, with accursed chains of slavery clanking around the necks of the latter."[6]

The 116th was much like any regiment during the Civil War. Many of the men had a fondness for whiskey. Private James Dalzell noted in his post-war book about his war experiences that many farm hands in his part of Ohio would not work for a farmer unless he had some whiskey to serve his help, and this proclivity no doubt carried over to the army. Corporal Benjamin Dye's letter to his brother Mahlon dated February 8, 1864, indicated that the boys were prone to celebrate on paydays:

> It is a fine morning here this Monday morning. We were paid off yesterday evening. We got two months' pay and the boys have plenty of green backs this morning. Consequently we feel a little elevated and likely some of us will take a little high if there is rotgut enough to be found...

Whether it was "rotgut," " tanglefoot," "bug juice" or "pop Skull," it all meant the same. There always seemed to be time and place for drinking from General Grant down to the most humble private; and many soldiers brought the habit home, struggling with alcoholism for the rest of their lives.

The regiment was assembled at Martinsburg on March 1, 1864, in preparation for the campaign season. The Administration was anxious to initiate a final massive effort to end the war. Lieutenant Colonel Wildes received a letter dated March 3, 1864, from General Milroy who was in Washington. The general expressed his desire to return to the seat of war and his hope for a command in the Valley. But Milroy was finished in the Valley, because, according to Wildes, "General Milroy was under the ban of the ogre General Halleck, and could not expect a command as long as Halleck controlled army affairs."[7]

With the coming of spring, a new commander was assigned by the Administration to lead the next campaign in the Valley—a new commander who would prove by far the most incompetent to ever command an army to which the 116th was assigned. In an all too common refrain, the men of the Valley would suffer for the Administration's propensity to appoint political generals at the expense of the men who had to follow them.

TO FIGHT "MIT SIGEL"
8

General Robert Milroy's letter to Lieutenant Colonel Wildes from Washington coincided with the appointment of General Ulysses S. Grant to supreme command of the Federal Armies. Grant's promotion was propitious news for Milroy and for the cause of the Union, but it spelled doom for the Southern Confederacy. Unlike his predecessors, Grant would take the risks required to achieve victory.

Even so, there was a dearth of effective leaders available to serve under the new chief. Some of the most promising Federal officers had been killed in battle and others lacked experience. In the months following Ulysses Grant's promotion to Lieutenant General and overall command, only a handful of Federal generals proved capable of providing the type of leadership and ingenuity required for independent command. There were perhaps only three other senior Federal generals besides Grant who possessed the qualities necessary to push the rebels into collapse. William T. Sherman, George Thomas, and Phillip Sheridan, all Major Generals in the United States Army, were the men, other than Grant, who provided the leadership in decisive battles and campaigns that brought final victory to the Federal Government. The key quality each of these generals possessed was nerve—the willpower to take risk and stand fast under the most trying battlefield conditions.

The problem with the Federal Army in 1864 was the lack of generals with nerve or, for that matter, even the competence necessary to plan and execute directives from the General-in-Chief. Simply stated, the Federal Government had appointed far too many incompetent "political generals" to function effectively. These politicians turned generals were the scourge of the Federal Armies, and it was especially evident in 1864.

Ulysses S. Grant was only the second American to be appointed to the full rank of Lieutenant General, only George Washington had previously held that title. Soon after assuming the rank and responsibilities, Grant devised a grand strategy to defeat all of the major rebel armies and end the war. General Grant had overwhelming forces at his disposal, 662,000 men in twenty-two Corps.[1] His plan called for a simultaneous movement against all major sectors of the Confederacy beginning with the spring campaign of 1864. In a letter to General Sherman dated April 4, 1864, the general explained, "It is my design...in the spring campaign, to work all parts of the army together, and somewhat towards a common centre."[2]

Grant's plan called for coordinated campaigns against Richmond, Virginia, and General Lee's Army; Atlanta, Georgia, and General

Johnston's Army; the Shenandoah Valley and Mobile, Alabama. Major General William T. Sherman was assigned the task of capturing Atlanta. Major General Benjamin Butler and the Army of the James was to assail Richmond from the south side of the James River. Forces were to be collected from General Banks' command, following the Red River Campaign, to move against Mobile. Major General Franz Sigel was to commence a movement up the Shenandoah Valley to deny the rebels the use of that natural granary. Finally, General Grant himself would accompany the Army of the Potomac on a Campaign devoted to the destruction of General Lee's Army of Northern Virginia—the capture of Richmond being a secondary objective for the Army of the Potomac.

Unfortunately for the 116th and the VIII Corps, one of the most ineffective political generals, Franz Sigel, was assigned the important task of commanding the Shenandoah Campaign in the spring of 1864. Franz Sigel was a thirty-nine year old German immigrant with important political ties to the German-American community. Sigel had been director of schools in St. Louis, a city with a large German population. When the war began in 1861, Sigel helped unify the German immigrant sector in support of the Union. He was also an effective recruiter of immigrants for the Federal Army.

While Sigel had some military experience, he had graduated from a military academy and served as a junior officer in the service of Duke Leopold in Germany, his most polished ability was leading an organized retreat. In one of the first fights of the war at Carthage, Missouri, he had led a brilliant retreat from superior enemy forces. In his next battle in August 1861 at Wilson's Creek, Missouri, he was routed and forced into an ignominious flight to escape capture. The only truly successful action of his career was at Pea Ridge, Arkansas, on March 8, 1862. In action near Elkhorn Tavern, Sigel's Division broke through the rebel line. Subsequent behavior by Sigel revealed that his remarkable success was spurred by his desire to break loose and retreat to the north into Missouri. At Pea Ridge, "Sigel was determined to beat a hasty retreat into Missouri with his two divisions. Whether the rest of the army followed was none of his concern."[3]

Sigel did nothing noteworthy following the Battle of Pea Ridge. General Halleck admitted that Sigel's behavior had "destroyed all my confidence in him," and he feared that Sigel might absent himself at a "critical moment" in battle.[4] Nevertheless, President Lincoln gave Sigel command of the Department of West Virginia in 1864 because of political considerations. Lincoln had always courted the immigrant vote, and Sigel had considerable clout with the German community nationally. Sigel fostered strife between his immigrant staff officers and non-immigrant officers in the army, and he stirred up the German community sufficiently to coerce the President into appointing him to his new command. Colonel David Hunter, a native of Virginia and staff officer serving under Sigel, understood the situation and sarcastically noted it in his diary, "The Dutch vote must be secured at all hazards...the sacrifice of West Virginia is a small matter."5

The 34th Massachusetts Infantry arrived at Martinsburg on March ninth, and its colonel, George Wells, assumed command of the forces there. The 34th had been assigned to garrison duty in Washington, D.C. Henceforth the 34th would share the rigors of field duty with the 116th until the close of the war. Colonel Wells was an excellent officer, and his regiment was well drilled, disciplined, finely uniformed, and well equipped. A photograph of the 34th Massachusetts on parade appears in many books about the Civil War. At first the newcomers looked upon the 116th and the rest of the brigade with disdain. An officer from the 34th wrote, "It looks as if we were to suffer from the connection," with the 116th and the First Brigade.6 But after fighting beside the 116th and First Brigade until the close of the war, "the 34th Massachusetts regiment felt as much pride in the history the First Brigade had made for itself, as was felt by any regiment in it. It was not then ashamed of the 'connection' formed fourteen months before, nor was there an officer or man in it who felt that he had 'suffered by the connection'." 7

On April twelfth the 116th joined by the 123rd Ohio marched to Harper's Ferry and encamped on Bolivar Heights. Five days later they returned to Martinsburg. Colonel McReynolds, who had once tried to arrest Colonel Wildes, had returned and had been assigned command of Martinsburg by General Averell. For a few days Colonel Wells continued to act as Post Commander, and the 116th took orders from Wells, "owning to the utter dislike felt by everybody for McReynolds."8 Fortunately for the 116th and Colonel Wildes it wouldn't matter for long, because the 116th was assigned to a reorganized First Brigade which included the 18th Connecticut Infantry, 28th, 116th and 123rd Ohio Infantry. Colonel Augustus Moor of the 28th Ohio was placed in command of the brigade.

General Grant's planned offensive in the Shenandoah Valley would utilize two columns, one under command of Brigadier General George Crook and the other under Major General Sigel. Grant did not believe he could expect much from Sigel, so he assigned the bulk of the work to Crook. Grant met with Crook and explained his intentions for the campaign. Crook was to lead a force from Charleston, West Virginia, to destroy part of the Virginia and Tennessee Railroad south of Lynchburg, Virginia. To keep the rebel forces under Major General John C. Breckinridge from concentrating against Crook, Grant ordered Sigel to advance up the Shenandoah Valley toward Staunton, a simple enough mission. Once Crook finished his work on the railroad, Grant wanted the two columns to meet at Staunton to advance on Lynchburg. Grant himself would take the offensive against Lee's Army of Northern Virginia while Butler and Sherman initiated their movements against the rebels. Thus was Grant's Spring Campaign to be set in motion on all fronts nearly simultaneously.

The 116th and the rest of Sigel's Army moved out of Martinsburg on April 29, 1864. Sigel moved his army cautiously, stopping at Bunker Hill and then at Winchester. Colonel Wildes noted that he observed more display of the national flag at Winchester on this trip than ever before. The army remained in camp just south of Winchester for several days. Men from the 116th wandered over the battlefield of June 1863 and found that the rebels had poorly buried some of the Federal dead after the battle. They selected a nice spot and reburied their comrades properly. Wildes also mentioned that the Federal cavalry burned a house there, because a cavalryman had been killed by a shot fired from the house a few days previously.

On May fourth the men were ordered to pack all of their spare clothing and non-essential items into knapsacks to be sent to Martinsburg. Sigel was preparing his army for the advance and wanted everything ready for battle. On the following morning Sigel ordered field maneuvers, brigade drill and a mock battle. The officers of the brigade, having had no opportunity to learn and practice for nearly one year, were not up to the task, and the result was, in Wildes' own words, "the funniest farce ever witnessed anywhere."9

Colonel Moor of the 28th Ohio (also a German immigrant) had been appointed commander of the First Brigade. The 28th Ohio was a predominately German unit, one of many such ethnic units to serve in the Civil War. Many states had units with a majority of their members hailing from a foreign nation. The 10th Ohio Infantry, for instance, was an Irish regiment. Lieutenant Colonel Wildes explained how the foreign leadership affected the outcome of the maneuvers:

> A whole field full of Generals, Colonels and staff officers were present to witness the performance. General Sigel and Colonel Moor had a lot of Dutchmen on their staffs who could hardly talk English, and who knew nothing about communicating orders on the drill ground...One of the first things that was done was to deploy and start out the 34th Massachusetts as skirmishers...Our own regiment, for instance, was ordered through something like this: The right wing was ordered to advance, firing, to a fence pointed out, and there to lie down and keep on firing. Then, when it was thought our right wing was out about long enough to be

pretty badly cut up, the left was ordered to charge, without instructions how far to go in its wild career, or what to do next...As soon as we reached the left of the other wing it jumped up and charged, too, the whole regiment yelling like fiends. The 'recall' was sounded by General Sigel's bugler, but of course we didn't hear it, and away we went up the Valley, clear out to the picket line. Now came on the gallop three or four leather breeches Dutch staff officers after us, who finally overtook us and ordered a halt. But the 34th Massachusetts skirmishers! What had become of them? Here we had gone to the picket line and had not come up with them. It seemed they had been forgotten in the general muss, and had been allowed to advance some distance beyond the picket line before they were thought of and recalled.10

Thomas Wildes did not spare his criticism of General Sigel as he had with General Milroy. Sigel eventually changed his party allegiance from Republican to Democrat; thus, the "ardent Republican" Wildes had no incentive to shield Sigel's reputation. That given, it should in no way detract from the validity of his opinion of Sigel's military abilities as noted in the following paragraph from his book:

Talk about your 'corn stalk militia,' and 'general trainings' of ye olden times! There was never anything seen half so ridiculous, and it bred in everyone the most supreme contempt for General Sigel and his crowd of foreign adventurers. Not an officer or a man retained a spark of respect for, or confidence in, him or any of the leather breeches retinue of staff officers with which he had surrounded himself. So that for all the good that army would or could do under him, it might as well, and better, have returned at once to Martinsburg.11

By May of 1863 the 116th had begun its atrophy, as was common to all Civil War regiments, but still the regiment numbered nearly 800 effectives at muster. Of the 200 gone from the regiment, many were dead from disease or disabled by wounds or disease. A few were still in rebel prisons. A few others were detailed away from the regiment. Three of the officers from the 116th on detached duty were Lieutenant Milton Ellis, who was with the Signal Corps, Lieutenant John Welch with the Pioneer Corps and Lieutenant Ransom Griffin with the Ambulance Corps. The numbers at muster would continue to dwindle from all causes until at the close of the war only a fraction would remain from the original 1,000.

Companies F and K, the two companies that had required additional recruiting at Camp Putnam before mustering in, were sent to guard signal posts about seven miles from Winchester on May sixth. By then General Grant had crossed the Rapidan River with his 122,000 strong Army of the Potomac and was engaged with Lee's Army at the Battle of the Wilderness near Fredericksburg, Virginia. On May ninth the rest of the 116th and Sigel's Army advanced to Strasburg. Two days later Sigel's Army moved up the valley to Woodstock.

While Sigel crept up the valley, General Crook had defeated the rebel force protecting the vital New River Bridge on the Virginia and Tennessee Railroad at the Battle of Cloyd's Mountain. Crook's men destroyed the bridge and then retreated back to West Virginia. Crook was supposed to link up with Sigel's Army at Staunton, but Crook feared that rebel reinforcements would cut off his column before he could get there. Crook's retreat allowed Rebel General Breckinridge to concentrate his efforts against Sigel's Army.

Colonel Wildes mentioned a "neat rebel trick" used to try to capture a large portion of the army's wagon train. According to Wildes, "A note had been written and handed to the Division Wagon Master, purporting to come from the Chief Quartermaster, and to be in his hand writing, ordering a large train to the rear, with which were also to go the returned Sutler's wagons."12 An unguarded train left camp headed north before the Quartermaster realized what had happened. The rebel raiders Mosby and McNeil were waiting for the unguarded train a few miles down the road. The Quartermaster raced off on a horse and managed to catch the train before it reached the ambush point. This time the train returned safely, but Mosby and McNeil would increasingly prey on supply trains for the rest of the year. Soon, "No party of less than 50 men was safe a mile from camp," because of the savage raids by partisan bands led by these men.13

The army left Woodstock on May fourteenth and marched south to Mount Jackson. Colonel Moor was ordered to assume command of a force of three infantry regiments, 1,000 cavalry and six guns to "ascertain and feel the position and strength of the rebels..."14 The infantry in Moor's force included the 34th Massachusetts, 123rd Ohio and 1st West Virginia. Only the 123rd Ohio was from Moor's own First Brigade. Moor pushed south all the way to New Market, where he engaged a rebel force in a furious exchange of artillery fire. Moor held his position at New Market until dusk, when a rebel attack was repulsed. Moor reported that the rebels lost five killed and several wounded during the engagement. Moor and his force remained in place overnight without campfires.

The following day, May 15, 1864, the 116th was "left with the trains, the first and last time during the war, until about the middle of the afternoon, when some cavalry relieved us, and we were moved to the front on the double quick."15 May 15, 1864, was the date of probably the most famous small battle of the entire Civil War at New Market, Virginia.

The Battle of New Market is famous among Southerners, especially Virginians, because of the gallant participation of the cadets from the Virginia Military Institute (VMI). Taking nothing away from General Breckinridge and the rebels at New Market, the Federal troops were severely handicapped because of General Sigel's leadership. The battle commenced at about 8 a.m. in a heavy rainstorm and was fought in ankle-deep mud. At the start of the battle Colonel Moor's force faced Breckinridge and his army alone, Sigel and the rest of his army did not arrive at New Market until noon. When Sigel arrived he tried to persuade Colonel Moor to retreat. Sigel showed no enthusiasm for the fight and made numerous mistakes, the worst of which was to feed his army piecemeal into the battle.

A series of further errors by Sigel doomed his army and nearly resulted in its destruction. At one point, "Sigel tried to organize an infantry counterattack...But in the excitement he lapsed into German, and many of his shouted orders were incomprehensible to his American subordinates."16 By afternoon Sigel's Army was in full retreat with many units scattered in a disorganized flight.

The timely arrival of Captain Henry A. DuPont helped save Sigel's hapless survivors. DuPont arrived as Sigel's Army was scattering, and he placed his single battery in action at 500-yard intervals along the pike. One section would fire into the rebels as long as possible and then fall back to cover the other section up the pike. In this manner DuPont bought time for Sigel's men to escape.

The 116th also did its fair share to help save the defeated army. Colonel Moor learned during the battle that his "two finest regiments," the 28th and 116th Ohio, were with the train at Mount Jackson.17 Moor sent his staff officer to order them to march at the double quick to the scene of the fighting. Some cavalry relieved the 116th at the train, and Colonel Washburn pushed his men to the front on the run, meeting General Sigel near Rude's Hill. Along the way Washburn "ordered bayonets to be fixed to clear his way on the pike up to the battle-field through disgraceful fleeing masses of cavalry and straggling infantry."18 The 116th ran four miles to reach the front and arrived nearly exhausted. Colonel Moor formed the 116th on each side of a battery on the pike; here the 116th covered the retreating army, being, along with the battery and some cavalry, the last troops to leave the field. Moor reported that the 116th "brought up the rear in good order" in spite of the chaotic conditions during the retreat.19

Sigel's Army crossed the rain-swollen river near Mt. Jackson. General Breckinridge had hoped to destroy the bridge before Sigel could get there, but the rebel cavalry had been unable to reach the bridge. After the army crossed, a military engineer from Sigel's command attempted to blow the bridge to slow the rebels. Powder kegs were exploded atop the bridge with little effect. Since the 116th had brought up the rear, the men went to work to destroy the bridge with axes and crowbars and accomplished what gunpowder could not. The rebels remained south of Mt. Jackson and celebrated so loudly that they could be heard for miles.

There was reason for the rebels to celebrate; they had driven Sigel's larger force from the field and inflicted heavier casualties than they had sustained. The Federals had not fought well at New Market. Only the 34th Massachusetts, in their first combat experience, had much to be proud of. They had stood their ground when the other Federal regiments on their flanks had broken for the rear, and they had paid a high price in blood for their determination. Unfortunately for the 34th, they had the dubious distinction of being battered by the VMI cadets, who hit them hard with an enfilading fire. The 123rd Ohio, another regiment that served with the 116th until the war's end, performed poorly. Many of the officers from the 123rd were still in rebel prison camps, and the lack of leadership showed. The terms "less than stalwart" and "hapless" described their performance at New Market.20

Since the 116th had arrived at the front just as the army was beaten and in retreat, only a few men were wounded. It was probably fortunate for the 28th and 116th Ohio that Sigel had not managed to grind them up as he had the rest of his army. Sigel had simply fought the battle too conservatively. He had fed his regiments into the fight instead of striking with concentrated force. At the point of combat, Breckinridge had held an advantage in strength. The men seemed to sense that they had been betrayed by poor generalship as noted by Colonel Wildes: "Very few of us wanted to fight any more 'mit Sigel.' His army was beaten in detail." 21 Wildes' comments were an obvious barb referring to a wartime ballad inspired by the devotion of Sigel's German followers and titled "I'm Going to Fight Mit Sigel."

Some of the bridges on the retreat route were washed out from the furious rains during the day of the battle, so the retreat was far from orderly. Nevertheless, the army was not vigorously pursued and managed to reach Cedar Creek by May seventeenth. Private James Dalzell of Company H slipped away from the column during the retreat from New Market for some personal foraging. Private Dave Sheppard also of Company H accompanied him. Dalzell wrote an account of his wartime experiences and included the excursion he made on this occasion. The following excerpts are from his description of this foraging diversion:

Sigel was *on* his famous retreat from Woodstock...The truth of history compels me to state that we were about a mile ahead of the retreating column—at the heels of Sigel and his generals, making good time, that hot afternoon, in the direction of Cedar Creek...Not the most powerful gun in the Confederacy could have reached Dave, me, or the general who lead that *Segelopoedia!* We got tired of the main road, and in the confusion and disorder of the mad, and senseless, and utterly causeless retreat...now was our chance to resume our old operations against hen-roosts, distilleries, and things.

We were hungry...Every house near the road was already looted...On we went, discussing the situation, until, just as we emerged from the wood again into the open fields, we came upon an antiquated darkey, viewing the retreating army from the hilltops...Our parley with Sambo was short, sharp, and decisive. We told him we would shoot, hang, burn, and destroy him from the face of the earth, if he did not instantly pilot us to where we could get provender. He looked solemn...lied in his throat, and swore, '...don't know where you can get a bite.' We quickly assured him this would not do, and fixing bayonets...bade him trot ahead and show us our desired food or he would soon be weltering ankle deep in his own gore. This was all put on...

The poor old fellow told us we should find what we wanted, and we let him go, for after we were gone it would be death to him, sure, if what he had done should be discovered. A solitary woman and baby kept the hut...We were not the men to rob a lonely woman. So we bought three canteens of milk, and two loaves of bread, the only eatables she had about the premises, and gave her a five-dollar greenback out of my pocket-book, and went on our way rejoicing.[22]

Dalzell explained that such foraging expeditions were dangerous, but hunger was so compelling that danger and even behavior that was regrettable could be and were ignored. He explained, "We had some conscience, though a hungry stomach speaks in such tones of thunder, under such circumstances, that nothing less than the failure to find prevents the overt act..."[23]

When the 116th and Sigel's Army reached Cedar Creek, they had ample opportunity to reorganize and refit. The rebels did not press them; instead, General Lee ordered General Breckinridge to join his army in its operations against Grant at Hanover Junction. Private Dalzell noted that over 300 wounded men were at Cedar Creek after the Battle of New Market. He recalled a chance encounter with a dying man: "One poor fellow shot in the abdomen—a stranger to me—called piteously for water. I filled my cup hastily in the creek and raised it to his lips. He drank eagerly, rolled over, shuddered, and died before I got out of the ambulance."[24]

Commander-in-Chief Grant had expected more from Sigel. He wrote the following in his memoirs: "...just when I was hoping to hear of good work being done in the Valley I received instead the following announcement from Halleck: 'Sigel is in full retreat on Strasburg. He will do nothing but run; never did anything else'."[25] General Halleck suggested that Major General David Hunter should replace Sigel. It was obvious that Franz Sigel would not do, before the battle and even more so afterwards. So General Grant turned to someone he personally knew, someone with ties to the Republican Party, appointing General David Hunter to command of the Department of West Virginia.

"THEY STOOD THE TERRIBLE TEST MAGNIFICENTLY"
9

The day after the 116th Ohio reached Cedar Creek, Lieutenant General Grant, upon the suggestion of General Halleck and Secretary of War Stanton, removed General Sigel from command and appointed Major General David Hunter as commander of the Department of West Virginia. General Grant wrote in his memoirs, "Not regarding the operations of General Sigel as satisfactory, I asked his removal from command, and Major-General Hunter was appointed to supersede him."[1] The transfer took place on May 19, 1864; and according to Colonel Wildes, General Hunter assumed command on the twenty-first.

Major General David Hunter was an unfortunate choice to supersede General Sigel. He was yet another Federal general who owed his high rank to his political connections. As noted in the previous chapter, there was a very short list of effective and qualified generals available for command of the Federal armies in 1864. There were more capable officers available to replace Sigel from the Army of the Potomac and from General Sherman's Army in the West. But rather than calling upon the generals vital to the operations of these armies, Grant turned to the inactive General David Hunter, one of the most senior generals in the Federal Volunteer Army.

David Hunter was an intense, dichotomous man, evil in the opinion of many and yet favorable in the judgment of others. He was born into a prominent family, the grandson of one of the signers of the Declaration of Independence. He had many relatives from Virginia, and many believed he was born into a Virginia family, but, in fact, Hunter was a Northerner. Following his graduation from West Point in 1822, Hunter served in the army, with the exception of a six-year hiatus, until the outbreak of the Civil War. During his army career he served with future Confederate President Jefferson Davis and became the confidant of future President Zachary Taylor. Hunter had hair so black that many believed he dyed it. He had a swarthy complexion and lineaments similar to a Native American. Because of his dark features, army comrades called him "Black Dave." This sobriquet caught on with the troops serving under him in the Shenandoah Valley in 1864.[2]

While stationed at Fort Leavenworth, Kansas, in 1860, Hunter "initiated a correspondence with the newly elected President Lincoln, which won for him an invitation to travel on the inaugural train to Washington in February, 1861."[3] The President had received word from Hunter of an assassination plot, and he wrote to Hunter about potential Southern defectors: "it occurs to me that any real movement of this sort in the army would leak out, and become known to you. In such case, if it would not be unprofessional, or dishonorable (of which you are to be judge) I shall be much obliged if you will apprize me of it."4 While on the inaugural train tour with the President, Hunter was injured trying to protect Lincoln from a jostling crowd in Buffalo, New York. His thoroughly Republican ideology and connection to Lincoln proved highly beneficial in his ascension to high rank.

Hunter was wounded at First Bull Run and subsequently was sent through a series of assignments. While commanding the Department of the South in May 1862, he attempted to abolish slavery in the area under his jurisdiction. He also organized one of the very first regiments of African-American troops. The rebels were outraged and initially planned to execute Hunter should he be captured.

During the Chattanooga Campaign in November 1863, Hunter served under General Grant and formed a friendship with him. Grant subsequently assigned Hunter as an observer on the Red River Campaign. When a replacement was needed for Sigel, Grant quickly approved Hunter's selection. Once again politics and personal connections had determined who would command the 116th and the loyal men fighting in the Shenandoah Valley.

To his credit "Black Dave" Hunter immediately went to work to implement General-in-Chief Grant's orders and plans for the Shenandoah Campaign. Chief of Staff Halleck wired Grant's orders to Hunter, which called for the capture of the rebel supply center at Staunton, Virginia, and a subsequent movement against Charlottesville, Virginia. Hunter quickly took measures to improve the condition of his army and to prepare it for the advance against Staunton. He immediately ordered Brigadier General George Crook to move against Staunton with a view of joining forces to concentrate overwhelming force against that place.5

On May 22, 1864, General Hunter issued General Order Number 29 through Assistant Adjutant General Halpine. The order exhorted the men to do their best to support General Grant's campaign and gave instructions for preparing the army for the march. Hunter ordered the army to subsist off the country but placed restrictions on foraging. Among other things the order called for the men to carry an additional pair of shoes and 100 rounds of ammunition. The problem was that many men were doing without shoes. In fact, Quartermaster Sergeant Ezra Walker reported that 175 pairs were needed for the 116th, and Walker was forced to look for knapsacks because the regiment had sent theirs back to Martinsburg on orders from Sigel. Captain Keys was sent to Martinsburg to retrieve the stored knapsacks and found that they had been lost or destroyed. While Keys ordered new knapsacks, Walker was able to gather about 200 knapsacks from other regiments so the 116th

could carry all the extra ammunition. On the subsequent march an officer riding by the 116th asked, "What troops are these?" The reply came from Jim Hall of Company A, who yelled, "Troops! This is Hunter's ammunition train."6

The 116th and Hunter's Army took up the march for the new campaign on May 26, 1864, only nine days after the retreat form New Market. A brand new regiment, the 160th Ohio Infantry, had been added to the First Brigade, as was the First Battalion of the 5th New York Heavy Artillery. The 160th had only mustered in on May twelfth and would only serve until September 1864.7 Apparently the 160th was like many of the Ohio regiments raised in 1864 that joined only "to avoid the stigma of the draft."8 "The 160th Ohio protested so much against going to the front that it was sent back, on the 30th, from Rude's Hill."9 That regiment would finish up its short tour of duty guarding the army's trains.

Four days later the army reached the recent battlefield at New Market and encountered a horrifying and sickening sight. The rebels had thrown the Federal dead into a pile in a hollow and only partially covered them with dirt. "Feet arms and heads were protruding at all points of this festering mass."10 The men were outraged and swore revenge.11 An unfortunate burial detail endured the terrible stench of the decomposing bodies to properly bury them, and the army moved on.

Quartermaster Sergeant Ezra Walker wrote a letter from Staunton giving an account of the march. The following is from a portion of his letter:

> We left Cedar Creek May 26th, after having sent back all our tents and everything else that could not be carried on our backs. Passing through Strasburg, General Hunter ordered the men to burn several buildings from which several of our men had been bushwhacked. The folks were allowed to take nothing from the houses. Hunter says 'this bushwhacking has got to be stopped,' and you may depend upon it he will stop it. Many of our men were obliged to march without shoes, and it was really a pitiful sight to see them marching along, leaving marks of blood on the ground. We were put on half rations of bread from the very start, and for several days had been without any. May 29, marched from Woodstock to Mt. Jackson, where we encamped on the same ground on which we fought two weeks ago. Passing through Edinburg we found a great quantity of salt, which we took. Just before leaving the town, one of the men went into a garden to get some onions, and a woman came out and drove him out with rocks...June 3rd, marched from Mt. Jackson to Harrisonburg...Our foraging parties searched the houses and

stores for flour, meat, etc., taking all they found...We also destroyed three printing offices. June 4th, we expected to go directly up the Valley towards Staunton, but turned off the pike to the left soon after leaving the town, and passed the old Cross Key's battle ground, and so on to Port Republic...12

As Walker noted, the army turned off the Valley Pike and took the road to Port Republic. This was because Hunter had discovered that the rebels had dug in at Mt. Crawford, where the Valley Pike crossed the North River. Hunter decided to outflank this force and join Crook to capture Staunton. His plan would have succeeded except that the army was delayed at a river crossing at Port Republic. The army had to wait for a pontoon bridge to be thrown over the South Fork of the Shenandoah River. By the time the army was across the river at Port Republic, the rebels had discovered Hunter's move and were in place to block Hunter's advance on the Staunton Road near Piedmont, Virginia.

The rebel force at Piedmont was commanded by the 116th's old nemesis, General William "Grumble" Jones. He had led the rebels against the 116th in the regiment's first battle at Moorefield. Since that time Jones had exhibited considerable talent as a cavalry commander and had proven himself worthy of an independent command. He had helped save General Lee's best cavalry commander, General J. E. B. Stuart, from a beating at the Battle of Brandy Station just before the Battle of Gettysburg. After a transfer and a series of successes, the *Richmond Whig* proclaimed him to be "the Stonewall Jackson of East Tennessee."13 Now General Lee depended on Jones to defend the Valley. Jones had to defeat Hunter's superior force and then turn about to face Crook's column approaching from West Virginia. He could not allow Hunter to unite his two forces.

The impending battle at the tiny hamlet of Piedmont, Virginia, had assumed the proportions of a high stakes gamble. The Federal Government desperately needed a breakthrough victory for General Grant's coordinated spring campaign. On all fronts the Federal Armies were stalled. Grant's operations with the Army of the Potomac had cost over 38,000 casualties without achieving significant progress. General Sherman's Atlanta Campaign had also met with inconclusive results with casualties exceeding 5,500. General Butler's campaign along the James River was a miserable failure. The Lincoln Administration sensed that Northern support for the war was eroding; a victory of any kind was as crucial at this point as it had ever been.14

The 116th marched through Port Republic and went into camp in a piece of woods near the road for the night of June fourth. The men were hungry and didn't know what the morrow would bring. Hunter had ordered them to pack eight pounds of hard bread and ten rations of sugar and coffee. Now most of the men were out of rations, so they boiled their coffee and lay down for the night without supper.

Early on the morning of June 5, 1864, the 116th was called out of camp without the usual morning coffee and breakfast. After waiting in a rain for over an hour, the First Brigade took up the march at about half-past five. It was soon obvious that a fight lay in store. Colonel Augustus Moor's First Brigade marched on the west (or right) side of the Staunton Road and was followed by Colonel Joseph Thoburn's brigade. Colonel Moor ordered Major Henry Peale of the 18th Connecticut Infantry to deploy Companies A and B from his regiment and two companies from the 5th New York Heavy artillery as skirmishers in advance of the First Brigade. The 123rd Ohio Infantry was deployed as skirmishers on the east of the road to cover the advance from that quarter.

At about 6 a.m. the sharp crackle of carbine fire was heard just to the south. The advance Federal cavalry had run into Rebel General Imboden's cavalry pickets at the crossroads near Mt. Meridian. There was no time to boil coffee; the men would have to fight without breakfast.

The 116th wanted to prove beyond doubt that it could fight. Milroy's defeat at Winchester had left the 116th with a stigma it did not deserve. The newcomers of the 34th Massachusetts had shown disdain for the 116th, as had General Franz Sigel and his entourage. Sigel believed the 116th was poorly organized and "entirely useless."15 As we have seen, it was Sigel who was worthless. Before this day, June 5, 1864, was over, the 116th Ohio Infantry would prove beyond any doubt its resolute courage and determination under the very heaviest hostile fire. It would emerge from a terrible storm of lead and iron with a reputation for steadfastness to rival any regiment during the war.

A cavalry battle had developed around the crossroads near Mt. Meridian, and the 116th along with the rest of Brigadier General Jeremiah Sullivan's Infantry Division halted north of the crossroads and watched the action. Soon the Federal cavalry drove Imboden's troopers back, and the 116th resumed the advance toward Piedmont. General Jones, having learned of Imboden's retreat, sent Major R. H. Brewer and his battalion of dismounted cavalry into a wood atop Northwest Hill (three quarters of a mile north of Piedmont) to slow the advancing Federals. Meanwhile the bulk of Jones' force hurried to fortify their position just north of the village of Piedmont.

Major Brewer had considerable military expertise; he was a graduate of the class of 1858 at West Point. He placed his men in concealment behind a rail fence at the edge of the timber atop Northwest Hill. Brewer's Battalion consisted of approximately 500 men.16 The battered remnants of Imboden's Brigade re-deployed on the right, east of the Staunton Road.

When the tiring Federal cavalry reached Brewer's position at Northwest Hill, they were checked by Brewer's fire and could not drive the rebels off the hill. Major General Julius Stahel, commanding the First Cavalry Division, sent word to General Hunter that his cavalry was stalled. Hunter directed General Sullivan to send in his infantry to relieve the weary troopers and carry Brewer's position.

Sullivan ordered Colonel Moor to lead his First Brigade into action against Brewer's line. Moor sent his skirmishers under Major Peale forward and formed three regiments from his brigade in columns of battalions. The 18th Connecticut Infantry formed on the right, the remainder of the battalion of the 5th New York Heavy Artillery formed in the center and the 116th formed on the left of Moor's attacking front. Each regiment presented a front the width of one company, and Moor ensured that enough space was provided between the columns to allow the regiments to deploy in line of battle.17

As Moor's columns approached the woods where Brewer's troopers waited, Moor wheeled his regiments into line of battle. Behind the 116th, Captain Alfred Von Kleiser's 30th New York Independent Battery, another German unit consisting of four 12 pounder Napoleons, unlimbered to cover the infantry. Moor ordered the 28th Ohio, his own regiment, to support these guns. The term of service for the 28th expired within the month, so Moor's assignment was most welcome for these short timers due to return home for discharge.

Shells fired from a long-range rebel battery near Piedmont began to explode around the skirmishers as they advanced over the rough ground, sending dirt and debris high into the air. Suddenly Brewer's men opened fire from their concealment and shook the skirmish line. The skirmishers recoiled and Moor ordered them to fall back on the main line. Moor then sent his entire battle line forward under rebel fire.

The New Englanders and New Yorkers to the right of the 116th quickly ran into trouble and made little progress. However, the 116th overlapped Brewer's position along the Staunton Road; and while the right wing of the 116th engaged the rebels near the wood, the remainder of the regiment flanked the rebels and poured a demoralizing enfilade fire into their right and rear. Brewer's line gave way, and the 116th "had several opportunities, of which it availed itself, of enfilading the rebels as they fell back."18 Lieutenant Gottlieb Sheifley of Company K wrote that this first charge by the 116th at Piedmont "dislodged the Johnnies from a piece of pine timber and drove them behind their breastworks; this was about 11 o'clock."19 The 116th pushed ahead and punished Brewer's disorganized troopers as they streamed across an open field in retreat.

Brewer's Battalion suffered very heavy casualties at Piedmont, many no doubt falling from the musket fire of the 116th.

The fragments of Brewer's Battalion scurried into the main rebel line north of Piedmont and took cover inside the "bull pen" already prepared by Jones' main force. The "bull pen" was a line of rail and earth breastworks thrown up along the edge of another heavier wood where Jones had posted most of his infantry. This wooded area was west of the Staunton Road and ran parallel to Walker's Lane, a farm road leading to the Walker home one mile to the west. The rebel line inside the woodland faced an open clearing which offered an excellent field of fire upon the approaching Federals. Jones had posted from left to right the 36th Virginia, 45th Battalion, 45th Virginia, and the Thomas Legion inside this fortified line that extended from the Staunton Road to the bluffs on the Middle River. Brewer's bloodied and disorganized Battalion was placed in line next to the Thomas Legion on the rebel right. There they regrouped and awaited Moor's approach.20

After Brewer's Battalion was driven from Northwest Hill, Brigadier General Sullivan rode to the front to confer with Colonel Moor about the rebel positions that lay ahead. General Hunter apparently did not know just where the main portion of the rebel army was deployed; the wooded area just ahead of Moor's Brigade concealed the rebel troops positioned there. While Imboden and Brewer were delaying Hunter's advance, Jones had put his men to work along a rail fence at the north edge of the wood. The rebels had dug shallow trenches, piling the dirt upon fence rails and logs. This quickly constructed breastwork gave the rebels good cover and protection from Federal minie balls. Moor ordered his men on the right to fire into the woods and breastworks. When the rebels failed to reply, Moor decided that his brigade could easily clear the woods. General Sullivan agreed and ordered Moor to attack.

Moor, believing that the woods ahead were no major threat, led the 18th Connecticut, 5th New York Heavy Artillery and the 116th Ohio into the open field just north of the woods. Moor's decision to send his brigade forward without a reconnaissance was a blunder that cost scores of needless casualties that day. A probe of the woods with a skirmish line would have developed the strength of the rebel position. Instead, Moor led his three regiments into a well prepared and strong rebel position with about the same results as leading them into an ambush.

Colonel Washburn led approximately 692 men from the 116th Ohio into the fight at Piedmont.21 The 116th was still on the left of the brigade, just as it had been earlier during the attack on the pine timber at Northwest Hill. When the 116th was well into the open field and within seventy-five yards of the rebel breastworks, a sheet of orange flame burst out along the length of the tree line. Sprays of wet soil and turf appeared in the field just beyond the front rank; bullets whizzed overhead or thudded into the bodies of the surprised Buckeyes, spattering their comrades with blood. Colonel Washburn—a perfect target mounted on his horse—kept the men moving toward the rebel works.

Washburn and his men probably believed they would penetrate the rebel works, because the 116th pressed on despite the terrible rebel fire until near the edge of the wood. Washburn's horse was hit and fell beneath him, but he escaped unhurt and kept pressing the attack. To the right of the 116th, the "cookie regiment" (18th Connecticut) was being pummeled. The 18th "fought desperately and at some disadvantage, being entirely in the open field," like the 116th.22 Soon after the rebels opened fire, the 18th Connecticut "lost its cohesion," and "confusion reigned in their ranks."23 The New Englanders scattered and streamed back to the cover of the pine timber. When the 18th recoiled, the New Yorkers were hit with a heavier fire, and they too quickly fell back.

Intense rebel fire at point blank range was raking the 116th near the edge of the wood. Men fell shot through the bowels, writhing on the ground. Others fell wounded in the shoulder, side, thigh, and head. The bullets seemed to fly as thickly as large hail in a driving storm. With the other units in retreat and facing a concentrated fire, the 116th had to pull back from the rebel works. The 116th, apparently under orders, fell back to the more sheltered area between the two wooded portions of the field. There Colonel Washburn and his officers reformed the lines under rebel musket and artillery fire.

After Moor's attack was repulsed, the rebel artillery roared into the fray with full fury. The Augusta Battery near the Staunton Road fired 20 pounder Parrott shells and 24 pounder spherical shells into the 116th. General Jones reinforced the Augusta Battery with a twelve-pounder howitzer and a three-inch rifle from the Lewisburg Battery, and soon these guns added their weight to the barrage on Moor's front. A shell, probably from one of these guns, burst within four feet of Lieutenant Gottlieb Sheifley of Company K, and a fragment struck him on his left thigh. Sheifley noted the time was approximately 11 o'clock. He was hit a second time by a shell fragment that struck his chest. According to Sheifley the hit "mashed in three ribs on my right breast and knocked me down as completely as I ever was in my life."24

The rebel artillery near the Staunton Road kept firing at a brisk pace. Since the 116th was the nearest Federal unit targeted by the rebel guns, they were visible to the men as the 116th attempted to regroup. Lieutenant Sheifley noted, "I saw with my own good eyes two of their guns on their extreme right, in position not alone, but firing at us at an astonishingly rapid rate, and we could plainly see every flash."25 If the barrage continued unchallenged, it would demoralize Moor's battered brigade and allow the rebels to take the offensive. General Hunter directed Captain Henry DuPont, his chief of artillery, to position his guns to silence the rebel artillery. Captain DuPont was an exceptionally gifted artillery commander, and he was able to assess the terrain and place his batteries very effectively. Soon DuPont's batteries "literally formed a ring of fire around the right flank of the Confederate left wing."26 DuPont's guns concentrated their fire on the rebel guns nearest to the 116th. Soon six of the rebel gunners had been killed, and three guns were abandoned near the road. With the Augusta Battery silenced, Captain Von Kleiser's New York battery along with other Federal batteries to the east of the road hammered the Lewisburg section until it was also withdrawn.

With the rebel artillery effectively out of the fight, General Hunter decided to launch another attack on the rebel left. Just before 1 o'clock, Hunter directed General Sullivan to coordinate with General Stahel's cavalry to again assault the rail pens. Two more infantry regiments would be added to the attack, and Colonel John Wynkoop's Second Cavalry Brigade would guard the Federal extreme right. Hunter had decided not to risk committing Colonel Joseph Thoburn's Second Infantry Brigade to the attack, fearing to expose his left to a counterattack.

This attack, like the previous one against the rebel works, was doomed before it began. In the first attack the defending rebels actually outnumbered Moor's attacking force. There were over 1,400 well-protected rebels, armed with Springfield and Enfield rifle muskets, facing the attack. Additionally, Moor's linear attack formation spread the force along a wide front, rendering it nearly impossible to punch through the rebel fortifications. The situation was very much like what occurred a few days earlier at Cold Harbor, Virginia. There, Grant's Army was smashed against well-prepared rebel trenches resulting in heavy Federal losses. Experience had shown that an overwhelming numerical advantage was required to launch a successful assault on an entrenched enemy.27 With the rebel artillery silenced and Thoburn's Brigade positioned to cover a counterattack, a more compact strike down the Staunton Road, much like Emory Upton's assault at Spotsylvania, might have succeeded. But Moor simply repeated the same method used in the first assault.

Colonel Moor brought up his own 28th Ohio from supporting Captain Von Kleiser's Battery and added his short timers to the assault line on the right of the 116th. The 5th New York Heavy Artillery was next on the right, then the 18th Connecticut and finally the 1st West Virginia Infantry, Colonel Thoburn's regiment, was last on the right flank.

General Jones repositioned the withdrawn section of the Lewisburg Battery behind the rebel line about 300 yards into the wood, and Brigadier General John Vaughn's 1st, 39th, and 59th Tennessee regiments were also sent to bolster the rebel left. The Tennessee regiments were probably not on the line when the second Federal charge commenced at approximately 2 o'clock.

As the brigade bugler sounded the charge, the 116th again moved toward the dreaded rebel "bull pens" with the left wing nearly reaching the Staunton Road. The 116th aimed for the portion of the rebel line manned by the Thomas Legion, an eight-company regiment led by Major William Stringfield and a five-company battalion commanded by Lieutenant Colonel James McKamy, totaling approximately 390 men. According to one soldier from the Thomas Legion, they "never fired at a longer range than seventy-five yards" during the battle.28. This is attributable to the fact that the 116th was partially sheltered by a rise or hill as it approached the rebel works.

The second charge was nearly identical to the first except even more men were hit this time, because the 116th stood in the open field and exchanged shots with the rebels. The color guard was especially hard hit. According to Colonel Wildes every color bearer and all of the color guard were wounded during the battle. Sergeant Reese Williams exhibited extraordinary valor during this charge for which he was promoted to a lieutenancy. Williams was hit in the side while carrying the flag. Though bleeding profusely, Williams refused to yield up the colors and defiantly held them in the face of the obviously concentrated rebel fire. Williams continued to hold the flag until he passed out from loss of blood and was carried to the rear. At that point another act of heroism was seen. Color Sergeant David Barrett of Company C, already suffering from a severely wounded arm, took the flag from Williams and carried both standards with his remaining arm. Captain Mann of Company C noticed Barrett's mangled arm and took one of the flags from him.

As devastating as the close range rebel fire was, it seemed particularly concentrated towards mounted officers and color bearers. Colonel Washburn's horse went down in the first charge, Colonel Ely of the 18th Connecticut had a horse shot from under him, and General Sullivan had *three* horses shot beneath him during the battle.

The 116th stubbornly clung to the blood-spattered field until it was littered with their dead and wounded. Lieutenant Sheifley believed that the rebel works could have been carried during this charge: "The second charge we made about 2 o'clock, and were recalled before we got to the rebel works, for reasons never yet known to me. I believed then, and do now, that we could have taken the Johnnies as well at 2 o'clock as we eventually did at 4 o'clock. 29

On the right of the 116th, Moor's 28th Ohio was being cut to pieces as well. The regiments farther to the right soon fell back and this allowed

Piedmont Battlefield. The rebel line attacked by Moor's Brigade was posted along this field during the battle.

Marker for the Battle of Piedmont on the Staunton Road near the spot where General Jones was killed. Thoburn's men attacked from the field in the foreground.

Examples of artillery projectiles for Federal artillery at the Battle of Piedmont. Left to right: Spherical shell fragments, U.S. 12-pounder spherical shell with Bormann fuse, 12-pounder canister, 3-inch Schenkl shell, 3-inch Hotchkiss shell with percussion fuse, 3-inch Hotchkiss shell with brass fuse plug, Hotchkiss shell fragments. A Colt Model 1860 revolver for size comparison. (Relics courtesy of Leroy Burgess)

Examples of artillery projectiles of the caliber fired at the 116th at Piedmont. Left to right: 3.67 inch Schenkl shell for the 20-pounder Parrott Rifle, 3.67 inch Parrott shell, another 3.67 inch Parrott shell, C. S. 24-pounder smoothbore shell with Bormann type fuse. A Colt Model 1860 revolver for size comparison. (Relics courtesy of Leroy Burgess)

the rebels to concentrate their fire on the 28th. The 28th "went down flat on their bellies" for cover from the terrible leaden storm. 30 At this point the 116th fell back "to a slight cover of a rise of ground" where it halted and lay down within "within short rifle range of the enemy's works."31

When Moor's Brigade retreated this second time, the rebels rushed out from their works to attack the right portion of the Federal line screaming "New Market, New Market!"32 But the rebels didn't last long out in the open field either, and they quickly repaired to the cover of their works. This attack was made in the direction of the 18th Connecticut. Colonel Ely of the "cookie regiment" then requested that some artillery be brought forward: "Seeing an excellent opportunity to use cannon I dispatched an orderly with a request for two howitzers, which came promptly and did excellent service, in knocking the rail pens in splinters amid great slaughter."33

The two guns mentioned by Colonel Ely were 12 pounder Napoleons brought forward from Captain Von Kleiser's New York Battery and placed in a sheltering depression on the ridge near the 18th Connecticut. Colonel Wildes wrote about the effective work of these guns: "The demoralization which every shot created in their ranks could be plainly seen, crowds of the enemy fleeing from the spot where a shot struck the rails, when our infantry would open fire upon them the moment they showed themselves, the guns of the battery also saluting them at the same time with grape and cannister."34

While the 116th lay in front of the rebel works, First Sergeant Joseph Purkey of Company H was hit and severely wounded in the leg. The sergeant immediately jumped up, leaned on his musket, shook his fist, and was heard screaming at the rebels, "Now, ---- you, I suppose you think you've done it." 35 The men on the line chuckled at Purkey's defiant display, but the rebels had the last laugh as the wounded sergeant fell into their hands after the battle.

With two failed assaults and a rebel counterattack to discourage him, General Hunter was considering a retreat. However, Hunter decided to attempt one more assault, having learned of a weakness in the rebel center near the Staunton Road.

Hunter sent orders to Colonel Thoburn directing him to lead a force from his brigade against the rebel weak spot just south of the rail pens. A ravine sheltered Thoburn's approach, and when his force appeared it was in perfect position to flank the rebel line facing Moor's Brigade. Between 3 and 4 o'clock the 116th saw Thoburn's men charging the rebel flank, and shortly thereafter orders came to charge the rail pens one more time.

At about this time a shell fired from the Lewisburg Battery on the rebel right nearly killed Colonel Wildes. He wrote about the incident after the battle as follows:

Just before the last charge a shell struck the ground within two feet of me, plowed the ground up under me, throwing me headlong, and ricochetting out again, passed on and hit Captain Teters in the leg, wounding him quite badly. It didn't explode till it had passed us ten feet or more. Had it exploded where it first struck the ground, the loss of life could not have failed to be great.36

Sergeant Reese Williams had returned to the line from the surgeon's dressing table and had reclaimed the national colors. When the charge was sounded, Williams attempted to go forward with the flag but couldn't keep up. As Captain Mann again came forward to take the flagstaff, Williams kissed the colors "and swung his cap and feebly cheered as he saw them carried over the rebel works."37

Thoburn's force succeeded in flanking the rebel works in the woods, and General Jones was forced to pull troops from the rail pens to oppose Thoburn's attack. Brewer's troopers were pulled out of the rail pens and sent against Thoburn. As the 12th West Virginia Infantry advanced with Thoburn's right, the 116th advanced and opened fire on the Thomas Legion. This subjected the Thomas Legion to fire from two fronts. With the 12th West Virginia pressing the rebel flank, the 116th rushed across the open field and leapt over the rail breastworks. Men from the 116th quickly captured scores of rebels from the Thomas Legion, 60th Virginia and Brewer's Battalion. As Thoburn's force pressed in from the 116th's left, the rebel line crumbled. Lieutenant Sheifley later asserted, "In this last charge my regiment (the 116th Ohio) alone took about 500 prisoners..." 38

General Jones attempted to rally his troops along the Staunton Road to prevent the developing disaster. As his line disintegrated, Jones galloped toward Thoburn's front with a group of reserves. A bullet struck Jones in the middle of his forehead, knocking him from his horse and killing him instantly. Another rebel officer attempted to rally the beaten rebels, but he too in turn was shot and killed. Thoburn's men rushed past the body of Grumble Jones without stopping, probably without recognizing it.

Just who shot General Jones became a controversy immediately after the battle. The identity of that soldier is still in question. "If every boy who later claimed to have shot him (Jones) had put a bullet in him, why, he would have been so heavy it would have taken a four horse team to have moved his body off of the battlefield," according to a Pennsylvanian.39 According to Colonel Wildes, "His body was found directly in front of the position of the 116th."40 An article written years

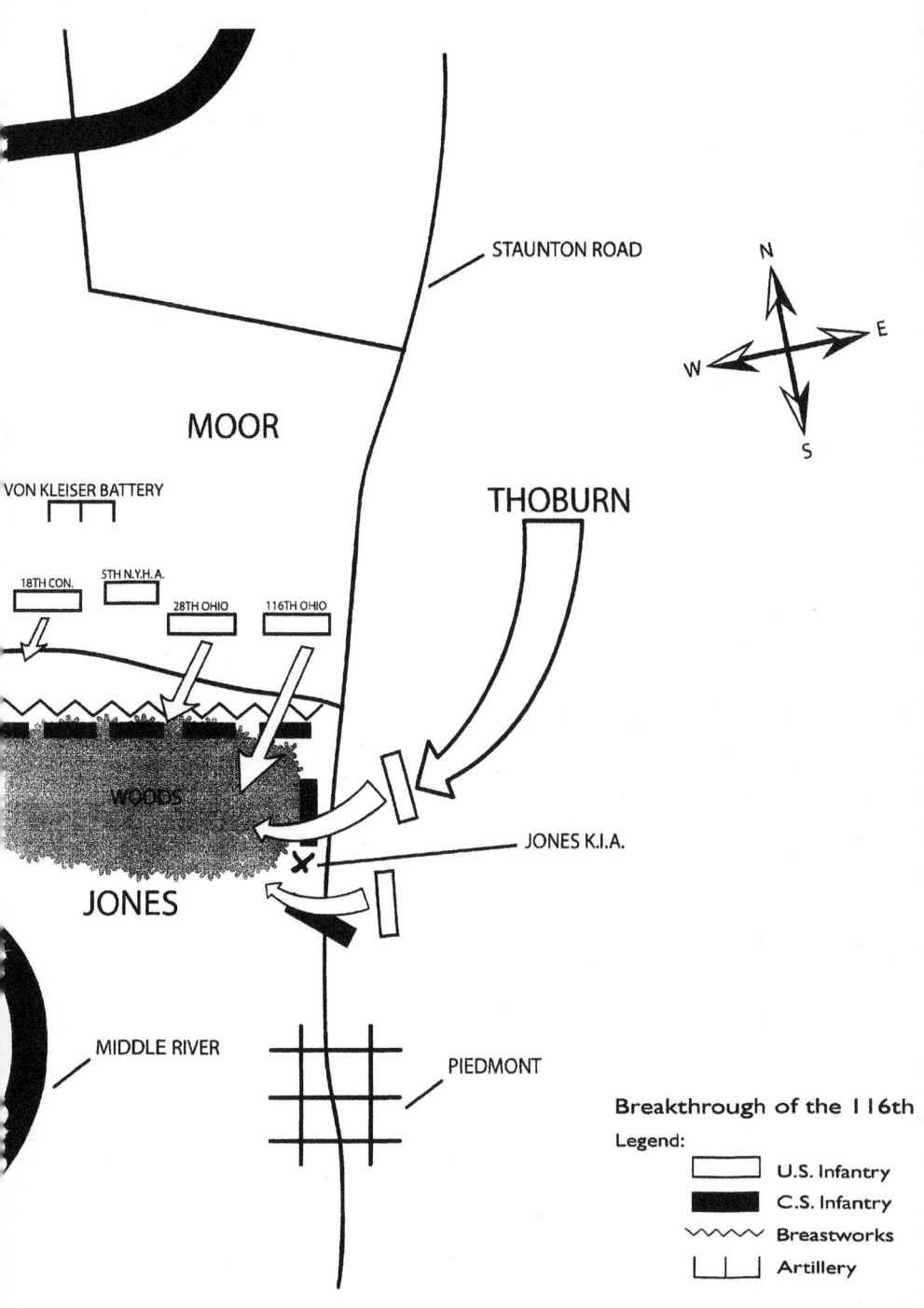

after the war claimed that Private Henry Stevens of Company E shot the general. Samuel Tschappat, a veteran of the 116th, wrote, "Cols. Washburn and Wildes and other officers said it was Henry Stephen's shot that killed Jones."[41] Private Stevens may have shot a rebel officer, but he probably was not the man who shot General Jones. At least four other Federal regiments were in the immediate vicinity where Jones fell, and the officer Stevens supposedly shot was struck in the breast—not in the forehead.

After General Jones fell the right portion of the rebel line in the wood collapsed. Thoburn's force pushed into the wood while the 116th was capturing hundreds of rebels along the rail pen. The 28th Ohio broke through the rebel line shortly afterwards, and then the entire rebel line scattered and ran. Federal pressure funneled the fleeing rebels toward a ford of the Middle River on the eastern edge of the wood. As the rebels struggled to escape across the ford, many were picked off by Federals shooting from the bluffs above the river. Part of Moor's Brigade and some of the 116th participated in the fight at the ford, where many rebels were killed and captured.

Private Mike Manning of Company H, an Irishman of small stature, caught a large rebel Irishman hiding along the riverbank and took him prisoner. As Manning marched his captive through the Federal lines at bayonet point, he berated his charge for being a "rebel and an Irishman, too." Soon Manning and the rebel were arguing points about succession in "true Irish style, with good strong brogue and both generally talking at once," to the amusement of the soldiers nearby. Some of the soldiers, looking for a little fun in their victory flush, grabbed Manning and allowed the rebel to give him a good shaking. Manning and the rebel "both possessed the keenest kind of Irish wit, and many a poor wounded soldier forgot his pain in laughing at the comical scene."[42]

The Rebel Army had been split in two and escaped in separate directions. Thoburn's attack nearly succeeded in capturing the entire rebel left posted in the wood. Only General Jones' sacrificial counterattack and a precipitate flight across the Middle River saved the rebel left. The remainder of the Rebel Army withdrew to New Hope and on to Fishersville. Rebel casualties at Piedmont were approximately 600 killed and wounded and over 1,000 captured.[43] Rebel killed and wounded were probably higher than this estimate because the rebel reports were incomplete.

Federal casualties at Piedmont were approximately 165 killed, 620 wounded, and 39 captured.[44] The 116th Ohio suffered worse than any other unit on the field according to Fox's book on regimental losses.[45] The dead were buried on the field, and the severely wounded remained at Piedmont when the Federal Army moved on to Staunton the following day. The wounded that could be moved went with the army to Staunton and were later sent north with a wagon train from Staunton. A post war article by Sergeant B. C. Drake of Company H, who was severely wounded in the leg at Piedmont, mentioned the Federal wounded at Piedmont. Soon after Hunter's army left the field, a rebel force moved in and took charge of the wounded still at the battlefield. A young rebel doctor tended to the Federals. Drake noted that the doctor was "a splendid young man, and he did everything that he could for our comfort."[46] Those who survived and could be moved were sent to Staunton after Hunter's Army moved on.

The Battle of Piedmont is barely mentioned except in the most comprehensive works on the Civil War. Yet the battle was one of the most fierce and furious of the war. There were also important strategic concerns and implications at stake at Piedmont: "The upper valley was opened to invasion for the first time in the war, with serious psychological and economic implications for the Confederacy. In the North the victory solidified President Lincoln's position at the Republican convention then in progress in Baltimore."[47] William F. Fox wrote that battles are memorable in proportion to the casualties resulting from the combat. It is true that great battles are remembered as much for the extent of their bloodshed as anything. Nevertheless, Piedmont accomplished more and was of greater strategic importance than many of the better-remembered battles of the war.

Casualties in the 116th were staggering. "The 116th lost 181 men killed and wounded, forty-one being killed and thirteen afterwards dying of their wounds," according to Colonel Wildes.[48] Fox's book on regimental losses listed the casualties for the 116th Ohio at Piedmont as twenty killed and 156 wounded.[49] Colonel Washburn compiled a list of the killed and wounded for the 116th at Piedmont while the regiment was at Staunton on June 9, 1864. Colonel Washburn counted eighteen killed on the field, four died shortly after the battle, and 156 wounded.[50] The Official Roster for the 116th Ohio Infantry lists at least twenty killed, twenty mortally wounded and twenty-eight captured at Piedmont.[51] The men listed as captured were almost certainly wounded men taken by the rebels at Staunton and Piedmont after Hunter's Army departed. Drake's article substantiates this.

Colonel Wildes' list of Piedmont casualties appeared in his book written almost twenty years after the war and contained some errors. Colonel Washburn's list was compiled just days after the battle; and while it may contain a few omissions, it is probably the most accurate list available. The following is from Washburn's letter to the Ohio A. G. dated June 9, 1864:

Staunton Va. June 9, 1864,
B. R. Cowen
A. G. of Ohio

Sir. Enclosed you will find the list of casualties in my Regt. in the recent battle of Piedmont, Va. With regard to the part taken by my command in the battle, the official report of the Maj. Genl. Commanding, and the list of casualties will bear testimony. I send this under "Frank" as there is not a post stamp in the whole regt.

I am respectfully yours
James Washburn Col.
116th O. V. I.

B. R. Cowen)
A. G.   )

(Killed)

Company A—Nathaniel D. Hayden, Addey Brock.

Company B—Sylvester Shumway.

Company C—John Latchaw, Fredr. Neptune.

Company D—Corp. Robert Armstrong, John Derwiler, Robert H. Dyer, Elias B. Brock, Joseph Summons.

Company E—Francis Swartz.

Company F—Corp. William King, Matthew (Morris) Krouse, Garrison Miracle, James Hughes, Richard Phelps, (George Johnson: from Roster).

Company H—Stephen C. McCoy.

Company I—Richard B. Miller.

(Wounded)

Company A—Corpl. Benj. F. Dye, hip; Fred'k R. Rose, severely, shoulder; William Brock, severely, shoulder; Robert Smith, arm; John Smith, neck; 1st Sgt. Mann Smith, severely, knee; Musician Albert Gates, leg (captured); Jacob Keyler, severely, hip; Corpl. Newton Meeks, severely, bowels; James Hall, leg; John Harman, leg; James Kimpton, severely, shoulder; Elijah Bennett, severely, head (died 6-24-64); David Barcus, severely, wrist; Sgt. Daniel Hurd, severely, arm; Cyrus Sprague, severely (captured); Jacob Zimmerly, severely, thigh (died 7-1-64); Sam'l Zimmerly, severely, thigh (captured); Sam'l Tidd, severely, thigh; Robert McCammon, severely, side.

Company B—George Keyes, severely, hand; Marion Coleman, severely, leg (captured); John Baker, back; John Anderson, face; Sgt. Uriah Hoydt, leg; 1st Sgt. Wm. H. Bush, leg; Wells Grubb, arm; Davis Watson, arm; John Doland leg.

Company C—1st Sgt. John Heald, severely, lungs; Sgt. John Beach, hip; Color Sgt. David Barrett, severely, arm; Sgt. Mathew Maris, severely, leg; Corpl. John Barrett, severely, leg (died 8-19-64); Adam Rodecker, side, (died 6-5-64); Franklin Barnes, leg; William Barnes, arm; Emmon Beardmore, wrist; Elwood Chambers, severely, foot (died 6-23-64); Miles Davis, head; Isaac Barrett, severely foot (died 7-10-64); George Gannon, body (died 6-5-64); George Kestner, severely, arm; James Mobberly, severely, hip (died 7-12-64); John Montgomery, severely, arm; Henry Pfiefer, bowels (Died 6-5-64); James Preshaw, severely, shoulder (captured, died 11-3-64 at Atlanta, Ga.); Riley Thornberry, hip; Albert Vickers, head; Edward Yockey, severely, leg (captured); John Buchwald, severely, shoulder; William Metz, head; Phillip Schoupe, leg.

Company D—1st Lieut. Richard Chaney, foot, William Flowers, severely, head (captured, died 11-5-64 at Atlanta, Ga.); Sam'l Alford, severely, Lungs (died 6-15-64); C. M. Blowers severely, shoulder; Josiah Norris, arm; Richard Mahoney, severely, leg (died 6-15-64); James Headly, severely, hip & ankle (captured); Scott Dix, leg (captured); H. B. Hixenbaugh, severely, bowels (captured); Washington Bryan, severely, arm (died 6-16-64); James Sinclair, severely, arm; John Winland, severely, arm; John Hall, severely, arm; Jacob Hall, side (captured, died 12-29-64, Salisbury,N.C.);
Eldridge Moffett, severely, hand; Daniel Bennett, shoulder; Henry Mowder, hip; Hugh Thompson, leg; Sam'l Forsyth, hand; Jesse Stine, head; Joshua Nixon, shoulder; Peter Hickman, head; Alford Gray, hip; Peter Schultz, leg; Thomas Rowley, arm; Sgt. James Drum, head. (Roster: David Conger)

Company E—Sgt. Joseph Skiles, severely, groin; Moses McCollough, severely, leg (died 6-5-64); Ephraim Henthorn, severely, severely, leg; Madison Miller, severely, leg (died 9-15-64); Harrison Cochran, severely, foot (captured); Charles Palmer, severely, leg; William Fisher

(Tisher), severely, shoulder (captured); Lewis Barcus, severely, leg (captured); Joseph Hall, arm; Corpl. John Atkinson, arm.

Company F—1st Sgt. Stephen Brown, severely, arm; Corpl. Robert Martin, severely, arm; William Sutton, severely, leg amputated; James Carson, severely, hip; Elijah Bunting, severely side, (captured); Samuel Stephens, leg; Jacob Dillon, severely, thigh; Jasper Rake, severely, leg; Wesley McGee, side; George Johnson, severely, leg (roster lists as KIA); Thos Peterson, severely, foot; Emanuel Okey, shoulder (captured, died in Sultana disaster); James Piggot, head; Lienjenius Efaw, thigh.

Company G—Alex McFarland, hip; John Rawlings, leg.

Company H—Capt. W. B. Teters, severely, leg; 1st Sgt. Joseph Purkey, severely leg (captured); Sgt. Benj. Drake, severely, leg; Sgt. Reese Williams (Color Bearer), severely, side; Sgt. Henry Arnold, knee; Corpl. Benj. Tilton, severely, ankle (captured); Jacob Gregg, thigh (died 4-23-65); J. C. Wilson, severely, leg (captured); Nathaniel Butler, severely, arm; David Brock, hip; Dighton Bates, mouth; William Cain, heel; John Groves, severely, abdomen (captured); Wesley James, severely, shoulder (captured); John Cackley, foot; John Keyser, severely, thigh (captured); Eli Kirkbride, ankle; John Larrick, severely, bowels (captured, died 9-12-64 at Savannah, Ga.); John Mott, severely, hand; William McBride, severely, thigh & leg; Andrew Powell, wrist; Solomon Rich, severely, thigh (died 7-1-64); Simon Secrist, side; Thos Spear, arm (captured); James Harrison, severely, lungs (died 6-6-64).

Company I—Sgt. John Chick, hip; Jesse Annon, arm; Bradly Barrows, arm; Luther Cayton, head; S. P. Fleak, side; Ephraim Frost, severely, shoulder (died 1-15-65); Consider Frost, severely, both legs, (died 6-29-64); Edwin Fuller, severely, thigh; James Gilchrist, severely, leg; J. C. S. Gilbert, severely, face (captured, died 10-9-64 at Savannah, Ga.); Nathan Hatch, severely, face & shoulder; Mark McAfee, arm; Saml. McCollock, severely, knee; Joseph Morrison, severely, both legs (captured); Elijah Patton, severely, arm; Fayette Paugh, severely, leg; Rufus Stanley, leg; George Tasker, groin; Fredk. Warren, severely, bowels, (died 6-10-64).

Company K—1st Lieut. Gotlieb Shiefley, side; Edward Henshaw, severely, bowels (captured); Nelson Clements, wrist; Saml. Spencer, thigh; John Kulow, leg; Thomas Witham, arm; George Lyon, head; Andrew Cagg hand (captured, died 1-7-65 at Florence, S.C.).[52]

The 116th Ohio was involved in fifteen battles during the Civil War and some of the fiercest fighting seen anywhere during the war. Piedmont was the toughest fight the 116th experienced. Colonel Wildes emphasized this in his book nearly twenty years later. Three days after the battle Wildes wrote a letter expressing these sentiments:

> ...I am all right, except a bruise from a spent ball on the right knee. It was a stirring time for us. I will write you more fully soon of the splendid conduct of the regiment. This has really been the first battle that thoroughly tested the mettle of our officers and men. You will be proud to know that they stood the terrible test magnificently... 53

Wildes continued his praise for the regiment in his book after the war:

> I never saw greater bravery than was that day displayed by the color bearers and color guard of the 116th regiment. But to see them all wounded, some we feared mortally, at the close of the battle, brought tears to the eyes of everyone who had witnessed their splendid behavior. Nothing could exceed the heroism of the whole regiment in this engagement.54

While Thomas Wildes made no secret of his pride in the 116th Ohio, he was not given to hyperbole. The 116th Ohio proved in the standup fight at Piedmont that it was as dependable as any regiment in the service, and its subsequent proud record for gallantry validated this fact. They had charged rebel breastworks across open ground three times in a matter of hours, each time taking serious losses. Their bravery and determination compared favorably with any regiment in the Civil War.

Colonel Wildes made special mention of the bravery of Captain Mann of Company C who carried the Colors while leading his company during the last charge. He also mentioned Lieutenant Chaney of Company D for continuing to lead his company throughout the battle despite a wounded foot. Orderly Sergeant Adam Meyers was second in command behind Chaney and assisted the Lieutenant greatly. Wildes accused Captain Mathew Brown of Company F of cowardice. Nevertheless, Colonel Wildes acknowledged that Lieutenant Wilson Martin led Company F well during the fighting, and it behaved gallantly in spite of Brown's behavior.

Piedmont brought vindication to Milroy's Boys and revenge for New Market and Winchester. But the carnage in the shattered wood and bloody clover field had a sobering effect. The dead were gathered for burial, the wounded were collected, and the next morning the army moved on. During the following ten months the 116th would experience fighting at an unprecedented pace as the Federal Armies closed out the war. Piedmont was the gate of the road to victory.

"Black Dave's" Folly
10

"Black Dave" Hunter had just succeeded where every other Yankee general sent by President Lincoln had failed. He had thrashed a rebel army in the Shenandoah Valley so thoroughly that the Valley was open to Federal occupation for the first time in the war. President Lincoln was in Baltimore for the National Union (Republican) Convention, and news of Hunter's victory at Piedmont brought "rolls of applause and shouting" in celebration.1 Hunter's victory, coming at such a crucial time for the country, was cause for celebration in itself. But Piedmont was more significant than a success in a small battle. "The Valley was open. Lynchburg could be taken. The supplies to Richmond could be cut."2 In sum, because of Piedmont, the Federal Government had an opportunity to squeeze off supplies to Richmond and Lee's Army and cause their defeat in a matter of weeks.

General Grant had important plans for Hunter's Valley Campaign. On May 25, 1864, he had outlined his plans for Hunter in a message to Chief of Staff Halleck. Grant wrote:

> If Hunter can possibly get to Charlottesville and Lynchburg, he should do so, living on the country. The railroads and canal should be destroyed beyond possibility of repairs for weeks. Completing this, he could find his way back to his original base, or from about Gordonsville join this army.3

With the rebel army in retreat from Piedmont, Hunter could march his army to Charlottesville and initiate the destruction of the Virginia Central Railroad. If he encountered a superior force sent from Lee's Army, he could retreat back through the Valley and keep the Valley (a natural invasion route) covered from rebel intrusion.

General Hunter's first course of action was to march to nearby Staunton, Virginia. The 116th along with the rest of Sullivan's Infantry Division arrived at Staunton the day after the Battle of Piedmont. The Federal Government's tremendous opportunity to shorten the war immediately began to unravel. A series of inane and inapt decisions by Hunter eventually squandered his chance to cut off General Lee's supply line from Lynchburg.

Hunter delayed at Staunton to unleash "an orgy of destruction."4 A considerable amount of military property was destroyed, but soon looting broke out by "mixed mob of Federal soldiers, Negroes, mulatto women" and town "riffraff."5 The 116th apparently was not a participant in much of the destructive work in town, having been "sent out to tear up the railroad track west of Staunton."6

From Cold Harbor on June 6, 1864, the day Hunter arrived at Staunton, General Grant sent orders for Hunter:

> It would be of great value to us to get possession of Lynchburg for a single day...if this letter reaches you in the Valley between Staunton and Lynchburg, you immediately turn east by the most practicable road until you strike the Lynchburg branch of the Virginia Central road. From there move eastward along the line of the road, destroying it completely and thoroughly until you join General Sheridan.7

On June eighth General Crook's column arrived at Staunton to join forces with Hunter, increasing Hunter's strength to approximately 18,000 men. Colonel Moor and his 28th Ohio were due for muster out, having joined in the summer of 1861. The colonel and his men departed in charge of the train going north. The 34th Massachusetts replaced the 28th Ohio in the First Brigade, and Colonel Wells of the 34th replaced Colonel Moor as brigade commander. The 116th was thenceforth in brigade with the 18th Connecticut Infantry, 5th New York Heavy Artillery, 34th Massachusetts and 123rd Ohio Infantries.

By June tenth Hunter had made up his mind to move against Lynchburg via Lexington rather than following General Grant's orders to proceed immediately to the Central Virginia Railroad in the direction of Charlottesville. He detached a cavalry force to feint towards Waynesboro to confuse the enemy and mask his intention to move against Lynchburg. Hunter's entire army departed Staunton on the morning of the tenth, leaving about 300 wounded and sick men behind. Many of the men from the 116th who had been severely wounded at Piedmont eventually were captured and sent to rebel prisons because of Hunter's decision to ignore Grant's orders.

The 116th was the last regiment to depart Staunton. After marching about seven dusty miles behind Hunter's army, the 116th was ordered to countermarch and meet a huge supply train at Staunton. Upon meeting the train near Staunton, the train was found to have a supply of coffee and hardtack. At dark the men drew rations from the train and devoured their first full meal in a week. The train also carried mail, and after supper the men were given the mail intended for them. The mail was "as great a luxury as the supper we had just eaten," according to Colonel Wildes.8

A long and weary night march was required to catch the rest of the army. The 116th toiled on the road most of the night before meeting the army as it took to the road for the new day's march. Hunter sent permission for the 116th to rest until 10 a.m. After resting the 116th followed in the wake of the army. About noon the regiment encountered a group of women standing beside the road near a house. The women called out asking for the colors to be unfurled so that they could have one more look at the Stars and Stripes. The flags were unfurled and the soldiers gave three cheers for these loyal Virginia women. "As the men started up 'The Union Forever,' the women joined their voices with theirs, which was the first time for several months many of them had heard a woman's voice in the harmony of song."9

As the 116th reached Lexington on June 12, 1864, General Lee was launching a relief force to check Hunter. Lynchburg was extremely important to Lee's army, so he weakened his position at Petersburg to save it. General Breckinridge, who had been sent to join Lee with his force after the Battle of New Market, was ordered to return with his force to Waynesboro. Lee then ordered Lieutenant General Jubal A. Early to take his II Corps from the Army of Northern Virginia and go after Hunter. These two forces would cooperate to protect the railroad and Lynchburg. Time was running out for Hunter, and the advantage gained at Piedmont was now all but lost.

At Lexington "Black Dave" indulged his favorite preoccupation—the destruction of rebel property. Much of what Hunter ordered at Lexington was punitive vandalism. Hunter ordered the burning of the Virginia Military Institute, arguably as a reprisal as much as a military consideration. He gleefully watched the burning of the Institute and then ensured that former Virginia Governor Letcher's house was also incinerated.

Hunter also did little or nothing to restrain the sacking of Washington College in Lexington. The college had been endowed by President George Washington and was named in his honor. "The name and memory of its great founder should have saved it from the vandalism of Turks," wrote Wildes, "and what can be offered in palliation of the act when committed by American soldiers?"10

Colonel Wildes in his book did not mention the role of the 116th at Lexington. He neither admitted nor denied any participation by the regiment in the repugnant acts mentioned here. The acts of Hunter at Lexington were censured by many of the ranking officers at the time the destruction occurred, and in later years it was a reproach to the men who had served under Hunter. In Hunter's own view it was simply applied justice.

General Hunter dallied at Lexington to satiate himself for two precious days before moving on Lynchburg. During the stay at Lexington Hunter received several reports indicating that his situation had changed.

He learned that Sheridan had retreated and that rebel reinforcements were heading toward the Valley.11 This meant that Hunter could not fulfill General Grant's orders, and that he would have to hurry to capture Lynchburg before approaching rebel forces could unite there. Under these circumstances Hunter might have been better advised to return to Staunton and await another opportunity to strike Lee's supply line.

Once again the 116th was in the rear guard when Hunter's army departed Lexington on the fourteenth. By late afternoon the army had reached Buchanan. Rebel General McCausland's cavalry had burned the long bridge across the James River at Buchanan over the protest of the citizens. The conflagration had spread to the town, and several buildings were destroyed as a result of McCausland's pyromaniacal proclivities. The army was able to ford the river anyway and was across by midnight. The 116th did not reach Buchanan until 3 A. M. and had to do without anything to eat, because the regiment's cooking utensils were in the train across the river.

On June fifteenth the 116th forded the river and started for Liberty. The road was blocked in areas by felled trees, rock piles and even diverted streams intended to delay Hunter. A dead man was seen lying beside the road along the way. The men had become hardened to such sights; Colonel Wildes wrote, "It would shock anyone to repeat the trifling remarks made by the men as they passed him."12 By evening the 116th had marched past the famous Natural Bridge (one of President Jefferson's favorite sites) and went into camp just beyond the Peaks of Otter.

General Lee's Army had suffered heavy casualties during Grant's Overland Campaign in May and June. The rebel wounded had been sent to the Lynchburg area, and Wildes noted that the region was at that time one massive hospital. As the 116th passed through Liberty on June 16, 1864, the town was "almost nothing but a rebel hospital," and the homes and barns in the surrounding area for miles were "filled to repletion with wounded men."13 The 116th remained at Liberty until the seventeenth while the Virginia and Tennessee Railroad was destroyed there. For the past two days the 116th had been on half rations; and when the quartermaster informed the men that there would be no rations the next day, they told him that he would be the one suffering if he couldn't produce something to eat.

General Breckinridge had arrived in Lynchburg by a forced march from Rockfish Gap. With the assistance of General D. H. Hill, the rebels frantically worked to fortify the town. Nevertheless, Lynchburg was in no condition to withstand a determined assault on June sixteenth. General McCausland and his cavalry had done wonders in delaying the Federal advance, but Hunter could have pushed his force into Lynchburg by the sixteenth by "hard marching."14 Instead, Hunter wasted that day tearing up the railroad station at Liberty.

On June seventeenth, the 116th broke camp three miles south of Liberty and started for Lynchburg. By 10 A.M. rebel cavalry blocked the way. A skirmish line was sent forward, and the rebels fell back steadily. As the army approached a bridge, the rebels made a stand long enough to destroy the bridge before retreating. An engineer was ordered out to reconstruct the bridge; but the engineer proved so exacting and meticulous that he created a delay, trying everyone's patience. When the 116th arrived at the scene, Captain John F. Welch "prevailed on the engineer to let him try his way of building a bridge 'in a hurry,' and calling for a number of good choppers from the 116th, which it contained in abundance, as he knew, they went into a woods close by and began cutting timbers...and in less than an hour the artillery was crossing..."15

Heavy firing was heard in the direction of Lynchburg, and the 116th hurried to the scene of the fighting near an edifice known as Quaker Church, about five miles southwest of the city. Imboden's cavalry had thrown a defensive line across the road near the church, and Crook's Division was attempting to push through to Lynchburg. The 116th came up on Crook's left. Most of the fighting occurred on Crook's front, so the 116th did not participate in the main breakthrough on the rebel left. Imboden's troopers broke for the rear when Federal cavalry appeared on their flank, leaving an open path for the Yankees to enter Lynchburg. Towards evening the 116th pushed ahead to the outskirts of Lynchburg. Here the rebels had prepared breastworks and entrenchments to defend the city.

General Early had commandeered all available trains at Charlottesville to transport his army on the Central Railroad to Lynchburg without delay. Early rushed to Lynchburg with Ramseur's Division and one brigade from Gordon's Division. Arriving at Lynchburg at about 1 p.m., Early sent two brigades out on the Salem Road toward the sound of the fighting at the Quaker Church. The remainder of his Corps would arrive as trains became available.

When Jubal Early reached Lynchburg, Hunter became the hunted. Early was arguably one of the top four generals serving in the Rebel Army. Early's skill and ability on the offensive may have in fact ranked behind only Robert E. Lee and Thomas "Stonewall" Jackson. Certainly in June 1864 he was the best general available to Lee for an independent command. Most importantly, Early had the aggressive instinct and nerve that both Hunter and Crook lacked to succeed in an independent command.

Jubal Early was a highly experienced and talented commander. He was a graduate of the Class of 1837 at West Point and was a veteran of the Seminole and Mexican Wars. At West Point Early was bright enough to attain high academic standing without exerting himself. As a soldier at the Point, Early admitted that he was far from exemplary. He explained, "I had very little taste for scrubbing brass, and cared very little for the advancement to be obtained by the exercise of that most useful art."16

Twice Early had resigned from the army and returned to his native Southwest Virginia where he was a capable and successful attorney. Possessed of a keen wit and biting sarcasm, Early was "a bundle of inconsistencies and contradictions."17 "Arbitrary, cynical, with strong prejudices, he was personally disagreeable," and as a consequence of his personality he made few friends.18 Nevertheless, Early was liked and respected by the soldiers who served under his command. Having experience serving under Robert E. Lee as a brigade and then division commander in nearly all of the major battles of the Eastern Theater, Early easily overmatched Hunter *and* Crook at Lynchburg.

The troops sent forward by Early from Ramseur's Division made contact with Federal troops as Imboden's troopers fell back from the Quaker Church. General Early led Ramseur's skirmishers forward, shouting at the Federals, "No buttermilk rangers after you now, you ---- Blue—Butts!"19 When General Hunter arrived to assess the situation it was nearly dark, and he decided to renew the attack in the morning. Crook's soldiers understood that the delay would only give pause to enable the rebels to strengthen their defenses. A private in the 91st Ohio noted that the officers and men were angered by Hunter's decision: "The curses that greeted this order were long and deep and loud."20 This final delay by Hunter erased all possibility of victory for the Federals at Lynchburg.

Crook's division went into camp after dark, having been relieved by troops including the 116th. All through the night the 116th lay on the picket line very close to the rebel trenches. At about 10 p.m. the sounds of a locomotive chugging and whistling emanated from Lynchburg. Colonel Wildes explained, "we could hear trains arriving, and after daylight could see large bodies of troops moving out of the city towards our position, and hear bands playing..."21 This was all part of a ruse employed by General Early to convince the Yankees that he was receiving reinforcements. In fact, Early was still outnumbered because the rest of his Corps "did not get into Lynchburg until late in the afternoon" of the eighteenth.22 Colonel Wildes was apparently hoodwinked, because he described Early's nighttime "reinforcement" in his book nearly twenty years after the battle. Hunter also mentioned Early's train ruse in his official report and indicated that he was unsure of the number of rebels defending Lynchburg.

On the following day the 116th participated in the most significant fighting of the Battle of Lynchburg. Crook had taken part of his division to reconnoiter on the Federal right. During the morning the rebel artillery pounded the Federal positions with accuracy superior to anything the 116th had yet seen. Rebel sharpshooters also raked the Federal lines with accurate fire. During the morning hours the 116th supported a battery on the Federal left and hunkered down to wait for developments.

While Crook was seeking a weakness unsuccessfully on the rebel left, Early skillfully massed his infantry behind their entrenchments for an attack. At approximately 2 p.m. Early launched a ferocious attack on Hunter's center and left. The rebel yell was heard amid a storm of musketry all along the line. The 116th and the battery it was supporting were pulled from the left and sent to support the line at the point of the rebel attack.

As the 116th was re-deploying, the rebels approached through a wood on its flank. Two Federal regiments went forward to meet the advancing rebels and were driven back through the ranks of the 116th. As the 116th prepared to face the onslaught, ranks were opened to allow the disorganized and retreating regiments to pass through. General Sullivan rode up and ordered Colonel Washburn to charge the attacking rebels. The 116th "immediately formed for the charge," and struck the rebels " just as they were ascending a hill."23 The commander of the nearby 5th West Virginia Infantry was ordered to charge if the rebels gave way. With the advantage of charging down slope, the 116th quickly routed the rebels, who "broke in wild confusion to their breastworks."24

Seeing the rebels recoiling before the 116th, the 5th West Virginia joined in the chase across open ground beyond the woods. Both regiments were on the heels of the startled rebels as they reached the rebel rifle pits. These were veteran rebel troops, fresh from the killing fields of the Wilderness, Spotsylvania and Cold Harbor. But they could not resist the determined Buckeyes and fled into a second line of works. (This work was called Fort Early, and it still stands in Lynchburg.)

Color Sergeant Fred Humphrey waved the colors for the rest of Hunter's army to see as he led the regiment over the earthen wall of Fort Early. The rebels unleashed a barrage of canister from a battery placed less than 100 feet away in the nearby works. Sergeant Humphrey was struck in the neck and shoulder and fell "terribly wounded."25 Another member of the color guard took up the flag and the 116th swarmed over the rebel works.

As the 5th West Virginia approached the works they too were hit by a storm of rebel fire and recoiled before reaching the works. According to the regiment's official report, the 5th West Virginia got within "a few yards of a strong fortification, from which the enemy opened a very severe fire," and then the Mountaineers were "compelled to retire."26

All along the rebel line artillery roared into action and hammered the Federal positions across the open space between the lines. The 116th was isolated within the rebel works, and soon Early sent two regiments after the Buckeyes. A New York officer watching from Hunter's lines noted that he saw the 116th scrambling into the rebel fort and thought the Buckeyes held on from pride in their achievement.27 Colonel Wildes and his men sensed they had achieved something grand and clung to the dirt walls while the canister balls and bullets pelted them incessantly. They "fought hard against desperate odds," wrote Wildes, "waiting for help, which we felt would surely come, until we were assaulted on both flanks by infantry, and by grape and cannister from a battery, planted not five rods in our front."28

The 12th and 23rd North Carolina Infantry charged the 116th on each flank within the works, as mentioned by Wildes.29 Captain Edwin Keyes was holding his Company B against the rebel attack on the left when his left knee was hit and shattered. In danger of being overrun, the 116th began an orderly withdrawal from the rebel works under a terrible shower of lead and iron. The already severely wounded Captain Keyes was hit again, this time shattering his left elbow, as his men began to fall back. Keyes was carried along by some of his men as they fell back with the rest of the regiment. Somehow the 116th held together under the deadly rebel fire long enough to reach the first line of rebel rifle pits and took cover.

The 116th was stranded in a no man's land, with a large open space swept by rebel artillery and rifle fire to cross before reaching friendly lines. No support was forthcoming, so the 116th lay in the rebel rifle pits and fired back at the Tar Heels. A large rebel force worked its way under the cover some timber on the left flank of the 116th until it was in position to outflank the Buckeyes. So far the 116th had held together under the intense rebel fire without breaking, bring most of their wounded along. When the rebels emerged from the woods and hit the left flank, the 116th pulled back across the open space to the cover of the same woods where they had chased the rebels earlier. Once into the woods, the 116th formed lines facing the rebels, ready to repel an attack.

After waiting in the trees for what seemed a long time, with no sign of the rest of Hunter's army, and no orders, the 116th pulled back to where the Federal lines had been. By 5 p.m. Hunter had called for a retreat, and his infantry had begun to retrace their steps down the Salem Pike under the cover of cavalry skirmishing. Colonel Wildes simply noted that the 116th cleared the woods at the crest of the ridge "only to find that the retreat had commenced."30 At about 7 p.m. the 116th moved out and followed the retreating army. The Lynchburg Campaign had ended in failure.

No other regiment on either side fought better at Lynchburg than the 116th Ohio. The men deserved better results. Other regiments during the Civil War earned eternal fame for deeds no braver than those of the 116th that day. The 116th had sent a message to Jubal Early: *these* Yankees can fight. Early "knew that he was lucky," had the rest of Hunter's troops fought as well as the 116th, the rebels might have been driven into Lynchburg.31

Hunter had little to boast of in his official report for the battle. However, he did mention the 116th: "In the eagerness of pursuit, one regiment (One Hundred Sixteenth Ohio) entered the works on the heels of the flying enemy, but being unsupported, fell back with trifling loss."32 He failed to mention why he did not send support for the 116th to exploit the breach in the rebel line. Instead he explained his hypothesis that Early outnumbered him.

But the losses for the 116th were not really trifling. Captain Keyes and the other severely wounded men could not be moved, and so they were left to the rebel's care. Upon learning of the Captain's serious wounds, "the officers and his men gathered about him to bid him farewell, for it was evident he could not be moved far."33 Captain Keyes died in Lynchburg the next day from the effects of his wounds, and his remains were interred at the Lynchburg National Cemetery after the war. The official tally of casualties for the 116th at Lynchburg was five killed and thirty wounded.34 Colonel Wildes wrote that the losses of the 116th during the charge were twelve killed, twenty-two wounded, and ten prisoners.35 His totals contained a few errors. The following is from Wildes' casualty list for Lynchburg, with corrections for those listed as killed:

KILLED

Privates James A. Boyd and Jefferson Gatten, Co. A; Charles C. Davis, Co. B; Geo. B. Blair and Geo. M. Coulter, Co. E; William Fisher, Co. F; Gilbert Van Horn, Co. I; and Evander B. Hamilton, (actually mortally wounded) Co. D.

WOUNDED

COMPANY A—Corporal John W. Devore, foot; Henry Harmon, thigh; Daniel P. Hubbard, bowels.

COMPANY B—Captain Edwin Keyes, knee and elbow, (died 7-19-64); Color Sergeant Fred E. Humphrey, shoulder and neck; Royal Daines, side, (captured); Phillip Feiger; William E. Lafaver.

COMPANY C—Corporal Walter Tacker, leg, (captured); John Egger, leg.

COMPANY D—Corporal Alexander Straight, arm; James G. Dally, leg; Isaiah Mozena.

COMPANY E—Sergeant John G. Reithmeller, side; Joseph Connor, hip.

COMPANY F—William Allen, right arm amputated; Jacob Martin, head.

COMPANY G—Corporal James B. Miller, ankle; David A. Moore, (died at Andersonville, 8-14-64).

COMPANY H—Isaac Russell, side;

COMPANY I—Corporal William Scott, head.

COMPANY K—Corporal Carmi Allison, lungs; Corporal John Young, foot; Corporal Perry Gardiner, neck; William Hunter, finger.

MISSING IN ACTION PRESUMED KILLED

Micajah Gowdy and Moses F. Starr, Co. D.

CAPTURED

Captain Edwin Keyes, Sergeant Fred E. Humphrey, Horace McNeal, Wells Grubb, William Lefever, Nelson Watson, Royal Hoyt, (died at Andersonville), Alex (Haddock) Warren, all of Co. B; Albin Vickers, Co. C, and John Vickers, Co. D.

Total: Eight Killed, two mortally wounded, two MIA, twenty-four wounded, and thirteen captured.

(The Colonel's list may contain some inaccuracies regarding the wounded, as the Roster did not show some of the men on his list as being wounded at Lynchburg. However, the Roster sometimes contained omissions. Some of the men who were listed on reports as wounded were not so listed in the Roster.)

Colonel Wildes described the scene in the woods as the 116th prepared to leave the field: "The rebels were now shelling the woods with great fury, and being still within range of their grape and cannister, also the rattle of small arms, the hurling and crashing of flying missles, the explosion of shells, and the yells of the victorious enemy, combined to make one of the wildest battle scenes we ever witnessed."36 Quartermaster Sergeant Walker wrote an account of what he witnessed on the eighteenth in a letter written on July 1, 1864:

…Captain Keyes, of company B, was wounded in the left knee and left elbow, and, it is feared, it will be necessary to amputate both the arm and leg; if so, he cannot possibly live. I could not keep from shedding tears when I saw him the first time, and yet he would, while lying there on his back, sing in a cheerful tone, 'Rally Round the Flag,' and talk to others to cheer them up…We also had another 'color bearer' wounded, making in all three that have been wounded during this raid. Our flags, too, are beginning to look the worse for wear…I saw no less than a dozen amputations performed, and there are others that would have to be performed the next day…I do hope and pray I may never be called upon to witness the horrors of another battle field…Lee and I busied ourselves, trying to make the men of our regiment as comfortable as possible. We carried them into a large barn that had been prepared for a hospital, where we made beds of new mown hay. Every man we moved was covered with blood, and by the time we were through we were about as bloody as the wounded men. 37

Hunter had become convinced that Early outnumbered him and decided to retreat. Obviously, Hunter had taken into account that a retreat from Lynchburg was a possible scenario; and that should he retreat, he would be forced to march through the mountains of West Virginia to Charleston rather than down the Shenandoah Valley. He knew when he failed to destroy the railroad from Charlottesville, as ordered by General Grant, that the rebels would be able to use the railroad to trap his army if he attempted to march down the valley in retreat. He apparently turned to General Crook for advice as to the retreat route to be used. Crook had retreated over approximately the same route following his victory at the Battle of Cloyd's Mountain the previous month. Crook had shown even

Illustration of the regimental flag carried by the 116th Ohio Infantry, one of several variations used by Federal infantry regiments during the Civil War. (Courtesy of the Ohio Historical Society)

Captain Edwin Keyes, Company B. Captain Keyes was mortally wounded at the Battle of Lynchburg. He died of his wounds the following day, June 19, 1864. (Courtesy of Mark D. Okey)

less fortitude than Hunter had, so it should be no surprise that he would recommend the safest route.

As Hunter arranged for his retreat, General Early was pondering when to attack. The remainder of his Corps had arrived by rail, and he intended to take the offensive. "His combat instinct told him...to assail the enemy at once," and the people of Lynchburg expected him to punish the "Vandal" Hunter.38 Fortunately for the 116th, which had been left out on the firing line without knowledge of Hunter's intention to retreat, Jubal Early decided to yield on the side of caution. Part of Lynchburg was undefended, so Early wanted to be certain of Hunter's intentions. Early wrote, "Pursuit could not, therefore, be made at once, as a mistake...would have been fatal."39

The 116th followed Hunter's retreating army all through the night of June eighteenth. All of their sweating, marching, fighting, bleeding, fear and exaltation during the campaign had been for naught, and that night they were ravenous. The men had "had but one cracker apiece in two days, had marched all one of these, fought all the other, and stood picket during the intervening night."40 Still they managed to march all night and overtake the train before daylight. At about 6 a.m. they stopped to make coffee at their previous campsite near Liberty and found that the local blacks were flocking to the army, many of them heavily loaded with provisions. Some of the blacks willing shared their provender, and others led a foraging expedition to where bacon, flour, meal and other food supplies were concealed. With the help of the local blacks, the 116th was able to get a meal and save a few provisions for later.

Early's troops intruded on the interlude at Liberty, so the 116th was forced to make yet another all night march. Fatigue had long since set in on the men, many were so weary that they slept while walking in the ranks, "only awakened by making a wrong step, or something of that sort."41 The retreat continued through Salem by the twenty-first. On the night of the twenty-second, Companies A and B were left on picket atop Pott's Mountain. The two companies were inadvertently left behind and were attacked by a much larger rebel force. Only a determined stand saved the two companies from capture. Gilbert G. Webster, of Company B, was wounded in the arm during the fighting. On the afternoon of the twenty-third, Companies A and B rejoined the rest of the 116th, thoroughly exhausted.

The retreat from Lynchburg was a dreary, privative ordeal. The route took the 116th through White Sulphur Springs and on into the West Virginia Mountains. On Thursday June 23, 1864, Jubal Early decided to lay aside retribution and obey his commander's orders, as Hunter should have done. Early and his army turned back toward the unguarded Shenandoah Valley and commenced the most daring major raid of the

Civil War. Hunter and the 116th struggled on through the "dry, inhospitable West Virginia Mountains to Charleston."42

By June twenty-seventh the men of the 116th had been without bread for four days, living on fresh beef and coffee. Day after day they climbed through the steep mountains. Hundreds of mules and horses gave out under the strain. At least fifty wagons were burned for this reason, and 300 draft animals were shot because they couldn't keep up and would have been taken by the enemy. Nevertheless, the men worked to save the animals by unhitching them, grazing them, and then loading them with guns and packs, which enabled some of the animals to keep up. On the twenty-seventh, having passed Meadow Bluff, the 116th went into camp. A supply train rumbled into camp, and the men, those who were still able, rejoiced as never before, grateful for their deliverance from privation.

Two days later the 116th passed the famous "Lover's Leap," and the magnificent "Hawk's Nest." The view from "Hawk's Nest" is truly inspiring, overlooking the rapids of the New River in a gorge between two mountains. The unique vista was perhaps the only pleasant moment the men experienced on the dreadful retreat. Two more days on the tortuous road brought the 116th into Gauley Bridge, where supplies were plentiful. A more dirty and ragged set of men could not have been found anywhere, but the worst was finally over.

The problem of unequal rations, the result of unauthorized foraging as mentioned previously, was probably most noticeable during this campaign. Soldiers like Private Dalzell who had special connections managed to get their share of food when others did without. Colonel Wildes made a subtle mention of this in his chapter about the Lynchburg Campaign. Speaking of rations he wrote, "Some had none, others a little, and a few lucky fellows who always had enough, no matter what happened, had an abundance."43

For two days the 116th enjoyed an essential respite at Gauley Bridge. Provisions were abundant for the first time in weeks. Quartermaster Sergeant Ezra Walker noted in his diary, "rations here are very plenty, we have drawn again today. I am sure I do not know what they will do with so much, poor fellows! I wish they could have had some of this nice pork and Hard bread a week ago while we were out among the mountains of Virginia."44

On July 2, 1864, the 116th left Gauley Bridge for Camp Piatt where steamboats waited to transport the regiment to Parkersburg. The 116th camped that night about five miles above Piatt after marching sixteen miles that day. Sergeant Walker wrote, "Many of the men fell out sick. The Doctor says from eating too much—they have not got used to it since getting back from the raid."45

At Camp Piatt the 116th embarked on steamships for the trip to Parkersburg. Conditions were dry, and the river was low. Several times the men were required to march around shoals because the boats could not pass through. Quartermaster Walker took the trains overland to Parkersburg while Colonel Wildes took charge of two companies of the 5th New York Heavy Artillery aboard a steamboat. Colonel Wildes described the appearance of the regiment as it debarked at Parkersburg:

> As rough and uncouth as was our appearance when we first entered Parkersburg, in September 1862, it was far worse now. The clothing of the officers and men was in tatters and dirty, half were barefooted, and all worn down by the hardships of the expedition. To add to their misfortunes, the camp diarrhoea had set in before we left Gauley Bridge, and had prostrated a great many men. We were truly 'forlorn and shipwrecked brothers.'"46

Being so near home, a great many of the men were met by family and friends at Parkersburg. Many of the men from Companies B, G and I were given permission to make a quick detour to their homes in Meigs and Athens Counties, Ohio, on the Fourth of July. Also while at Parkersburg, Colonel Charles Halpine, Hunter's adjutant general, held a dinner for the officers of the 116th Ohio and the 5th West Virginia to honor their splendid charge at Lynchburg.

Thomas Wildes in his book about the 116th made a lengthy digression to defend General Hunter and put the Lynchburg Raid in its best possible light. He had made a similar presentation in defense of General Milroy's defeat at Winchester. Again, Hunter was a partisan Republican with connections to General Grant and President Lincoln. Wildes, as a participant in the Lynchburg Raid and as an "ardent Republican," had every motive defend both Hunter and the raid. Wildes made perhaps his most valid supportive point when he wrote, "An expedition attended with such important results cannot, in truth, be called a failure."47 Nevertheless, with all respect to Wildes, his explanations for Hunter's decisions and delays during the Lynchburg Campaign amounted to little more than flimsy diversions from fact. The fact that Hunter mishandled the Campaign.

"Black Dave" Hunter in the Valley was like a fool in his folly. There is much evidence to indicate that Hunter put his passion for revenge before his devotion to duty. There can be absolutely no doubt that Hunter understood what General Grant wanted before the campaign commenced. In a message to the U. S. Army Adjutant-General on May 21, 1864, Hunter wrote, "I have directed Generals Crook and Averell to move immediately on Staunton. I hope to meet them there and then move directly east, via Charlottesville and Gordonsville."48 Yet, as we have seen, Hunter chose to move on Lynchburg via the Valley. By this route he could burn and pillage at will, all the while ignoring the fact that his army could be sealed out of the Valley by a strong rebel force.

Hunter's arduous retreat to Parkersburg took his army out of the Valley and out of the war for nearly a month. Meanwhile, General Early took his army into Maryland and whipped a hastily gathered force under General Lew Wallace at the Monocacy River on July 9, 1864. Early then moved against Washington, forcing General Grant to rush the XI Corps from Petersburg and the XIX Corps from New Orleans to protect the Capitol. Even so, Early put a severe scare into Washington. And because Hunter's Army was not in position to protect the Valley, Grant was forced to pull a large portion of his available force out of the Petersburg Campaign.

General Grant was reserved in his appraisal of Hunter. Long after the war Grant wrote the following comment in his memoir:

Had General Hunter moved by way of Charlottesville, instead of Lexington, as his instructions contemplated, he would have been in a position to have covered the Shenandoah Valley against the enemy, should the force he met have seemed to endanger it. If it did not, he would have been within easy distance of the James River Canal, on the main line of communication between Lynchburg and the force sent for its defence.49

Grant had explained that Hunter was forced to retreat from Lynchburg for want of ammunition. General Early, in his memoir, offered a different appraisal of Hunter's performance:

Had Hunter moved on Lynchburg with energy, that place would have fallen before it was possible for me to get there. But he tarried on the way, and when he reached there, there was discovered "a want of ammunition to give battle."50

There can be no doubt that "Black Dave's" folly in the Shenandoah Valley was costly. Costly to Hunter's reputation, costly by prolonging the war, costly by allowing Early to advance on Washington, and costly to the image of American soldiery. The 116th had done everything possible to make the campaign a success and was deserving of a better fate. But the long parade of Federal "political generals" commanding in the Shenandoah Valley rendered defeats there an immutable fact.

Somebody Else's War
11

While General Early and his army were thrashing General Wallace's hastily assembled Federal force along the Monocacy River south of Frederick, Maryland, on July 9, 1864, the 116th was filing into railroad cars for the last leg of their route back to the Shenandoah Valley. Leaving Parkersburg by rail, the 116th reached Cherry Run on the tenth. The tracks east of Cherry Run had been torn up, so the men detrained and marched on to Martinsburg, West Virginia, about fifteen miles. Martinsburg was a most welcome home away from home for the 116th. The citizens there seemed to favor the 116th over the rest of the Yankees. In fact, according to Colonel Wildes the citizens had shown many favors, including hiding the regiment's convalescents from raiding rebels and gifting the men with food and clothes. But with Early at the gates of Washington, the 116th was allowed to camp at Martinsburg for only a single day, the twelfth, before moving again.

There was good reason for the 116th to be on the move. Jubal Early was putting quite a scare into the Administration on July twelfth. That day his troops probed the defenses of the Capitol, and only the last minute arrival of the Federal VI Corps from Petersburg kept his army out of the city. Upon discovering that the entire VI Corps was manning the Washington defenses, the rebels had no choice but to fall back into the Valley. The logical task for Hunter's Army and the 116th was to cut off Early's retreat route. Accordingly, on the thirteenth the 116th took up the march for Harper's Ferry. By the fourteenth the 116th had passed by Harper's Ferry and camped at Sandy Hook. As previously mentioned, the 116th at this point had been almost constantly in motion since the last of May. Their uniforms were in tatters, and most of the men were either bare-foot or nearly so. The next day the 116th was ordered to proceed to Hillsboro, Virginia. Some of the men remained in camp, because their shoeless feet were too battered to allow them to continue.

The expedition to crush Early's retreating army was complicated and fraught with dangers. The Federals had more than sufficient forces in place, but these forces had to be coordinated and carefully positioned to ensure success. A skillful and aggressive commander familiar with the area of operations and forces at his disposal was essential for success. Obviously, the first priority was to get Early's Army out of the Washington vicinity without suffering any kind of setback; and lacking an aggressive commander on the scene, this priority monopolized the Government's attention.

On the fourteenth General Halleck sent the following message to General Hunter: "Major-General Wright (VI Corps Commander) has been placed by the President in supreme command of the forces operating on this expedition, and the Secretary of War directs that all your available forces, as soon as the junction can be affected, be placed under his direction."[1] That night General Wright informed General Hunter that he had arrived at Poolesville, Maryland, with troops from the VI and XIX Corps and directed Hunter to proceed to Leesburg, Virginia, across the Potomac from Poolesville. The 116th reached Hillsboro on the fifteenth and went into camp for the night. Meanwhile, Early's army was slipping away from Wright, passing through Leesburg and into Purcellville, just a few miles from the 116th and Sullivan's Division at Hillsboro.

For some reason, Wright and Hunter did not coordinate their efforts, and Wright remained in Poolesville until the sixteenth. Consequently, the 116th was "obliged to halt and allow the rebel army to pass across our front almost unmolested, for Wright did not proceed to Leesburg at all..." until Early had escaped.[2] The opportunity to cut off the retreating rebel army was lost because of a lack of communication between the two Federal forces. Hunter's troops, including the 116th, could not block Early's retreat without support, and Wright did not act with alacrity to cooperate with Hunter's forces. The 116th remained at Hillsboro until the afternoon of the sixteenth while Early's Army hurried towards the Shenandoah Valley.

General George Crook arrived at Hillsboro on the afternoon of the sixteenth to replace General Sullivan. Special Orders from General Hunter directed Crook to assume command of "all the forces proceeding from this department to form a junction with Maj. Gen. H. G. Wright..."[3] Crook immediately turned the army onto Early's trail, but the prey had already escaped. The 116th was sent after a rebel train at Waterford, east of Hillsboro, but upon arriving there found that the rebels were gone. Fortunately for the 116th the people of Waterford were loyal, as noted by Colonel Wildes:

> It was very hot, and our men called for water as they marched rapidly through the place. Very soon many women and children came along the marching column with buckets and pitchers of water, which they dipped out to the men. Flags were also thickly displayed.[4]

Meanwhile, Hunter was chaffing under the orders placing the junior General Wright in command of his army. Crook's appointment to command of Sullivan's troops effectively placed him in charge of the bulk of Hunter's troops. Hunter felt that he was being made the scapegoat for Early's mischief and asked to be relieved immediately; he reasoned that the command changes undermined his authority and credibility with his army. Hunter wrote to the President asking to be relieved and received the following reply:

> It seemed to be General Grant's wish that the forces under General Wright and those under you should join and drive at the enemy, under General Wright. Wright had the larger part of the force, but you had the rank. It was thought that you would prefer Crook's commanding your part to your serving in person under Wright. That is all of it. General Grant wishes you to remain in command of the department, and I do not wish to order otherwise.5
>
> A. Lincoln

Hunter would continue in command of the department but merely as a figurehead. His decision-making role diminished steadily until his position was practically meaningless.

Crook's infantry including 116th followed after Early's train to Purcelville. Federal cavalry under General Duffie struck the rebel trains there and captured eighty-two wagons, 117 draft animals and about sixty prisoners just before the infantry arrived. The 116th then went into camp for the night at Purcelville. Crook and Wright's columns converged at Purcelville that night, "just in time to let Early, with all his plunder, slip through between them."6 Colonel Mulligan, now commanding an infantry brigade, went forward with Duffie and found Snicker's Gap in possession of the rebels.

Once Early's Army reached Snicker's Gap, its escape was a certainty. Early now had a myriad of options and opportunities to create mischief. The first priority of Wright's expedition was to chase Early away from Washington. General Grant then intended for Wright's troops, including the XIX Corps, to return to Petersburg. Hunter's Army, now commanded by Crook, was to follow Early down the Shenandoah Valley and, if possible, move against Gordonsville, as Grant had originally intended. Halleck relayed these instructions to Hunter on July seventeenth, and quoted Grant's instructions for the Federal Army to "eat out Virginia clear and clean as far as they go, so that crows flying over it for the balance of the season will have to carry their own provender with them."7

The 116th remained at Purcelville until the morning of the eighteenth when it advanced to Snicker's Gap. As the men passed over the summit at the gap, a beautiful view of the Shenandoah Valley unfolded before them. The flat multi-colored floor of the valley contrasted to the resplendent blue of the distant mountains. Beneath the gap flowed the shimmering Shenandoah River, or "Shinning Door" as the men called it, snaking its way down the valley toward its confluence with the Potomac. Weary men trudged down the mountainside beyond the gap, appearing like a huge blue caterpillar against the dark green mountainside.

When the 116th reached the foot of the mountain at Snicker's Ferry, the Federal generals were still looking to strike a blow against Early's retreating army. General Crook, "believing that only the enemy's cavalry were holding Snicker's Ford," ordered Colonel Thoburn to move about two miles down the river to cross at Island Ford.[8] Crook expected his infantry to easily flank the rebel cavalry and clear the crossing for the rest of his army. The 116th was among the first troops to cross with Thoburn's Division, "under a severe fire from some rebel skirmishers, who were under cover of bushes skirting the west bank of the river."[9] After crossing the "Shinning Door," Companies B, C, D and K of the 116th, commanded by Lieutenant Colonel Wildes, were thrown out as skirmishers to locate the enemy.

A rebel captain and fifteen men were captured at the crossing. These prisoners admitted that General Early and most of his army were within a mile of the crossing, and it wasn't long before Colonel Wildes encountered advancing rebels. Colonel Thoburn sent this information to General Crook who ordered him to find a strong position, hunker down, and wait for the reinforcements he was expecting from the VI Corps. Colonel Thoburn posted his infantry in two lines, the first behind a bluff about seventy-five yards in advance of the second line, which he posted in an old roadbed behind a stone wall along the riverbank. Colonel Wells commanded the First Brigade, including the 116th, on the left. Colonel Thoburn held the right with the Second Brigade, and the Third Brigade held the center.

About an hour after Colonel Thoburn had established his position, the rebels sent a strong skirmish line to probe the Federal left and center. Simultaneously, a strong flanking force consisting of two lines of battle struck Thoburn hard. Thoburn's front line on the right fell back to the extreme right, which was held by about 1,000 dismounted cavalrymen. When the front line, punished by an enfilading fire, fell back, the cavalrymen panicked and stampeded across the river, taking part of Thoburn's infantry with them. Almost the entire front line crumbled, and Colonel Thoburn knew he was in trouble. Realizing that he needed dependable troops to steady his right, Thoburn sent for the 116th. He ordered Colonel Washburn to rush the 116th from the left to bolster his threatened position on the Federal right.

Snicker's Ferry Battlefield. View of the field from the rebel line facing the Shenandoah River.

Colonel James Washburn. The "old colonel" was shot in the left eye, the ball passing out behind the right ear, at the Battle of Snicker's Ferry. (Courtesy USAMHI)

Colonel Washburn hurried his men to Thoburn's relief, forming them next to the 4th West Virginia Infantry as it fought to hold its position "against desperate odds."10 Colonel Washburn was at the head of the regiment leading it into the fight when a rebel minie ball fired at close range smashed into his face. The ball entered the colonel's left eye, coursed downward through the colonel's head and exited behind his right ear. When the colonel fell Lieutenant Colonel Wildes hurried to the front to steady the men. He quickly sent two companies under Captain Mallory beyond the wall on the riverbank to counter the rebels who were punishing the 4th West Virginia. The captain led a charge that drove the rebels back. Then his men frantically threw together a log and stone breastwork for cover and opened such an effective fire on the rebels on that flank that they withdrew. The rest of the 116th took cover behind the stone wall along the riverbank and furiously opened fire at the rebels on their front.

Another stone wall ran out at a right angle to the wall along the riverbank. The rebels were using the wall for cover to fire into the flank of the 116th. Sergeant Silas King, of Company F, was sent with ten men to silence this enfilading fire. King and his men emerged from the riverbank on the opposite side of the wall from the rebels, at point blank range, and opened fire on them. These rebels were from Rhodes Division, probably veterans of the brutal fight in the breastworks of the "Bloody Angle" at Spotsylvania. But King and his squad prevailed after a bitter fight, killing and wounding the rebels "almost within the length of their guns."11 The sergeant was cited for his coolness, determination and bravery for this action that secured the flank of the regiment.

Colonel Thoburn in his report mentioned that when the 116th appeared, "the panic was over. The attack was bravely met and the enemy driven back."12 But the rebels weren't through. General Rhodes made another attack against the wall. The Federals fought back desperately, knowing that with the river at their back a retreat would set them up for slaughter. There was no option except to drive the rebels back. Colonel Thoburn moved along the wall encouraging the men and urging them to hold fast. "He was the coolest man on the field."13

With the 116th fighting for its life behind the stone wall, Sergeant Edgar Humphrey, of Company I, fought for his manhood. Some of the boys had called him a coward. So in the thick of the fight the sergeant would stand "in plain view of rebel line, load and fire as deliberately and coolly, as if engaged in target practice."14 Colonel Wildes noticed Humphrey's rash behavior and was going to Humphrey to order him to take cover when the sergeant was hit and fell. Kneeling beside the fallen sergeant, Wildes heard him say faintly, "Colonel, I guess they won't call me a coward again, will they?"15 The sergeant survived, but he had nearly thrown away his life because of a careless spiteful remark.

Some of Mallory's men returned to the firing line along the wall to help repulse the rebel attack. The rebels were at a disadvantage as they were attacking across cleared fields before the wall. Unable to reach the stone wall through the intense Federal fire, the rebel column fell back a third time, this time for good, leaving Thoburn's men in possession of the field. A cheer went up from the 116th as they saw the rebels disappear behind a hill in retreat, their fallen comrades dotting the open field.

As the field quieted with the lull, the roar of artillery fire sounded from across the river. The rebels were trying to plant their guns into position to shell Thoburn's line along the stone wall. Federal artillery posted on higher ground commanded the rebel guns and soon forced the rebel artillery to withdraw. The Federal gunners then shifted their aim to the rebel infantry, not far advanced from the stone wall. According to Colonel Wildes, "The lines were so close to each other that some damage was done to our men by shells from our batteries."16 But the artillery fire was effective enough to keep the rebels under cover, and they did not attempt another attack.

General Crook had requested help from the VI Corps, and the men from the 116th could see across the river the "long lines of the Sixth Corps drawn up on the mountain's side and in the fields at its foot."17 Elisha Rhodes of the 2nd Rhode Island Infantry (part of the VI Corps) was with the column sent to Snicker's Ferry. He recorded the scene in his diary: "Hurrying down the slope we found that a part of General Hunter's Army had crossed the river and had been driven back, losing many men. A Rebel Battery discovered us and opened fire but fortunately did no injury to our Brigade, but several were killed and wounded in our 3rd Division."18

The men of the VI Corps remained on their side of the river and watched somebody else's war, hearing all the while the "booming of cannon and the sharp rattle of musketry."19 General Crook wrote in his report, "General Ricketts, commanding the corps, did not think it prudent under the circumstances to cross his men..."20 To the men of the 116th the battle must have seemed reminiscent of their charge at Lynchburg one month ago to the day. Again, as at Lynchburg, they found themselves in a tight spot facing the enemy, only to be left unsupported while available reinforcements stood by and watched. It no doubt seemed to like a developing pattern that nobody liked.

With no support forthcoming from the VI Corps, General Crook sent orders to Colonel Thoburn to withdraw his division back across the river. Colonel Wildes mentioned that the 116th did not attempt to cross the river until long after dark to conceal the movement from the rebels. All of the wounded men from the 116th were carried along during the crossing. Colonel Washburn, expected to die from his horrible wound, had been carried over the river during the battle. Thoburn mentioned that many of the wounded from other regiments were left to the enemy because a rebel battery was shelling the ford where those regiments crossed.

"I never read of a battle in which so many different regiments claimed to be the 'last to leave the field'," wrote Colonel Wildes.21 The regimental historian for the 18th Connecticut made the claim that the "cookie regiment" was on the right when flanked and was last to cross the river. Colonel Wildes, wanting to set the record straight, noted that the 18th Connecticut was not on the right, and the right was never flanked anyway—thanks to the 116th. However, Colonel Thoburn in his report mentioned that "detachments" from some other regiments including the 18th Connecticut helped hold the right along with the 116th, and together they "saved the command from a complete rout."22 Colonel Thoburn singled out the 116th Ohio and the 4th West Virginia with special praise for "firm and gallant conduct"; and he noted that when Colonel Washburn fell, "His place was promptly and worthily filled by Lieutenant Colonel Wildes..."23

Jubal Early barely mentioned the battle in his memoir, writing only a single paragraph about it, and he did not list his casualties. The official report of the Federal casualties was sixty-five killed, 301 wounded, and fifty-six missing, while the rebels, "at their own estimate," lost over 600 killed and wounded.24 The 116th lost four killed and ten wounded. The excellent cover provided by the stone wall undoubtedly kept the 116th from suffering much heavier casualties, as the fighting was very intense. According to Colonel Wildes the 4th West Virginia lost heavily before the 116th arrived to help. The following is the list of casualties for the 116th Ohio at the Battle of Snicker's Ferry or Cool Spring:

KILLED

Samuel L. Hayes, Company B; Joshua Farley, Company G; William Stoneman, Company I; George Lamp, Company H.

WOUNDED

Colonel James Washburn, severely in the head; Sergeant James Hunter, Company A, severely, head; Sergeant Edgar Humphrey, Company I, severely, neck; Privates James Saxton, Company G, severely, neck; Joel B. Cummins, Company G, severely, shoulder; Samuel Dobbins, Company C, severely, side; James McElroy, Company B, severely, thigh; E. S. Clithero, Company D, severely, leg; Leander Eddy, Company A, severely, leg; and Francis M. Byers, Company I, severely, leg.

Colonel Wildes wrote the following paragraph describing the men killed in the battle for his book:

> We again lost several good men killed and wounded. All the killed were choice men. Samuel L. Hayes was a beautiful young boy, only eighteen years of age, whom everybody loved. He was killed on the skirmish line and his body carried back by his comrades. George Lamp, of Company H, was another fine boy of the same age. William Stoneman was one of the very best men of Company I, only 21 years of age. Joshua Farley, of Company G, was but 24 years of age, an excellent soldier and a fine man. His captain, H. L. Karr, writes of him: 'Joshua Farley, of Silver Run, Meigs county, was as brave a soldier and as brave a patriot as ever shouldered a musket in defense of his country. His comrades carefully and tenderly laid him in a soldier's grave, a few feet from where he fell, and Company G, officers and men, never had heavier hearts, than when they marched from the grave of that brave soldier.'25

After the war the United States War Department arranged to have the battlefields gleaned for the bodies of Federal soldiers for reburial in National Cemeteries. Often the task of identifying the dead was difficult or impossible. Sometimes a board stuck into the ground at the gravesite provided identification. In other cases engraved objects like watches, identification tags, or diaries found with the bodies provided the names of a soldiers from battlefield graves. Soldiers on the battlefield were often hastily and only partially buried with no attempt to identify their bodies. The remains of Joshua Farley, William Stoneman, and George Lamp were recovered from their graves on the battlefield after the war and reburied at the Winchester National Cemetery. Their graves were identified, but a cursory study of the known burials in National Cemeteries indicated that probably over half of the men killed in action from the 116th were either not recovered from the battlefields or were buried under an "Unknown" marked headstone in a National Cemetery. This, of course, was customary, because the majority of the battlefield dead reburied in many National Cemeteries are unknown.

Six men were specially mentioned by Wildes for fighting with great bravery during the battle: Captain Mallory, of Company A; Lieutenant Moseley, of Company H; Lieutenant Bidenharn, of Company C; Lieutenant Martin, of Company F; Sergeant Silas King, of Company F; and Sergeant Edgar Humphrey, of Company I. Conversely, Captain Mathew Brown of Company F was censured by Wildes for behaving in

Grave of Joshua Farley, Company G, at Winchester National Cemetery. Joshua Farley was killed at the Battle of Snicker's Ferry on July 18, 1864.

Grave of Captain Wilson S. Martin, Company F, at Newport, Ohio. Wilson Martin was mentioned for gallantry at the Battle of Snicker's Ferry.

"a most cowardly manner in the battle of Snicker's Ferry."[26] Wildes already considered him a coward after the affair near Romney. He noted that the captain showed the "white feather" at Piedmont and behaved badly at Lynchburg. After the battle Wildes recommended that Brown be dismissed from the service for cowardice and forwarded the paperwork up the chain of command.

Amazingly, Colonel Washburn was still living when the men crossed the Shenandoah after the battle. In fact, the brave colonel was conscious and actually asked how the regiment had performed during the battle. Still not expecting to survive, Washburn gave his sword, belt, watch, pocket book, papers, etc. to Lieutenant Colonel Wildes, requesting that they be sent to his family. Washburn was well liked by the men. He had been a carpenter in Monroe County before the war, with a wife and four daughters. Many of the officers and men passed by to see him with tears in their eyes, and during the night several men maintained a vigil near his tent.

From all accounts, Colonel Washburn was an exceptional man who earned the affection and respect of his men. One story about the colonel told of his concern for his men. During the march to Lynchburg, the month before his grievous wound, Washburn was said to have allowed Private William Lafavor to ride his horse while he carried the private's musket and walked. Lafavor was having problems with a leg and was unable to walk.

By morning Washburn showed signs of a possible recovery. He was borne by a party of strong men to Harper's Ferry and ultimately fought off infection and survived his terrible wound. Within sixty days he reported for duty! He never recovered sufficiently to assume command of the regiment, having lost his left eye and suffering from partial paralysis to his face. But on October 26, 1864, the colonel visited the 116th at Cedar Creek and was given a wonderful reception. A dress parade was held in his honor after which the following address from Washburn was read to the regiment:

> The Colonel of the regiment embraces this opportunity of tendering his thanks to, and expressing his pride in, the brave officers and men of the 116th regiment. On account of a severe wound he received at Snicker's Ferry in July last, he has not been with you throughout the entire campaign, but he feels proud to say that he belongs to a regiment which has bravely withstood, in the memorable campaign just closed, all the hardships, privations and perils of the march, the bivouac and the battle field. While it was his honored privilege to lead you, he ever found you ready to obey orders; since he has been separated from you he has anxiously and proudly watched your movements. In three of the most stubbornly fought battles of the summer, he has found you always where duty called you, and where good soldiers ought

to be, and he has heard only unstinted praise of your conduct. You have made for your regiment a name that will outlive you all, and to which your children and your children's children will point with pride in the years of the future.
James Washburn, Colonel 27

Wildes described James Washburn as a leader of men, bluff, frank, and courageous but "too kind-hearted to be a good disciplinarian."[28] He was motivated by patriotism and principle not out of desire for glory and renown. He remained in service as commandant of the Post at Wheeling, West Virginia, by order of General Sheridan. The triumph of his will and determination over his frightful wound mirrored the testimony of his service while commander of the 116th Ohio Infantry.

General Early decided on the day following the battle at Island Ford to pull his army back to the Strasburg vicinity; he believed that his line along the Shenandoah rendered his trains vulnerable to attack from Harper's Ferry. On the twentieth while Early's Army was moving south, one of his divisions under General Ramseur was roughly handled at Carter's Farm just north of Winchester. Ramseur's men were routed, losing four guns before Ramseur managed to get his troops in hand near Winchester. Early took Rhodes Division and marched to reinforce Ramseur. When the Federals did not press the attack, he and his two divisions then fell back to Cedar Creek.

Thus ended the expedition to crush Early and his army. General Wright turned back for Washington from Snicker's Ferry on the twentieth, taking his VI Corps and the XIX Corps with him. Crook concentrated Hunter's Army of West Virginia (VIII Corps) around Winchester. Grant apparently believed that Early and his army were through with threatening the North and would return to Lee's Army. Thus, Grant expected Crook's troops to follow Early up the valley and then destroy the Virginia Central Railroad as far as Charlottesville.

Colonel Wildes believed that the responsibility for the expedition's failure belonged to General Halleck. Wildes felt that Halleck had persecuted General Hunter while attempting to cast all the blame for Early's mischief on Hunter. When General Grant refused to censure Hunter, Halleck simply refused to order anything in relation to the expedition against Early; he only relayed Grant's orders from City Point. Wildes possibly mistook Halleck's trait of shirking responsibility for something more sinister. For his part, Halleck repeatedly informed General Grant that he had not heard from General Hunter. The tone of his messages indicated that he possibly felt that Hunter was indifferent. If this were true, he could not be expected to coordinate the movements of General Wright and General Hunter against Early.

According to Wildes, Halleck deliberately failed to take initiative during the expedition and thereby ultimately ensured its failure:

The result was seen in the blundering and blind pursuit of Early, by Wright from Washington, and Hunter from Harper's Ferry. With the two armies of Wright and Hunter within fifteen miles of each other, the one in Early's rear at Poolesville, and the other on his flank at Hillsboro, neither knew of the other's position during a whole day, and neither would move on the enemy, because Halleck received no orders to move from Grant at City Point. Thus that campaign, ending at Island Ford, was managed. The evil genius of Halleck hovered over it, with an eye single to the defeat and discomfiture of Hunter, whose success would have been his defeat and chagrin, and hence the worst handled and most fruitless campaign of the war.29

Students of Civil War History will know that General Henry "Old Brains" Halleck was truly in character during the expedition against Early. Gideon Wells very aptly described Halleck in his diary by stating that Halleck "originates nothing...takes no responsibility, plans nothing, suggests nothing, is good for nothing."30 President Lincoln clearly understood Halleck's limitations and flaws. The President could not even rely on Halleck for advice in making difficult military decisions. He remarked that Halleck was "little more than 'a first rate clerk'—useful in his way, but not in the way the president had hoped."31 So Colonel Wildes was in some measure correct in blaming Halleck. His contention that Halleck deliberately sabotaged the expedition, however, is another matter. Perhaps Wildes himself was seeking a scapegoat, or perhaps his own bitterness over the cost and outcome of the expedition clouded his appraisal of Halleck's role.

The day after the battle the VI Corps departed with the intention of returning by ship to Petersburg. On the twentieth the 116th crossed the Shenandoah at Snicker's Ferry and remained in camp at that place until the twenty-first. General Crook decided to concentrate his army at Winchester, so the 116th marched to Winchester and camped at the old campground it had occupied in May during Sigel's campaign. Winchester was the most important base of operations in the entire valley. It provided a staging point for rebel raids and invasions when occupied by the rebels. When occupied by the Federals, it provided a launching point for incursions up the valley and also served to increase security for the B & O Railroad. "Winchester would change hands no fewer than 72 times during the war."32 There were still more changes of occupation yet to come; Jubal Early was not through in the valley yet.

"Old Jube's" Revenge
12

While General Hunter remained at Harper's Ferry as commander of the Department of West Virginia, Brevet Major General George Crook commanded the department's troops in the field. He now became the *third* general to command the Army of West Virginia and the 116th since May. General Crook, it should be noted, was an improvement over the previous generals under whom the 116th had served, but subsequent events would prove that he was not talented enough to defeat Jubal Early and his army on equal terms. George Crook, like so many other Federal Generals including Ulysses Grant and William T. Sherman, was a native Buckeye. Born near Dayton, Ohio, on September 8, 1828, he attended common schools in Ohio before his appointment to West Point. Crook "was graduated from West Point in 1852, ranking thirty-eighth in a class of forty-three."[1] While at the Point, Crook formed a close friendship with Phillip Sheridan, another Ohioan who would later eclipse him. Remaining in the army until the outbreak of war, Crook was named colonel of the 36th Ohio Infantry in 1861. By 1864 he had gained some experience as a division commander and also had commanded an independent force at the Battle of Cloyd's Mountain. George Crook was an able tactician and an excellent officer, but he lacked the confident determination and innate aggression required for success as an army commander. His familiar, almost homespun ways and features led to the nickname "Uncle George," as the men surreptitiously called him in his army.

On the twenty-third, two brigades of Crook's infantry were sent south of Winchester on a reconnaissance looking for Early's Army. The 116th was part of the reconnaissance, which also included General Rutherford Hayes (a future President of the United States) and his brigade. Few rebels were seen, and the infantry returned to camp confident that no sizeable rebel force was in the vicinity. This information was forwarded to General Crook.

The reconnaissance brought welcome news to Crook. General Grant was trying to keep track of the situation in the Valley from his headquarters at City Point, near Petersburg. Grant was probably hoping that Early would rejoin Lee at Petersburg, and the results of the reconnaissance seemed to indicate his return. However, the canny President Lincoln smelled trouble. On the morning of the reconnaissance, Lincoln telegraphed General Hunter to ask, "Are you able to take care of the enemy when he turns back upon you, as he probably will on finding that Wright has left?"2 General Hunter quickly replied, "My force is not strong enough to hold the enemy should he return upon us with his whole force. Our latest advices from the front, however, do not lead me to apprehend such a movement."3 Hunter went on to say he would take care not to be surprised.

Lieutenant General Jubal A. Early, Crook's adversary in the Valley, was at the apex of his military career. Like Civil War veteran and Supreme Court Justice Oliver Wendell Holmes, Early understood that "the reward of a general was not a bigger tent; it is command."4 To General Early, command was synonymous with action. Perhaps no other general at this stage of the war, save General Robert E. Lee, possessed Early's level of calculated aggressiveness. Others may have been more rashly aggressive, but Early usually attacked only after careful consideration.

Early carried an apt nickname given by his men. Stories of his profane and acerbic wit abounded in his command. That and the fact that his men were amused by his "old-fashioned name" and "his air of premature age," led to them to call him "Old Jube."5

On the twenty-third, the day of Crook's reconnaissance, Old Jube received a report from his cavalry that General Wright was returning to Washington and "that Crook and Averill had united and were at Kernstown near Winchester."6 Upon receipt of this intelligence he immediately decided to attack. President Lincoln's question to Hunter was about to be answered. Hunter's intelligence was faulty, and Early would make him pay for his mistake.

Sunday, July 24, 1864, began peacefully with the 116th in camp. Quartermaster Sergeant Ezra Walker wrote in his diary, "We hoped we would be permitted to remain in camp all day and had made preparations accordingly. Everyone was engaged writing letters or washing clothes…till an order came to fall in immediately as the enemy were coming down the valley in full force.7 General Crook did not anticipate a full scale attack; he thought that Early had moved too far south to attack Winchester. Thinking the approaching rebel force was only a reconnaissance, Crook ordered out one of his divisions to drive the rebels away. Colonel James Mulligan, an old friend who had helped drill the 116th at New Creek, was given the job. The fiery Mulligan sent his division straight at the advancing rebels. To his surprise, Mulligan ran into General John B. Gordon's full division and was repulsed. Mulligan was immediately in trouble, but Crook did not yet know it.

General Early sent Ramseur's Division to attack Crook's right while Gordon engaged Mulligan in the center. Old Jube soon learned that Crook was vulnerable on both his flanks, especially on his left, so he ordered General Breckinridge to launch Brigadier General Wharton and his division against Crook's left. Meanwhile the 116th moved to the front with the left portion of Colonel Thoburn's (First) Division, near the Valley Pike. Colonel Wells, commanding the First Brigade to which the 116th was attached, was ordered to throw out a strong skirmish line.

The 116th probably provided a portion of the skirmish line sent in advance of Thoburn's Division. Crook ordered Thoburn to advance toward the rebel center behind the skirmishers. As he prepared to follow Crook's orders, Thoburn observed General Ramseur's men closing on his right flank and hesitated so that he could inform Crook of this development. At this point Mulligan's troops were struck on their left flank and rear by General Wharton's division. Mulligan's line began to buckle. Men in blue began streaming to the rear in large numbers. As Colonel Mulligan rode among his men trying to rally them, he was hit five times by the vicious rebel fire and fell mortally wounded. Some of Mulligan's boys gathered him up, but the bellicose Irishman testily ordered them to put him down and instead save the colors.[8] After Mulligan fell General Hayes and his brigade backed up Mulligan's men to save the left from a complete rout. General Crook finally realized that he was outnumbered and ordered a general withdrawal. Hayes and Thoburn's steady troops provided cover for the retreating army.

As Colonel Wells gave the order to withdraw, a large rebel force attacked the First Brigade. According to Wells, "Immediately upon our withdrawal a very heavy force appeared in our immediate front, and another body, sweeping in from the right, cut off my entire skirmish line from the main body, and succeeded in capturing a large number, those who escaped only saving themselves by running far to the left."[9] The 116th fell back in good order along with the First Brigade. The troops on the left and right of the First Brigade suffered far heavier casualties. The First Brigade occupied a more secure position than the troops on the flanks and thus was probably subjected to less intense rebel fire. Colonel Thoburn stated in his report that the skirmish line allowed the division to "move in low ground under cover from the enemy's fire," and only the skirmish line suffered heavy casualties.[10]

Colonel Thoburn ordered the First Brigade to form on Fort Hill in Winchester, but Colonel Wells received orders to accompany the wagon train on the retreat to Martinsburg. The 116th covered the retreat on the left side of the pike, frequently clashing with rebel cavalry forays against the train. "Our regiment behaved splendidly throughout the retreat," wrote Wildes, "scarcely a man straggling from his place."[11] There was, however, a large body of disorganized troops mingling with the train during the retreat, probably most of them from the broken infantry regiments and stampeded cavalry units. Quartermaster Sergeant Ezra Walker described the scene for his diary:

There was considerable confusion and fast driving while getting the trains on the road, stragglers came back in great numbers and the fields on either side of the road were <u>filled</u> with them. Some had been on the skirmish line and got off from their regts, others were barefoot and had been <u>sent</u> back, but there were a great many stragglers.12

A rumor circulating through the retreating column that rebel cavalry was capturing the train caused a panic among the teamsters. According to Quartermaster Sergeant Walker several wagons were abandoned by frightened teamsters who cut loose the teams and rode or ran away. "Our own teamsters," wrote Colonel Wildes, "Dye and McKnight, always cool, took their teams through in good shape. There was no such thing as stampeding them."13

The train managed to reach Bunker Hill by 9 P.M., despite the rebel cavalry sent by Early to harass and capture the train. Time had to be bought in order to evacuate supplies from Martinsburg. So the 116th made a stand at Bunker Hill on the evening of the twenty-fourth. A very heavy rain curtailed any further action during the night. On the morning of the twenty-fifth, the 116th skirmished with a large force of rebel cavalry. The skirmishing in the Bunker Hill vicinity lasted until about 9 A.M. when the 116th began to pull back towards Martinsburg.

Again the 116th held the rear guard for the train on the twenty-fifth. The skirmishing with rebel cavalry continued until Martinsburg was reached around noon. Just south of town the 116th formed a line of battle and sent out a strong skirmish line against the rebels. By occupying the rebels south of town, the stores were evacuated from the town and the trains retreated to Williamsport, near Hagerstown, Maryland. At about 4 P.M. the 116th fell back through town. The rebels soon moved in to occupy Martinsburg. Uncle George shrewdly guessed that the rebels were unprepared for his men to turn back upon them in town, so Crook ordered the 116th with Thoburn's Division and part of the Second Division to charge into town. The surprised rebels were sent scrambling out of town and some were taken prisoner. With this accomplished, Crook's troops built campfires south of town to deceive the rebels and then fell back to safety across the Potomac at Williamsport.

Casualties for the 116th at Kernstown were remarkably slight: one mortally wounded, a few slightly wounded, and three captured. Charles Schafer of Company E died from the wound he received at Kernstown on October 17, 1864. William Clark of Company K, Joseph Gerlds of Company H and Benjamin Patterson of Company B were captured. James Earley of Company F was reported missing in action on July 24,

Stone fence on the Second Kernstown Battlefield. The 116th advanced from the fields on the right.

Opequon Church on the Second Kernstown Battlefield.

1864; he returned to his company on August 31, 1864, at Charlestown, West Virginia. Joseph Gerlds was exchanged in August and also returned to the regiment. Benjamin Patterson died in rebel prison at Danville, Virginia, on February 18, 1865. Colonel Wildes listed seven others as captured. These men were not so listed in the Roster; they, like Earley, may have been missing in action and later returned. Arthur Gibson of Company G was listed as captured on July 25, 1864. Colonel Thoburn in his report for Kernstown listed his casualties as six killed, fifty-two wounded, and 108 missing. " Many of the missing," he wrote, "may have escaped to points on the Baltimore and Ohio Railroad west of Martinsburg, and have not yet been able to join their regiments."[14]

Thomas Wildes revealed his opinion of the Federal command, without referring to Crook or anyone in particular, in his book years after the war:

> We were pretty sick of this sort of campaigning. If the pursuit of Early, in the Loudon Valley, was unskillful, this pursuit, in the Shenandoah, was incautious and reckless...Had there been a better understanding, and more unity of action between Hunter and Wright, there can be no doubt that many of the blunders, from the 14th to the 24 of July, could have been avoided. As it was, no campaign of the war was more disjointed, more fruitless and demoralizing.[15]

On July twenty-sixth the 116th marched to Sharpsburg and by the twenty-eight had returned to the Harper's Ferry vicinity to camp at Halltown. Quartermaster Sergeant Walker described the scene of the Antietam Battlefield, noting that little remained to indicate that a terrible battle had occurred there less than two years before. "Passed over a portion of the Antietam battlefield," he wrote, "the old church has been fitted up and white washed the field in front and beyond ploughed and but little remains to show that a great battle was fought there, but few graves can now be seen where last year there were so many!"[16] A few days later, on August fourth, Jubal Early passed through the Antietam Battlefield with some of his troops. He noted in his memoirs that he saw few traces of damage remaining when he visited the portion of the field he had fought upon in 1862.

At Halltown requisitions were submitted for desperately needed shoes and clothing. Over 150 men, according to Ezra Walker, were shoeless. Wildes wrote years later of the pitiful condition of the men: "Considering the worn out condition of the shoeless men when we reached the Valley on the 12th (July), their terrible condition now must be left to the reader's imagination, for, even at this distance of time, we have no heart to describe it."17 On the twenty-ninth the Quartermaster spent the entire day issuing clothes and shoes to the regiment.

Old Jube's victory at Kernstown provided him with numerous opportunities for mischief. The Administration had no way of knowing where Early would go next, but now familiar with his audacity, it was expected that he would strike again. Washington, D.C., Cumberland, Maryland, and Southern Pennsylvania were the obvious targets. The high command gave priority to protecting Washington, so Crook's troops were ordered to proceed to Monocacy Junction, near Fredrick, Maryland, to join with the VI and XIX Corps to protect Washington. On the thirtieth, the 116th took up the march for Monocacy Junction. "No one on that march will ever forget the fearful heat of that July day," wrote Wildes.18 Scores of men in the marching army fell during the day with sunstroke, but apparently Colonel Wildes slowed the pace, because no men succumbed from the 116th. The march took the 116th through Middletown, Wolfesville and Frederick, and on to the Junction, where the 116th camped on August fourth.

Meanwhile Old Jube was doing a fair impersonation of "Black Dave" Hunter. His army moved into the Martinsburg vicinity and commenced destroying the recently repaired railroads there. Hunter's depredations were etched into Early's psyche. Referring to Hunter's burn policy in the valley, Early wrote, "I came to the conclusion it was time to open the eyes of the people of the North to this enormity, by an example in the way of retaliation."19 The target chosen for retribution was the town of Chambersburg, Pennsylvania. Early had already extorted $200,000 from the City of Frederick, Maryland, during his Washington raid. He sent Brigadier General John McCausland with two brigades of cavalry to Chambersburg with a demand. The town fathers of Chambersburg were told they must pay either $100,000 in gold or $500,000 in currency to save their town from incineration. When the citizens of Chambersburg failed to meet the demand for ransom, the fire relishing McCausland torched the town.

News of Chambersburg's destruction spread throughout the country. The presence of Early's Army on the Maryland border, already a cause of great concern, now became a priority. On July 31, 1864, the day following the Chambersburg raid, President Lincoln met with General Grant at Fort Monroe, Virginia. Grant pressed the President for permission to appoint a single commander to take charge of the four separate departments involved in the Washington-West Virginia area. Grant recommended Major General Phillip Sheridan to command all the troops assigned to the task of defeating Early. Grant wanted General Sheridan "to put himself south of the enemy and follow him to the death". 20

Sheridan's appointment to the Army of the Shenandoah heralded the "dawn of a new era in the valley."21 On August 7, 1864, the Administration merged four separate military departments into the Middle Military Division with Sheridan in command. His command would consist of the veteran VI Corps from the Army of the Potomac, a portion of the XIX Corps, Crook's Army of West Virginia (VIII Corps) and a Cavalry Corps of two divisions from the Army of the Potomac with Averell's Division. With this powerful force Sheridan would outnumber Early's Army by nearly two to one. Despite this preponderance of strength being amassed against Early, President Lincoln held doubts about the prospects for victory. In a telegraph Lincoln cautioned Grant to be vigilant:

> ...please look over the despatches you may have received from here...and discover, if you can, that there is any idea in the head of any one here, of 'putting our army south of the enemy,' or of following him 'to the death' in any direction. I repeat to you it will neither be done nor attempted unless you watch it every day, and hour, and force it.22

The situation in the Shenandoah Valley had forced General Grant to send the very best officer available to take charge. General William T. Sherman and General George Thomas were occupied elsewhere, and all the remaining generals in the Federal Army were, in truth, not equal to the task. Nevertheless, when Grant appointed the thirty-three year old Phillip Sheridan to the vital Middle Military Division, it was by no means an obviously infallible choice. Sheridan had never held such a large and important command.

Phillip Sheridan was born to Irish immigrant parents on March 6, 1831. The exact place of his birth was never recorded. His family moved to Somerset, Ohio, while he was an infant or small child. By his teen years Sheridan had determined to pursue a career as an army officer, and he sought an appointment to West Point. It was only by propitious circumstances that he gained his appointment to West Point; the first choice appointee failed his entrance exam. Though he was an average student and was suspended for one year, Sheridan managed to graduate with the class of 1853. During the years before the Civil War, Sheridan served in the army in the Far West.

During the first year of the war Sheridan served mainly as a supply officer. When he finally did obtain a combat command, he was successful and proved exceptionally able. He quickly received promotions and increased responsibility, and at each level he continued to impress. While Sheridan was a capable strategist, he was an average tactician whose greatest asset was his battlefield presence.23 Sheridan was accustomed to overcoming great odds all of his life, and this trait carried over on the battlefield where, in terms of nerve and determination, Sheridan had few peers.

General Grant arrived at Monocacy Junction from City Point while the 116th was camped there. At Monocacy Junction Grant "found Hunter's command encamped along the Monocacy River, presumably protecting Washington but making no effort to flush out and engage Early."24 Grant immediately called for Sheridan to meet with him at the Junction. At that meeting Grant issued orders for Sheridan to proceed to Harper's Ferry and commence operations against Early. In effect, Grant told Sheridan to find Early and push him up the Valley, destroying all forage and provisions along the way so that nothing would "be left to invite the enemy to return."25

While at Monocacy Junction on August fifth, the 116th was reissued canteens and haversacks. A deserter was executed on the evening of the fifth, and the circumstances were related in Quartermaster Sergeant Walker's Diary:

> There was a man shot this evening for desertion, he deserted from the 23rd Ohio, went over to the rebels, was captured at Cloyd's Mountain, made his escape, made his way to Columbus where he hired as a substitute (getting $500.) was assigned to this Dept and by the Genl. assigned to the 23rd Ohio and by the Col. to his old company. He was recognized immediately by his old comrades put in irons till he was brot out to be shot this evening. He either stood or kneeled on his coffin when executed.26

General Grant ordered all of the troops of Hunter's command to be concentrated at Harper's Ferry to commence operations against Early. On August sixth the 116th broke camp before dawn and started the return trip to the Shenandoah. The enervating march over the previous week had accomplished nothing, except, perhaps, to reinforce Grant's awareness of his need for Sheridan. The 116th had to wade across the Monocacy; Walker noted that it "looked so funny to see a whole Division of 10,000 men with their pants rolled up as high as they could get them."27

By August eighth the 116th had returned to the Harper's Ferry vicinity. On the previous day, General Hunter, realizing that he was only functioning as a figurehead, had asked President Lincoln to be relieved from command. A few days earlier, Hunter had mentioned to Grant that he ought to be relieved; to which Grant replied, "very well then," and called for Sheridan.28 Soon Hunter simply faded from the scene, requesting leave of absence. The energetic Sheridan would have full command with minimal interference and no figurehead, other than Halleck, to endorse his plans.

Word of Captain Mathew Brown's dismissal from the service for cowardice arrived in camp on the eighth. Colonel Wildes had considered Captain Brown a coward long since, but he had been unable to address the situation. On July 25, 1864, a message from General Halleck to General Hunter established a streamlining process for weeding out recreant officers: "The Secretary of War directs me to say that summary punishment, by drum-head-court-martial, should be imposed upon those of your command who are guilty of cowardice in the face of the enemy."29 The new policy apparently enabled Colonel Wildes to get what he wanted. According to Wildes:

> He (Brown) had acted badly at Piedmont and Lynchburg, and now his peremptory dismissal from the service was recommended by his regimental, brigade, division, corps and army commanders, and on the 9th of August, the order of the War Department arrived dismissing Captain Mathew F. Brown from the service. We had no time for courtsmartial in those days, especially when an officer was guilty of cowardice. The captain, himself, explained his dismissal by saying it was because he 'couldn't swallow the nigger without grease.' The example of such men was intolerably demoralizing, and Secretary Stanton made short work of them, by arbitrarily and peremptorily dismissing them from the service.30

It is impossible to know what would have happened in Brown's case had Colonel Washburn not been wounded and absent. Brown had escaped official sanction until Washburn was out of the picture, but now it may not have mattered. In any case, command of Company F devolved upon First Lieutenant Wilson Martin after Brown's dismissal. Martin did not receive his promotion to captain until February 15, 1865.

On August tenth the 116th marched from Halltown on a yet another "raid" up the Valley. Sheridan's Army expected hard marching and fighting, but no one could have known that this departure inaugurated the campaign that would end rebel occupation in the Shenandoah Valley forever. The heat was again oppressive on the first two days of the march; but according to Quartermaster Sergeant Walker, the 116th kept "up better than any other (regiment) in the command."31 The line of march took the 116th to camp near Berryville on the evening of the first day.

An unfortunate accident claimed the life of a soldier from the 116th on the morning of the eleventh near Berryville. The men had just been given an order to load, and a soldier from Company E was placing a cap on the cone of his musket when it accidentally discharged. Private Nathaniel Ady, of Company E, was struck and killed, and two others were slightly wounded. It was the third accidental shooting death in the regiment, but it would not be the last. Such accidents were avoidable only by the strictest diligence on the part of every soldier and officer. Under circumstances of fatigue during the march and stress under fire, such mishaps occurred even more often than they were reported.

Quartermaster Sergeant Walker saw General George A. Custer, another native Ohioan, riding by on the evening of the eleventh and gave a surprising description of the young general. "He is quite a young man," wrote Walker, "and dresses very plain. Green velvet pants with stripes and dark blue shirt and an old slouch hat no one would take him for a general in the U.S. Army to see him riding by."32 Custer is often remembered for his fancy and unique outfit. Walker did not mention Custer's long curly hair or the braid running almost the length of his jacket sleeve. Sketches of Custer in the Valley by famed artist James Taylor for *Leslie's Illustrated Newspaper* show Custer arrayed in his fancy jacket and red scarf. Apparently the boy general was not decked out in his best on this hot day.

Sheridan's army now greatly outnumbered Early's, and the move to Berryville required Early to pull back or be cut off from his supply route. By August twelfth Early had deftly retreated to Hupp's Hill, just north of Strasburg. The 116th and the Army of the Shenandoah followed to Middletown and formed a semi circle along Cedar Creek in front of the rebel position at Hupp's Hill. The two armies skirmished during the evening, and some shots from rebel sharpshooters struck amid the 116th, wounding one man.

Signs of battle fatigue were beginning to show up in the 116th. This was a topic almost totally ignored by Thomas Wildes. Indeed, the subject was not well understood at the time Wildes wrote his history of the 116th. Nevertheless, the 116th had been in constant motion for three months, enduring severe marches under the most demanding circumstances possible. The men had fought in four engagements during that period and had been regularly exposed to danger on the skirmish and picket lines. They had seen their friends, neighbors and sometimes their relatives mangled in the bloodbath at Piedmont and again in the other sharp fights they had endured. With only a very few days in camp since May and no time for recuperation, the men had to be nearing their limits.

Quartermaster Sergeant Walker gave a picture of the effects of the constant strain in his diary written on the lines near Cedar Creek:

Some of the balls from enemy sharpshooters came over on the hill where we are, wounding one man in our regt., two in the 170th and one other thro the hips...(someone in) Co "A" tried to fall out but Col. Wildes made him come along, after we fell into line he laid down and began to moan & cry and carry on at a great rate; poor fellow! He is more to be pittied than blamed.33

Colonel Wildes was a patriotic man serving his country in its time of greatest need, not a career army officer. Yet he would never allow the 116th to falter, and he could not allow a sign of weakness to undermine his authority.

Early fell back to Fisher's Hill, just south of Strasburg. Fisher's Hill was known as "the Gibraltar of the Valley" and was practically impregnable when properly manned.34 Perhaps the best natural strongpoint in the Valley, Fisher's Hill is a rocky ridge connecting on the east with the North Fork of the Shenandoah River and stretching across the valley floor. A small stream called Tumbling Run flows at the base of the hill. Early had established a signal and observation station on nearby Massanutten Mountain, a towering peak near Strasburg running for miles through the center of the valley. From there he could observe the movements of Sheridan's army.

Jubal Early mentioned in his memoirs that his signal station was attacked by some of Sheridan's troops. On August fifteenth the 116th and the 14th West Virginia tried to capture the mountain where a signal station had been established near Strasburg. The attempt proved unsuccessful; the rebel force holding the mountain was too strong to drive off the mountainside. There was more skirmishing on that day, and the 116th remained on picket at the foot of the mountain until the next morning.

Sheridan received word from Grant that Early was being reinforced; Grant believed that soon Early would be too strong for Sheridan to attack him, especially at Fisher's Hill. "To meet the requirements of his (Grant's) instructions," Sheridan later wrote, "I examined the map of the valley for a defensive line-a position where a smaller number of troops could hold a larger number...I could see but one such position, and that was Halltown, in front of Harper's Ferry."35 Sheridan should have known that Early's army could not outnumber his, without massive reinforcements. Apparently he believed his position at Cedar Creek was too weak to give battle. On August sixteenth Sheridan set his army on the road for Halltown where he planned to establish a strong defensive line.

The 116th left camp about 9 P.M. on the sixteenth in the direction of Winchester. It seemed to the men in the 116th that the rebels held some sort of mystical grip on the Valley south of Winchester. With two additional Corps along to help, it must have been a mystery why

Sheridan would retreat. On through the weary night the 116th marched, halting about 2 A.M. at their old campground near Winchester. Immediately the exhausted men lay down and slept until wakened after dawn to resume the march.

After a hurried breakfast the men fell in and resumed the march, passing through Winchester and turning east toward Berryville. Winchester's women stood in their doorways laughing at the Yankees as they marched through the town, apparently in retreat.36 Heavy palls of smoke billowed up on the horizon from farms where the cavalry was burning hay and grain to deny it to the rebels. It was just the beginning of a policy that would be remembered for years to come as "the burning."

By evening the 116th reached its old campground near Berryville and went into camp. On the eighteenth after a short march of four miles, the men went into camp in a wood. For two days the 116th remained in camp. Foraging parties brought in an abundance of fresh vegetables and meat. Feasting on the relative plethora of fresh food, many of the men enjoyed their best meal in months. Parties of men went to the nearby farmsteads and helped themselves to fruit, honey, hogs, and about anything else they wanted. One soldier worried that he had become too accustomed to helping himself to other people's property. "I am getting hardened so, to taking whatever I see that I want," he wrote. "I am afraid I shall feel loath to give up the practice when I get home, if I live to get there."37

The ever-aggressive Early had immediately followed Sheridan's army from Cedar Creek. Jubal Early, then and ever afterwards, believed that Phillip Sheridan, or "Little Phil" as his men knew him, was weak, timid and lacking in resourcefulness. Even in the North, Sheridan was being criticized for withdrawing to Halltown. The retreat was so reminiscent of other Federal failures in the past that the Northern people feared the worst. Old Jube moved his outnumbered army into position to challenge the Yankees; to him, Sheridan was just "one more incompetent scoundrel whose time would come."38

On the twentieth the 116th moved to a small wood within two miles of Charlestown. The next day the 116th shuffled around, first starting out to guard a forage train and then returning to yet another different camp. No sooner had the men started to pitch their tents than they were ordered to fall in and march. A line of battle was formed about two miles west of Charlestown. At this stage of the war the men on both sides had learned the value of cover, so the soldiers quickly threw a rail breastwork together for protection. Early attacked that day with Rhodes and Ramseur's divisions in the vicinity of Charlestown. The firing became general along the lines, but the heavier fighting took place to the right of the 116th's position. Well after dark the 116th fell back from the breastworks to a camp near Halltown. As the troops passed through

Charlestown, the bands played "John Brown's Body," because this was the place where the fanatical abolitionist was hung. Apparently this was a common practice for Federal troops marching through the town.

Early learned from the fighting near Charlestown on the twenty-first that the Federal positions were much too strong for a frontal attack. On the twenty-second Sheridan's Army concentrated in the Halltown vicinity behind a line of breastworks stretching from the Potomac to the Shenandoah. Quartermaster Sergeant Walker described the works in his diary:

> Crooks command occupies the extreme left resting on the Shenandoah 19th Corps the center and 6th Corps the right resting on the Potomac. There has been heavy skirmishing along the lines all day with some little cannonading. We have been fortifying all day and now have a line of works extending from the Shenandoah to the Potomac with numerous flanks extending and giving us in all some six or eight miles of fortifications.[39]

Sheridan was unsure of Early's strength and was exercising extreme caution. He felt more pressure to prevent another defeat than to destroy Early's Army. There was good cause for Sheridan's respect for his adversary. Although his forces vastly outnumbered Early's Army of the Valley, he was still facing "one of the most formidable fighting organizations in American History."[40] The rebel division and brigade commanders were some of the best in the rebel army, accustomed to working near miracles on the battlefield. Sheridan knew from his experience with Grant against Lee that superior numbers were not a guarantee of success against the tough veterans of the Army of Northern Virginia.

Conversely, Jubal Early was completely disdainful of Sheridan. In fact, Early was recklessly over-confident as illustrated by his actions on August twenty-fifth. Early pulled nearly all of his forces out of the Halltown front and feinted toward Shepherdstown. He left General Anderson behind near Halltown with only Kershaw's Division and some cavalry. Early apparently hoped to draw Sheridan out from behind his strong works at Halltown. Had Sheridan called Early's bluff, Anderson's force would have been annihilated.[41] Instead, Sheridan refused to leave the security of his Halltown lines.

A reconnaissance by Crook's troops on the twenty-fourth attempted to probe the rebel lines and bring on an attack. Quartermaster Sergeant Walker noted, "in the latter we failed, our artillery did some splendid shooting...causing them to run in all directions."[42] On the twenty-fifth a heavy rain fell and some artillery firing was heard by the men of the

116th. Early slipped most of his army out of the Halltown lines, but even Quartermaster Sergeant Walker got word that the rebels were moving toward the vicinity of Shepherdstown.43

Again on August 26, 1864, General Crook sent out a reconnaissance against the rebel lines near Halltown. The ensuing nasty little fight proved costly to the 116th. In his report General Crook mentioned the fight: "August 26, still another reconnaissance was made on the enemy's right…One brigade from Colonel Thoburn's division was sent out at the same time in front, making a feint of attack in that direction."44 Colonel Wells commanding the First Brigade of Thoburn's Division, to which the 116th was attached, was ordered to drive the rebels from some woods and to burn some wheat stacks in preparation for the reconnaissance. The 116th along with the 5th New York Heavy Artillery were sent to clear the woods while the 34th Massachusetts was to burn the wheat stacks in the field.

The rebels were quickly driven out of a small patch of woods in front of the Federal works by a skirmish line. But when the main portion of the 116th and 5th New York Heavy reached the small patch of woods, another rebel line behind breastworks opened a very heavy fire upon the two regiments from across a road at the edge of another wood. Colonel Wells wrote, "a strong skirmish line firing from these (woods) within easy range, and directly upon our flank, made the small piece we were ordered to hold almost untenable. Our line quickly changed front to the right, and a portion of it charged across the pike, driving the enemy back from the edge of the woods."45 The right wing of the 116th made the charge across the pike that drove the rebels back. It was here that the 116th lost several men.

Colonel Wells then pulled the two regiments back to a wooded area along the pike and exchanged fire with the rebels. The 34th Massachusetts quickly fired the wheat stacks while the other two regiments occupied the rebels. The rebels held the upper hand in the firefight along the pike. Colonel Wells noted that he was "losing men fast" while the rebels were "protected" and probably lost few men.46 During the fighting the intrepid Sergeant Silas King of Company F was hit and nearly killed. A rebel bullet struck King in the mouth, passed through his neck and exited between his shoulders. With rebel bullets buzzing thickly about them and their comrades falling steadily, the men sought cover and scattered along the woods.

As soon as Colonel Wells saw that the 34th Massachusetts had finished its job, he gave the order to withdraw. The 116th and 5th New York Heavy Artillery pulled back to the original lines in good order. A few dead were left behind, almost all from the New York regiment. There were no stretchers present with the advance, so bringing off the severely wounded was difficult under fire and painful for the wounded. In his report, Colonel Wells listed his casualties as nine killed, fifty-six wounded and one missing.47

Both Colonel Wells and Colonel Wildes praised the 116th for its conduct during the fight. Colonel Wells mentioned in his report that the 116th was "steady and gallant, as usual."48 In a letter written on August 27, 1864, the day following the battle, Colonel Wildes proudly noted that the "whole regiment behaved gallantly."49 The affair at Halltown was undoubtedly more severe and trying than what was anticipated, but the 116th and the other regiments had done all that had been asked of them. What Wildes didn't mention was that the constant exertions of campaigning and strain of combat were beginning to tell upon the men.

Losses in the 116th were surprisingly heavy, really excessive for what was accomplished: one killed, four mortally wounded, twenty-three wounded and one captured. Wildes, in his letter of August 27, 1864, mentioned that 103 rebels were captured, and he noted General Hayes' report that 150 rebels were killed and wounded during the fighting that day.50 Below is a list of casualties for the 116th Ohio Infantry at Halltown:

KILLED

Private George W. Matchett, Company C.

MORTALLY WOUNDED

Corporal Jacob Sidders, Company I, Privates Elza J. Hill, Company A, Miles Davis, Company C, Charles Dirkes, Company E.

WOUNDED

Sergeant Major William J. Lee, side; Corporal Jerome McVeigh, Company A, right hand; Corporal J. C. Sidders, Company I, broken leg, (Died of Wounds); Elza J. Hill, Company A, right arm, (Died of Wounds); Emanuel Keylor, Company A, thigh; John A. Harmon, Company A; Corporal Abner G. Carlton, Company C, thigh, severely; Miles H. Davis, Company C, (Died of Wounds); Charles D. Watson, Company C, hip, Sergeant A. G. Jackson, Company D, hip; Sergeant James K. Drum, Company D, side; Isaac Price, Company D, thigh; William Morris, Company D, shoulder; James D. Ferrill, Company D, knee; Charles Dirkes, Company E, knee, severely, (Died of Wounds); Christian Miller, Company E, bowels; Martin Thoner, Company E, Knee; Sergeant Leander Shahan, Company F, head; Sergeant Mathias

Rucker, Company F, foot; Corporal (Sergeant) Silas King, Company F, very severely; Amos Jones, Company F, (Captured and Died as a POW, March 1865); L. Efaw, Company F, leg; Sergeant Benjamin F. Sammons, Company H, hip; Sergeant William A. Arnold, Company H, knee, severely; James R. Finley, Company I, leg; Charles Watson, Company I, shoulder, Jesse Burton, Company I, side.

CAPTURED

Amos Jones, Company F. 51 (Died 03-12-65 as POW at Richmond, VA.) Roster

The regiment's major, William T. Morris of Monroe County, showed up in camp on the twenty-sixth in civilian clothes. He had been at home on leave, saying that there was illness in his family. While on leave, Morris had tendered his resignation, and on the twenty-fourth it had been approved. Colonel Wildes had been unaware of the major's intention to resign; nevertheless, he did not criticize him for it. According to Wildes, "Major Morris was an excellent officer, always prompt in the discharge of every duty, and as a man, was courteous and gentlemanly toward all, officers and men alike."52 Morris had shown pluck and had earned praise for his conduct during the fight at Bunker Hill in June 1863. However, some of the men held a different opinion of him. Quartermaster Sergeant Walker mentioned Morris' resignation in his diary:

> Major Morris came back today but in <u>citizens clothes</u>. He has played out most beautifully while we were along the B&O. R.R. out of the way of <u>danger</u> he was willing to stay but as soon as we go into the field, where there is a prospect of a fight, he suddenly learns that his family requires his presence at home and resigns, very well, he was never of much account as an officer though he was a pleasant man to be with, how unlike the Col. or Lt. Col. 53

Commissary Sergeant William T. Patterson also mentioned that Morris arrived in camp on the evening of the twenty-sixth. Patterson wrote about Morris in his diary: "…his copperhead proclivities are too strong for the army particularly at a time like this, very affable man and has been quite popular among the boys."54 Wildes may very well have shared the same opinion, but he gave no indication of it in his post war account of the 116th. Major Morris was the brother of the Democratic Congressman from the district of Southeast Ohio. Patterson and Walker were quite possibly biased against Morris because of his political persuasion.

Corporal Abner Carlton, Company C. Corporal Carlton was severely wounded at the Battle of Halltown on August 26, 1864. (Courtesy of USAMHI)

Grave of Abner Carlton at Beloit, Kansas.

Skirmishers from the 116th were sent out the day following the fight at Halltown. They fired a volley and advanced toward the rebel lines only to find that the enemy was gone. Anderson had withdrawn his division and had marched to Stephenson's Depot. Early's infantry pulled back from feinting towards Maryland and moved to Bunker Hill. Most of the twenty-seventh was spent verifying Early's troop dispositions. The cavalry under General Wesley Merritt drove Early's cavalry back from Leetown, assuring General Sheridan that "Early had abandoned the projected movement into Maryland."[55]

Marching orders arrived directing the 116th to proceed to Charlestown. The 116th marched through the town and then back to the same campground occupied the previous week in a wood near town. "It must be borne in mind," wrote Colonel Wildes, "that we never passed through Charlestown without singing: 'John Brown's body lies a moulding in the tomb, His soul goes marching on'."[56] Colonel Wildes and his boys were not going to allow the locals to forget that Brown's cause had now become their own.

For the next few days the 116th finally caught a break, hearing firing in the distance but not being called into action. The men were sorely in need of rest and a thorough refitting. Stragglers and recovered wounded soldiers were returning to the regiment, and the number present exceeded 400. While at Charlestown the little Irishman Mike Manning of Company I "was tied to a tree under guard for several hours for impudence to the Lt. Colonel."[57] The little fellow had bought the men a good laugh at Piedmont with his antics as he marched in a burly Irish rebel prisoner. His Irish temper was no doubt blamed for his misfortune at Charlestown. Manning, it seems, was the regiment's stereotypical Irishman, so often portrayed in Civil War lore.

By September third, Sheridan had decided to advance again to the "Clifton-Berryville line, and that afternoon Wright went into position at Clifton, Crook occupied Berryville, and Emory's (XIX) Corps came in between them, forming almost a continuous line."[58] Having just marched south from Charlestown, the 116th was going into camp for the evening near Berryville when the routine was most rudely interrupted. General Crook had learned that a rebel force was approaching from Winchester and ordered his divisions to fall into line. This rebel force was Anderson's troops on their way to Ashby's Gap to return to Lee's army at Petersburg. Anderson did not know that Crook's Corps was at Berryville, and General Crook did not know that Anderson and his command were on their way back to Petersburg via Berryville.

The resulting clash caught everyone by surprise with embarrassing results for the Thoburn's Brigade and the 116th. After throwing down their kettles and camp equipment and forming a line, the 116th took position and went prone to await developments. The following is from Thomas Wildes' post war account of the battle:

> Suddenly a terrific fire opened on the regiments on our right and left, our brigade having been thrown into a gap existing between our second division and the 19th corps. The regiments fired upon stampeded in a panic, which, for the moment, also seized ours, and for the first and only time during its term of service, it fell back without orders. It was rallied by the officers a few rods to the rear, however, when we all had a good laugh, at our own expense, over our 'panic.' The men were more ashamed of being caught in a 'panic,' than of any and all the little escapades of their lives, and never quite forgave themselves for it.59

Crook was forced to use his Second Division to shore up Thoburn's position after the "panic." It seems from all accounts that the greatest blame for the embarrassing stampede fell upon the Second Eastern Shore Maryland Infantry, the 15th West Virginia Infantry and the 123rd Ohio Infantry. Thoburn in his report noted that the Maryland regiment fled and the 123rd Ohio "also failed to made a stand."60 He did not mention any failure by the 116th, probably because Colonel Wildes and his officers quickly got the 116th in hand and faced the enemy. In effect, there was no official blot on the record of the 116th for what occurred at Berryville.

After rallying most of the 116th, Colonel Wildes pulled the regiment back under the cover of a stone wall. Anderson's attack was repulsed easily by Crook's line. The 116th then drove the rebels out of a nearby stone house and, according to Wildes, "made good use of it in driving the (rebel) line in rear of it back a safe distance from our front."61 Crook's men lay on the field in line of battle all through the night. In the morning the Federals built a line of works, something they had become quite proficient at by this stage of the war.

Anderson's force was in extreme peril, being outnumbered by Crook's troops and within striking distance of Sheridan's army. Had General Crook sensed his advantage, he could have destroyed Anderson's force before Early could prevent it. As it was, Early brought up three infantry divisions in the morning to rescue Anderson. The ever-aggressive Early even entertaining a notion of attacking Sheridan's line before realizing the strength of the Federal works. After consulting with Anderson, Early gathered his force and on the fifth pulled back west of the Opequon. Crook's corps and the 116th marched back to the main defensive line and camped at Clinton.

Four men from the 116th had been wounded at the Berryville fight: Leonard Craig of Company H was severely wounded in the leg, John

Harman of Company A was wounded on the nose, George Bates of Company I was severely wounded in the hand, as was Benjamin Larrick of Company H. Benjamin Larrick died of his wound at Frederick, Maryland, and was later buried at Antietam National Cemetery. No other casualties were recorded. The rebels were believed to have suffered heavier casualties, because they attacked against the Federals who were protected by a stone wall.

Commissary Sergeant William Patterson recorded the events of September third in his diary. He was baffled by the conduct of Thoburn's troops. The following is a portion of his entry for the third:

> ...our left had not yet formed altogether ere the "Johnny's" were on us; they charged our whole line vehemently and I regret much to say, that for some reason our division broke, how this could be, what could do it, what magic power the enemy could employ to make effeminate our daring soldiers to paralyze their courage particularly the 116th, which had never failed before is wrapped in deep mystery to me...They didn't retreat far, however, till the officers succeeded in rallying another line. Quite a number though ran clear away leaving their commands, good many of the 116th, there too that never flinched before. Why they did so this time is a query; their conduct is an anomaly.62

Even the regiments most famed for their valor and resolution had their embarrassing moments during the four hard years of combat in the Civil War. For example, the 20th Maine Infantry, known as the heroes of Little Round Top at Gettysburg, once "got frightened and 'skedaddled' ...like a flock of frightened sheep."63 But even in late 1864 the 116th remained a very proud regiment. The soldiers of the 116th truly sensed that their regiment was a manifestation of their collective manhood. They were all neighbors, friends, and relatives; should the 116th behave untowardly, their personal reputations would suffer.

Despite Patterson's consternation, the 116th was not under some "magic power" of the rebels. The men were bone weary from the constant marching and edgy, perhaps even nearing fatigue, from the incessant skirmishing with Early's gritty veterans. But there would be no repeat of the "panic" of Berryville. Honor and the iron will of Colonel Wildes would be the cement hardening and bonding the 116th until the end of the campaign. No influx of draftees and bounty men ever affected the efficiency of the 116th. Until the war ended the 116th remained what it always essentially was—a plucky collection of steadfast Ohio yeomen fighting for their country.

In the weeks ahead the 116th would have a hand in closing out Old

Jube's career. Old Jube's days of threatening the North were now over. General Lee's "bad old man" was facing overwhelming odds, and he knew it. But Old Jube would never comprehend that his adversary was capable of defeating him. His disrespect for Phil Sheridan would cost him dearly in the months ahead, although he never would admit it.

"TELL COLONEL WILDES TO COME ON!"
13

The first week of September 1864 heralded the long awaited confirmation that the Unionists would win the war. On September second General Sherman's army, having defeated General Hood's rebel army, occupied Atlanta. This momentous news came on the heels of an announcement that the Federal Navy had silenced the last of the rebel forts in Mobile Bay. Now only the port of Wilmington, North Carolina, remained open for rebel shipping. With General Grant and the Army of the Potomac slowly strangling the rebel capital, the end of the war was coming into focus. The only suspense concerning the war now was just how fast the Confederacy could be closed out and at what cost. Rumors of the two Federal victories had been circulating for days as Sherman closed in on Atlanta; now the soldiers of the 116th saw the rumors confirmed in the newspapers.

While the 116th was in camp near Clifton on the fifth, Colonel Mosby's guerilla band attacked and captured an ambulance train under the command of Lieutenant Ransom Griffin, of Company H, who had been assigned to the ambulance detail. The train had departed Harper's Ferry without an armed escort. Some officers from other commands were with the train when Mosby's men attacked. Lieutenant Colonel Kellogg, of the 123rd Ohio, was with the train and managed to get away. Kellogg found a Federal cavalry outpost and gathered about twenty cavalrymen to follow him back to the site of the attack. When Kellogg appeared, Mosby's men abandoned most of the ambulances but escaped with Lieutenant Griffin and three ambulances.

During the next two days the 116th stayed near Clifton. Lieutenant Griffin showed up in camp "much to the surprise of all" on the sixth.[1] He had somehow escaped from Mosby's band during the night of his capture. On the seventh, Lieutenant Colonel Wildes took the 116th out of camp to drill during the evening. After drill he spoke to the assembled men, sternly "telling them he wanted to see no more running and deserting of colors in time of action!"[2] He commended those who had rallied quickly at Berryville on the third, but he warned everyone that he would not brook running from the enemy again, telling those who might run to "beware!"[3] Colonel Wildes was to a great extent responsible for the good name the 116th had earned. His gallant and reasoned conduct in the thick of all the regiment's battles had provided an example for the men to emulate, and his speech on the seventh wasn't overweening, it was simply a verification that he would not allow the 116th to fail.

The VIII Corps moved to the extreme right of Sheridan's defensive line on September eighth, placing the 116th about mid-way between Bunker Hill and Charlestown. News of Captain Edwin Keyes' death at Lynchburg finally reached the 116th by a letter from Sergeant Humphreys, who was at home recovering from his Lynchburg wounds. Captain Keyes had been left behind because of serious wounds that would require amputation of an arm and leg. He had died the day after the battle. Some of the officers drafted a notice of sorrow and grief to be sent to the newspapers in Monroe, Athens, Noble and Meigs Counties in Ohio. Also on the eighth, the regimental sutler brought his wagon into camp for the first time since the Lynchburg raid. One soldier noted, "it was a sight to see the men crowding around anxious to pay the highest prices for things of no earthly use to them."4

The one remaining hope the rebels held for victory was the nomination on September 8, 1864, of General George B. McClellan as the Democratic Party Candidate for President. While McClellan refused to label the war a failure, he held ideas for peace "considerably different from those of the Republicans." While Lincoln's party demanded rebel capitulation and recognition of emancipation, McClellan insisted that the rebels could rejoin the Union with full rights as assured before the war.5 In effect, the rebels were hoping for the election of McClellan, because they believed that his election would signal that the North was tired of war and ultimately willing to accept Southern independence.

Another tragic accidental shooting occurred on the night of the thirteenth. A camp guard, half-awake, unexpectedly fired his musket and wounded two men from Company A. Private Milton Danford's leg was severely wounded, requiring amputation. He died on September twenty-fourth. The unfortunate sentry was never convicted of misconduct, being found insane.

Lieutenant Gotlieb Sheifley, of Company K, succeeded in obtaining a release from the army in a novel way. Sheifley obtained a leave of absence on the grounds that his wife was seriously ill. He then immediately traveled to Washington and requested to see the President. During the war President Lincoln was known to have been very disposed to allowing a brief audience to soldiers who came to the White House to see him. When the President heard Sheifley's story, he "looked at him a moment, and then sat down and endorsed his resignation as follows: 'Accept this man's resignation. An officer who will tender his resignation in person to the President, does not know enough to be in the service'."6 When notice of Sheifley's resignation, effective September seventeenth, reached the 116th, it was met with supreme contempt. In the years following the war Sheifley moved to Illinois.

General Early was convinced that General Sheridan was incapable of assuming the offensive, so he was willing to return Anderson's troops to Lee. On the fifteenth General Anderson and his portion of the Confederate I Corps departed for Petersburg. This time, to avoid another clash like the one at Berryville, Anderson marched up the valley and through Thornton's Gap. Within one day Sheridan had received intelligence of Anderson's departure. It was the news Sheridan had been hoping for, "He immediately began preparations for a movement by the army toward Newton, beyond Early's flank and against his communications."7

General Grant was coming under increasing pressure to deal with Early's army in the Lower Valley. Accordingly, on the eleventh he informed Chief of Staff Halleck that he would visit Sheridan, and that he expected things to remain quiet around Petersburg until he resumed the offensive.8 According to Wildes, "On the 16th of September, the army was visited by General Grant, though few knew it until long afterwards outside of General Sheridan and his staff."9 Commissary Sergeant Patterson, however, noted Grant's presence at Harper's Ferry on the seventeenth.10 In any case, Grant met with Sheridan, as noted by Wildes, on the sixteenth. Grant came with plans of his own to drive Early from the Valley; but when the two met, "Little Phil" did most of the talking.11 Sheridan assured General Grant that he now intended to attack Early's weakened army, to which Grant replied, "Go in."12

Before General Sheridan could initiate his movement to the south of Winchester, the monumentally overconfident Early divided his army yet again, as he had done at Halltown in August. On September seventeenth Early took two divisions of his infantry and marched north with a view of destroying the B & O Railroad near Martinsburg. Ramseur's and Wharton's divisions remained in the Winchester vicinity. General Averell's cavalry observed Early's column moving toward Martinsburg, and the intelligence was forwarded to Sheridan on the afternoon of the eighteenth. Sheridan changed his plans, deciding to attack the vastly outnumbered rebels remaining at Winchester.13 Upon receipt of this remarkable news, Sheridan wrote orders to move on Winchester the following morning. Thus the pivotal Battle of Opequon resulted from a sudden change of plans.

On the eighteenth the 116th made ready to move at a moment's notice. All the regiment's wagons and the sutler were sent to the rear. The men drew rations and packed up their haversacks in preparation for the move. Afternoon passed into evening with no orders to fall in and march; the movement was delayed until before dawn. That evening the surgeons held a sick call to determine if any men were too ill or disabled to go into action. Private Charles Fulton, of Company E, and others went to the sick call requesting to be sent to the rear. After examining Fulton, Surgeon Shannon refused to excuse him from combat duty. As Fulton trudged back to his tent, he suddenly collapsed and died. News quickly spread through the camp, and the men angrily denounced the surgeon for his apparent callousness and incompetence. Further investigation revealed that the private had died from heart disease, that Surgeon Shannon was unaware of his condition and thus had not excused Fulton from duty. When the men learned that Surgeon Shannon had acted in good faith, the anger subsided

Sheridan's Army began to stir after midnight on the nineteenth. Sheridan's battle plan called for General James H. Wilson's cavalry to move out before dawn on the Berryville Pike. Wilson's cavalry was to clear a path for the VI Corps through Berryville Canyon, east of Ramseur's defensive line. The VI Corps and the XIX Corps were to proceed through the canyon and attack the rebels just beyond. While the infantry fought in the hills east of Winchester, the cavalry divisions of Merritt and Averell were to circle to the north of Winchester and attack Early's left flank and rear. Crook's troops were to be held in reserve and, if unneeded, sent south of Winchester to block Early's retreat route. Sheridan was planning a double envelopment—a classic battlefield maneuver "that generals dream about but rarely succeed in bringing off."[14]

Events on September nineteenth unfolded quite differently than Sheridan had envisioned. Wilson's cavalry succeeded in opening a lane for the VI Corps to clear Berryville Canyon and deploy, but the VI Corps had brought its ambulances and supply wagons along, blocking the narrow route through the canyon. When the XIX Corps followed into Berryville Canyon, it was delayed by the tangle of wagons and artillery from the VI Corps. Without support the VI Corps could make no progress against Ramseur, and it was over two hours before the XIX Corps managed to clear the canyon. The delay gave Old Jube the time he desperately needed to prepare for Sheridan's attack.

As mentioned previously, Early had taken two of his divisions to Martinsburg on the eighteenth. "At Martinsburg," Early wrote, "where the enemy had a telegraph office, I learned that Grant was with Sheridan...and I expected an early move."[15] Early knew enough of Grant to expect an attack. Although he did not write it, Old Jube knew that he must reunite his army at once or run the risk of losing Ramseur's Division. Accordingly, he sent Rhodes and Gordon hurrying in the direction of Winchester. Early and Rhodes returned to Stephenson's Depot that evening, and Gordon arrived there at dawn on the nineteenth.

While Sheridan's infantry struggled to clear Berryville Canyon, Early's two divisions arrived and deployed on the high ground east of

Winchester. Because of the delay at the Berryville Canyon, Early had his army deployed and ready "an hour before the Union assault."16

The creeping pace of the Federal deployment allowed the rebels time to strengthen their defensive lines and prepare artillery positions before the attack began in earnest. Early's position was not extremely strong: there was no system of trenches as Lee employed at Cold Harbor and Petersburg. Nevertheless, Early had managed by 10 A.M. to have his army in position and prepared to meet Sheridan's attack, something Sheridan had not anticipated.

The VI and XIX Corps fiercely battled Early's divisions into the afternoon without conclusive results. By 2 P.M. a lull "settled over the field, and General Early concluded that the fighting was over."17 And why not? Old Jube had seen this pattern before. McClellan did not use his reserve at Antietam when he could have crushed Lee; nor did Meade use his final reserves at Gettysburg. And Hunter had retreated from Lynchburg with less of a fight.

Here Sheridan proved he was worthy of command and of Grant's confidence. Disregarding his original battle plan, Sheridan ordered Crook's Corps into the fight.

The 116th had marched at daybreak on the Berryville Pike to the crossing of the Opequon and there waited in reserve. All through the morning the men could hear the roar of the fighting ahead, sweating it out, wondering when they would be called into the maelstrom. "We could hear the cheer of the troops as they charged, and something I never heard before," a soldier from the 116th wrote, "the brass bands discoursed ' sweet music' during the hottest of the fight."18 By noon the sound of the fighting had increased to a "steady roar," and everyone knew that this was a severe battle, not just another skirmish.19

At about 2 P.M. the 116th was ordered to the front, and the regiment hurried through the clogged gorge at Berryville Canyon. Once again the signs indicated a severe battle: "The road was crowded with artillery, caissons, ammunition wagons, ambulances, prisoners, wounded men," leaving no doubt about what lay ahead.20 Once through the narrow gorge the 116th moved into a wood about two miles beyond the Opequon, taking position on the right of the battered XIX Corps. Patterson described the scene in his diary:

> As we went up we met Gen. Sheridan & Staff, the Gen waved his hand and says 'go for 'em boys' whereupon Lt. Col. Wildes calls for three cheers for Gen Sheridan, which was heartily responded to by the 116th. Our command moved on to the field in the best order imaginable and about 2 O'clock became engaged.21

"Scarcely were our guns loaded, and our bayonets fixed," wrote Wildes, "before the bugles sounded the charge, which was repeated by every officer in the two lines, and, with a loud cheer, our whole corps threw itself with desperate valor upon the enemy's left wing and flank."22 As the 116th forged ahead across open country, it was raked by a flanking fire from a wood on the left. Colonel Wells, commanding the brigade, realized that the rebels in the wood held an advantage, and he "pointed out the danger" to the commander of a trailing regiment, the 10th West Virginia.23 Colonel Wildes saw the 10th charging the woods and went to its assistance, changing front under fire and charging in behind the rebel works in the wood. Now the 116th held the advantage, and its "bullets were whistling down" the rebel line.24 The 116th drove the rebels from their works at bayonet point, the rebels retreating to a stone wall nearly a quarter mile beyond.

The rest of the brigade had pushed on, following the rebels as they retreated across the open ground towards the stone wall. This high stone wall ran west in the direction of the Martinsburg pike, with artillery and infantry posted behind it. In the rear of the wall, "upon a knoll, was an earth-work with rifle-pits, in which were two guns. About 400 yards in front of this line and parallel with it was a short, low stone wall."25 Wells ordered the brigade to hunker down behind the low wall to rest and await the next assault. Soon the 116th emerged from the wood and took position on the left of the brigade.

A brigade of troops from the XIX Corps, including the 116th New York, was on the left of the 116th following the charge into the wood. Fire from the 116th and the XIX Corps troops forced the rebels on their front to move farther down the wall. After catching their breath, the men were impatient to resume the attack. Corporal Henry Johnson of Company H was the color bearer that day, and he stepped out from the rest of the regiment, waving the flag as he ran toward the rebels. Johnson turned and yelled for the men to follow him. When asked years after the war what he was thinking, Johnson replied, "Thoughts! I had no thoughts...Who could think there with that old banner waving over him in the center of the battle?"26

Colonel Wildes could not send the regiment forward against the wall without orders and support. He screamed at Johnson to bring the colors back within the lines, fearing that both Johnson and the flag would be captured. Johnson wouldn't budge. Wildes then sent part of the color guard to bring Johnson and the colors in, but the agitated corporal sent them back with a message for Wildes. "Tell Colonel Wildes to come on! We can finish the job just as well as not," was one version of the message.27 Another version had Johnson saying, "Tell the colonel to come-on I'm commanding this Reg't."28 Johnson was furious at the rebels for concentrating their fire upon the flag, conspicuous in the open field, and he would not back away. Rebel bullets tore through the flag, riddling it with holes. Johnson took a severe wound in his arm; it hung limply at his side while he grasped the colors with his remaining hand, "blood pouring down his blouse sleeve and over his pantaloons."29

Meanwhile Colonel Wells waited for the remainder of Crook's troops to arrive on the right. Colonel Duval's Division had approached from the opposite side of Red Bud Run, a marshy little creek that flowed roughly parallel to the Berryville Pike, and had to cross the swampy banks to reach the fighting. When Duval's men finally went into position on the right, the firing swelled into a crescendo. The roar and flame from thousands of firing muskets in opposing lines created a cloudy storm with man-made "thunder and lightening."30 It seemed as if hours passed amid the thundering volleys, and all the while Corporal Johnson clung to his bullet riddled flag between the lines.

The fact that the rebel right was probably exposed to fire from the 116th may have saved Johnson's life. At length the whole line rushed the rebels behind the high wall, and as the 116th went forward, Johnson was gathered in, "still clinging to his colors with one arm. No one had the heart to punish him for disobedience of orders."31 The fearless corporal ignored his painful wound and went with the 116th as it overran the rebel line along the high wall. All along Thoburn's line the Yankees went forward with a cheer, "and the rebels were driven from the wall in utter rout."32

Some of the rebels fell back to the knoll beyond the high wall, manning rifle pits and allowing the artillery to remain in place, pouring shell and small arms fire into the 116th and Crook's men. A soldier recorded the subsequent action in his diary:

> ...the Col (Wildes) with the quick perception of a soldier seeing their present position very precarious and that much more could be done by advancing and also the position that could be taken there would be much less dangerous, he ordered the 116th to advance, which they did, by crawling carefully on the ground...they reached a slight elevation in the ground, which afforded shelter. From this position our boys by double charging their pieces were enabled to reach the rebel battery, which was silenced in consequence thereof, horses being killed and cannoniers driven from their guns.33

Colonel Wells mentioned this movement in his official report, noting that the 116th had "an excellent position on the left, from which they were enabled to fire directly upon the piece and horses."34 According to

Colonel Wildes, the 116th would have charged the knoll and the rebel gun, except Colonel Wells sent an aide to the 116th reprimanding Wildes for moving "forward without orders," and directing him to wait for orders to advance.35

As previously noted, Sheridan's battle plan called for a cavalry attack to sweep past the rebel extreme left flank. As the sun began to set, while the 116th was keeping the rebel gunners pinned down, the full fury of the Federal cavalry struck from the north along the Martinsburg Pike. Gordon's tired veterans crumbled before a stampeding horde of saber wielding troopers. Wildes described the scene of the final attack: "At this juncture, Custer came gallantly sweeping down the right, inside the enemy's works. Then it would have required more than orders to keep us from attempting to be the first to reach those guns, and away the regiment dashed in splendid style..."36 It was a race to capture the guns atop the knoll, with the entire line swarming into the rebel works.

Once into the rebel works atop the knoll, the 116th found a brass twelve pounder and a caisson full of ammunition. Two wounded horses and a dozen dead ones lay there, and another caisson was abandoned beneath the knoll with all of its team killed.37 As the smoke cleared and the cacophony of battle subsided, Colonel Wells reorganized the brigade and prepared to move into Winchester. Wells ordered a detail from the 5th New York Heavy Artillery to take charge of the captured artillery, leaving the New Yorkers in place while the brigade moved by the left flank into Winchester.

The women of Winchester, no doubt, were a little less smug in their appearance upon seeing the 116th march though their town this time, as opposed to their behavior the previous month when Sheridan's Army was falling back from Strasburg. Early's troops were driven through the town in no gentle manner, leaving no doubt as to the severity of their defeat. Winchester's residents had witnessed more than their share of fighting and the misery that accompanies it. "I have seen more sad scenes of the war since coming to Winchester than ever before," wrote a veteran of the VI Corps who had seen battlefields from Bull Run to Petersburg.38

Crook's Corps chased the retreating rebels through town and a few miles beyond before darkness set in. The 116th went into camp for the night on their old campground about two miles south of Winchester. General Sheridan rode into Winchester to telegraph news of the victory to Washington and to General Grant. The news provoked the only display of exhilaration Grant's staff had ever seen from the general. He went out and threw his hat into the air, knowing that Sheridan's victory "was the beginning of the end."39

Casualties at the Battle of Opequon were severe. Sheridan's Army suffered 5,019 casualties, of which 698 were killed, 3,983 wounded, and

338 missing.40 The rebel losses were approximately 4,000, of which half were killed and wounded.41 Casualties for the 116th at Opequon were four killed, one mortally wounded and twenty-eight wounded as listed below:

KILLED.

Orville S. Hetzer, Company B; Lewis C. Secoy, Company B; John A. McIlwee, Company H; George Sigler, Company K.

MORTALLY WOUNDED.

Corporal Peter Yoho, Company F. (Died 10-22-64)

WOUNDED.

Corporal Jerome McVeigh, Company A, neck; John Drake, Company A, foot, severe; John Hay, Company A, thigh, severe; James H. Stewart, Company B, Stomach; Corporal D. F. Sears, Company C, severe; Emmon H. Beardmore, Company C, head, severe; Jacob Mishack, Company C. thigh, severe; William Montgomery, Company C, thigh; W. W. Wheaton, Company C, groin; Second Lieutenant W. H. Mosley, Company H, thigh, severe; Corporal Henry T. Johnson, Company H, arm, severe; Mathew R. Moore, Company H, leg, severe; John W. Williams, Company H, leg, severe; Isaiah Tribby, Company H, shoulder, severe; Yoho Watson, Company H, head, severe; Israel Hamilton, Company D, leg, severe; Peter Beaver, Company D, thigh, severe; Sergeant Mathew Atkinson, Company E, leg, severe; Milton Mosena, Company E, head, severe; Dallas Gillmore, Company E, side, severe; Corporal Lewis Mosena, Company E, arm, severe; I. Phelps, Company F, groin, severe; Joshua Mercer, Company F, ankle, severe; Samuel B. Halliday, Company G, leg, severe; J. H. Harman, Company G, finger; John J. Norris, Company I, foot, severe; William McNeil, Company K, arm, severe; Daniel D. Weddle, Company K, knee, severe.42

On the day after the battle, President Lincoln sent a message in cypher to General Sheridan:

Executive Mansion,
Washington,
Sep. 20, 1864,

Have just heard of your great victory. God Bless you all, officers and men. Strongly inclined to come up and see you.

A. Lincoln 43

The victory, following as it did Sherman's victory at Atlanta, ensured Lincoln's reelection. Even the enlisted men sensed the significance of the battle. Commissary Sergeant Patterson scribbled in his diary as the fighting ended: "How easily the good and great Lincoln will be reelected!"44 Patterson's words seem so perspicacious through the haze of time, yet the joy of victory revealed the inevitable to the sergeant at that moment in time.

Uncle George's Splendid Day
14

At about 7 A.M. on the morning of September 20, 1864, the 116th took to the road in pursuit of Early's Army of the Valley. The cavalry was in the vanguard, moving out around 5 A.M. Crook's troops followed the other two corps of infantry south on the Valley Pike to Middletown, marching the twenty or so miles to that place by 5 P.M. Beyond Middletown Sheridan's Army of the Shenandoah spread out in camps along Cedar Creek just north of Strasburg. After dark the 116th quietly disappeared into a wooded hollow to a camp concealed from the rebel's observation. As the men moved silently through the trees, the glimmering campfires of the VI Corps dotted the landscape in the distance, a spectacular sight against the dark mountainside looming beyond.

Old Jube knew he had been lucky to escape from Winchester with his army intact. Years later he wrote, "When I look back to this battle, (Opequon) I can but attribute my escape from utter annihilation to the incapacity of my opponent."[1] To some extent Early was correct, things certainly could have been much worse for the rebels. Though soundly defeated, his army remained intact and was soon ready to give battle. According to his report dated October 9, 1864, his army had only lost three pieces of artillery. The only piece actually captured in the fighting was from the battery that had its horses shot down by the 116th, as Early noted, "the horses were killed and it could not be brought off."[2]

Early decided to make a stand at Fisher's Hill, just as he had done the previous month, hoping to bluff Sheridan into allowing him to remain in the Lower Valley. "To have retired beyond this point," wrote Early, "would have rendered it necessary for me to fall back to some of the gaps of the Blue Ridge, at the upper part of the Valley, and I determined therefore to make a show of a stand here, with the hopes that the enemy would be deterred from attacking me in this position, as had been the case in August."[3] So Old Jube set his army to work on the twentieth and twenty-first strengthening his old fortifications and constructing "bull pens" like the ones faced by the 116th at Piedmont.

Fisher's Hill was a very strong position when sufficiently manned, but the rebels did not have enough infantry to make it impregnable. For some reason, never explained, Early placed his least dependable troops in the weakest position of his line. He placed his cavalry, which had collapsed at Winchester, on his left, where he was most vulnerable to attack. He posted his infantry along the pike behind a "solid wall of towering rocks", and this combined with a line of strong fortifications presented a very daunting front to the Federals.[4] But with his left flank poorly defended, Early offered Sheridan an excellent opportunity to drive him from the strongest natural position in the Valley.

On the night of September 20, 1864, while the 116th was preparing to go into camp, General Sheridan met with his corps commanders at a tent pitched near the pike beyond Cedar Creek.5 Sheridan called the meeting to develop a plan to drive Early off Fisher's Hill. All of his generals agreed that a frontal assault against Early's line would likely fail. A movement against Early's right was impracticable, because the attacking force would be observed and steep terrain protected Early's right flank. Uncle George Crook, exhibiting his tactical ability, suggested a flank attack against Early's left, utilizing the heavily wooded terrain to conceal his approach. The less perceptive General Wright of the VI Corps and General Emory of the XIX Corps did not agree. Sheridan then called for Colonel Thobun and Colonel Hayes, Crook's division commanders, and asked their opinion. At some point during the meeting, General Sheridan decided to approve Uncle George's plan. However, he never really gave credit to General Crook for suggesting the plan of attack. In his memoirs Sheridan took almost all of the credit:

> ...I resolved on the night of the 20th to use again a turning-column against his (Early's) left, as had been done on the 19th at the Opequon. To this end I resolved to move Crook, unperceived if possible, over to the eastern face of Little North Mountain, whence he could strike the left and rear of the Confederate line, and as he broke it up, I could support him by a left half-wheel of my whole line of battle. The execution of this plan would require perfect secrecy, however, for the enemy from his signal-station on Three Top could plainly see every movement of our troops in daylight. Hence, to escape such observation, I marched Crook during the night of the 20th into some heavy timber north of Cedar Creek, where he lay concealed all day of the 21st.6

On the morning of the twenty-second, the 116th was positioned in a heavy wood north of Hupp's Hill, having marched into the wood under the cover of darkness on the previous night. Here the 116th waited with the rest of Crook's Corps while Sheridan positioned the rest of his army for the attack. Before dawn Sheridan's army was aligned as follows: the XIX Corps was in line on Sheridan's left along the Valley Pike north of Strasburg, Wheaton's Division of the VI Corps was aligned right of the XIX Corps troops with Getty's VI Corps Division further right, west of the Middle Road, and Ricketts VI Corps Division was still further to the west. Averell's cavalry was placed along the back road to screen

Crook's approach to Little North Mountain on the extreme right of the Valley floor.7

Just past noon General Emory sent some of his XIX Corps against the "bull pens" on Early's right. At about the same time, Crook's Corps and the 116th began their movement against Early's extreme left, under the cover of heavy woods and ravines north of Hupp's Hill. Crook's two divisions, the 116th included, had initially moved out around daybreak, the 116th halting about two miles away on the west side of Fisher's Hill. Now and then a bullet or two whirred overhead as the men waited in the pine and cedar woods. General Crook, wearing a plain uniform with no insignia, had personally led the column, taking caution to hide the movement from a rebel signal station across the valley.8

As the 116th and Crook's troops prepared to move into the cover of the heavily wooded Little North Mountain, Averell's cavalry drove in rebel skirmishers and formed a screen to cover the movement. At the base of the mountain, the 116th removed knapsacks and all superfluous gear, "arranged canteens and bayonet scabbards so that no noise would be made by them, and in the lightest kind of marching order, started up the steep, thickly wooded side of Little North Mountain."9 Uncle George formed his corps into two parallel columns, "each division in two lines, side by side."10

The march across the side of Little North Mountain was difficult, over rough ground covered with dense cedar and pine forest and outcroppings of rock. A cleared area along the route exposed Crook's men to the view of the rebels on Fisher's Hill, and a rebel picket line opened fire. Rebel Brigadier General Bryan Grimes noticed Crook's two lines moving across the clearing and reported this to General Ramseur. However, only a few artillery shells and some scattered shots were fired at Crook's column, and Ramseur apparently took no action following Grime's report.11

By about 3 P.M. Crook's column was in position to outflank Early's extreme left. The men started quietly down the mountainside and prepared for the attack, as described by Colonel Wildes:

> The 116th, now being in its old position, on the extreme left, and in the front line, could now see, through an occasional open space, that we were going in with our left just inside the rebel works. It gave us a fair prospect for some hard fighting, and every man nerved himself for the shock soon to come. But now we were discovered, and the enemy opened on us with shot and shell.12

The Battle of Fisher's Hill was decided the moment Crook's corps burst from the woods at the base of Little North Mountain. "Had the heavens opened," said one rebel officer, "and you been seen descending, no greater consternation would have been created," than the appearance of Cook's divisions on Early's left.13 The 116th roared with an unearthly yell and charged into a line of rebel works "like a western cyclone, every man for himself, firing whenever he saw a rebel..."14 Crook's charging troops struck Lomax's rebel cavalry, guarding Early's flank, scattering the rebel horsemen "like the swine with an overdose of devils."15

Soon after emerging from the woods, the 116th encountered an open slope with manned earthworks. Colonel Wells recorded in his official report that the regiments in his brigade raced to be first into the rebel works. A rifled cannon "was fired at less distance than 100 yards into the One hundred and sixteenth Ohio," wrote Wells, "but they rushed on without an instant's hesitation, capturing it in the very smoke of its discharge."17 The gun was from Captain Kirkpatrick's Battery and was one of the few indisputable captures of artillery involving Crook's Corps that day.18

Clearing this line of rebel works, the 116th pushed on along the enemy works with the 34th Massachusetts under the direction of Colonel Wells. Crook's Corps, the 116th included, had lost most of its unit cohesion during the initial charge due to the rough and wooded terrain. "Being closest to the works, we were confronted and stopped at several points by small bodies of the enemy," Wildes explained, "but such stops were only momentary, for as soon as a little sharp firing was heard...the men would...concentrate there, and in a few moments would be rushing on again."19 The 116th passed through a series of ridges manned by artillery, fighting through pockets of resistance. Colonel Wells noted that Crook's men captured several rebel guns on these ridges: "I saw and touched four brass and more than as many iron guns before any, except men of this (Crook's) corps, had reached them."20

Captain Teters, of Company H, almost single handedly captured a rebel battery along the way. Teters was a very determined soul (as noted previously, he nearly arrested the stubborn colonel of the 40th Ohio at Gallipolis). In the confused fighting at Fisher's Hill, Teters was separated from most of his men when he encountered a rebel battery. When he couldn't gather enough men to charge the "nearly deserted" battery, Teters rushed the rebel guns by himself, shooting "one of the rebels off of a horse."21 Most of the rebel gunners fled, but one stood his ground, challenging the captain. Drawing his sword, Teters demanded that the rebel surrender and threatened to cut off the rebel's head. This drew an angry response, as the gunner immediately swung a rammer at Teters. A violent fight ensued with Teters warding off the blows with his sword until he was able to pick up a musket and knock the gunner down.

Another Federal soldier, seeing the desperate struggle, came to the captain's assistance and "thrust a bayonet" through the downed rebel.22

Two North Carolina infantry regiments, the 32nd and 45th, and the 2nd North Carolina Battalion faced the 116th and the rest of Colonel Wells' troops on the ridges of Fisher's Hill.23 Shortly after hearing the firing from Crook's assault, General Ricketts launched his division against the face of Fisher's Hill, just north of where the 116th was making headway. As the 116th was fighting through the rebel works, pushing toward the Valley Pike to the east, Colonel Keifer's Brigade of VI Corps infantry swarmed over the works on the north face of the ridge. Two Ohio regiments that once were in Colonel Washburn's Brigade with the 116th, the 110th and 122nd Ohio, now in the VI Corps, "came over the works, as the 116th and 123rd were running along inside," and joined their voices in giving "the well known 'West Virginia yell.'"24 Now the North Carolina regiments battling the 116th were in "a cauldron of fury," being pummeled by musket-fire from three sides."25

The Tarheels, having no other recourse, scattered under the hail of bullets. General Early rode up as the rebel line was collapsing on this section of the field. Old Jube was ordering up General Wharton's Division from his right flank to shore up this portion of his line, and he was furious to find his largest division in complete rout before Crook's troops. The unaccustomed sight of panicked Southerners so infuriated the crusty general that he ordered the nearby 13th Virginia to fire at the Tarheels. The Virginians declined and instead took to *their* heels.26

With the flight of the 13th Virginia, Pegram's flank was exposed to attack from three directions. When the VI Corps hit Pegram's front, the rebel defenders broke and ran for their lives.27 The rest of Sheridan's infantry was now sweeping over Fisher's Hill; Early's army simply turned and ran south on the Valley Pike or scattered into the mountains. It was only the second time a sizeable rebel army had been driven in disorder from a strong line of works to this point in the war, the other time involving Bragg's army on Missionary Ridge, Tennessee, in November 1863.

Once the rebels were driven off the ridge near the Valley Pike, the day's work was over for the 116th. It was the cavalry's job to chase Early's shattered army. Yet again the 116th had performed superbly in battle. Colonel Wildes was praised for his efficiency in the brigade commander's official report for the battle. Colonel Wells also singled out the 116th for praise in his report: "I would especially call attention to the gallant charge of Colonel Wildes' regiment in the face of the artillery fire."28 Wildes and the 116th were being mentioned for gallantry in nearly every brigade level battle report, clearly more often than any other regiment in the First Brigade.

Uncle George Crook was largely responsible for the Federal victory at Fisher's Hill. He had conceived the battle plan and sold it to the army commander, and his corps had behaved magnificently, doing everything expected from it. At both Winchester and Fisher's Hill, "it was Crook's corps that played the decisive combat role" of outflanking and routing the rebels.29 Yet Crook was largely ignored, because Sheridan took credit for the tactical planning. History, nevertheless, has now recognized the vital role Crook's tactical facility played in both battles. September 22, 1864, was truly Uncle George's splendid day, the best of his career.

General Crook himself, unlike Sheridan, was unassuming and willing to give credit to subordinates. In his report for the battle, Crook noted that the victory "was mainly owing to the individual bravery of the officers and men, who are entitled to great credit."30 Crook's selfless dedication during the battle itself resulted in controversy over whose troops captured several rebel guns on the ridges of Fisher's Hill. Some of the VI Corps troops apparently came upon cannon already captured by Crook's troops that had been left unguarded. Crook explained: "I did not permit any of my men to remain with the artillery, from which we had driven the enemy in our advance, so as to get credit for its capture, as I needed every man at the front to make the rout of the enemy as total and complete as possible, and not at the rear to guard captured guns."31

Casualties for both armies at Fisher's Hill were remarkably light. Sheridan reported only fifty-two killed, 457 wounded and nineteen missing, a total of 528.32 Colonel Thoburn reported only one killed and seventy-seven wounded in his division, to which the 116th was attached, the one man killed was from the 116th.33 General Early reported thirty killed, 210 wounded and 995 missing, for a total of 1235.34 Losses in the 116th were one killed and ten wounded as listed below:

KILLED.

Sergeant (Acting Sergeant Major) Edmond P. Tiffany, Company B.

WOUNDED.

Corporal James M. Hartley, Company B, head, severely; Corporal James H. Stewart, Company B, arm, severely; John McElroy, Company B, arm, severely; Thomas Smith, Company C, severely; Sergeant James K. Drum, Company D, thigh, severely; Christian Rhimes, Company F, foot, severely; Corporal Edward Lowry, Company G, hand, severely; Andrew Powell, Company H, hip, severely; Corporal Joseph Sechrist, Company H, severely; Samuel H. Cramblitt, Company I, elbow, severely.

Sergeant Tiffany was killed at the close of the fighting, when it was nearly dark. He and Lieutenant Martin, of Company F, were talking, when a seemingly random shot hit Tiffany in the head, passing completely through and killing him instantly. "All thought there was no danger," wrote Commissary Sergeant Patterson of the incident.35 According to Colonel Wildes, the sergeant was buried on the field; his body was later claimed by friends and re-interred in Meigs County, Ohio.

Colonel Wildes related two incidents at Fisher's Hill that serve as excellent examples of the "brother against brother" and "father against son" nature of the American Civil War. Wildes mentioned in his book that the 116th captured a rebel lieutenant colonel. This rebel officer by chance met his son who was a private in the 13th West Virginia, the regiment in the line behind the 116th. "They shook hands, embraced and parted, the father to go to a Northern military prison, the son to continue in the contest, with his Union regiment."36 Private Leroy D. Brown, of Company H, had a brother-in-law in a Federal cavalry regiment. "He had a brother," wrote Brown, "who belonged to a rebel battery which we captured. After the war closed, it was ascertained that this brother was killed at Fisher's Hill."37

On the morning after the battle, the 116th marched off Fisher's Hill and took its place with its division. Soon the rest of Thoburn's men moved on to follow Early's army, but the 116th and the First Brigade were kept on the battlefield to bury the dead and take charge of captured men. Part of the job involved collection of captured and abandoned cannon, weapons, accouterments and material amid the debris of battle. It was evening before supplies came from the rest of the army, and the 116th drew rations from a train. The rebel prisoners were brought under guard by the 116th in the empty supply wagons.

It was after 10 A.M. on the morning of September twenty-fourth before the 116th took to the road to catch up with the rest of Sheridan's army at Harrisonburg. The men must have pondered what the near future would bring while on the march that unusually warm autumn day. Would Early leave the Valley and return to Lee's army? Would the 116th join the Army of the Potomac, as Grant originally intended, or would the VIII Corps simply remain in the Valley and go into winter quarters? One thing practically everyone knew—there was still plenty of work to be done in the Shenandoah Valley, and Early's army lay somewhere along the road ahead.

A TRIUMPH OF MORAL COURAGE
15

On the day following the Battle of Fisher's Hill, while the 116th Ohio was collecting captured materiel on the battlefield, Sheridan's army pursued the broken rebel army up the Valley. The pursuit was a failure. If one examines the campaigns of the Civil War, only two army commanders were truly successful in following up a victory by crushing a rebel army in the field. General Ulysses S. Grant, at the close of the war, was the only commander to run down a rebel army and capture it. General Sherman practically duplicated the feat under somewhat different circumstances. Sheridan put the blame for his failure squarely on his cavalry, and there is good evidence that his cavalry was ineffective and a hindrance in the pursuit. In truth, however, it appears that little Phil did not push hard enough to ground Early. "General Sheridan followed our retreat very languidly," wrote rebel General John B. Gordon of Early's army.1 While Sheridan's army was tired, so was Early's, and even from the haze and distance of time, it appears that Sheridan could and should have done more.

At Rude's Hill, a few miles north of New Market, Sheridan attempted to engage the rebels as they made a temporary stand on September twenty-fourth. Before Sheridan could bring on a fight, Early withdrew south of New Market. Sheridan followed beyond New Market and went into camp around 5 P.M. With Sheridan's infantry in camp that night, Early made his getaway. By evening of the twenty-fifth Early's infantry had reached the mouth of Brown's Gap, east of Grottoes in the Blue Ridge. Early was then reinforced by Kershaw's Division and some cavalry. After further maneuvering Early fell back to Rockfish Gap, near Waynesboro.

Sheridan gave up his pursuit and concentrated his infantry in the vicinity of Harrisonburg, Virginia. The 116th caught up with the rest of Crook's Corps at Harrisonburg "on the 26th, in charge of a large train."2 Wildes noted in his account that supplies and rations were scarce for the large concentration of troops at Harrisonburg. This coincides with General Sheridan's dispatch to General Grant, explaining that it was difficult to supply the army, and his army could not forage enough to subsist without army supply.3 While at Harrisonburg for a few days, the headquarters of the 116th, at least, was sufficiently supplied by foraging parties led by Quartermaster Sergeant Walker. "Foraging trains were sent out daily, and with these Walker and Orderly Webster were sure to go," wrote Wildes.4 The sergeant brought in bread, vegetables, chickens, sweet potatoes, and honey.

General Grant held differing views from those of General Sheridan in regard to the next move. Sheridan admitted in his memoirs that Grant "advocated the wholly different conception of driving Early into eastern Virginia, and adhered to this plan with some tenacity."[5] Halleck wired Sheridan on the twenty-seventh to inform him that Grant expected Sheridan to move on Charlottesville.[6] Sheridan resisted Grant's plan, suggesting that his army should burn out crops in the Valley and move on after rendering the area a "barren waste."[7] History sides with Grant. Like Hunter, Sheridan had an opportunity to shorten the war in the East by months by following Grant's instructions. Instead, he contrived his own puzzling strategy, a strategy clearly inferior to Grant's.[8]

On September 30, 1864, Company A of the 116th was assigned to guard a mill near the town of Dayton, Virginia, about four miles southwest of Harrisonburg. The rest of the regiment marched to Dayton on the afternoon of October second. The residents of the village were kind to the 116th; many of the residents were pacificist Dunkards who did not participate in the war. According to Colonel Wildes, "the people of Dayton were as fine and loyal a people as we had met anywhere in the South."[9]

Lieutenant John R. Meigs, Sheridan's engineer, was in Dayton on the third conducting a military survey. The young Lieutenant was the son of U.S. Army Quartermaster General Montgomery Meigs and was a valued member of Sheridan's staff. Near dusk the Lieutenant rode out of Dayton to return to camp. In a driving rain Meigs encountered about six riders he took to be Federal cavalrymen. What happened next still remains a matter of dispute. One fact is certain—Meigs was shot in the head and killed by one of the riders. A soldier from the 116th noted the news in his diary that night:

> ...(Meigs) was waylayed by some half dozen rebels dressed in our uniform and killed, he had orderlies with him one of them supposed to be killed the other had his horse shot-under him, but was not hurt—and he found his way back to our camp in the dark and brought the news. It was raining hard.[10]

Colonel Wildes also wrote an account of the killing in his book. Wildes noted that one of the men riding with Meigs came to the camp of the 116th after the shooting. According to Wildes, "A strong detachment of our regiment was sent out on the double quick to the place, where his body was found by the roadside. Shortly afterwards a large body of cavalry came out from Sheridan's headquarters, and placing his body in an ambulance, carried it back to Harrisonburg."[11]

When General Sheridan heard the report of the incident that night from one of the men who accompanied Meigs, he was furious. He sent a party of cavalry to the site of the shooting almost immediately to burn a barn belonging to the resident farmer. By afternoon of the fourth, an order from Sheridan came to the 116th directing Colonel Wildes to burn the village of Dayton. Sheridan ordered every house within five miles of the site of the shooting to be burned. It was not the first instance of retaliatory burning, but Sheridan's orders involved more houses and a larger area than usual. Sheridan explained his orders in his memoirs: "The fact that the murder had been committed inside our lines was evidence that the perpetrators of the crime, having their homes in the vicinity, had been clandestinely visiting them, and been secretly harbored by some of the neighboring residents. Determining to teach a lesson to these abettors, of the foul deed—a lesson they would never forget—I ordered all the houses within an area of five miles to be burned."[12]

General Custer and his cavalry went to work on the morning of the fourth burning homes in compliance with General Sheridan's order. A witness at Sheridan's headquarters reported that Custer had vaulted into his saddle when Sheridan gave the order, exclaiming: "Look out for smoke!"[13] In Dayton, on the afternoon of the fourth, the residents removed property from their homes, as reluctant soldiers from the 116th informed them of Sheridan's order. The cavalry had reached the outskirts of Dayton by nightfall, as described by a soldier from the 116th, "The whole country around is wrapped in flames; the heavens are aglow with the light thereof."[14]

Sheridan's order did not set well with the 116th. Sergeant Patterson's diary entry explains how difficult it was to see the town preparing to burn and why:

Such mourning such lamentation, such crying such pleading for mercy I never saw nor want to see again. Some were wild, crazy, mad, some cry for help while others would throw their arms around Yankee soldiers necks and implore mercy…If it was at Berryville, Charlestown or Winchester I would say burn in retaliation of Chambersburg, but this place is the most loyal or at least most innocent of any I have seen in the Valley…An old soldier of 1812 with his old woman were compelled to sleep out in open air. Many who were sick did the same. It is certainly hard. Truly war is cruelty.[15]

As the sun rose on October 5, 1864, time was running out for the residents of Dayton. Their personal effects and property had been removed from the houses, and many residents had spent the night in the fields with their possessions. Colonel Wildes "wrote a statement to General Sheridan of the character of the people of the place, and urged and begged him to revoke the order in so far as Dayton was concerned."16 Wildes sent his note to Sheridan by a messenger, telling him to hand it to the general in person. When the messenger reached Sheridan's headquarters, staff officers wanted to take the message and an argument ensued. The persistent messenger somehow managed to pass through the staff officers and guards until he handed the message to Sheridan in his personal quarters. "The General read the note and swore, read it again and swore, examined and cross examined the messenger."17 At length Sheridan yielded and sent the messenger back to Dayton with an order exempting the village of Dayton from burning. The vicinity, however, became known as the "Burnt District." Patterson noted that "Scarcely a house (was) left between Dayton and Harrisonburg."18 Custer's cavalry apparently did that work.

At Dayton, Colonel Wildes had put off burning the village as long as possible. All of the houses were empty; men from the 116th had helped carry out the last of the residents' goods and effects. Smoke billowed up from burning dwellings in the surrounding outskirts of Dayton. No one wanted to be first to set fire to the Dunkard people's homes, to exchange evil for good.

With everything prepared for the burning, the messenger finally returned to Dayton with Sheridan's permission to spare the village. When the officers and men went to inform the villagers of Sheridan's reversal, the villagers believed the worst, "and the screams of women and children were perfectly heart rending. But the joy that succeeded as soon as their mission was understood, was so sudden and overcoming that many of the poor women fainted, and the clapping of hands and shouts of gladness of the little children over the good news was too much for even the grim and sturdy old soldiers."19 Soldiers helped the villagers carry their belongings back into their homes, glad to have escaped a terrible blot on their souls.

It had taken more than a feeling of compassion to save Dayton from the wrath of General Sheridan. By 1864 the war had reached a level of brutality usually reserved for war on a foreign enemy. The little-known events at Dayton are a stark contrast to what General Sherman would exhibit in his well-known "March to the Sea" through Georgia in November 1864. That Colonel Wildes was able to intercede on behalf of a hamlet in the middle of bushwhacker country is a testimonial to the reputation that he had earned. Wildes proved at Dayton that he was as morally courageous as he was physically courageous; his civic action at Dayton was a triumph of moral courage.

The people of Dayton did not fail to show their appreciation. They heard that the 116th was preparing to move in the morning, so they showered the officers and men with "a great quantity of provisions and delicacies."20 Wildes always believed that any soldier from the 116th would forever be welcomed in Dayton. He was surely right, because in the years that followed, "the town of Dayton, Virginia erected a bronze plaque to the memory of the commander of the 116th who refused to burn the community to the ground on orders from General Sheriden."21

Lieutenant John R. Meigs was laid to rest in a very special place. Quartermaster General Montgomery Meigs had just that spring opened a new cemetery for the Federal dead near Washington, D.C. The new cemetery was located on the estate of Mrs. Robert E. Lee, called Arlington. General Meigs had his son buried in Mrs. Lee's rose garden beside the Lee family's fine mansion. Today that estate is the burial place for our nation's heroes; it is known as Arlington National Cemetery.

Another unfortunate incident occurred while the 116th was in the Harrisonburg vicinity that September. The incident relates to Captain John Varley of Company E. Captain Varley was unfairly dismissed from the service following the Battle of Fisher's Hill. Varley had tendered his resignation just after the regiment's bitter little fight at Halltown on August 26, 1864. As noted in the case of Captain Brown, the army was at that time cracking down on officers showing cowardice in the face of the enemy. While Captain Varley had tendered his resignation on the grounds of family sickness, it was construed as cowardice, because he resigned directly after a battle. Several officers from the 116th signed a letter to be sent to Secretary of War Stanton requesting that Captain Varley be discharged honorably. The officers verified that Varley was not a coward and had proven himself a gallant officer in subsequent battles. Unfortunately for Varley, it was not until after the war that his status was changed to honorably discharged.

"A SHARP LITTLE FIGHT WITH THE JOHNNEYS"
16

Colonel Wildes went to Harrisonburg on the night of October fifth, possibly to explain more thoroughly the reason why he had not burned Dayton. He left orders for the 116th to march into Harrisonburg before dawn to join the rest of the First Brigade on a march back to Fisher's Hill. Only burnt rubble remained where houses once stood along the road to Harrisonburg, few houses had survived the burning ordered by Sheridan. When the 116th reached Harrisonburg, most of Sheridan's army had already departed. Colonel Wells' brigade and the 116th brought up the rear on the entire march.

Sheridan's rationalizations prevailed over General Grant's plans for the Army of the Shenandoah. Sheridan's victories at Winchester and Fisher's Hill had elevated his influence, apparently, because Grant acquiesced to his views. "I being on the ground," wrote Sheridan, "General Grant left to me the final decision of the question, and I solved the first step by determining to withdraw down the valley at least as far as Strasburg, which movement was begun on the 6th of October."1 Sheridan planned to burn out all the stores of grain between Harrisonburg and Strausburg, leaving only enough to supply his own army. He probably did not expect more trouble from Early, because he intended to return at least the VI Corps to Grant's army after reaching Strausburg.

The march on October sixth was difficult, a total of twenty-eight miles. Near Mt. Jackson the 116th halted for the night, drawing rations until past midnight. One soldier noted in his diary that the men were "very tired"; and the day had been "warm and dusty."2 While the 116th marched, the cavalry set fires all across the Valley. General Sheridan noted, "...many columns of smoke from burning stacks, and mills filled with grain, indicated that the adjacent country was fast losing the features which hitherto had made it a great magazine of stores for the Confederate armies."3

General Early, having been reinforced by Kershaw's Division and a cavalry brigade under General Rosser, became emboldened to attack Sheridan. As Sheridan withdrew toward Strasburg, his cavalry burning as it went, Early grew aggressive and sent his cavalry to press the withdrawing Federals. The rebels harassed the Yankee cavalry and skirmished with the rear guard on October seventh. By the eighth Rosser had followed on the heels of Sheidan's army far enough to distance his command from any possible infantry support from Early.

The 116th was nearing Fisher's Hill on the ninth when General Sheridan unleashed his cavalry on Rosser. Being in the rear guard, the

116th prepared for action and moved in the direction of the cavalry fight. General Sheridan was watching the fight from an elevation called Round Top, a mile of two south of Fisher's Hill. Colonel Wildes described the cavalry action:

> From our position on Round Top both cavalry fights, which were going on at the same time, were in plain view...The low, rumbling, steady roll of resounding hoofs, which fairly shook the earth, the reports of artillery, the explosion of shells and the quick thudding sound of heavy carbine firing, added to which were the cheers and shouts of the pursuing host, combined to form the most animating and exciting scene we ever witnessed. In all our experience and observation in the war, nothing approached the grandeur and sublimity.4

The cavalry battle witnessed by the 116th was officially known as the Engagement of Toms Brook. Rosser's troopers, whom Rosser called the Laurel Brigade, were soundly thrashed and embarrassed—the whole rebel cavalry force was routed and chased for over twenty miles. Early admitted to losing nine pieces of artillery, although it may have been more.5 To the citizens of the vicinity and to the men who fought it, the battle was known as the Woodstock Races. And Old Jube added insult to injury with a remark he aimed at Rosser's brigade, "The laurel is a running vine."6

On the following day, the 116th camped on Fisher's Hill and set pickets. Sheridan sent his army into camp again along Cedar Creek, so the 116th moved across Cedar Creek and camped at Cedar Hill on the eleventh. Thoburn's Division, including the 116th, camped on a long hill about a half-mile east of the Valley Pike crossing of Cedar Creek. (The exact location of the camp at Cedar Hill may have been closer to Cedar Creek initially.) About a mile to the southwest lay the outskirts of Strasburg and farther south loomed the peaks of the massive Massanutten Mountain, green and golden with early autumn foliage.

Elections for state and county offices were held in camp on the eleventh in accordance with a law allowing the many thousands of soldiers from Ohio to participate in elections. President Lincoln, in fact, was very supportive of the soldier vote. General Sheridan and General Crook, both Ohioans, voted with the 36th Ohio Infantry. Most of the soldiers from the 116th were from the same congressional district of Southeastern Ohio. James Morris, a Democrat, was the incumbent. Monroe County usually voted Democratic, and Morris was popular with the 116th. His brother, William T. Morris, had been the major of the 116th, and the congressman had helped recruit the 116th in 1862.

However, Congressman Morris had supported Clement Vallandigham, a vehemently anti-war Democrat and suspected Copperhead. The returns from the 116th for the election were:

$$\text{Plants (Republican) -------- 220}$$
$$\text{Morris, (Democrat) ---------- 70}$$

7

As shown above, the Republican won the regiment's vote by a better than three to one margin. The vote, nevertheless, reflected a limited but continued loyalty to the majority party of Monroe County, in spite of the fact that a vote for Morris was seen as a vote for the Copperheads, fairly or unfairly. Most of the soldiers understood that a vote for the Democrats was an anti-war vote. An entry in Commissary Sergeant Patterson's diary illustrates the soldier's perception of Morris votes: "...Copperhead votes... How strange that Union soldiers will vote to help the rebs."8

A calm seemed to settle on Sheridan's camps at Cedar Creek. On the twelfth the 116th drew rations and loafed around camp while it rained a little. Little Phil fatuously believed that Early and his army were whipped.9 With that in mind he decided that the VI Corps could be spared, and on the thirteenth ordered it to move to the east enroute to Petersburg. Sheridan was now nearly as overconfident as his adversary had been before the Battle of Winchester.

Old Jube, however, was far from ready to quit. Always aggressive, he believed that with the return of Kershaw's troops and a few days rest that his army was again ready for a fight. Early learned that Sheridan was sending part of his army back to Grant, so he moved down the Valley to Fisher's Hill by the thirteenth. By 10 A.M. on the thirteenth, Early had most of his infantry in position at Hupp's Hill, just south of the Federal camps. Sheridan's attention was focused on deciding how to answer General Grant's views regarding a movement against Charlottesville and on to Richmond. Meanwhile, Early was looking and hoping for an opportunity to pounce on Sheridan's army, knowing that one victory would set things right. What followed on the thirteenth was an apparently unintentional clash that took both commanders by surprise.

October 13, 1864, dawned cold, crisp and quiet. No one from the 116th anticipated any activity for the day or anything significantly different from the previous day. At about 2 P.M. the deep boom of artillery sounded from the direction of Strasburg, and shells thudded into the camp of the Third Brigade. Moments later shells were exploding near the camp of the 116th. The sudden incoming shellfire was a surprise to all. One soldier later recalled that nobody thought the rebels were within fifty miles of Strasburg and the shelling was as unexpected as "lightening out of a clear sky."10

Uncle George Crook quickly ordered Colonel Thoburn, whose camp was nearest to the rebel artillery, to send out his First and Third brigades on a reconnaissance to develop the enemy. In pretty short order Thoburn formed his two brigades and sent them off, hoping to add more artillery captures to his division's already impressive tally. The 116th moved out on the left over "a piece of low, open ground, which the batteries swept," steadily advancing while the shells burst overhead and sprayed the earth around them.11 The two brigades moved swiftly across the open ground, crossed Cedar Creek and moved into a line of battle along the Valley Pike. The 116th was on the left of Wells' Brigade on the south of the pike, and the Third Brigade under Colonel Thomas Harris moved toward the batteries from the north of the pike, an interval of about two-hundred yards separating them.12

As Thoburn's two brigades moved over a hill under a steady and accurate artillery fire, a wooded area on a hillside separated them and obscured each brigade from the other. To this point the rebel artillery looked like an easy target for the advancing 116th. But suddenly a large rebel infantry force appeared in the thick underbrush just yards ahead of the First Brigade. The rebels were Conner's Brigade of six South Carolina infantry regiments and the 3rd South Carolina Battalion. Taking cover behind a low stone wall, the 116th and Wells' Brigade fired a searing volley at close range into the approaching South Carolinians. One of the shots brought down General Conner, smashing his knee. Soon his replacement, a colonel, was hit and fell mortally wounded. The rebels were driven back with a major now commanding Conner's Brigade.13

Meanwhile the Third Brigade encountered an overpowering force of rebel infantry preparing to counterattack. The rebels were from General Gordon's rebel division, and Colonel Harris reported, "…it soon became apparent the he (Gordon) was there in such force as to enable him to turn our right…"14 Colonel Harris ordered a withdrawal and sent an officer to inform Colonel Wells that he should also fall back. Unfortunately for the First Brigade, Harris' retreat was rapid and disorganized, giving the rebels a clean shot at the First Brigade's right flank. Apparently, Colonel Harris "…withdrew ere suffering much damage."15

The 34th Massachusetts was holding the right flank of the First Brigade's position along the wall. A belt of woods on the right of the 34th prevented the New Englanders from seeing Harris' rapid retreat, and the messenger sent by Colonel Harris, Lieutenant Ballard, "had his horse shot" and did not manage to reach Colonel Wells with the order to fall back.16 The left wing of the 116th moved out along another perpendicular stone wall to enfilade Conner's rebels and helped drive them back again.

But the 34th was hit on the right flank by the large rebel force that had driven the Third Brigade back. The rebels emerged from the woods unexpected and crushed the right wing of the 34th Massachusetts.

Colonel Wells knew his brigade had to fall back or be surrounded. Wells, a very able soldier, was capable of extracting his men, even with his flank broken. But before Wells could give the order to retreat, a rebel bullet struck him in the chest. Captain Karr of the 116th was on Wells' staff and was present when the colonel fell. A soldier from the 116th recorded the scene:

> When Col. Wells fell he spoke to Capt. Karr and directed him to move the command out of there by the left. The Capt. asked the Col. if he would be able to ride his horse off the field. He made an effort and says I can go no farther, lay me down here in a good place I can live but a little while, my wound is mortal.17

Command of the brigade devolved upon Lieutenant Colonel Wildes, who wrote, "At this juncture, a large force came down upon the left occupied by the 116th, and the whole brigade was driven back amid a furious shower of balls."18 Wildes probably did not have time to assume command when the wave of rebels swept over his flanks. The First Brigade had to run a gauntlet of musket balls and artillery shells across an open field to escape. The survivors gathered in the cover of a wood on the opposite side of the field, and Federal artillery opened on the rebels, bringing a conclusion to the strange and unexpected battle.

General Early arrived at the scene of the fight in time to see Colonel Wells being carried to the rear as a prisoner. The rebels had quickly overrun the place where Wells fell and captured many from the 34th Massachusetts. Old Jube ordered up an ambulance for the colonel, but Wells died as he was being placed in it.19 His body was returned "under a flag of truce and sent to his home in Massachusetts" following the battle.20

The combat was called the Battle of Stickley's Farm, as it was fought near the Stickley house. It is very likely that the entire fight was unintentional, perhaps the result of an over-eager rebel artillery officer. General Early certainly had no purpose for giving away the presence of his army to Sheridan, thus losing the advantage of surprise. Once the rebel artillery drew Thoburn's response, the rebels had no recourse except to send out their infantry to protect the guns.21 After Thoburn's troops withdrew, Early ordered the artillery limbered up and his force fell back to his old fortifications on Fisher's Hill.

The fighting at Stickley's Farm was intense and costly for a reconnaissance. Colonel Harris' uncoordinated withdrawal allowed the

The 116th held a position behind the stone fence shown in the photograph above during the Battle of Stickley's Farm on October 13, 1864. At the time of the battle the area was an open field. Rebel Colonel William Rutherford of the 3rd South Carolina Infantry was mortally wounded when a soldier, probably from the 116th, shot him near this fence. The bullet tore through Rutherford's belt buckle and passed through his stomach. Flanked out of this position, the 116th retreated through a ravine behind and to the left of the regiment. (Courtesy of Rodger Lemley)

rebels to nearly annihilate the First Brigade; casualties in the First Brigade ran three times those of Harris' Brigade. Losses were heaviest on the right of the First Brigade where the 34th Massachusetts was hit by flanking fire, losing over 100 men.22 Casualties for the First Brigade were one officer and fifteen men killed, two officers and sixty-eight men wounded, three officers and seventy men missing for a total of 159. The Third Brigade lost six killed, forty wounded, and four missing for a total of fifty. The combined loss for Thoburn's Division was 209.23 Rebel losses for the battle were twenty-two killed and 160 wounded, including Brigadier General Conner.24 The rebels lost considerably more men wounded than did Thoburn's troops; in all probability, most of the rebel casualties occurred along the wall held by the First Brigade.

Casualties of the 116th were one killed, seven wounded and five captured. The man killed was Corporal Dickerson Archer, 36, of Monroe County. He left a wife and two daughters behind. Archer's remains were later re-interred at Winchester National Cemetery. Casualties for the 116th were as follows:

KILLED.

Corporal Dickerson Archer, Company E.

WOUNDED.

Royal Phelps, Company G; Jesse Frazer, Company G, arm shot off; Corporal James E. Bullock, Company G; Jehiel Graham, Company G, Hip, disabled for life; John W. Hall, Company D, arm; Leroy D. Brown, Company H, knee; John Rush, Company E.

CAPTURED.

Corporal Wm. A. Ferrell, Company D; Samuel King, Company F; First Sergeant Charles A. Cline, Company E; George W. Wiley, Company E; Joseph A. Hall, Company E.25

In effect the Battle of Stickley's Farm was just another costly and pointless sacrifice. At the cost of 209 casualties and the death of perhaps Crook's best brigade commander, nothing was gained except the knowledge of Early's return to the Strasburg vicinity. The 116th had been lucky; fate had selected the 34th Massachusetts for the greatest suffering. A typically laconic diary entry by a corporal in the 116th perhaps best illustrates the view of the men in the ranks: "at ceder hill had a sharp little fight with the Johnneys and was repulsed and had to fall back."26

Nevertheless, Little Phil re-evaluated his perception of the threat posed by Early and his army. Fortunately, he recalled General Wright and the VI Corps; the VI Corps returned to camp on the fourteenth. Sheridan ordered out some of Custer's cavalry and Emory's infantry for a reconnaissance the following day, learning that Early held the high ground south of Strasburg. But Sheridan was being pressured to complete the campaign that General Grant had envisioned since May—the movement against Charlottesville. Asked to meet Secretary Stanton and General Halleck in Washington to discuss Grant's plans, Sheridan decided to leave for Washington on the fifteenth. By then he had dismissed the action at Stickley's Farm as simply a brusque gesture from his feeble rebel opponents. To Sheridan, the more important matter was convincing Washington that his plans for future operations were better than Grant's.

Perhaps Colonel Wildes had a better grasp of the threat Early posed. After the fight on the thirteenth, Wildes knew that Old Jube was totally unpredictable. Wildes had experienced first hand the fury still burning in the rebels. Wildes later wrote of his surprise at the vicious rebel attack, wondering, "what would be the next thing in order for old Early to treat us to."27 He would remain vigilant in the days ahead, watching for the unexpected, unlike the army commander.

Colonel Wildes was now acting commander of the First Brigade, and Captain Wilbert B. Teters, of Company H, commanded the 116th. Teters would remain in command of the 116th until the close of the war. The new CO was not one to shrink from danger. He could be depended upon to lead the regiment into the most trying combat. If anything, Teters may have been over-anxious for opportunities to demonstrate his daring.

Before General Sheridan departed for Washington, he looked over the position at Cedar Creek, hoping to make the position ready in case Early should attack. The Cedar Creek encampment was not a strong position to fight a defensive battle. Still Sheridan decided to send his cavalry off on a raid against the Virginia Central Railroad while he was at the Washington meeting. Shortly after Sheridan left camp, a ruse message from General Longstreet, commander of the rebel I Corps, was intercepted. The message called for Early to join forces with Longstreet for an attack at Cedar Creek. General Wright, who had been left in command at Cedar Creek, forwarded the message to Sheridan. The commanding general decided to return his cavalry to Cedar Creek. Later Sheridan explained that he "abandoned the cavalry raid toward Charlottesville, in order to give General Wright the entire strength of the army, for it did not seem wise to reduce his numbers while reinforcement for the enemy might be near..."28 For some unexplained reason the cavalry, after its return to Wright, was not effectively utilized to guard

Monument to the 34th Massachusetts Infantry at Winchester National Cemetery. A bust of Colonel George Wells, commander of the 34th, tops the monument.

Grave of Corporal Dickerson Archer, Company E, at Winchester National Cemetery. Dickerson Archer was killed at the Battle of Stickley's Farm on October 13, 1864.

the fords of Cedar Creek. This incomprehensible lapse would soon yield disastrous results.

ONE OF ONLY TWO
17

While General Sheridan was away on his trip to Washington to meet with Secretary Stanton, General Early was faced with a difficult decision. For three days following the fight at Stickley's Farm, Early remained at Fisher's Hill "observing the enemy, with the hope that he (Sheridan) would move back from his very strong position on the north of Cedar Creek, and that we would be able to get at him in a different position..."[1] Early was apparently unaware of Sheridan's departure. In fact, as an element of his battle plan he intended to have a brigade of his cavalry (Payne's) attempt to capture Sheridan at his Belle Grove headquarters.[2] Early's greatest concern was what to do with his army. "I was now compelled to move back for want of provisions and forage," wrote Early, "or attack the enemy in his position with the hope of driving him from it, and I determined to attack."[3]

By October first Early was laboring in the Valley under extreme pressure, there were important men clamoring for his replacement. General Lee did not fully appreciate the odds Early was facing, and he hinted that Early should take the offensive. In a dispatch General Lee reminded Early that he had sent reinforcements that weakened his own army with a view of gaining a victory commensurate with the risk to his own situation.[4] Time was running out on Early. He realized that he would have to strike Sheridan's vastly superior force by surprise or fall back and return most of his army to Lee.

On October seventeenth, General Early's most able subordinate, General John B. Gordon, was sent to the signal station on Massanutten Mountain along with Early's topographical engineer, Captain Jed Hotchkiss. After ascending the rugged mountainside, the two men were able to clearly see every detail of the Federal camps and their approaches. General Gordon saw that the Federal left was the weakest defended, and from his lofty observation point he devised a plan to attack it by surprise. Captain Hotchkiss drew a map of the federal camps, and that evening he presented the map and Gordon's findings to Early.

Gordon's plan called for rebel infantry to move along the base of Massanutten Mountain to a ford over the Shenandoah River. The rebel infantry could move unobserved into position to attack the camp of the Second Division of the VIII Corps and move into the rear of Sheridan's army. On the eighteenth Gordon and Hotchkiss found a path to enable the rebel infantry to reach Bowman's Ford and cross the river undetected. General Early approved of the plan and made preparations to attack at Cedar Creek before dawn the next day, October 19, 1864.

Meanwhile the 116th had spent the four days following the Battle of Stickley's Farm in camp at Cedar Hill. On the sixteenth the 116th began building fortifications to protect their camp, although few expected an attack. The mountain and river seemed to make an attack on their camp impracticable. The seventeenth found the 116th still "at Ceder crick and very busy a fortifying..."5 On the eighteenth General Crook sent the Third Brigade under Colonel Thomas Harris out on a reconnaissance towards Fisher's Hill. Harris went only as far as Hupp's Hill and didn't encounter any rebels. Part of Wildes' Brigade also made a reconnaissance on the left, "but no sign of any movement on the part of the enemy was discovered."6

General Sheridan had reached Washington by about 8 A.M. on October seventeenth. There he met with General Halleck and Secretary Stanton until around noon, convincing his superiors that he should build a defensive line to hold the Valley and protect Washington. This would allow him to and return a large part of his army to General Grant.7 Sheridan took two engineer officers with him to plan the defenses and boarded a special train bound for Martinsburg, West Virginia. On the morning of the eighteenth, Sheridan rode south to Winchester, where he and the engineers surveyed the heights around the town as a possible location for his planned defensive line. Receiving information that all was quiet at Cedar Creek, Little Phil spent the night at the Logan house in Winchester.

On the afternoon of the eighteenth, while Sheridan was riding south from Martinsburg, Early perfected his plan of attack and issued his orders. His plan of attack was as follows: Early would personally lead the divisions of Wharton and Kershaw through Strasburg. Wharton would continue north and attack along the pike. Kershaw would move east, cross Cedar Creek at Robert's Ford, and attack Thoburn's First Division at Cedar Hill. Gordon would take the three divisions of the II Corps by his concealed route to Bowman's Ford. In the pre-dawn darkness Gordon's force would cross the Shenandoah and press the attack against the 2nd Division of the VIII Corps. As for his cavalry, Early ordered Rosser to take his brigade and Wickham's north on the Back Road to assail the Federal cavalry on the Federal right. Lomax was ordered to move by way of Front Royal to the Valley Pike and engage the Federals as he found them. Colonel Payne's Brigade would secure the ford in advance of Gordon's attack and then make a rush for Sheridan's headquarters at Belle Grove.8

The speed with which Early's plans were implemented was remarkable, especially when compared to the lumbering pace of Sheridan's attack at Winchester. From the afternoon of the eighteenth to the pre-dawn hours of the nineteenth, Early's men moved to their respective positions to await the pre-arranged time for the coordinated attack. After nightfall on the eighteenth, Gordon began moving his divisions along their concealed path to Bowman's Ford. The II Corps was in position and waiting to cross the Shenandoah hours before dawn. Kershaw's Division was in place and concealed by the trees along Cedar Creek at Robert's Ford, undetected in the darkness. Everything had unfolded according to plan, while Sheridan's Army slept.

With the first easing of darkness on the morning of October 19, 1864, General Joseph B. Kershaw launched his attack at Robert's Ford. Fog wafted up from the creek bottoms in the cold, still air, blanketing the woods and hillsides, spilling over Thoburn's camp. At 5 A.M. only the Second Battalion of the 5th New York Heavy Artillery stood between Kershaw's whole division and the camp of the 116th. The fords and roads along Cedar Creek and the Shenandoah were unguarded except by an occasional vidette and the New Yorkers. Cavalry pickets should have been in place, but they weren't. The "front door" to Sheridan's camps was wide open—Gordon and Kershaw bolted through. Kershaw's men overran the 5th New York Heavies in minutes, with hardly a shot fired. Thus Thoburn's advance guard was gobbled up so fast that an effective alarm wasn't given.

On Gordon's front, Payne's Cavalry bounded across the Shenandoah, scattering the few videttes along the bank. Gordon's divisions quickly followed, splashing across the river and hurrying past Thoburn's camp towards the Second Division camp beyond. About a mile past the ford Gordon brought his fast moving column into line near the Cooley house. From there his men quickly smashed trough the camp of the 9th West Virginia Infantry and pressed on towards Hayes' camps.

According to Colonel Wildes, "Our brigade was aroused by our camp guard, which we never failed to keep, about 4 o'clock, as the rebel columns struck our pickets in our front, when there occurred enough firing to give the alarm."9 Other accounts have Captain Wilkes of the 5th New York Heavy Artillery informing First Brigade Headquarters of suspicious sounds and movements along the creek. Wilkes made a second visit to Wildes after 4:45 A.M. By then Colonel Wildes was getting his men prepared to meet an attack.10 Two other accounts credit Captain Hamilton Karr, of Company G, as being first to give the alarm. Karr himself recalled the events of those pre-dawn hours:

> I have been an early riser all my life, and that morning was up sometime before daybreak, and in the quietude of that hour I heard the slow and careful tread of the rebels forming in line very near and in front of us. I immediately awoke Col. Wildes, the commandant of our brigade. He readily comprehended the

situation, and in the fewest minutes we had our brigade under arms in line of battle.11

Lieutenant Ransom Griffin, also of Company G, noted in a post war account of the battle, "...H. L. Karr, of the 116th Ohio was apparently the first to hear the enemy, and rushing out, had the whole brigade in line, and most gallantly repulsed the enemy."12

According to Colonel Wildes, his pickets were not fired upon, and the rebels advanced so rapidly that only a few shots were fired as the pickets fell back through the fog. Wildes' explanation agrees with the record of Kershaw's orders, which called for no firing until the attack on Thoburn's works.13 As soon as Wildes arose, he ordered the teams hitched and the regimental wagons sent to the rear. His quick thinking saved the 116th's wagons and teams, only "a mule and a few goods" were lost.14 Skirmishers were also sent out over the works to meet the attackers moving silently through the fog.

Wildes sent Captain Karr to division headquarters, and he with Lieutenant Dissoway, of the brigade staff, rode quickly to the Third Brigade camp to give the alarm. Captain Karr rode to find Colonel Harris, the commander of the Third Brigade. He found Colonel Harris sleeping in an ambulance far to the rear of his brigade. When Captain Karr woke Harris and told him of the impending attack, Harris answered, "That cannot be."15 Karr told him, "...you must not doubt or dispute me in such an emergency, but had better stir yourself."16 Colonel Harris did not stir himself in time to reach his command before it was overrun. In his report he suggested that he was unable to reach the front because his headquarters was "some distance to the rear of the works..."17 He did not mention Captain Karr; instead, he reported that he was "...awakened by the report of the firing of our pickets."18 Harris had ample reason not to mention Karr's attempt to awaken him; thus, Karr's account seems more believable. Colonel Wildes was likewise unable to stir Harris' camp: "Seeing we could do nothing with these sleepy fellows, we rode rapidly back to our brigade, which we had scarcely reached before the storm burst in front and on both flanks."19

"The mist and fog was so heavy that you could hardly see the length of a regiment," wrote Wildes.20 When the rebel line appeared through the fog before the 116th, it completely overlapped both flanks. To the right of the 116th, the Third Brigade was in complete chaos. Many of Harris' "half-dressed" men managed to man their works and fire a few volleys, but his brigade soon fled. 21The 34th Massachusetts held the right of the First Brigade, but the panic in Harris' camp allowed Kershaw's men to again crush that regiment's right, as had happened at Stickley's Farm. Soon the Massachusetts men were caught up in the stampede of Harris' troops and flushed to the rear in disorder. There were reports of partially dressed and shoeless men bolting for the rear, many without their guns.22

But Colonel Wildes did not falter, nor did the 116th. The 123rd Ohio was next in line on the right, and the two regiments opened a fierce fire on their front. It was an effective and galling fire that checked the rebels on the brigade's front and allowed the two regiments to fall back in good order. Wildes had made his point to the 116th after the fight at Berryville, and it would not repeat that embarrassing performance. Although constantly pressed on front, flank and rear, the two regiments delivered an effective counter-fire, holding firm to allow the trains to escape. The regiments moved through a ravine behind the camp and reformed in a field beyond. Here they opened fire into the rebels climbing out of the ravine in pursuit, checking them again. The fog was now clearing on the high ground, and the gray light of dawn was overspreading the landscape.

Along the top of the ridge beyond the camp, the two regiments were soon in serious trouble. A large rebel force was pressing from a wood on the left, so Wildes was forced to move off the high ground towards the Valley Pike. Wildes intended to pull back into a wood to the rear to make another stand, but the rebels were already there. "The enemy now pressed us hard until we reached the pike," he wrote, "but not a man broke from the ranks, and we rose on to the pike with a firm line."23

As the 116th emerged onto the pike, the rebel II Corps was smashing Crook's Second Division's camps. Colonel Hayes had some time to prepare for Gordon's onslaught, having heard the firing when Kershaw attacked Thoburn's camp. Despite the additional time to prepare, his division was quickly swept aside and battered, probably worse than Thoburn's was. Fugitives from Hayes' camp tumbled across the pike and across the open field towards Belle Grove; still others fled north along the pike. Most of Hayes' men soon recovered, but they were apparently psychologically beaten and determined to go to the rear.24 Most were through for the day.

Meanwhile General Emory and General Wright met along the Valley Pike on the left flank of Emory's XIX Corps. Emory had just sent Thomas' Brigade from Brigadier General James W. McMillan's Division into the fray to buy time for his corps to meet the rebel onslaught. McMillan's men bravely closed with the rebels in a wood near the place where the 116th emerged onto the pike. In minutes of hand-to-hand combat, Emory's boys were driven back onto the pike, losing nearly a third of their number.25

General Emory saw Colonel Wildes, who reported with his two "battered" Ohio regiments.26 Out of the nine regiments in Thoburn's division only these two, the 116th and 123rd Ohio Infantries, remained intact, and now Emory would have to call upon these stalwart fellows to

Site of the First Brigade camp at Cedar Creek. It was here that the 116th met Kershaw's attack on October 19, 1864.

The ravine where General Wright led the 116th and 123rd Ohio in a desperate charge during the Battle of Cedar Creek.

buy him more time.27 Colonel Wildes "informed him (Emory) of what was coming, and of the situation of affairs on his left."28 Emory did not hesitate to give Wildes his reward for fighting his way through the terrible maelstrom of Kershaw's attack; he ordered Wildes to turn his two regiments around and charge Evans' rebels approaching through a ravine along the pike.

If Colonel Wildes was dismayed, he didn't own up to it. He immediately formed his line for the charge, the 116th on the left. The men pulled their bayonets and attached them to the muzzles of their Springfield Rifle Muskets. Wildes knew what Emory was thinking—the sacrifice of his men to save an army, not unlike the First Minnesota at Gettysburg. It was the supreme test of their mettle, but he and his men really had no other option. "Every officer and man in our little band knew he was going to meet overwhelming numbers in those woods," explained Wildes, "but they never hesitated."29 They had slipped through the rebel horde like wet ice; now they would defy the odds and meet them head on.

Across the pike on their left was the objective, a wooded ravine shrouded in milky fog and gray smoke, crawling with rebels. Wildes moved them out, across the pike and down the steep slope, the men venting their tension with the West Virginia yell. Suddenly a mounted officer galloped out ahead of the two regiments—it was General Wright! The army commander was leading the 116th into the ravine. Rushing through the opaque, foggy air, the two regiments flashed across the bottom of the ravine and scrambled up the opposite slope, their mouths screaming out the yell. "We advanced close to the edge of the woods," remembered Wildes, "where we met with a terrible fire and a counter charge from ten times our number, which swept us back again to the pike."30 A bullet grazed the general just above his chin; blood flowed, matting the whiskers on his chin. He rode back to the pike amid the scrambling debris of Wildes' brigade.

Wildes soon emerged onto the pike, his two regiments having been "dashed to pieces against the strong lines of the enemy in this charge..."31 To the north along the pike fugitives from Hayes' and Kitching's commands were streaming across the plain in the direction of Belle Grove, the imposing gray stone plantation house used as Sheridan's headquarters. The XIX Corps was under heavy attack and was disintegrating all along its line of works. Rebel artillery finally joined in the fray, sending shot and shell into Emory's works. It was probably at about his time that Captain Teters was hit by a shell fragment in his right shoulder. He relinquished command of the 116th to Captain John Hull, of Company K.

The battle had begun less than two hours before, but already about half of Sheridan's Army had been crushed. Most of Crook's Corps was demoralized and scattered, out of action for the rest of the day. Colonel Wildes rallied his two regiments along the pike after escaping the beasts in the ravine. The men had clumped together in groups and squads, and he quickly gathered and organized the survivors into their respective regiments. His command was continually shrinking, like summer hail on warm grass. The 116th had counted 378 officers and men present the previous month. Now probably less than that number from his entire brigade followed him along the Valley Pike.32

"Reaching the pike," recalled Wildes, "our broken ranks rallied, and hearing that General Crook had made a stand at a point near Sheridan's headquarters, a short distance beyond the pike, we fell back there."33 At Belle Grove Wildes found that General Crook and his staff had gathered remnants of the VIII Corps around Sheridan's headquarters. Crook hoped to hold until the trains could carry away the contents of army headquarters. Scores of ambulances and wagons also were gathered at Belle Grove, and this "patchwork" force mentioned by Wildes held until the vehicles were brought off.34 Now the XIX Corps line completely gave way and flowed by the left flank of the 116th through the open fields around the mansion. Wildes described the action at Belle Grove:

> We checked the advance of the enemy, and pushed him back a short distance, and I think the very hardest and most stubborn fighting of the day took place here. We were fighting Kershaw's and Wharton's (Gordon's and Ramseur's) rebel divisions. The proportion of officers to the number of men in our line was very large. Probably not over 1,500 enlisted men of Crook's whole corps were engaged, while there was fully one-fourth that many line and staff officers. A great many line and staff officers took muskets, and lay down in the ranks of the men, while all mounted officers used their holster revolvers. The position was held for over a half hour, which gave time for the trains to move out of the way and Sheridan's headquarters to be emptied of everything of value, and also for the 6th and 19th corps to form a new line further to the rear.35

The army's vehicles, from Belle Grove and from the camps, had to pass through Middletown to escape the rebel tide. As the wagons and ambulances drove through the village, they came under fire from rebel cavalry.36 It was during this action near Middletown that Crook's best division commander was shot. According to a soldier from the 116th who escaped from Thoburn's camp with the train, "Rebel cavalrymen came in to Middletown as the train was passing and fired into it—wounded Lieut. Welches' horse..." He continued, "Col. Thoburn was also wounded here...Dr. Shannon (surgeon of the 116th) was badly wounded there, some think he was shot out of windows & probably Col. Thoburn."[37]

Another account of the Thoburn shooting stated that Thoburn was "assailed in Middletown by the cavalry of the enemy, who from being dressed in our overcoats were enabled to approach him closely without exciting his suspicion, and received a mortal wound."[38] Nearly the entire train managed to get through Middletown to safety, only a few wagons were abandoned when their draft animals were hit by rebel fire.[39]

Back in Winchester General Sheridan had been awakened at about 6 A.M. and informed of the sounds of cannon heard to the south. Sheridan dismissed the noise as part of a reconnaissance scheduled for that morning by the XIX Corps. Sheridan remained in bed but could not sleep. By 8 o'clock he was dressed and eating his breakfast, having ordered his horse saddled and brought up. At this point his army was soundly beaten at Cedar Creek, and he was totally unaware of it. After breakfast he mounted his now famous steed Rienzi and started south, around 9 A.M.

Just south of Winchester Sheridan learned that his army had been attacked and driven back from its camps. Initially Sheridan decided to meet the retreating army at Winchester, rally it, and fight if Early followed.[40] But his pugnacious nature would not allow that. Though not a great tactician, the general was a true "war dog."[41] He would push on to Cedar Creek and determine if his numerically superior army could still win the day. In minutes he was spouting orders, making plans and pushing Rienzi up the pike and into legend.

After Wildes and the 116th were driven back from Belle Grove, the crucial stage of the battle unfolded. Early's rebels had ripped through Crook's camps and completely scattered his corps. Kershaw and Gordon had then blasted the XIX Corps apart. The VI Corps, having ample time to prepare a defense, was next to be hit and driven back. Early's plans had been executed to near perfection, with his divisions striking in concert with overpowering force at each stage of the battle. The rebels had inflicted heavy casualties, concentrating overwhelming firepower in each assault. The Federal Army, essentially an uncoordinated collection of disjointed commands lacking a commander to gather and direct them, was outgunned at each phase of the battle. Early's troops had pushed past Belle Grove into Middletown, securing the village and the pike. At this point Old Jube made a costly mistake.

The thick early morning fog had been a great asset to the rebels, allowing them to hit each Federal position with a degree of surprise. Now the fog was lifting. But combined with the smoke of battle, the fog

Belle Grove mansion on the Cedar Creek Battlefield.

U.S. 3-inch Ordinance Rifle. This type of cannon was used extensively by the Federal Artillery in the Shenandoah Valley.

obscured the alignment of the VI Corps from Early's generals, and they hesitated. Early had two relatively fresh infantry divisions remaining, Wharton's and Pegram's. While the VI Corps was regrouping, after the fight at Belle Grove, Early should have sent Wharton's division through Middletown. Instead, Early used his two remaining divisions to fruitlessly batter the VI Corps. Had Early secured Middletown and the pike beyond, he could have threatened the Federal's rear and controlled their line of communications.42

Retreating to a new defensive line beyond Belle Grove, Wildes noticed that the rebels held Middletown. There in the fields west of Middletown, he encountered Colonel Harris, who had assumed command of Thoburn's First Division. While Wildes and the 116th had spent the hours facing the rebel onslaught time and again, Harris had flowed with the detritus of battle, gathering up squads of men and individuals from Crook's command. General Wright ordered Harris to send his little band of VIII Corps fellows into the fight to help buy more time for the VI Corps to regroup north of Middletown. Colonel Harris spotted Wildes and his remnant from the First Brigade and directed Wildes to "the edge of the woods beyond the ravine in which the Sixth Corps train had become blocked up."43 "Here we had another hard struggle for another half hour," wrote Wildes, "finally being driven back by the masses of the enemy in our front and on our flanks. We now fell back again to the position beyond Middletown, the remnant of our little corps still clinging to the left, which it stubbornly refused to yield amid all the dreadful assaults of the morning, the 6th on our right in the center, and the 19th now on the extreme right of the line."44

By the time the 116th had reached its last position north of Middletown, the tide of battle had turned against the rebels. It was approximately 9 A.M.; General Sheridan was on his way from Winchester. The Federal line would soon stabilize north of Middletown, and the Federal cavalry was finally starting to take part in the main battle. Hundreds and perhaps thousands of Early's famished men were plundering the Federal camps, absenting themselves from the battle lines. Those still at the front were jaded from their overnight march and hours of combat. General Gordon later argued that Early should have continued with an all-out assault during this period, but the state of affairs on the field after 9:30 A.M. contradict Gordon's notion. Early, in hindsight, would have better served his army by collecting his over 1,800 prisoners and twenty-four guns and then falling back to Fisher's Hill.45

Thousands of soldiers remembered witnessing Sheridan's ride. A few men from the 116th later wrote about it. Years after the war Private Moses Edgar, of Company C, recalled the battle and Sheridan's arrival: "By this time we had got broken up, and went behind the Sixth Corps to reform. A squad of my company was standing beside the pike, and I among them, when Gen. Sheridan rode up from Winchester. Some of his staff's horses were falling under them. General Sheridan called to us to 'go back and get ready to thrash them, and that we would sleep in our own tents'."46 The time was approximately 9:45 A.M. Lieutenant Griffin and Captain Karr both reported seeing Sheridan, and Karr noted that the time when Sheridan arrived was not later than 9:30 A.M.47 This was confirmed by a member of the Topographical Engineers, who happened to look at his watch as Sheridan rode through the VIII Corps position. Following Sheridan's escort, he noted that "the General crossed the pike in front of the Second Division of the Sixth Corps at not later than 9:45," although other reports had the time as 10:30 A.M.48

After gathering stragglers, under direction from Colonel Harris, Wildes marched the 116th and the remnants of the First Brigade across the pike to support two batteries. The sound of cheering was audible over the scattered shots and occasional booming cannon, coming from the north and growing constantly louder. It was the voices of the stragglers, the wounded, and the bummers along the pike shouting for joy at the appearance of Sheridan. Soon Sheridan galloped up to General Crook who stood with his shattered corps.

Colonel Wildes, a former newspaper editor, wrote perhaps the best account from the 116th of Sheridan's arrival at Cedar Creek. The following is from his post war history:

> His great black horse, immortalized in song, was covered with flecks of foam and dripping sweat. Throwing the reins from his hand, he jumped to the ground. 'Well, Crook, how is it?' he asked. 'Bad enough, bad enough,' answered Crook, pointing to the hand full left of his corps. 'Well, get ready now, we'll lick them out of their boot yet before night,' was Sheridan's quick reply, as he nervously and vigorously cut off the tops of weeds and grass with his riding whip. Hardly a minute elapsed before he was in his saddle again and off down the line in a hard gallop, the cheers of the men as he passed along telling just where he was. 'We are now going back to our camps, boys.' We'll have all those camps and cannon back.' We'll soon get the tightest twist on them you ever saw.' 'Get ready, boys, to go for them.' 'We'll sleep in our old camps to-night.' Such are some of the quick, crisp sentences he spoke to the men as he passed down the lines.49

A lull settled over the field after Sheridan's arrival. The fog had lifted enough for the rebels to see the Federal positions and that Federal cavalry hovered on their flanks. As the hours passed, Early grew less confident of his ability to push the Federals farther. He still believed the battle was won—that eventually the Yankees would fall back. Past experience favored his line of thinking. However, the battles at Winchester and Fisher's Hill should have initiated Early to the fact that Sheridan was a different kind of animal from what the rebels usually encountered. Somehow Old Jube retained his contempt for Sheridan, and he decided to wait it out. Apparently Early decided to hold his ground in hope of a complete victory, gambling that the Federals would not counterattack.

At about 1 P.M. Early sent the divisions of Gordon, Ramseur and Kershaw against the Federal line, hoping another push might send the Yankees tottering away toward Winchester. But the rebels were spent, and their efforts were feeble. Like a tiring fighter in the late rounds, the rebels were fading while the Federals waxed stronger, preparing for a final surge. The probing attack only served to confirm the reality that Early could not possibly drive the realigned Federals from their position.

After the weak rebel attack was repulsed, before 2 P.M., Sheridan probably wanted to counterattack. However, he continued to make preparations and to wait for his stragglers to come up. Another reason Sheridan delayed was that a report came in that another rebel force believed to be reinforcements from General Longstreet was moving toward Winchester.50 These rebels were apparently Lomax's cavalry, but the report was enough to cause Sheridan to delay his attack.

Colonel Wildes later described the interval before the final attack was made:

> It was wonderful to see the enthusiasm and confidence the presence of Sheridan inspired. There was real magic in it. Up to 4 o'clock all was silence on both sides, and preparation, organization and deep suspense on ours. Sheridan continually rode along the front, studying the ground, encouraging the men, arranging and strengthening the lines. Every minute was adding strength (returning stragglers) to our lines. 52

Finally, around 4 P.M., Sheridan loosed his pent-up army on Early's tired butternuts. The XIX and VI Corps smashed into the strongest rebel positions, while the remnants of the VIII Corps followed on the Federal left. Initially the rebels fought back fiercely from behind stone walls and wooded ridgelines. But when General Custer's cavalry appeared on Early's left flank, the rebels panicked and fled. The fighting was almost a complete duplication of what had occurred exactly one month previously at Winchester. Fearing that the cavalry would ride them down from behind, the rebels broke at a dead run from left to right. One rebel later wrote that the rebel line splintered in a "moment," and the "stampede" was worse than the Federal rout that same morning.52

By 5:30 P.M. the battle had made a complete circuit, it was now the rebels who were running for their lives. Here and there an island of rebel resistance kept the Federals from annihilating Early's shattered army. The infantry followed after the fleeing rebels to Cedar Creek, where the cavalry took up the chase.53 Along the way the 116th moved through the detritus of battle in the fading sunlight. Ghastly corpses, dead horses, broken and shattered vehicles, discarded muskets and the ubiquitous battlefield smoke and trash covered the landscape. The crushed and matted fall grass showed pools of blood and "zigzag trails of blood," and the hard limestone soil would not soak it up to mercifully remove it from view.54

As General Sheridan had promised, the 116th returned to its camp at Cedar Hill that night. The rebels had ransacked the camp, but the 116th was more fortunate than the rest of Crook's troops, because early that morning the men had time to grab their canteens and haversacks. Wildes described the condition of the camp that night, "...our tents, blankets, rations, etc., were gone, the rebels having made clean work of our camps, and no rations came up to us until the next morning, when we ate as hearty a breakfast as we ever did in our lives. We found our dead stripped of their clothing, the hyena conduct of which the rebels were almost universally guilty whenever by fortunes of war our dead fell into their hands."55

Of all the battles in which the 116th fought an assessment of its participation in this battle is most difficult. Several factors account for this. First, Colonel Joseph Thoburn, division commander, was killed, and thus he never wrote an official report for the battle. Second, Colonel Thomas Harris, who succeeded Thoburn and wrote the report for the First Division, was not in a position to observe the 116th during the early phase of the battle. Also it was in Harris' best interest to downplay the part of any unit from the First Division that would compare favorably to the performance of his own brigade. Third, General Crook also did not observe the 116th during its orderly retreat and subsequent charge during the opening phase of the battle.

One fact seems certain: the 116th was one of only two regiments from the First Division to maintain an orderly retreat from Thoburn's camp, and being prepared, offered effective resistance to the rebel attack. Even the 34th Massachusetts, "one of the very best regiments...as steady as a rock in battle," was scattered and sent scurrying from camp, but the 116th held together.56 This fact was substantiated when General Wright found the 116th and 123rd in solid enough condition to lead them in a countercharge after their escape from Thoburn's camp. A correspondent on the scene verified this: "Lieutenant Colonel Wildes, of the 116th Ohio...reported the 116th and 123rd to General Emory, and was sent into the fight, where he and his noble men made a glorious record."57

Casualties at Cedar Creek were heavy. As noted previously, the rebels were able to fight the battle according to their own plan throughout the morning. By deploying superior numbers at the point of attack and by the advantage of surprise, the rebels were able to inflict nearly twice their own casualties upon the Federal Army. The official report of Federal casualties at Cedar Creek totaled 5,665: 644 killed, 3,430 wounded and 1,591 missing.58 Early's army gave up forty-three cannon and suffered at least 320 killed, 1,540 wounded and 1,050 missing, for a total of 2,910.59 Losses in the 116th were miraculously light. The early morning fog, the regiment's effective counter-fire, and the effective guidance of Colonel Wildes combined to save the 116th from severe losses. The numbers reported by Captain Teters in his post action report do not match exactly the numbers given later by Colonel Wildes. However, at least two men from the 116th were killed, two mortally wounded, fifteen wounded and six captured, as listed below:

KILLED.

Francis Caldwell, Company B; David Bruny, Company E.

MORTALLY WOUNDED.

Dr. Thomas J. Shannon, Regimental Surgeon; Aaron Weekley, Company A.

WOUNDED.

Lieutenant Colonel Thomas F. Wildes; Captain W. B. Teters, Company H, shoulder; Lieutenant R. T. Chaney, Company D; Lieutenant J. C. H. Cobb, Company G; Color Sergeant Charles P. Allison, Company K; Corporal Alexander Strait, Company D; Abel C. Barnes, Company C; Milton Mozena, Company C; Robert Carpenter, Company F; James Earley, Company F, left arm (Pension File); James Wilson, Company F; Samuel R. Halliday, Company G; William S. Parrott, Company I; Orlando Griffith, Company K; and Pardon Hewett, Company K.

CAPTURED.

Corporal James H. Stewart, Company B; Daniel Bennett, Company D; John Rawlings, Company G; James Whitman, Company G; Jacob Carpenter, Company H; and William S. Parrott, Company I.[60]

Colonel Wildes would have agreed that the outcome of the Battle of Cedar Creek was changed not by one regiment, but by one man. "Our army," he wrote, "after having sustained a decided defeat, totally routed the victors without receiving any reinforcements, save one man—Sheridan!"[61] It was Jubal Early's misfortune to have misjudged Sheridan by failing to recognize his one salient quality. Early might have been correct in judging Sheridan as his inferior in terms of tactical and intellectual ability, but he failed to comprehend that Sheridan with his huge superiority in men and material would win with dogged determination. Sheridan's battlefield presence inspired his army with confidence, all they needed to defeat "the choice troops of the South, with which General Early had entered the Valley, and threatened Washington in July."[62]

The reputation of the VIII Corps, burnished somewhat by successes at Winchester and Fisher's Hill, lost some of its luster at Cedar Creek. It should be noted, however, that the appearance of General Sheridan reinvigorated the corps later in the morning after its setback. Having served under a succession of uninspiring commanders, it is understandable that the men anticipated defeat after being surprised and routed from their camps. In terms of reputation, the VI Corps benefited most from the fighting at Cedar Creek. While that corps indeed fought splendidly, fate had spared it the surprise battering inflicted on the VIII Corps. Circumstances favored the VI Corps but disadvantaged Crook's boys on October 19, 1864.

In the days following the great battle the 116th remained camped at Cedar Creek. A soldier noted that the men had "lost about all their blankets the morning of the attack and suffer much consequently."[63] Within a few days supplies arrived, and the men were issued new clothing, tents etc. The men did some picket duty and some foraging. The days passed quietly in camp; Sheridan had no intention of following after Early up the Valley. To the ordinary soldiers the days were lost to diary entries such as, "at cedar crick nothing of importance."[65]

Colonel Thoburn's death was a severe blow to Crook's Corps. The able Irishman was well respected and sincerely grieved, as illustrated by Colonel Wildes' tribute:

Captain Hamilton Karr, Company G. (Courtesy of Mark D. Okey)

First Lieutenant John Cobb, Company G. Lt. Cobb was wounded at the Battle of Cedar Creek. (Courtesy of Mark D. Okey)

The greatest loss we met was in the death of Colonel Thoburn. No better or braver officer ever lived. Every man in his division fairly loved him. Firm, yet kind hearted as a child, he impressed every one who met him as an honest, patriotic, Christian gentleman. As a man he drew around him a pleasant circle of friends, constant and affectionate, who deeply and inconsolably mourned his loss. In disposition he was frank, manly, kind, and always cheerful. He was the soul of kindness to those he commanded, and the very soul of honor itself in all the relations of army life. He did not possess an impulsive nature. He was not a thunder-bolt on the field. He was a rock, rather. Fiery floods might break upon him, and yet he was always the same, always cool, strong, intrepid, brave and firm.65

Following the Battle of Cedar Creek, General Grant informed Sheridan that he wished him to immediately move against the Central Railroad, saying that he believed that cutting off Southwest Virginia from Richmond was of "great importance."66 Sheridan, however, believed that Early had been reinforced, and he did not believe he could make the march because of supply difficulties. Again Sheridan's views prevailed. The Federal Army of the Shenandoah would return to Winchester and establish a defensive position there. There would be no campaign to fulfill Grant's objectives planned since spring.

On October twenty-sixth Colonel Washburn, as mentioned in a previous chapter, visited the 116th and was warmly received. The regiment held a dress parade in his honor, and a message from the colonel was read to during the proceedings. Colonel Washburn stayed with the regiment for several days, but he was not sufficiently recovered form his terrible wound to resume field duty. He was assigned by General Sheridan to command the Post at Wheeling, West Virginia.

On Tuesday, November 8, 1864, the last day that the 116th camped at Cedar Creek, the regiment voted for President. Apparently several men had returned to the regiment during its stay at Cedar Creek, as 462 men voted. Abraham Lincoln received 374 votes, and George McClellan received eighty-one from the 116th.67 The candidates did not excite everyone, as is always the case in elections, as indicated by one soldier's diary entry: "The polls opened at headquarters of the O.V.I. parts of four Rgts. Voted here. I did not vote at all, but I was almost forced to vote for Abe."68

The following day the 116th broke camp and began the retrograde movement to Winchester. Fighting in the Shenandoah Valley was finally over for the 116th. Early's army would be returned to Lee in increments until it no longer posed a threat to Washington. General Sheridan intended to fortify the Winchester vicinity sufficiently and then return much of his army to Grant at Petersburg. The Battle of Cedar Creek brought a decisive and conclusive victory for the North in the Shenandoah. Soon the 116th would move on to the final fighting of the war.

ANSWERING GRANT'S CALL
18

As the 116th marched away from Cedar Creek on November 9, 1864, the war had passed its zenith and now entered its terminal phase. Everywhere the Confederacy was in decline, soon to meet its nadir. Sherman was preparing for his March to the Sea, where he would cut a swath of destruction through Georgia and later through the Carolinas. Sheridan's victories had deprived the bounty of the Shenandoah from Lee's army. Yet perhaps most devastating to the rebel cause was Abraham Lincoln's re-election that November.

The Lincoln Administration won re-election by only a fifty-five percent majority in the loyal states. Despite the relatively close margin, only three participating states, Delaware, Kentucky and New Jersey, voted against him. Thus, Lincoln won by the huge majority of 212 Electoral votes to twenty-one. The President did much better with the soldiers, winning seventy-eight percent of their votes. With an almost uncanny coincidence, the 116th voted the exact same proportion as the rest of the Federal Army, twenty-two percent for McClellan.1

Stopping at Newton for the night, the 116th continued to Kernstown on the tenth and went into camp at that place, just south of Winchester. Some of the men had been expecting, indeed hoping, that the army would go into winter quarters since September. Having whipped Early three straight times, the men probably expected a hiatus for a few months from active campaigning. But Old Jube somehow managed to march down the Valley once more to probe Sheridan's positions. On the eleventh and twelfth the men heard skirmishing as Early's cavalry felt Sheridan's lines.2 "Discovering that the enemy continued to fortify his position," wrote Early, "and not being willing to attack him...I determined to retire, as we were beyond the reach of supplies."3

November 12, 1864, proved to be the last threatening day for the 116th in the Shenandoah Valley. For the next five weeks the 116th would enjoy a much-needed respite, performing picket and guard duty near Winchester. Early fell back to New Market, where Kershaw's Division returned to Richmond on the fifteenth. Three weeks later General Gordon took his division and Pegram's to Waynesboro to board trains for Petersburg. Later Bryan Grimes would take Ramseur's old division, the last troops of the great rebel II Corps, back to Lee.4 It seemed obvious that Sheridan would not advance on Lynchburg, so Early was left with a token force in the Upper Valley—no threat to Washington.

The 116th idled at Kernstown for several days. On the sixteenth the First Brigade held its first dress parade since Sigel's leather britches days. The previous six months had been one continuous blur of battles and enervating marches, with no opportunity for military routines. On the eighteenth, as the regiment prepared to move again, Rev. E. W. Brady resigned from the chaplaincy. Private James Logan of Company C, who was also a minister, was chosen by the regiment and commissioned by the Governor as the new chaplain. The Rev. Logan had distinguished himself by volunteering to carry the colors in battles when the color bearer had fallen, and he held the respect of the men in the ranks. Reverend Brady had served the 116th well, officiating for religious services, tending the wounded, helping at the hospitals, and serving as regimental postmaster. He left the 116th with the best wishes of the officers and men.

The First Brigade moved out of Kernstown on the eighteenth, marching to Opequon bridge to guard the railroad and bridges there. Before leaving Kernstown the men of Company I had "raised a subscription, and sent it to Mrs. Matilda Secoy," widow of Lewis Secoy of Company B who was killed in the Battle of Opequon on September nineteenth.5 Along the Opequon the days were passed with camp life and picket duty. Many of the men no doubt went foraging when the opportunity presented itself. Thanksgiving Day, November twenty-fourth, was memorable, because a shipment of 10,000 turkeys arrived by rail that day from Ohio and New York. "The train stopped at our depot to-day," wrote one soldier from the 116th, "and put off 1,000 pounds of turkeys for this brigade..."6

Rainy and cold weather soon set in, and the men went to work building log huts to shelter themselves for the winter. Before long the camp had assumed the proportions of winter quarters as if the men expected to stay. November passed into December with only picket duty and camp routine to occupy the troops. One soldier wrote in his diary on December fourteenth, "I pass away my idle time reading novels, which relieves the monotony and dread which belongs to camp life."7 November was the first month since April that the 116th did not see battle and casualties. But the 116th was not destined to enjoy the garrison life and log huts for long.

News of General Thomas' victory over Hood at Nashville was celebrated by firing a grand salute on December seventeenth. Sheridan had begun sending his army back to Grant in December, because Early had already sent Kershaw's Division away. By mid December the VI Corps had been returned to Petersburg. On December 18, 1864, orders arrived directing the 116th to prepare to march on the morrow. General Grant called for "the best division in Crook's Corps" to move at once to join the campaign around Richmond with the Army of the James, "and in compliance with this order the 1st was selected."8 The sudden change of plan was not all that well received by everyone, as recalled by Thomas Wildes:

> What hardships the men of this division had endured in this Valley of Virginia. How often had its soil been baptized in the blood of its bravest and its best. What severe defeats they had sustained and what glorious victories they had achieved upon its soil. Scores of its best men were to be left behind in sanctified graves. From the Heights of Bolivar to the environs of Lynchburg, the roadsides, fields and forests were dotted with the burial places of its noble dead. In the hospitals of the army, lay hundreds of its maimed and disabled, and Oh, how many languished, worse than dead, in Southern Prisons! How faithfully had its men fought for the success of the great cause of Liberty and Union in this bloody Valley. Is it any wonder, then, that protests were entered to its removal? Not from its officers or men, but from army commanders and the authorities of West Virginia. Strong protests against its removal from the field upon which it had achieved its renown were sent to General Grant and the authorities at Washington. It was urged that this division was more familiar with the Valley than any troops in it, was better acquainted with its people and their character, had become identified with it in every sense more closely than any troops that ever occupied it.9

The orders, however, would stand. On December 19, 1864, the 116th broke camp and moved to Harper's Ferry, and there the regiment again filed into cars for another train ride, not knowing exactly the destination. Some of the men wondered if the train would move east or west. The men waited until after dusk to get their answer; the train chugged off toward Washington. The entire First Division of the VIII Corps followed to Harper's Ferry, with the First Brigade, Wildes', being in advance and first to board cars.

Darkness set in shortly after the train pulled out of Harper's Ferry, and then the suffering began. Many of the men remembered this train ride as the worst of the war, surpassing even the ride from Parkersburg when fires were set in the cars to warm the men. It was damp, cold and very windy, and the men rode in boxcars and open cattle cars with no heat. Fortunately the ride to Washington was a short one, less than eighty miles. Reaching Washington in the predawn darkness, the men shuffled, cold and numb, off the train and formed ranks for the march across town. Wildes marched his brigade to the Potomac River landing where transports were waiting.

At the landing the 116th embarked on the *Lizzie Baker*, the 123rd Ohio and brigade headquarters on the *Keyport*, and the 34th Massachusetts on the *Massachusetts*. All three vessels were sidewheel steamers prepared as troop transports. The 5th New York Heavy Artillery, 2nd Battalion, formerly of the First Brigade, did not accompany it to the Army of the James. Most of the battalion had been captured at Cedar Creek, and a replacement battalion from the regiment was not sent forward. Thus, the First Brigade had only three depleted regiments when it left the Shenandoah for the Army of the James.

After loading and getting underway without delay, the transports steamed down the Potomac to Point Lookout, Maryland. There the captain dropped anchor, and the little flotilla spent the night off shore. A severe storm was brewing, and with dawn the conditions worsened. After delaying until almost noon, the captain steamed into the storm and turned south. Large waves driven by fierce, cold winds battered the transports. Soon the Buckeyes were "green to the gills" and fearing for their lives as the transports rolled violently through the pounding swells. Colonel Wildes, as brigade commander, was concerned for the rest of his troops, especially the 123rd Ohio aboard the older and less seaworthy *Keyport*. As twilight set in, and with the storm unabated, the captain hove to in the mouth of a creek south of Rappahanock. An U.S. Navy gunboat on patrol fired a shot across the bow of a transport, startling the already unnerved soldiers. But after pulling alongside, the Navy officers invited Wildes and his headquarters staff aboard for supper, which they gladly accepted.

Early the next morning the transports again sailed into the storm and endured a worse battering than the previous day. The *Massachusetts* disappeared in the haze and was not seen again that day. Even the crew of the *Keyport* became concerned; the vessel " was in real danger of foundering several times."10 The trip from Washington to City Point should have taken about one day, but the heavy weather had already consumed two days when Fort Monroe came into view. In smoother waters now, the transports passed the fort and steamed up the James River to within a few miles of City Point, where the captain dropped anchor for the night.

Finally on the twenty-third, the 116th debarked at James Landing, no doubt thankful to be on firm ground. The 116th crossed the wide James on a pontoon bridge and then marched to Camp Holly at Deep Bottom. This would be their camp while with the Army of the James, XXIV Corps. Still missing was the 34th Massachusetts, and some of the men from the 116th who were mistakenly put aboard ship with the Bay State boys. No word had yet been received of their fate; Wildes and his men worried that the *Massachusetts* had foundered in the storm.

That first night on the James was miserable, as the men had to sleep on the ground without tents. Since leaving their comfortable quarters along the Opequon, the 116th had endured nothing but hardship, severe enough to threaten health. In the morning the quartermaster and his staff were sent scurrying for rations and supplies. The men went to work building quarters and had them under construction when the 34th Massachusetts arrived. The *Massachusetts* had been driven into Cherry Stone Inlet during the storm, delaying her arrival for two more days.

"The Massachusetts men were not so handy with the axe, shovel and trowel as our western troops," wrote Colonel Wildes, "and made the erection of quarters irksome work. Our men were always ready to help them on such work, for they were good fighters, and for that our men liked them."11 The camp was situated on the Libby Plantation: the same Libby whose warehouse was used as a prison for Yankee officers. On the grounds where Libby's house once stood, the regimental quartermaster built his winter quarters.

On Christmas Day the men continued their building, carrying logs to camp, digging their floors, setting the logs in place, etc. There apparently was no time or opportunity to celebrate the holiday, and that evening the rebels probed the picket lines, probably in an attempt to determine who the new troops were. The brigade was sent into the works prepared for an attack most of the night. A reconnaissance went out the following morning, finding that the rebels had withdrawn. News came of Sherman's capture of Savannah on the twenty-sixth, for which salutes were fired, probably into the rebel works. The rebels responded and a heavy artillery duel ensued, lasting all day and night. Again the regiment was under arms and in line of battle on the twenty-eight, but nothing came of it.

After that first week in camp conditions calmed, and the 116th settled into a routine very different from the previous six months. Finishing their winter huts, the men then turned to improving the camp. There were many more inspections than before and some occasional drill. General Grant was a believer in keeping the men occupied during lulls, so there was considerable fatigue duty done along the James, mainly road work, cutting trees and corduroying roads. Major General John Gibbon had been appointed commander of the XXIV Corps, to which the 116th was now attached. He was a thoroughly professional soldier, already known for being largely responsible for the fame of the Iron Brigade, which he once commanded. The General visited the 116th for inspection and was very complementary of its orderly camp and the soldierly bearing of its officers and men.

Some officers received promotion just before New Years Day. The promotions were as follows: Captain W. B. Teters, to Major; First

Lieutenant J. Cobb, to Captain of Company H; Second Lieutenant Ransom Griffin, to First Lieutenant; and Second Lieutenant Wm. Biddenharn, to First Lieutenant. Company A was detailed to division headquarters on January ninth as provost guard, and Captain Mallory of that company was assigned as Provost Marshall. A soldier noted that, "General Grant rode through our camp" and that there was "great cheering at the fall of Fort Fisher," on January seventeenth.12 The cheering occurred when the regiment was assembled and read the news about the long awaited capture of Fort Fisher, which closed the Port of Wilmington and all foreign trade to the South. Doctor James A. Sampsell joined the 116th as an assistant surgeon two days later.

General Gibbon initially was prejudiced against volunteer troops, disliking their lack of discipline. By this stage of the war, however, he had long since learned to respect and motivate them. Under Gibbon there were many inspections, and there was an incentive introduced to motivate the men and spur competition. "Under a corps order," wrote Colonel Wildes, "our brigade had been competing for the first place in the corps in everything pertaining to the soldier."13 An inspection held on January twenty-second named the 116th the best in the First Brigade of the Provisional Division, XXIV Corps. The men were excused from fatigue and picket duty for one week—the incentive. Other recognition and rewards were given for the best man in the brigade, division and corps. Company B's Corporal James Stout was named best man in the 116th.

Two days later, January 24, 1864, a rebel gunboat flotilla sallied forth in an attempt to destroy the transports and base at City Point. According to an account by Colonel Wildes:

> It was a close call for the Army of the James, for had the rebel ironclads not grounded, the entire fleet of transports at City Point might have been sunk and the base of operations destroyed, in which event the Army of the James and Fort Harrison would have been isolated from the forces on the south side and greatly endangered...A large force of rebel infantry lay waiting in our front to attack and 'wipe us off the map,' had the ironclad expedition been successful. In failing, all soon became quiet on the James.14

At 9 A.M. on the twenty-fifth, General Harris, acting division commander, held yet another inspection. The 116th was declared best regiment in the division. Again the men were excused from fatigue and picket duty, this time for two weeks. As part of the festivities the regimental band of the 34th Massachusetts gave a serenade for the officers of the 116th. The numerous inspections were only possible

Corporal James Stout, Company B. Corporal Stout was named the best soldier in the 116th and the entire XXIV Corps during inspections at Camp Holly. (Courtesy of Mark D. Okey)

because the camp was much less subject to enemy fire and attack compared to the lines around Petersburg. Corporal James Stout, already named best man in the 116th, came out of a Sunday inspection on the twenty-ninth as best man in the entire XXIV Corps. Stout was given a thirty-day furlough and permission to take his gun and accoutrements home with him. Despite its earlier reputation as a ragged and poorly drilled unit, the 116th had proved that now, under equal circumstances, it was among the best of the veteran regiments in soldierly bearing, adding less meaningful laurels to its already established reputation as a gallant and dependable combat regiment.

Several officers resigned around the first week of February, opening several vacancies for promotions. Captains Dillon, Chaney, Cochran, and Adjutant Ballard all left the army at nearly the same time. Also Lieutenant Sibley, who had finally been exchanged from captivity and was in poor health, resigned. On February fifteenth Lieutenant Wilson S. Martin was promoted to Captain of Company F, taking Mathew Brown's place. Rees Willams, who had been severely wounded carrying the colors at Piedmont, was promoted to First Lieutenant of Company F. Sergeant William H. Bush was promoted to Second Lieutenant of Company B. Sergeant John Heald was promoted to Second Lieutenant of Company C, and Sergeant Charles A. Cline was promoted to Second Lieutenant of Company B.

News of the Thirteenth Amendment to the Constitution being forwarded for ratification reached the 116th in early February. Unlike the dissatisfaction so apparent when the Emancipation Proclamation was introduced, the soldiers this time celebrated this final solution to the divisive slavery issue. By this late in the war, most soldiers realized that as long as slavery existed there could never be peace. "The theme of punishment for treason became more pervasive as the war dragged on," so it seemed the best way to end the war was to "hurt the instigators and abettors of it," the slaveholders.15 "Everyone," wrote Wildes, "was ready to adopt measures that would forever put an end to American slavery, and was glad steps to that end were being taken. Salutes were fired, and officers and men cheered, shook hands, pulled and jerked each other about and fairly danced for joy."16

On February sixth Lieutenant Colonel Wildes, Major Teters, and Quartermaster Sergeant Walker left for home on furlough. Only Major Teters would return to the 116th. Thomas Wildes was to be promoted to Colonel of a new Ohio Infantry regiment, the 186th, then organizing at Columbus, Ohio. Wildes would take several good men from the 116th with him, including Quartermaster Sergeant Walker, who was promoted to quartermaster of the new regiment. Wildes was promoted to Colonel of the 186th on February 26, 1865, and on that day Teters was promoted to Lieutenant Colonel of the 116th in Wildes' place. The new Lieutenant Colonel returned to camp on the twenty-seventh in command of the 116th. So the gallant and able Wildes, who had led the 116th through its most trying times, moved on to a much more innocuous command, missing the last great battles of the war.

An unfortunate accident claimed the life of John A. Dennis, of Company I, on February 10, 1864. At Chapin's Farm, John Dennis was killed when a tree fell on him. Dennis was known as a good soldier who had always performed well, so it seemed especially hard that he would survive so many battles only to die in an accident. He was initially buried at nearby Fort Harrison.

When deaths occurred while the regiment was in camp, a letter would often be sent to the dead man's kin informing them of the circumstances. Sometimes the soldier's known relative was serving in the army; therefore, soldiers would receive as well as sent notices of deaths. Corporal Benjamin F. Dye, of Company A, received such a letter concerning his brother, Joshua, serving in another Ohio regiment. Dye's letter serves as a good example of how death notification letters were written. The following is an excerpt from Dye's letter:

> Joshua took sick when he was on Folly Island, but was getting better when he came on this (Morris) island. He went on duty too soon and in a few days was taken down again. That was about the first of August. We took him to the Regiment Hospital where he remained until the 21st of September when he came back to the company. We all thought he was going to get well. He stayed in the Company about 10 days when he was taken down again and had to go to the Hospital again for the third time. His disease was chronic diarrhea. The last time he was taken to the Hospital he took eripipelas. That and the above diseases took him from this vain world.
>
> Before he died he sent for me to come down to the Hospital which I did. He gave me his money which was $54.50. I asked him what he wanted me to do with it. He told me to send it to his Mother which I will, I will es press it in care of John Way in Woodsfield.
>
> Joshua was by rank a corporal. He was interred this morning at 9 o'clock with all honors due his rank. May his soul rest in peace and green be the grass that grows over his grave. He was a good soldier and respected by all his comrades and his loss is much regretted in the Company.17

The Southern Confederacy was in its death throes while the 116th camped along the James. Rebel deserters were crossing the picket lines in large numbers during the nights to give themselves up. In South Carolina Sherman's Army wreaked havoc, capturing Columbia and marching through the country at will. Charleston, South Carolina, the very birthplace of secession, also finally fell to Federal occupation. With news of each victory, the Federal guns would blast the rebels with a salute, bringing an angry response along the picket lines. By early March, General Lee was seeking a means of slipping away from the siege that encumbered his army. Lee called for General John Gordon, who now commanded the old II Corps that had followed Early in the Valley, and asked him to find a weak place in the Federal lines around Petersburg. Lee wanted to punch through and send a portion of his force to help General Johnston defeat Sherman. Ultimately, Lee hoped to unite his forces with Johnston to "deal with Grant."18 It was a last desperate bid, a forlorn hope, to stave off ultimate surrender at Petersburg.

While General Gordon was searching for an opportunity to attack at Petersburg, General Grant made preparations to finish off Lee's weakening army. In mid-March the commander in chief and Secretary of War Stanton reviewed the Army of the James. To the soldiers of the 116th the review must have seemed like a mass spectacle, the largest review they had yet seen. Within a few days Lincoln would travel to City Point to meet with Grant. The Administration needed to prepare for the obviously imminent collapse of Richmond and the war's conclusion. On March eighteenth, six officers from the 116th were promoted as follows: First Lieutenant John C. Heuthorn, to Captain of Company E; First Lieutenant Wm. Mosley, to Captain (not mustered); First Lieutenant John S. Manning, to Captain (not mustered); Second Lieutenant Charles Allison, to First Lieutenant (not mustered); Second Lieutenant Wm. J. Lee, to First Lieutenant; Second Lieutenant Joseph Purkey, to First Lieutenant.

"A MOST MURDEROUS FIRE"
19

On the evening of March 18, 1865, General Grant sent a message to General Edward O. C. Ord, commander of the Army of the James, informing him that General Sheridan had reached White House that day, returning from the Shenandoah Valley. As usual, Little Phil wasn't following his commanding general's wishes. General Grant had ordered Sheridan to destroy the Virginia Central Railroad and the James River Canal, attempt to capture Lynchburg, and then join General William T. Sherman somewhere in the Carolina's.1 As usual, Sheridan had won a victory, this time over the skeletal remnant of Early's army at Waynesboro, and then followed his own whim. His cavalry destroyed part of the railroad and canal as instructed by Grant, and then Sheridan decided to ride to White House, hoping to "take part in the final struggle of the war."2

Grant wasn't greatly displeased with Sheridan's decision to return to him rather than joining Sherman as instructed. He decided to wait for Sheridan's cavalry to join his army for operations south of the James. The rebels were also aware of Sheridan's approach, so General Ord was ordered to provide cover for Sheridan's weary troopers. Grant's message informed Ord that Sheridan would spend several days at White House to shoe up his animals and concluded with the following orders: "I want you to hold the crossings of the Chickahominy...It will probably be well for you to send a division of troops to meet Sheridan...If you deem a little infantry necessary for the support of your cavalry you may send it."3

Having idled for nearly three months at Camp Holly, the 116th finally broke camp on the morning of March twenty-fifth to fulfill Grant's orders concerning Sheridan. In company with Turner's Independent Division of the XXIV Corps, entrenching tools and a pontoon train, the 116th marched to the Charles City road. Cavalry was posted thickly along the route, which took the 116th through dense evergreen forests and past some of McClellan's battlefields to the Chickahominy. That afternoon the pontoon engineers went to work constructing a bridge over the river. A portion of Sheridan's force soon arrived and crossed over the pontoon bridge. Sheridan himself did not appear, much to the disappointment of the veterans of the Army of West Virginia, having crossed at a point down river.

That same day General Lee attempted to batter his way through the Federal lines at Petersburg. General Gordon, apparently believing as he did at Cedar Creek that an attack would always bring victory, devised and led the rebel assault on the Federal IX Corps lines at Fort Stedman. In this operation General Lee made a maximum effort, but the rebels were easily repulsed with heavy losses. Lee now realized that Petersburg was doomed; he would soon have to evacuate Richmond and Petersburg and attempt to join General Joseph E. Johnston somewhere farther south.

The following morning the 116th counter-marched to the James and went into camp for the night at Deep Bottom Landing. Rather than simply capturing the rebel capital, General Grant was determined to destroy Lee's army at Petersburg, so now with the arrival of spring he put his plans into operation. Grant would use General Warren's V Corps and General Humphrey's II Corps to flank the rebels southwest of Petersburg, "forcing them to come out of their trenches to protect their rear and the Southside Railroad."4 General Ord was instructed to send two divisions of General Gibbon's XXIV Corps and a cavalry division across the James to a position southwest of Petersburg. Once there, Ord's troops would man the lines vacated by the II and V Corps. The 116th would be among the troops sent south of the James.

On Monday March 27, 1865, the 116th began its final campaign that would culminate in the surrender of Lee and the Army of Northern Virginia. Before taking up the march, the men "stripped for battle, casting aside everything not absolutely necessary."5 The 116th had *never* marched so light, not even during the chase after Early's troops following the Washington raid. Commencing at about sunset, the 116th embarked on what General Gibbon called "one of the most remarkable marches on record, with very few stragglers."6 Crossing the James on pontoons near Deep Bottom, the 116th followed the river before turning right, entering a dense pine forest. Fires at intervals lit the pathway for the soldiers as they splashed along the muddy roads all through the night. Well before dawn the 116th crossed the Appomattox, probably on a pontoon bridge just below the Point of Rocks. The march continued until about 4 A.M., when the column halted along the Petersburg front. Despite the spiteful racket of a lively picket fight, the weary soldiers slept on the ground for three hours before resuming the march.

During the morning of the twenty-eighth, the 116th marched past the earthworks and forts of Petersburg. The regiment crossed paths with Sheridan's resting cavalry, passed General Meade's headquarters and went into camp beyond the Weldon Railroad at Fort Siebert, a distance of over fifteen miles. At daybreak on the twenty-ninth the 116th and Gibbon's other troops marched into the lines near Humphrey's Station, relieving the II Corps. Three officers from the 116th were promoted that day, but of the three only Richmond Knowles was mustered, as Captain of Company I. Knowles replaced Captain Alexander Cochran, who after finally being exchanged from rebel prison had been discharged in

February.

The weary march to the Petersburg trenches freed the V Corps to move against the rebel right. General Sheridan's cavalry was marching toward Dinwiddie Court House in conjunction with the V Corps operation. General Lee learned of the Federal movements, and "he was instantly aware of what they portended."7 Sheridan's cavalry could move against the South Side Railroad and in one movement cut off Lee's last supply line and his escape route. Lee could not evacuate his lines without a fight, so he sent Major General George Pickett's division and a 5,500 man cavalry force commanded by Major General Fitzhugh Lee to meet the new threat developing southwest of Petersburg.

Fighting began on the twenty-ninth that would continue until the rebels were driven out of Petersburg and Richmond. At about 5 A.M. on March thirtieth, the 116th with Turner's Division crossed Hatcher's Run to link up with a division from the II Corps.8 With Harris' Third Brigade connecting with the II Corps troops and the 116th with Potter's First Brigade on the right, Turner's division probed the approach to the rebel lines throughout the day. The skirmishing continued at a lively pace all day, a few men from the 116th being wounded.

Despite drenching downpours that hampered movements throughout the area of operations, the fighting intensified on the thirty-first. Early that morning the 116th along with Potter's and Harris' brigades attacked the rebel pickets along Hatcher's Run. Fighting over difficult terrain, through soggy woods filled with quicksand traps, Turner's men captured scores of rebels and drove their entire picket line into its works. "This was very gallantly done," wrote General Turner, "...giving us a very important advantage."9 By afternoon the 116th was within rifle range of the rebel works; by evening Turner's men had completely silenced the rebel artillery. General Ord reported to Grant that his men had captured 189 prisoners and two officers.10

Immediately after driving in the rebel pickets, Turner's men dug in, fortified and prepared for a battery to come up to exploit their gains. Although the 116th had accomplished everything General Ord had expected, the general remained cautious. In a message to General Grant, Ord reported that, "None of my officers have yet seen the enemy's line on account of swamps and woods and the quicksands, and the only approachable place on their front is reported impracticable as yet for artillery required to open passage."11 Grant understood Ord's situation and noted, "The quicksands of this section exceed anything I have ever seen."12

The two days of fighting along Hatcher's Run had cost the 116th eleven casualties. Below is a list of the men killed and wounded from the 116th on March 30 and 31, 1865:

KILLED.

John E. Smith, Company E.

MORTALLY WOUNDED.

Emanuel Byers, Company C.

WOUNDED.

Eranstus H. White, Company B; Corporal Abner G. Carlton, Company C; John M. Carlton, Company C; Andrew J. Morris, Company C; Jos. S. Johnson, Company C; James Agin, Company D; James A. Strong Company G; Minor Starkey, Company F; George Beach, Company I. 13

Although Corporal Abner Carlton was listed as wounded, his muster out file noted that he was wounded in his right foot at Hatcher's Run while cutting timber for breastworks on March 31, 1865. The wound was serious enough for Carlton to be sent to the General Hospital at Fortress Monroe, where he was discharged.

General Ord contemplated an assault against the rebel works on Turner's front to be carried out near dawn on April first. General Gibbon did not think the rebels would be inclined to allow Turner's force to retain its advantageous position, and General Wright forwarded a message to Ord that seemed to confirm Gibbon's assessment. Wright's message informed General Ord that the rebels had been strongly reinforced. "Possibly this concentration," he wrote, "may be to attack your front."14 To prepare for an assault on the rebel lines on the first, General Turner ordered Captain Mann of Company C to take a select group of forty men from the 116th for the purpose of cutting through the abatis fronting the rebel works. On the evening of the thirty-first, Captain Mann was summoned to Turner's headquarters and given his instructions. At about midnight the captain and his detail slipped into the darkness beyond the skirmish line to remain in concealment until the designated time for the assault.

A heavy artillery bombardment commenced after 10 P.M. and continued until about 4 A.M. on the first. Soon after the guns fell silent, a large rebel force appeared out of the darkness in front of Foster's Division and went crashing through the lines of Dandy's Brigade. Apparently the rebels decided to strike the XXIV Corps before Ord could mount an attack on them. Foster's Division was taken by surprise and was nearly routed. Turner's men were ready and instantly counterattacked the impetuous rebels. The 116th drove the rebels out of Dandy's works, sending the graybacks scurrying into the swampy woods beyond. A heavy artillery and musketry fire ensued along the XXIV Corps lines where Captain Mann and his brave forty had been concealed since midnight. "The battle raged right over the prostrate forms of the Captain's detail, many rebels being killed and wounded right among his men. They hugged the ground closely throughout the struggle, and when the rebels were repulsed," Mann and his men returned to the 116th "where they were greeted as if they had risen from the dead."15

General Ord reported the morning's results to General Grant, who could hear the firing from his headquarters near Gravelly Run. Ord mentioned that, "On Foster's front our pickets gave way and we lost 8 men. Turner's men behaved handsomely."16 He also reported that the rebels lost sixty men captured and several killed and wounded in the assault. The 116th, which charged into the rebels, had seven men slightly wounded. The names of the wounded from the 116th were not recorded, but James Earley of Company F may have been one of those wounded on the first. His pension file listed a wound of his side received in April 1865 at Hatcher's Run. Ord again reported to Grant, mentioning that his losses since arriving at Hatcher's Run amounted to 240 killed and wounded; the rebels had lost 300 prisoners and a number of killed and wounded.17 General Grant reported the morning's events to President Lincoln, who had arrived at City Point a few days before. He mentioned that Ord's losses during the fighting that morning were thirty killed and wounded, and that the rebels lost sixty men captured.18

There is no doubt that the 116th, and for that matter the entire First Brigade, impressed General Gibbon that day. Gibbon had the following message forwarded to General Turner's headquarters: "The major-general commanding desires that you express to Colonel Potter his satisfaction for the gallantry displayed by himself and troops this morning."19 Potter, of the 34th Massachusetts, had superseded Colonel Wildes in March as commander of the First Brigade. General Ord had basically reported Turner's success to General Grant, but it was Gibbon who realized that Potter's regiments were most worthy of praise. The First Brigade and the 116th, not surprisingly, had upheld the reputation earned in the Valley and carried it on after the departure of Colonel Wildes.

While Gibbon's men sparred with the rebels in the trenches near Hatcher's Run, General Sheridan fought and won a decisive battle a few miles west at Five Forks. The V Corps and Sheridan's cavalry combined to rout the force General Lee had sent to protect his right flank. The defeat was so severe, and the stakes so high, that a rebel captain described the battle as "the Waterloo of the Confederacy."[20] Upon receipt of the news, General Grant decided to make a full-scale assault on Lee's lines around Petersburg. Grant ordered General Meade, commander of the Army of the Potomac, to attack Lee with the VI and IX Corps at 4 o'clock the next morning, April 2, 1865.[21]

General Grant had originally planned to have the XXIV Corps participate in the "mass assault" scheduled at four o'clock.[22] The commander in chief did not expect much resistance on Ord's front. However, Ord reported that the ground in front of Foster's Division was a slough or morass that even the rebels could only cross on logs. Grant then reconsidered, telling Ord, "General Wright speaks with great confidence of his ability to go through the enemy's lines. I think as you have such difficult ground to go over your reserves had better be pushed well over to the right, so that they may help him or go in with you, as may be required."[23] Ord answered, agreeing with Grant and informing him that he would await developments, prepared to go to Sheridan's aid or Wright's as needed. That night Potter's Brigade was withdrawn from the firing line to the rear of a "belt of woods," leaving the pickets in place so that the rebels would not learn of the movement.[24]

The soldiers of the VI and IX Corps prepared themselves for the morning's desperate assault with "fatalistic determination."[25] The IX Corps in particular had participated in many ill advised and poorly executed assaults with disastrous, even nightmarish results—the doomed assault at the "Crater" being the most recent. Such nightmarish memories did not haunt the 116th. Although the regiment had experienced its share of assaults against breastworks, the terrible "bull pens" at Piedmont and Early's earthworks at Lynchburg, it had not been repeatedly led to wanton slaughter, as had been the case in the IX Corps. Having spent three months in camp recovering from the fatigue and effects of the Valley Campaign, the 116th was ready to finish the fight.

General Grant wanted to make this assault immediately upon learning of Sheridan's success at Five Forks; however, the report arrived too late and darkness precluded the effort on the night of the first. The delay held potential drawbacks for Grant, giving Lee additional hours to respond and even possibly concentrate his forces against Sheridan. Thus, the attack had to be pushed at first light on the second and with maximum effort. The II and XXIV Corps would hold in place, waiting to exploit any advantage gained by the other two corps farther on the Federal right.

This offensive did not resemble the bumbling assaults at Cold Harbor and Petersburg of the previous year. It hit the rebels on a wide front while they were reeling from a severe defeat. To soften up the rebel works in preparation for the assault, the Federal artillery laid down the heaviest bombardment of the entire siege.26 The furious shelling eased simultaneously with the onset of the Federal assault, about 4:45 A.M. First to be hit were General Gordon's rebels at Fort Mahone, by two divisions from the IX Corps. Moments later Wright's VI Corps attack got underway. Wright's attack struck a weaker portion of the rebel line held by General Wilcox of A. P. Hill's III Corps. While the IX Corps made only limited headway, Wright's troops soon breached the rebel line. A portion of the VI Corps forged ahead across the Boydton Plank Road. The remainder of the VI Corps turned left and swept down the rebel lines to link up with the XXIV Corps near Hatcher's Run.

As expected, Wright's success spurred the XXIV Corps into action. After breaking through Hill's lines, the VI Corps had scattered over a large area with many regiments resultantly disorganized. General Wright reported his breakthrough to Grant; then he added, "I must be re-enforced or I shall lose all that I have gained."27 Grant reacted by ordering General Ord to shift his XXIV Corps troops to the right to assist the VI Corps, as previously contemplated.

The 123rd Ohio Infantry, which had been brigaded with the 116th since Milroy's days, had spent the night of April first on the picket line after the 34th Massachusetts and the 116th withdrew for the night. Just after daybreak, perhaps an hour after the onset of the VI Corps assault, General Turner directed General Harris to advance his skirmishers against the rebel front. The tired men from the 123rd approached the rebel fortifications and, seeing that they were lightly defended, carried the rebel works. Harris' brigade was close behind. Most of the defenders had been siphoned off to oppose Wright's assault farther to the east. This attack hit the rebel works of Cooke's line northeast of Hatcher's Run.28 Holding up the First Brigade's honor, the 123rd got credit for capturing two cannon, two battle-flags and many prisoners.29 Interestingly, the two cannon captured by the 123rd had been taken from Milroy at Winchester in June 1863. "The flags," wrote Colonel Potter, "are old offenders, and furnish their own history."30

Just before 7 A.M. General Gibbon received orders from General Ord to send troops to support the VI Corps. In response, General Gibbon sent Foster's three brigades and the remainder of Turner's division—Curtis' Brigade and the 34th Massachusetts and 116th Ohio from Potter's brigade. Harris occupied the captured works until elements from the VI Corps arrived and then pushed on towards Petersburg, leaving the 123rd Ohio to take charge of the captured works. Foster's Division moved along the captured rebel works and emerged on the Boydton Plank Road. Turner and his men traveled on the outside of the VI Corps lines in the direction of the "Union signal tower near Fort Fisher."32

After reaching the Boydton Plank Road, Foster's troops encountered rebels near the Pickerell House.33 These rebels were Lane's and Thomas's brigades of Wilcox's Division. A brigade of Mississippians from Mahone's Division had also just arrived as an emergency reinforcement by direction of General Lee. Colonel Osborn's First Brigade of Foster's Division drove the rebels along the Boydton Plank Road toward Petersburg. General Wright by this time had turned his corps around, following Gibbon's troops towards Petersburg. The Federal II Corps too had driven the rebels from works in front of its lines near Hatcher's Run.

At this point General Lee had no real choice except to evacuate Petersburg without delay. If the rebels southwest of Petersburg could not buy time for Lee to bring up his forces from Richmond, Grant would have the ultimate victory he was seeking that day. Lee now was forced to depend upon a pair of small redoubts "named after the farms on which they were built—Forts Gregg and Whitworth."34

The two rebel forts had been built as a backup in case the outer works were to be breached. Fort Gregg was the more formidable of the two and the more completely finished with a trench fourteen feet wide and six feet deep protecting its earthen walls. A palisade of logs topped the walls with loopholes for riflemen and embrasures for a battery of six guns. On the opposite (north) side of the fort was a wall of thick pine trunks with loopholes. Ammunition had been stockpiled in abundance, and the defenders busied themselves loading extra muskets when Foster's troops appeared.35

The rebels driven back by Osborn's troops manned the two forts with a fatalistic fervor on par with the defenders of the Alamo. Some of the men from Lane's and Thomas's brigades manned Fort Gregg along with the 12th, 16th and 19th Mississippi regiments of General Nathaniel Harris' brigade. Harris himself deployed the 48th Mississippi and part of the 19th Mississippi in nearby Fort Whitworth. Lieutenant Francis McElroy brought two three-inch rifles from the famous Washington Artillery into Fort Gregg before the Federals arrived. Then General Wilcox rode up to Fort Gregg to address the defenders. With a loud voice he said, "Men, the salvation of Lee's army is in your keeping," and he went on to implore the defenders to hold for two hours.36 They were told not to surrender and that it was their duty not to give up, because General Longstreet was on his way. The rebels took Wilcox's words to heart in full measure.

General Grant moved his headquarters from Dabney's Mill, near Hatcher's Run, to the front. Before noon he had established his headquarters at the Banks House, located about a mile southwest of Fort Gregg.37 Grant was aware of the rebel force holding the two nearby forts, and he decided that Forts Gregg and Whitworth had to be carried. From the Banks House he could coordinate the efforts of the two corps from different armies operating in the vicinity, and he could observe the important assault first hand.

General Gibbon was placed in charge of the operation to capture the two forts. When Gibbon arrived, Harris' Brigade from Turner's Division was on the Federal left opposite Fort Whitworth, and Osborn's Brigade from Foster's Division was facing Fort Gregg. Foster's troops, being closest to the fort, would open the assault on Fort Gregg, supported by Curtis' and Potter's brigades from Turner's Division. The 116th along with the 34th Massachusetts waited in support about 800 yards from Fort Gregg. Gibbon sent his chief engineer scurrying to find artillery support. Two batteries, the 3rd Vermont and the 1st New York, were brought forward to a spot near a rebel work called Fort Owen to pound both redoubts before Gibbon sent his infantry against them.38

From inside Fort Gregg the rebels could see a vast blueclad host maneuvering with parade ground precision, their bright muskets and bayonets gleaming in the noonday sun. "Each defender had two or more rifles at hand," recalled one rebel.39 These extra rifles were loaded and placed within reach of the men at the loopholes, and throughout the battle the rebels worked frantically to load and hand rifles to defenders on the parapet. It was too late for the guns of the Washington Artillery to be withdrawn, so the gunners prepared for the inevitable assault with the same resolve as the infantry.

What really happened at Fort Gregg will never be known unequivocally, except for the final outcome and statistics. The rebel reports and stories differed from those of the Federal participants. There were also many differences and claims for honors among the Federal reports. Who was actually first into the fort, first to plant colors on the parapet, etc. cannot be determined, because each witness saw the battle, which unfolded with great tumult and violence, from his own position and perspective.

"At about 1 p.m., pursuant to orders, I directed the assault upon Fort Gregg," wrote General Foster.40 Osborn's and Dandy's brigades moved toward Fort Gregg from their position about 800 yards to the southwest. According to Colonel Dandy, "The assault was commenced at a distance of from 200 to 300 yards from the works, and was made at the double-quick, without a halt, under the most terrific fire of musketry and artillery I have ever witnessed."41 The rebel cannon in Fort Gregg, manned by the excellent Washington Artillery, blasted gaps in the attacking Federal lines. Other rebel guns positioned in works east of the fort soon added their weight to the iron storm. The rebels on the parapets had little suppressing fire to daunt them, and they peppered the approaching Federals with a merciless and accurate fire. Soon riflemen in nearby Fort Whitworth and in works along the road unleashed a leaden hail into the flanks of Osborn's and Dandy's men.

Though taking heavy losses, the Federals pressed on up to the edge of Fort Gregg. Some of the Yankees attempted to circle the fort and enter from the north side. Recent heavy rains had filled the trench at the rear of the fort with water so deep "that it was impossible to pass through it to the sally-port..."42 The soldiers milled beneath the parapets seeking an entry into the fort, constantly subjected to shots from the fort and the nearby rebel works. Confederate General Nathaniel Harris, commanding at Fort Whitworth, described the fight: "Gregg raged like the crater of a volcano, emitting flashes of deadly battle-fires, enveloped in flame and cloud wreathing our flag, as well in honor, as in the smoke of death."43

Reaching the walls of the fort was in itself an act of collective valor seldom surpassed during the war. The attacking Federals were as determined to capture the fort as the rebels were to hold it, but Foster's men were not making progress and apparently requested help. General Foster then sent in his supporting brigade, commanded by Colonel Harrison Fairchild. These troops made the dash across the open field subjected to the same scathing fire that met the first assault line. Fairchild's regiments rushed through the vicious gauntlet of fire and shouldered their way into the stymied mass of soldiers now huddled beneath the parapets of Fort Gregg. Close to the parapets the Federals escaped artillery blasts that raked the approach to the fort.

Now Turner's men prepared to go in. As the 116th moved into assault formation, the men saw a huge cloud of dark blue figures undulant against the impenetrable walls of Gregg. The contorted forms of the dead and seriously wounded dotted the muddy open field between them and their beleaguered comrades.

General Gibbon soon realized that Fort Gregg would not fold, so he immediately sent in his final reserve—Turner's Division. If Turner's men failed, he would have to order a retreat or call upon the VI Corps for help. General Thomas Harris' West Virginia brigade had so far done little, if anything, to reduce nearby Fort Whitworth. If Harris could carry the lightly defended Fort Whitworth, Fort Gregg could not hold.

Harris, it seems, failed for a third time to do a reasonable share of the fighting. Again, as he had done at Stickley's Farm, Harris took care of himself and his own brigade. Colonel Dandy remarked in his battle report that " a destructive fire was poured in upon the backs of our troops" from Fort Whitworth.44 While the rest of Gibbon's troops faced the murderous fire at Fort Gregg, Harris did not rush Fort Whitworth. Instead, he "contented" himself with firing a "perfect storm" of lead at Whitworth.45 As noted by Colonel Dandy, the "perfect storm" did not amount to an effective suppressing fire, and the Federals at Fort Gregg suffered severely as a consequence.

Nevertheless, General Turner sent his other two small brigades forward. Colonel Curtis' brigade would move against the west face of the fort while the 116th Ohio and 34th Massachusetts, commanded by Lt. Colonel Potter, formed on Curtis' right. The 116th prepared to follow across the same field of fire that had shredded two previous assault lines moments before. As the final attack got underway, Colonel Curtis rode among his troops, encouraging them to press on "despite the fort's brutal blanket of fire."46 The rebels, having little to fear from the disorganized and confused mass below, concentrated their fire on the vulnerable approaching lines. Colonel Potter described the advance of the 34th Massachusetts and 116th Ohio:

> I advanced by an oblique movement to the right, and then by a left half-wheel succeeded in placing one regiment of my command (the 116th) on the southern front of the fort. This gave me a direct fire on this front, and an enfilading one on the westerly front...we lay down and poured in a rapid and accurate fire. We suffered severely in reaching this point, but once here had the best of it.47

Ransom Griffin, writing about the battle years later, noted that a rebel battery punished the 116th while it lay along a road firing into Fort Gregg. Griffin explained, "but for a battery that took possession of a little fortification to our rear," the rebel artillery to the east "...would have soon cut us to pieces."48 The 116th was hit hard on the approach to Fort Gregg, and when the half-wheel was executed, "...the 116th bore the brunt of the movement and suffered a great loss."49 But now it would be the rebel's turn to suffer.

The 116th in previous battles had proven itself very capable of laying down an effective suppressing fire. Shooting down the rebel battery horses during the Battle of Opequon was an excellent example; the 116th again showed that ability at Fort Gregg. Griffin described the action, "Our men seeing a gun coming up would take aim at the right spot and soon we could see pieces of their hats flying like chips in the air."50 The men utilized the cover of a road bed on the southern face of the fort to shoot any rebel showing himself for over twenty minutes, "...succeeding in a great measure in silencing the enemy's fire..."51

To this point the 116th had been unable to reach the parapet of the fort because of troops from the first two charges lying in front of the fort and extending back about twenty-five yards.52 The 116th kept up its suppressing fire until few shots were being returned. Ransom Griffin takes up the saga from here:

As soon as the enemy was well forced down behind the works a few of us ran into the ditch. With my sword and Stephen Gilmore and W. J. Chase, with their bayonets, steps were dug up the embankment, up which we pushed Joseph Van Meter, Co. G, 116th Ohio, and upon the edge of which he stood, and, aiming at the first gun to come up, would shoot as the face appeared, pass his gun down and receive a loaded one, until, going up fourth, I had 16 men aligned along the edge of the fort.53

Now many men from the 116th began to shoulder their way into the moat and to fight their way up the steep and slippery parapet. The following description is from a post war account of the 116th at Fort Gregg:

There was scarcely a private soldier of our regiment who was not worthy of special mention and praise for his gallantry. Sergeant E. C. King, of Company F, is said to have been among the first to scale the enemy's works. He was promised a Medal of Honor, but for some reason never received it. There were numerous noted acts of bravery on the part of officers and men. A party of men, privates Williams and Reusser (?) of E, Samuel Forsythe of D, Joseph Van Meter of G, and Corporal Thompson of F, advanced in a squad by themselves under the lead of Sergeant Reithmiller (Ruthmiller) of E, to a bank close up to the fort, and lay down, watching for a chance to dash forward. Seeing the chance, all rose together to start, but that instant the brave Sergeant was killed. The rest of the party ran on, and digging holes in its side with their bayonets, climbed on to the parapet of the fort. In a moment they were joined by Corporal Stout bearing the colors, and the rest of the regiment.54

James Dalzell, of Company H, later described the actions of some of his comrades at Fort Gregg, including those of a young, swarthy farmer from Monroe County named Freeman Thompson:

A moment's pause, and Corporal F. C. Thompson, with thirteen other soldiers whose names history will cherish forever, clambered up the parapet. Almost at the top one was shot down and fell back into the ditch. Thompson was struck with a musket and fell, too, with several ribs broken, but in a moment climbed on a comrade's shoulder and was up again, fighting on the parapet against fearful odds. Close beside him were Clay Mountens (Mathews) and Joe Smith, of my company, until Clay's foot was shot off, and Joe shot clear through the neck, and both tumbled back into the ditch. Comrade on comrade's shoulders, up they climbed, fighting like demons. Some below loaded guns while the blood poured from wounds, and up they handed these muskets to Thompson and the rest who struggled on the parapet above, and soon the whole army swept in and the fort was ours.55

Thompson was knocked off the parapet a second time and fought his way back up. This time he found Joseph Van Meter, and together the two men lay down and fired into the fort with muskets loaded and handed up by their comrades, as described by Dalzell. For their valor at Gregg, Thompson and Van Meter were both awarded the Medal of Honor on May 12, 1865, and both accompanied General Gibbon to Washington with others who won the medal during the final campaign.56

While Thompson and the others struggled atop the parapet, Lieutenant Griffin marched his men towards the north face of the fort. About half-way there, probably on the west side, Griffin "rushed in, nearly jumping down upon Lieut. Sharboro, of Natchez, Miss., who happened to be rushing a few men to the south end."57 Sharboro immediately surrendered to Lieutenant Griffin and his men. According to Captain H. L. Karr, of General Turner's staff, Lieutenant Griffin was the first Federal officer to enter Fort Gregg.58

Another account from a veteran of the 116th mentioned that at some point after the regiment reached the mass of troops beneath Gregg's walls, someone gave the order to charge. "When the order to charge was given," the veteran wrote, "the third line was first on its feet and charged over and through the other troops, many of which joined in the charge. The colors of the 116th Ohio and the colors of the 10th Conn. were the first to be planted upon the parapet of the fort."59 Three separate accounts from veterans of the 116th reported the flags of the 116th and 10th Connecticut first on Gregg's parapet. No doubt several regiments also claimed that same honor.

The rebels fought back fiercely and inflicted heavy casualties upon the first intrepid Federals to reach the top of the parapets. The 116th suffered its "most serious loss in killed and wounded" atop the parapet.60 Many of the rebels threw bricks and even lit artillery projectile fuses and heaved the shells over the walls.61 Dead and wounded Federals tumbled down the steep walls after being shot, spattering the struggling climbers with blood, pieces of brain, shreds of flesh, and splinters of bone. Below the walls the struggling Federals raged at the sight of the slaughter above. Captain Jones, of the 16th Mississippi, heard a fearsome and unearthly roar from outside Gregg's walls: "The noise outside was fearful, frightful and indescribable, the curses and groaning of frenzied men could be

Monument in honor of the defenders of Fort Gregg placed outside the south wall of the fort.

Grave of Corporal Freeman C. Thompson, Company F, at Caldwell, Ohio. Corporal Thompson was awarded the MOH for gallantry during the Battle of Fort Gregg.

heard over and above the din of our musketry. Savage men, ravenous beasts!"62

Soon Gregg's walls were thick with enraged Federals, spilling over the ramparts into the fort. Nathaniel Harris, seeing that the situation at Gregg was hopeless, turned his men out of Fort Whitworth to scamper for the rebel lines farther to the east. The rebels had just received orders to evacuate Whitworth when Thomas Harris finally sent his West Virginia brigade against the fort.63 It was too late to evacuate Fort Gregg, now submerged beneath an angry blue wave. The rebels, determined to hold out for General Lee's sake, had fought Fort Gregg as if a black flag flew over its ramparts; the wrath of the battered XXIV Corps would be poured out with equal ferocity.

With Federals reaching the top of the parapets on all sides, several men from the 116th jumped off the walls and into the fort. Inside, Fort Gregg was quickly turned into a riot of hand-to-hand combat. Guns, knives, fists and bayonets were brought into play with full fury. A rebel captain was heard screaming to his men, "Never surrender to the ------ Yankees!" John Cole, of Company B, and Ephraim Williams, of Company E, instantly swung their muskets and felled the captain, quickly killing him. Another soldier from the 116th jumped over the parapet at the same moment and encountered a rebel leveling a musket at his head. The soldier brought his Springfield to bear and each man pressed the trigger at the same instant, the Ohioan being grazed and the rebel taking a bullet through the chest. Joseph Gerlds, of Company H, (who had himself been captured the previous July and exchanged), "seized a rebel officer on the parapet, and after a desperate struggle, compelled him to surrender his sword." Samuel Forsythe was one of the first men on the parapet with Corporal Thompson. "Forsythe was attacked by two big burly rebels. He bayonetted one, and was himself bayonetted in the leg by the other, just as the surrender was made."64

The scene inside Fort Gregg was something few men would want to remember and apparently few wanted to tell of it. In his report Colonel Dandy wrote, "I forbear to describe the scene inside that work after the surrender..."65 Most of the rebels continued the fight even after waves of Federals breached the fort's walls. The furious and tormented Federals felt no pity and had to be restrained by their officers from killing every rebel in the fort. One rebel who surrendered noted that "the cry was kill," and that only the Federal officers and the confused mingling inside the fort saved the rebels. He also reported that many Federals were hit by shots intended for rebels during the swarming melee.66

Joseph Van Meter yanked a flag away from a rebel color bearer moments before the few remaining uninjured rebels threw up their hands in surrender, and then it was over. The fighting inside the fort did not last long. According to Ransom Griffin, "Gen. Grant was soon there with his congratulations, stating that by his watch it was 27 minutes from the time of the charge until the fort was ours."67 Once the horde of Federals drove the rebels off the parapets, the rebels were quickly overwhelmed.

The remarkable rebel defense of Fort Gregg furnished General Lee with enough time to shuffle his troops into Petersburg's inner defensive line. General Grant did not continue the push against Petersburg that day, and Lee was thus allowed to evacuate Petersburg and Richmond before being trapped. The fighting at Fort Gregg would be remembered as a demonstration of incredible valor on both sides. General Gibbon, the veteran former commander of the famed Iron Brigade, praised the courage of his troops at Fort Gregg. He noted that his men, the 116th included, climbed the fort's parapets "under a most murderous fire," and he asserted, "This assault, certainly one of the most desperate of the war, succeeded by the obstinate courage of our troops, but at a fearful cost."68 The fighting at Fort Gregg was indeed some of the fiercest of the war.

Colonel Potter reported finding fifty-six dead rebels inside the fort, and he mentioned 250 rebels being captured there.69 A large majority of the captured were wounded. The tally of casualties for Gibbon's troops was 122 Killed and 590 wounded.70 Casualties for the 116th totaled ten killed, five mortally wounded, and thirty-three wounded out of approximately 350 men engaged.71 Company A, being assigned to provost duty, did not participate at Fort Gregg or any of the battles in April 1865. Casualties for the 116th at Fort Gregg were as follows:

KILLED.

Lieutenant William H. Bush, Company B; Sergeant Fred. E. Humphrey, Company B; Corporal James M. Hartley, Company B; William Hall, Company C; Sergeant John G. Ruthmiller, Company E; Corporal Louis W. Mozena, Company E; Martin Hysell, Company G; James Irwin Rogers, Company H; James Lindsay, Company K; David G. Groce, Company K.

MORTALLY WOUNDED.

Sergeant Myron R. Hitchcock, Company B; Corporal William H. Mobberly, Company C; Robert Hutchison, Company E; Gilbert McCoy, Company E; Samuel Rufener, Company E.

WOUNDED.

John P. Kibble, Company B; Otis P. Henry, Company B; Benj. F. McLain, Company B; Philip Feiger, Company B; John Truax, Company C; Geo. W. Sampson, Company C; Sergeant Wm. O. Belt, Company D; Corporal Samuel Forsythe, Company D; Eli Whitlach, Company D; John M. Bougher, Company E; Frederick Stephens, Company E; Levi Howell, Company E; Jacob S. Hurd, Company E; Andrew J. Curtis, Company E; John Schappat, Company E; David Amos, Company F; Corporal Edward King, Company F; Valentine Mahl, Company F; Henry Dillon, Company F; George Ray, Company F; Corporal David Longstreth, Company G; Corporal Edward Lowry, Company G; Samuel Barret, Company G; Sergeant B. F. Sammons, Company H; Henry C. (Clay) Mathews, Company H, right foot shot off or blown off by a shell; Corporal Jeremiah Swain, Company H; Joseph Smith, Company H; James R. P. Keyser, Company H; Nathaniel Butler, Company H; Corporal Armstrong Johnson, Company H; Isaac Yoho, Company H; Sergeant Geo. H. Bean, Company I; Charles Andrews, Company K.

Following the surrender of Fort Gregg, Gibbon's two divisions regrouped and awaited developments. The breakthrough around Petersburg was an electrifying success. General Ord was apparently content to rest and enjoy his "hard-won laurels."[73] But the 116th did not have time to mill around the battlefield. After nightfall the 116th was posted in front of Turner's division on picket. Colonel Potter instructed Colonel Teters to send out his sentries close up to the rebel works. Around 4 A.M. Teters discovered that the rebels had withdrawn from the fort on his immediate front. Teters sent a skirmish line into the fort without opposition and found sixty stand of arms but no rebels. The fort captured by the 116th that morning was known as Battery 45 or Fort Lee.[74]

Early that morning, April 3, 1865, news of Lee's evacuation of Petersburg and Richmond reached the 116th and Gibbon's Corps. There was a tremendous venting of joy with congratulations and backslapping. The men cheered the news roundly, but soon orders came to take up the chase after Lee's escaping army. The next few days would witness a race between the lean, weary, desperate rebels and the renowned ramblers from the Shenandoah Valley of Gibbon's Corps, known for their prodigious marching ability. It was an unequal contest, much like the Battle of Fort Gregg, but again nothing less than supreme effort would suffice; the 116th and Gibbon's troops would again meet the challenge.

"IN AT THE DEATH"
20

General Lee made good use of the time bought by the carnage at Fort Gregg. With Gordon's Corps still holding along an inner defensive line south of Petersburg, Lee made preparations to evacuate his army from Petersburg and Richmond. The irretrievable doom of the Confederacy was obvious. Yet some in the rebel hierarchy clung to the delusional hope of continuing the war. Even with the defenses of Petersburg collapsing, Jefferson Davis had to be convinced that immediate evacuation was required. Lee was compelled to send the following message to Davis on April second: "I think it is absolutely necessary that we should abandon our position to-night. I have given all the necessary orders on the subject to the troops, and the operation, though difficult, I hope will be performed successfully."[1] By midnight Lee was putting his orders for withdrawal into effect.

Lee's army began its retreat from Petersburg under the cover of darkness. "Silently and gloomily" Lee's weary troops marched out of their works and through deserted Petersburg, moving to the north side of the Appomattox River.[2] By early morning of April third, approximately 58,000 rebels were in retreat from Petersburg and Richmond, with Amelia Court House as Lee's immediate destination.[3] Lee's army traveled westward on five separate routes with a huge train of wagons, ambulances and artillery accompanying it.[4]

While the 116th was discovering that Fort Lee had been abandoned, other Federal units were moving into Petersburg without opposition. Well before dawn a squad from the 1st Michigan Sharpshooters entered Petersburg and hung Old Glory on the courthouse tower.[5] News of Lee's departure quickly reached Grant. The general rode into the abandoned city after dawn, but he had already formulated plans to bag the rebel army south of Petersburg.

Unlike previous Federal commanders, Grant would not delay or hesitate after fighting a severe battle, with or without a victory. He immediately set about planning to head off and capture Lee's Army southwest of Petersburg. Early on the morning of the third, Ord's troops were sent to the southwest in an effort to prevent Lee's escape. Grant additionally sent the II, V and VI Corps and part of the IX Corps in pursuit of Lee. Sheridan's cavalry, also in the chase, struck the retreating rebels on April third at Namozine Church west of Petersburg and drove the rebels back.

The 116th, as part of Turner's Division, was in the vanguard of Ord's column on the third. Early that morning the 116th marched down the Cox

Road to Sutherland Station. From there Turner's Division followed the South Side Railroad to Wilson's Station and camped at that place. General Grant accompanied Ord's column and established his headquarters at Wilson's Station. While General Meade and the Army of the Potomac marched toward Jetersville, the 116th and Ord's column marched toward Burkeville. Meade's objective was to catch and engage Lee's army. Grant, accompanying Ord's column, intended to beat the rebels to Burkeville and deny the rebels the escape route to Danville. As General Gibbon explained in his report, the 116th and his XXIV Corps troops were hurrying "to head off Lee's forces, which were trying to get round our left flank toward Danville."6

On April fourth the 116th continued the race to cut off Lee's Army. Corporal Louis Sulsberger, of Company C, wrote in his diary on the fourth, "We continued our march along the Southside R.R. we met about 500 prisoners taken by Gen Sheridan. The roads being swampy we only marched 15 miles..."7 The following day found the 116th marching along the railroad to Blacks and Whites, which was reached by 2 P.M. "Thence, the roads being very good," the 116th pressed briskly on to Nottoway, intending to go into camp for the night.8 But General Grant received an urgent message from Sheridan asking for an immediate meeting with the General-in-Chief. Grant rode out with an escort for Jetersville and directed Ord to continue the march to Burkesville that night. Finally reaching Burkesville around 11 P.M., the 116th wearily went into camp, having marched twenty-eight miles that day.

April 6, 1865, opened with a flurry of activity. Lee had realized on the previous day that he could no longer delay at Amelia Court House; thus, on the afternoon of the fifth Lee put his army in motion. Lee hoped to follow the railroad line on to Danville and points south, but the hard march of Ord's column had deprived Lee of that option.9 Lee decided to shift his retreat toward the west, hoping to use an operable stretch of the South Side Railroad at Farmville to link up with the supply depot at Lynchburg.10 On April sixth Grant pressed to capture Lee's army before it could reach Farmville for re-supply. As Army of the Potomac closed in on the rear of Lee's retreating column, General Ord dispatched a force to destroy two bridges over the Appomattox River near Farmville in an attempt to delay Lee's retreat.

"Early on the morning of the 6th, the 123rd Ohio, 54th Pennsylvania, a squadron of the 4th Massachusetts cavalry, and a large pioneer corps, all under the command of General Read, were hastened forward to either possess themselves of the bridges near Farmville, or destroy them."11 In company with the pioneer corps were at least ten soldiers from the 116th Ohio. The bridges targeted for destruction included the stupendous High Bridge, known for its incredible height and length. As the Federals marched towards the High Bridge, rebel scouts spotted them and reported their movements to General Longstreet. The rebel chieftain by chance met General Rosser and immediately ordered Rosser and his division of cavalry to intercept and destroy the small Federal column. Longstreet soon rounded up more cavalry under General Thomas Munford and sent them in support of Rosser, increasing the rebel cavalry force to about 1,200 horsemen.12

Before the pioneers could get well started on destroying the High Bridge, the rebel cavalry appeared, and a fierce cavalry fight ensued. Read led his Massachusetts boys in a gallant charge, and the troopers of 4th Massachusetts apparently fought well; but very quickly the New Englanders were overwhelmed and forced to surrender. Read was shot and killed in the cavalry melee. Then more rebel reinforcements arrived. Lieutenant Colonel Kellogg, of the 123rd Ohio, was in command of the infantry after Read and the cavalry failed to return from their foray against the rebel cavalry. According to an account from the 123rd Ohio, the two small infantry regiments fought the rebels for hours "till at last the boys began to get out of ammunition, and very soon that cry became general."13 Kellogg ordered the infantry to fall back toward the bridge, hoping that at least some of his men would escape into the nearby woods. The rebels attacked in force once the Federals began to fall back, and the Federals then "threw down their arms and surrendered to White's Battalion."14 Captain Randolph, of the 123rd Ohio, was reported killed by a rebel horseman after surrendering. The ten men from the 116th attached to the force as pioneers were also captured. As he was being led away by his rebel captors, one of the Federal officers flippantly remarked, "Never mind boys, Old Grant is after you! You will be in our predicament in forty-eight hours."15

General Grant directed Ord to send Gibbon's troops forward to Farmville to block Lee's path to that place. Grant gave Ord an additional instruction: "Let your provost-marshal or some one ascertain if there is any movement from Danville this way."16 Perhaps Grant wanted to be prepared in case General Johnston sent some of his forces north to help Lee. In compliance with Grant's instructions, the 116th was divided. Four companies from the left wing of the 116th remained with the First Brigade on the march to Rice's Station, while five companies from the right wing were sent southeast towards Danville to Meherrin Station. Thus part of the 116th was assigned the task of watching for any movement from Danville, as ordered by General Grant. Colonel Teters accompanied the right wing on the march from Burkeville to Meherrin Station. Early on the morning of the sixth the 116th divided, each wing of the regiment going its separate way.

While Gibbon's two divisions marched from Burkeville towards Farmville, the major action of the day was fought at Sailor's Creek, a few miles to the north. As Lee's Army retreated toward Farmville, with hopes of continuing to Danville, the Federal II and VI Corps and Sheridan's cavalry struck the rebels hard. The Federal II Corps hit Gordon's Corps, the VI Corps smashed a rebel force commanded by General Richard Ewell, and Sheridan's cavalry routed Anderson's Corps. By the time the fighting ended at Sailor's Creek, the rebels had suffered approximately 8,000 casualties including eight generals taken prisoner—Ewell, G. W. C. Lee, Kershaw, and five others. The Federal casualties amounted to about 1,800.17

Longstreet's Corps had not participated in the fighting at Sailor's Creek; these rebels had passed over Sailor's Creek in the morning on their way to Rice's Station to protect the railroad depot there from the Federals at nearby Burkeville.18 Part of the 116th along with the rest of Gibbon's troops hurried from Burkeville to Rice's Depot to head off Longstreet's Corps. When Gibbon's men arrived at Rice's Station, the rebels were already entrenched along the road to Farmville. As Gibbon's men approached the station on the evening of the sixth, two or three companies from the 116th were sent out on the skirmish line against the rebel right. The rebels confronting the 116th were from Heth's and Wilcox's commands now serving under Longstreet. Darkness put an end to the fighting, but not before the 116th had suffered at least four casualties.

The men from the 116th wounded at Rice's Station were William McFarland, Isaac Littleton, and Samuel McConnell, all of Company E, and Corporal Thomas Berry of Company K. The following is a list of the men from the 116th Captured at High Bridge on April 6, 1865:

Uriah Reddin, Company E; John Baker, Company B; John J. Walters, Company E; William Bassett, Company C; Jacob Dudley, Company H; John C. Bailey, Company I; John E. Ewers, Company I; Hopson L. Sherman, Company I; Perry Gardner, Company K; and James Lafever, Company A.19

Early the next morning when Gibbon prepared to advance, Longstreet had abandoned his works at Rice's Station and was marching to Farmville. The Federals, now including the VI Corps, soon followed Longstreet's rebels. Ord's men marched for Farmville while the Federal II Corps marched to the High Bridge in pursuit of Gordon's survivors from Sailor's Creek. The II Corps was able to gain possession of a wagon bridge before the rebels were able to destroy it, and by 9:15 A.M. General Humphreys had all of the II Corps on the north side of the

Appomattox in pursuit of Gordon. As Gibbon's XXIV Corps troops moved into the environs of Farmville, Longstreet had vacated the town to join Lee at Cumberland Church, destroying the bridges over the Appomattox River as he departed. The VI Corps followed into Farmville and by evening had crossed the river on a pontoon bridge to reinforce the II Corps operating against Lee's troops at Cumberland Church, a few miles north of Farmville.20

The heaviest fighting on the seventh occurred at Cumberland Church and did not involve the 116th and Gibbon's Corps. Lee's army managed to pull together at Cumberland Church long enough to fend off attacks by the II Corps during the day. The swollen Appomattox River separated most of the Federal army from Lee's army, and it was evening before the VI Corps was in supporting position near Cumberland Church. Lee waited for darkness and then retreated to the west toward Appomattox Court House.

The 116th spent the night of the seventh at Farmville, as did General Grant. The General-in-Chief, staying at the Prince Edward Hotel in Farmville, sent a message suggesting to General Lee that he should surrender his army to save both armies further needless and pointless casualties. He received a reply from Lee after midnight requesting terms of surrender without offering his surrender. Grant answered the following day, generously offering to parole Lee's Army.

At about 5 A.M. on April 8, 1865, the left wing of 116th moved out on the Lynchburg Road, participants in the most important race of the campaign. Turner's Division, including the companies from the 116th, was in the vanguard of the infantry. Two brigades of United States Colored Troops were placed under Gibbon's command on the seventh and joined the white XXIV Corps troops on the march that day. Colonel Woodward's Third Brigade of General William Birney's XXV Corps Division and Langdon's Artillery were assigned to Turner's Division.21 The men in both armies were now being tested at the limits of human endurance; only the toughest had survived this far, and these sinewy fellows wanted fervently to be, as General Phil Sheridan put it, "in at the death" of the Army of Northern Virginia.22

On the night of the seventh, General Lee had disengaged his troops at Cumberland Church and put his army on the road to Appomattox Court House without interference. On the morning of the eighth, the II and VI Corps followed Lee's army west. The task of cutting off Lee's escape route to Lynchburg fell to Sheridan's cavalry and Ord's infantry south of the Appomattox River. It was imperative for Ord's infantry to out-march Lee's army and block the road west of Appomattox Court House. The pressure was getting to General Grant. Stress and worry, perhaps about

Lee's refusal to surrender, brought on a sick headache, rendering the General-in-Chief ill throughout the day.

Ord's troops followed the road along the South Side Railroad to Prospect Station. A portion of Sheridan's cavalry was still at the station when the XXIV Corps arrived, and the V Corps approached the station about noon. Because General Ord was senior in rank to General Griffin, commander of the V Corps, Ord's troops took the lead in following the cavalry (Meritt's) to Appomattox Station.23 Ord's column followed the horse soldiers on the road to Walker's Church. The poor condition of the roads that day rendered the day's march an ordeal few could forget. Years after the war Ransom Griffin remembered:

> Never can we forget the terrible march from Farmville to Appomattox. Much of the road was red clay and slippery from recent rains...We started at sunrise, and never marched harder, and kept it up until 10 p.m., when we reached the Appomattox Station. The men equaled the Fifth Corps in swearing and growling, and even some officers were not amicable: but knowing who was leading them and the game we were after they 'footed it,' and I think every man in the four companies was there.24

General Grant was seen by the men of the 116th on the march "serenely smoking a cigar and pushing liesurely to the front on a small black horse."25 When the column turned to the northwest the men "seemed to realize that the end was near, and with renewed energies the men pushed on. The firing of the 2nd and 6th corps pursuing Lee became more and more distinct" as the 116th marched farther west, "and the eagerness of the men to get across Lee's track knew no bounds."26 General Ord was there to encourage the men with pity exhortations: "Legs will win this battle, men. This march will save all others. Whichever army marches best wins."27

The Buckeyes from the 116th had pulled some amazing marches in the Shenandoah Valley and had proven themselves among the best marchers in the Army of West Virginia. Like another veteran unit from the Valley, the 15th West Virginia, they too were "magnificent athletes" conditioned by grueling marches in the mountains of West Virginia.28 By about 11 P.M. the 116th was nearing Appomattox Station; Ord's column had achieved its objective—Lee's Army was cut off. The 116th had marched at least *thirty-eight* miles that day and maybe even more! This forced march was, simply stated, unsurpassed—even by the well remembered rebel "foot cavalry."29 "It was the hardest and best day's march, taking the state of the weather and condition of the roads into consideration, that was made by any troops during the war..."30

According to Lieutenant Griffin, every man in the four companies from the 116th was still in line when the halt was finally called in the darkness near Appomattox Station. Exhausted, the soldiers "quietly threw themselves down upon the ground to rest, in front of Lee's army, without the enemy's suspecting...that there was an infantry soldier within ten miles of them..."31 Lee himself did not suspect that Ord's infantry had sealed off his retreat route to Lynchburg. He knew that Sheridan's cavalry had pushed past his army, but he would not know until it was too late that Ord was within supporting distance of Sheridan, and that the V Corps was close behind.

Meanwhile the other five companies from the right wing of the 116th had marched to Meherrin Station, southwest of Burkesville. Jefferson Davis had just passed through Meherrin on his way south, and it was supposed that supplies or reinforcements could be sent to Lee via the rail line at Meherrin. Lieutenant Colonel Teters accompanied the men to Meherrin and then returned to Burkesville on the seventh. Captain Mann, of Company C, then took command of the detachment.

Several rebels were captured on the march to the station and a squad of rebel cavalry was there when the 116th approached. The captain sent out skirmishers and drove off the rebel horsemen. Then, "Breaking the road (track) was the work of but a few moments."32 Next the men were placed in concealed positions with a view of capturing any train approaching from the south. As expected, the sound of a locomotive was soon heard in the distance. Well before the train appeared, the sound of a whistle indicated that the train was stopping; then the rumble of the train grew faint and at last was no longer heard. It was supposed that the squad of rebel cavalry seen at Meherrin had warned the engineer that the 116th lay ahead, prompting him to turn back.

More rebel cavalry were seen that evening watching the station, and Captain Mann prepared for a night attack by setting the men to work fortifying his position. Chaplain Logan was with the five companies at Meherrin that evening. He went to Captain Mann and said, "Captain, we will no doubt be attacked during the night, and as John ____ never does us much good in a fight, I will esteem it a favor if you will give me his gun."33 Chaplain Logan had proven himself a brave soldier in the ranks during the campaigning in the Shenandoah Valley, and he was willing to bear hand in the fight that night in the tradition of a true "fighting parson." But the rebels did not return that night, and no rebels were again seen until the parolees from Appomattox passed through the area on their way home.

Back at Appomattox Station the left wing of the 116th was awakened before 3 A. M. on April 9, 1865, and put on the road again. This time the march was a short one, about three miles, to General Sheridan's headquarters. Foster's Division took the lead for the short march, and the troops form Doubleday's XXV Corps brigade followed Foster's men. Turner's Division marched behind Foster's command accompanied by Woodward's brigade of XXV Corps troops. General Gibbon directed that his troops should march into an open field around Sheridan's headquarters while he conferred with Sheridan and Ord. While at the meeting General Ord expressed his plan to Sheridan: "I will at once place Gen. Gibbon with his corps across the Lynchburg road and put Gen. Griffin with the 5th Corps on his right."34 The three generals agreed with Ord's plan and left Sheridan's headquarters. This decision placed the 116th in a crucial position in the event of a battle.

While waiting in the open field, their arms stacked, men from the 116th made fires and began boiling their coffee. "Hardly had the steam begun to rise before he (Sheridan) came to the door and said: 'I am sorry boys, but you can not wait for the coffee at such a time as this. Take arms and double quick it to the Lynchburg road."35 The 116th hurried towards the sound of firing in the direction of Appomattox Court House, taking position on the right of General Foster's division just south of the Lynchburg road.

Events unfolded rapidly on the morning of April ninth. General Lee, hoping that Federal infantry had not gained his rear, decided to send General Gordon's II Corps westward at first light. If Gordon could break through the Federal cavalry, and since it was cavalry he expected success, Gordon would move south of the road to protect Lee's escape route.36 Longstreet's corps confronted the Federal II and VI Corps a few miles east of Appomattox Court House. Even if Gordon's troops and the wagon train could break out to the west, the rest of Lee's army including Longstreet's command would have to escape from the Federals east of Appomattox Court House.

When General Gordon marched his corps west of Appomattox Court House around dawn on the ninth, he found Federal cavalry blocking his path as expected. Three Federal cavalry divisions deployed in his path: McKinzie's on the left, Crook's in the middle, and Devin's on the right. The flamboyant George Armstrong Custer and his men were in reserve.37 Despite the battered and weary condition of his troops, Gordon sent them forward fully expecting his men to brush aside Sheridan's large cavalry force hemming in Lee's army.

With Ord's infantry hurrying to his support, Sheridan instructed his cavalry commanders to fight a delaying action and make way for the infantry to make the final attack. Seeing the cavalry give way, Gordon's men gladly surged forward into a gap created intentionally by Sheridan's troopers. General Foster was by then deploying his infantry along the Lynchburg road. As Gordon's men crossed the crest of a ridge, Foster's infantry came into view on the hillsides ahead. The sight of the masses of blueclad infantry had an immediate and decidedly demoralizing impact. Most of the rebel supporting cavalry rode away from the fight towards Lynchburg, but Gordon could only prepare to skirmish with Ord's infantry and await Lee's orders.38

The 116th, as part of Turner's division, was initially intended to act as a support for Foster's troops. However, the firing intensified rapidly at the front, so Turner was directed to send his brigades through a stand of dense timber to form a line on Foster's right.39 Curtis' Second Brigade went in on the left of Turner's line next to the United States Colored Troops of Woodward's Brigade. Potter's First Brigade was next on the right, and Harris' Third Brigade was on the far right.40 After getting into its assigned position, the First Brigade advanced with Turner's battle-line, and the 116th was sent forward as skirmishers. Lieutenant Ransom Griffin described the scene at the 116th's last fight:

> I was ordered by Col. Potter, our brigade commander, by the right flank into the timber and to deploy my four companies as skirmishers and to send him word in five minutes what the enemy was doing.
>
> We got the word he wanted on time, as in less than 40 rods we found them packing rails for protection. 'Take trees and go for them,' was the order. As soon as they saw us, they knew it all. We could hear them yelling, 'Knapsack Cavalry; Knapsack Cavalry'...and, throwing their guns away, they went at top speed for their main camp.
>
> The prisoners told us that Gordon told them that there were no troops on their front but cavalry; that our infantry was 20 miles to the rear at sunset the night before, and that if they drove the cavalry they would have a clear road to Tennessee.
>
> They (116th) ran them nearly into Lee's camp. It was nearly a mile from the timber, mostly across a nearly level open ground, ending over a low hill on the top of which I looked back for the first time, only to see our line of battle just emerging from the timber, over half a mile to our rear.
>
> I was alarmed at the distance, and feared I could not stop them in time to save disaster. Seeing a high rail fence part way down the east slope of the hill, I ordered: 'Take the fence and lie down.' I intended to at once retrace a little, but one of the boys called out: 'Do you see that flag?' Stooping to look under the trees beyond the fence, I saw the white flag at Lee's headquarters about 250 yards distant, on a low hill beyond the ravine that was between us.41

The only recorded casualty from the 116th that day was hit just before the fighting ceased, as described by First Sergeant Francis Bartley, of Company G: "The last cannon Lee's army fired at us threw a shell into the woods as we were advancing. As it exploded, a piece of it knocked down James Davis, of Company G, merely stunning him, however, as he came up in ranks again in a few minutes afterward."[42] The rebel infantry, stunned by the appearance of Ord's infantry, apparently fired few shots at the 116th as it rushed across the fields toward the courthouse.

About twenty minutes after the 116th reached the rail fence mentioned by Lieutenant Griffin, the 34th Massachusetts arrived and took position on the left. A veteran from the 116th remembered, "we could see the courthouse and Lee's army in the valley below, and there we stacked arms."[43] A horseman, probably sent by General Gordon, was seen riding out from the rebel lines with a white flag. "As he neared the middle of the space between the lines, he was met by an officer from our side," wrote another veteran, "and at the same time the white flag appeared at different points along the enemy's lines."[44] The tension immediately drained from the soldiers on both sides, knowing, as they did, that the flags signaled a final conclusion to the bloodshed.

Hours passed while the men on both sides waited for the situation to unfold. General Crook came up during the lull and was cheered by the men he formerly commanded. He was heard to say, "There is not much use for my cavalry while this old West Virginia division is here."[45] Finally, after mid-day, activity in the nearby village revealed that something important was happening. According to Surgeon T. C. Smith, "We saw the Generals come separately—Lee first—riding up to the appointed place of meeting."[46] Another soldier from the 116th wrote, "Grant now soon came riding, rather faster than usual, up to Sheridan, held a brief conversation, and then rode forward to where Lee was said to be awaiting him. For a few moments there was a deathlike stillness, as though everyone was trying to comprehend and take in the full import of the scene before him."[47]

Wilmer McLean's red brick home was visible from the position where the 116th waited. It was there on the west end of the village that the two army commanders met to discuss the conditions for Lee's surrender. "During the interval," wrote Surgeon Smith, "the blues and grays were swapping hard-tacks and tobacco and no ill-will was apparent among them."[48] The terms of surrender were agreed upon, and they were liberal. Lee and his men would be paroled, and the rebels would be allowed to take the horses that they personally owned home with them. Both commanders signed the surrender document at about 3 P.M. From that moment the Civil War was for all intents and purposes over. General Lee

The McLean House at Appomattox Court House, site of General Lee's surrender.

Lieutenant Ransom Griffin, Company G. Lieutenant Griffin led the 116th on the skirmish line at Appomattox on April 9, 1865. (Courtesy of Mark D. Okey)

was easily the most influential commander in the Confederacy, having a George Washington-like status in the South, so naturally the rest of the rebel military forces would soon follow Robert E. Lee's example.

Once the result of Grant and Lee's meeting was revealed, "the whole army broke out in continuous, thundering, long-drawn-out cheering, yelling, screaming, which, beyond doubt, was the happiest, heartiest, gladdest ever listened to by mortal man. Officers and men threw up their caps and as they came down caught them on their swords or bayonets or stamped them into the ground. It seemed as though both sides were overjoyed and would never cease their noisy demonstrations."[49] However, General Grant, feeling somber following his meeting with his vanquished foe, ordered the celebrations to be curtailed. He did not want to demean General Lee and his army. The men present from the 116th would forever cherish the moment. To honor the left wing of the 116th, the following entry was written on the pay roll record of events for April: "This company...engaged in the pursuit and capture of Lee and his army at Appomattox, Virginia, April 9, 1865, this company being on the skirmish line at the time of surrender."[50]

EPILOGUE

Helping force Lee's surrender at Appomattox was a source of pride that the left wing of the 116th would cherish forever. Had the rebels escaped on the morning of April ninth, they would have reached the defenses of Lynchburg and doubtless would have prolonged the war. The unprecedented march that enabled Gibbon's Corps to head off Lee at Appomattox was the crucial phase of the Appomattox Campaign. The left wing of the 116th had the distinction of being the nearest Federal troops to Lee's headquarters when the shooting stopped. Ransom Griffin explained, "Gen. Gibbon...told me while he was in command of Vancouver Wash., that my four companies and the 34th Mass. were the nearest of our troops by half a mile to Lee's headquarters."1

Gibbon's divisions, the V Corps and McKinzie's Cavalry were chosen to remain with the surrendered rebels at Appomattox while the rest of the Federal army moved back towards Richmond. The 116th was part of the force selected to take charge of captured property and keep order while paroles were processed for the surrendered rebels. General Grant, in spite of his magnanimity, insisted on a formal surrender ceremony, which was arranged to take place on the morning of April 12, 1865. On that cold and gray morning, the rebels marched through the muddy streets of the village, their battle flags swaying with the cadence of their familiar route step, to the designated surrender point 2 Brigadier General Joshua Chamberlain, of the V Corps, hero of Gettysburg and other fields, was given the honor of presiding over the ceremony. By accounts it was an episode marked by melancholy; but when the Federals snapped a salute to their vanquished foes, the rebels, commanded by General John Gordon, responded—returning the salute with honor. Then the rebels stacked their muskets, furled their flags, and the Army of Northern Virginia passed into history.

At noon on the twelfth, Turner's Division and McKinzie's Cavalry marched out of Appomattox for Lynchburg. Finally Grant's troops took possession of the city that had kept Lee's army supplied during the Petersburg Campaign. By the April seventeenth, Gibbon had completed his task of "receiving the surrender of Lee's army and removing the public property to Farmville."3 The left wing of the 116th had marched to Lynchburg with Turner's men, while the remainder of the regiment remained at Meherrin Station doing light duties in that vicinity. On April twentieth the two wings reunited near Burkeville, and on the twenty-second the complete regiment started on the way to Richmond.

The 116th returned to Richmond, "keeping on the railroad most of the time," reaching the former rebel capital on April twenty-fifth.4 The Third

Division of the XXIV Corps had occupied the city since April third, and the troops of that division were drawn up to welcome their comrades who had grounded Lee's army at Appomattox. The 116th camped that night on the Lynchburg Pike about two miles beyond the city. From that time until mustering out of Federal service, the 116th remained in the same vicinity, only changing camps a few times.

By mid-June every major rebel command had been surrendered. With the expiration of their enlistment drawing near, the regiments recruited during the summer of 1862 were being sent home. Orders were sent to the 116th to prepare rolls for muster out; the 116th was going home a couple of months early. Company K had given some trouble in September 1862 when part of its men refused to be mustered into Federal service. Company F did not have enough men on its rolls to muster in with the rest of the regiment, so both companies had mustered into Federal service late. Now the authorities decided that the 116th would be mustered out, excepting companies F and K.

On June 12, 1865, the survivors from Companies F and K and all the surviving recruits who had joined the 116th after its mustering in were transferred into a veteran volunteer infantry regiment, the 62nd Ohio Volunteer Infantry, at Richmond. One of the veterans from the 116th remembered the bad feeling caused by this arrangement:

> The recruits felt that as they had cast their lots with the 116th, it was unjust for the Government to compel them to serve in a regiment, with whose history, glorious as it was, they had not been identified. Here was a severe test of the patriotism of these soldiers. They met to discuss the matter, and while all felt that they had been unfairly treated, they with a few exceptions, decided to accept the situation and serve out their time in the 62nd. A half dozen, however, leaving their arms and their uniforms behind them returned to their homes.5

Two days later the rest of the 116th was mustered out of Federal service. The regiment was drawn up in a hollow square following the ceremony, and Lieutenant Colonel Teters delivered a sincere farewell address to the men, thanking them for their cooperation and praising them for their accomplishments. He reminded the soldiers that they had never disgraced their colors and had won the praise of every army commander served under. He admonished them to be "as peaceful and honorable in civil life as you have been brave and glorious in battle."6

On June 15, 1865, at 3 A.M. the 116th broke camp and marched through Richmond to the wharf on the James River. There the men embarked on the *M. Martin*, once used as General Grant's boat, and steamed down the James to Fortress Monroe. The ship steamed past the forts, Dutch Gap Canal, Deep Bottom; places with names linked to the long siege of Richmond and Petersburg. "We could see Camp Holly from our vessel," wrote one soldier, "and the forts and earthworks we had watched with such vigilance so long. There were our log huts yet...it was a 'deserted village' indeed. It was hard to think that only a few weeks before, these opposing lines of works we were passing were held by hostile armies striving their very best to destroy each other."[7]

At Fortress Monroe the regiment caught another steamer bound for Baltimore, Maryland, reaching that place by 7 P.M. on the sixteenth. Staying aboard for the night, the men debarked the following morning and took railroad cars to Ohio. The regiment arrived at Columbus, Ohio, on the evening of June nineteenth. From Columbus the wayfaring veterans traveled to Camp Dennison, (Cincinnati) arriving on the morning of June twentieth.

For three days the men lay in camp waiting for discharge and final pay. Corporal Sulsberger wrote in his diary on the twenty-first, "At about 8 O.C. AM we turned in our guns & equipments over to the ordinance officer & layed in all day."[8] An article was published in the Monroe County newspaper announcing the return of the 116th to Ohio:

> Camp Dennison, June 20—The 116th O.V.I. arrived this morning. Col. Peters (Teters) commanding—22 officers and 377 men.—The rolls were ready for the Paymaster at eight o'clock, P.M. [9]

No mention of the transfer of Companies F and K was made in the newspaper article. Additionally the article did not mention the many other men from the 116th who were mustered out prior to June 1865. Many of the men who were released from rebel prisons were mustered out in separate groups after their release from prison camp.

On June 23, 1865, the survivors of the 116th, excluding two companies and the recruits, were discharged from the army and given their final pay. The men left for their homes, mostly by train. They rode to the station or stopping place nearest to their homes and farms. Crowds of friends and relatives often were waiting as the men stepped off the train, but there was no welcome home parade for the returning warriors. Nor had the 116th marched in the grand review in Washington, D.C.

The privates from Companies F and K remained with the 62nd Ohio at Richmond until August 8, 1865, when they too were finally discharged and made their way home. Many of the recruits, who had joined after the rest of the regiment had mustered in, remained in the army, eventually being transferred again into the 67th Ohio Volunteer Infantry, until that

Samuel Dinsmore's mausoleum at the *Garden of Eden* in Lucas, Kansas.

Effigy of a Union soldier at Dinsmore's *Garden of Eden*.

regiment was mustered out on December 12, 1865. "The Spartan mother who sent her son to battle, bade him to return with his shield in honor, or on his shield in death."10 These men joined the remnant that returned in June, also with Spartan honor.

There were too many who did not come home. Perhaps the saddest story of all the men from the 116th who did not return home from the war was that of Emanuel Okey from the hamlet of Stafford in Monroe County. Okey, a private in Company F, was slightly wounded in the shoulder at the fierce Battle of Piedmont. He stayed behind with the wounded when the rest of Hunter's army marched from Staunton during the Lynchburg Campaign and was captured when the rebels returned to the vicinity. Okey was sent to the worst prison camp ever seen on the North American Continent—Andersonville. After nine wretched months as a prisoner, he was released in April 1865. In company with released prisoners sent to Vicksburg, Mississippi, Okey embarked on the steamboat *Sultana* for the river trip home. On April 27, 1865, the grossly overloaded *Sultana* exploded on the Mississippi north of Memphis, engulfing the entire boat in flames. Emanuel Okey was one of at least 2,031 men who perished in that disaster.11 It was a viscerally sad fate to endure such unimaginable hardship only to die in that terrifying and tragic holocaust.

It is not within the scope of this book to summarize the post-war lives of the over 1,000 men who served in the 116th. Many of the veterans of the 116th remained in the same counties where they had lived before the war. But many of the veterans were caught up in the movement west that characterized the last quarter of the Nineteenth Century. One of the veterans noted during a reunion of the 116th that, "the boys of the 116th have become widely scattered...There is, perhaps, not a Western State or Territory in which some of our comrades do not reside."12

The most eccentric member of the 116th was one of those men who moved west. Samuel Perry Dinsmore, of Company B and Meigs County, moved on to Kansas years after the war. Dinsmore was a Populist politician with an artistic flare. He constructed his home or "cabin" from limestone "logs" and over the years fashioned a series of whimsical political effigies on his property, which he called *The Garden of Eden*. He remarried at age eighty-one to a pretty twenty-year old immigrant woman. Before his death he constructed a limestone mausoleum in which his body is placed and is on display in a glass-covered coffin.

In a strange twist of fate, Colonel James Washburn, so horrifically wounded during the war, outlived the younger Thomas Wildes who superseded him in command of the 116th. Wildes, like any reasonable man, had predicted that Colonel Washburn would never recover from his wound. "Doubtless," Wildes wrote, "it has shortened his life, which it has made a suffering one, until the end comes."13 James Washburn survived the war and later moved to a farm in Wisconsin; there he became a member of the Wisconsin Legislature. Lieutenant Colonel Wildes left the 116th to accept a promotion to colonel of a new infantry regiment, the 186th O.V.I. Soon after assuming command of the 186th, he was promoted to brevet brigadier general for gallant service at Cedar Creek. After the war Wildes graduated from the Cincinnati Law School (1866) and entered the practice of Law at Athens, Ohio. He later moved to Akron, Ohio, again practicing law in that city, where he unexpectedly died on March 28, 1883. The "Old Colonel," James Washburn, was still living in Wisconsin.

Another victim of untimely death was William T. Patterson, the Commissary Sergeant who kept an excellent diary during his service in the 116th. Patterson wrote the sketch of the 116th that appeared in the book *Ohio in the War*, and he was also preparing a text for a history of the 116th. After the war Patterson earned a degree from the University of Ohio and moved to Andover, Massachusetts, where he completed a theological course of study. Just after completion of his studies, he was stricken with fever and died on July 2, 1869.14

In the years after the war reunions became a tradition for many veterans of the 116th, especially those who had served in the ranks. James Dalzell, who became an attorney in Noble County, Ohio, after the war, organized reunions at Caldwell, Ohio. Dalzell became a politician, making speeches in different parts of Ohio. In a speech to veterans in Cincinnati in 1887, he reminded the audience of the nobility of their fallen comrades. Dalzell told them, "You are not as good men as they were, and I am not. The man does not live that is as good as the men who died for the flag."15 His words were expressive of the survivor's guilt so many of the veterans carried for the remainder of their lives as civilians.

In later years it became an annual event for the old veterans to hold ceremonies on Memorial Day at the cemeteries throughout Monroe County to remember their deceased comrades-in-arms. "A march to the graves by the survivors was a tradition. As they grew too old to walk they were transported by horse and buggy and later by automobile, until at last there were none to attend."16 Now the entire generation that fought the Civil War has long since passed, and like Abraham Lincoln, they too, because of the place they earned, belong to the ages.

The Union veterans of the Civil War are truly the paragon by which all our nation's veterans should be compared. They fought the noblest war in our nation's history and fought the most difficult enemy possible—Americans—their own countrymen, brothers, family and friends. The validation of their lives is assured today by the fact that all Americans live better, and *are* better, because they fought for the Union.

The men from the 116th and other Civil War volunteers from Monroe County, Ohio, established a tradition of military service that endures there today. The number of residents from that county serving in the military is one-third higher than the national average. During the Vietnam War, the town of Beallsville, in Monroe County, suffered the highest per capita losses of men killed in the nation.17

Thomas Francis Wildes wanted the examples of valor, duty, sacrifice and devotion to country so well associated with the service of his comrades from the 116th preserved for posterity. In this he succeeded. For he knew, and personally expressed his confidence, that future generations would never forget the legacy of the Union veterans. General Wildes believed that the unique saga of the 116th was worth preserving. The fierce pride he felt for his association with the 116th never wavered, "Many times subsequent to his leaving the regiment, did he express himself in no measured terms as to the bravery, efficiency and soldierly bearing of the regiment, and said it was an honor for any man to be able to say, 'I belonged to the 116th'."18

APPENDIX

The following is a list of grave locations for some soldiers and veterans of the 116th Ohio Volunteer Infantry. The names of soldiers buried in National Cemeteries were located in the *Roll of Honor* compiled by the U.S. Quartermaster's Department in 1868 or were located by the author. The names of veterans buried in non-government cemeteries were supplied by Doug Miller or were located by the author. Many other soldiers from the 116th who were killed during the war were listed as buried in National Cemeteries, but the *Roll of Honor* apparently did not list all their names. It is probable that many of the killed in action from the 116th were later interred as unknown.

Alford, Samuel Pvt. Co. D
    Staunton, VA
Allen, Jesse Cpl. Co. K
    Andersonville, GA: National Cem.
Andrews, Hiram Cpl. Co. K
    Garnett, KS
Archer, Dickerson Cpl. Co. E
    Winchester, VA: National Cem.
Arckenoe, Frederick Capt. Co. C
    Winchester, VA: National Cem.
Baker, Steven Pvt. Co. F
    Antietam, MD: National Cem.
Barrett, Isaac Pvt. Co. C
    Staunton, VA
Beach, John 2nd Lt. Co. C
    Kingfisher, OK
Bennett, Charles Pvt. Co. D
    Antietam, MD: National Cem.
Byers, Emanuel Pvt. Co. C
    Hampton, VA: National Cem.
Carlton, Abner Cpl. Co. C
    Beloit, KS: Elmwood Cem.
Cayson, Luther Pvt. Co. I
    Chanute, KS

Chaney, Richard Capt. Co. D
    Topeka, KS
Clark, William Pvt. Co. K
    Barnesville, KS
Clegg, Moses Cpl. Co. E
    Antietam, MD: National Cem.
Comstock, Josephus Mus. Co. G
    Antietam, MD: National Cem.
Conger, Daniel Pvt. Co. C
    Woodsfield, OH
Davis, Charles Pvt. Co. B
    Lynchburg, VA: National Cem.
Davis, Miles Pvt. Co. C
    Antietam, MD: National Cem.
Dennis, John Pvt. Co I
    Fort Harrison, VA: National Cem.
Dillon, Peter Capt. Co. E
    East Wheeling, WVA: Peninsula
Dinsmore, Samuel Pvt. Co. B
    Lucas, KS
Dirkes, Charles Pvt. Co. E
    Antietam, MD: National Cem.
Dobbins, Samuel Pvt. Co. C
    Bartlett, KS: Lakewood Cem.
Dumm, John Cpl. Co. C
    Council Grove, KS: Greenwood
Dye, Benjamin Cpl. Co. A
    Monroe Co. OH: Jericho Cem.
Earley, Alfred Pvt. Co. A
    Woodsfield, OH
Earley, James Pvt. Co. F
    Tyler Co., WVA: Oil Ridge
Eddy, Leander Pvt. Co D
    Lawrence, KS: Oak Hill Cem.
Eoff, Leander Pvt. Co. E
    Antietam, MD: National Cem.
Farley, Joshua Pvt. Co. G
    Winchester, VA: National Cem.
Frost, Consider Pvt. Co. I
    Staunton, VA
Fulton, Charles Pvt. Co. E
    Winchester, VA: National Cem.

Furguson, Edward Pvt. Co. I
    Texas Co., MO: Shafer Cem.
Gannon, George Pvt. Co. C
    Staunton, VA: National Cem.
Grandon, Matthew Pvt. Co. H
    Hutchinson, KS: Eastside Cem.
Groves, John Pvt. Co H
    Fairmont, NE
Hamilton, Evander Pvt. Co. D
    Lynchburg, VA: National Cem.
Harbin, John Pvt. Co. C
    Antietam, MD: National Cem.
Heck, Oswald Sgt. Co. C
    Winchester, VA: National Cem.
Hendry, Isaac Pvt. Co. G
    Kingman, KS: Walnut Hill Cem.
Hill, Elzy Pvt. Co. A
    Antietam, MD: National Cem.
Hill, Hezekiah Pvt. Co. A
    Hampton, VA: National Cem.
Hoyt, Royal Wagoner Co. B
    Andersonville, GA: National Cem.
Hubbard, Daniel Pvt. Co. A
    Evans, CO
Hull, Samuel Pvt. Co. H
    Antietam, MD: National Cem.
Hunnel, Thomas Pvt. Co. D
    Winchester, VA: National Cem.
Jefferies, Abram Pvt. Co. C
    Winchester, VA: National Cem.
Johnson, Joseph Cpl. Co. C
    Peabody, KS
Kalb, Abraham Cpl. Co. B
    Baldwin, KS: Oakwood Cem.
Keyes, Edwin Capt. Co. B
    Lynchburg, VA: National Cem.
King, Silas Cpl. Co. F
    Stafford, OH
Lamp, George W. Mus'n. Co. H
    Winchester, VA: National Cem.
Light, Matthias Pvt. Co. F
    Antietam, MD: National Cem.

Mahl, Valentine Pvt. Co. F
Laings, OH
Mahoney, Richard Pvt. Co. D
Staunton, VA: National Cem.
Martin, Wilson Capt. Co. F
Newport, OH
McCain, John Pvt. Co. F
Winchester, VA: National Cem.
McCoy, Gilbert Pvt. Co. E
Hampton, VA: National Cem.
McKenzie, James 1st Sgt. Co. G
Antietam, MD: National Cem.
McMillen, William Pvt. Co. I
Red Cliff, CO: Greenwood Cem.
Miller, Madison Pvt. Co. E
Staunton, VA: National Cem.
Mobberly, James Pvt. Co. C
Staunton, VA: National Cem.
Mobberly, William Cpl. Co. C
Hampton, VA: National Cem.
Montgomery, William Pvt. Co. A
Jamestown, KS
Mozena, Lewis Cpl. Co. E
Petersburg, VA: Poplar Grove
Okey, Gardner Cpl. Co. F
Stafford, OH
Patterson, Sampson Sgt. Co. D
Antietam, MD: National Cem.
Powell, Andrew Pvt. Co. H
Warrensburg, MO: Sunset Cem.
Powell, Lemuel Pvt. Co. G
Osage Co., KS.: Alpine Cem.
Rich, Solomon Pvt. Co. H
Staunton, VA: National Cem.
Rogers, Erwin Pvt. Co. H
Petersburg, VA: Poplar Grove
Rufener, Samuel Pvt. Co. E
Hampton, VA: National Cem.
Shumway, Sylvester, Pvt. Co. B
Staunton, VA: National Cem.
Sigler, George Pvt. Co. K
Winchester, VA: National Cem.

Smith, Samuel Pvt. Co. G
    Bourbon Co., KS: Rosedale Cem.
South, Thomas Pvt. Co. C
    Woodsfield, OH
Springer, James Sgt. Co. B
    Lebanon, NE: Hamburg Cem.
Steele, Samuel Pvt. Co. A
    Tulsa, OK: Rose Hill Cem.
Stoneking, James Pvt. Co. H
    Antietam, MD: National Cem.
Stoneman, William Pvt. Co. I
    Winchester, VA: National Cem.
Sutton, William Pvt. Co. F
    Staunton, VA
Thompson, Freeman Cpl. Co. F *M.O.H.*
    Caldwell, OH: Olive Cem.
Van Matre, Joseph (Van Meter) Pvt. Co. G *M.O.H.*
    Middleport, OH: Hill Cem.
Wildes, Thomas Lt. Col.
    Ravenna, OH: Maple Grove Cem.
Wilson, Joseph Cpl. Co. H
    Cleo Springs, OK
Wilson, Richard Cpl. Co. F
    Peabody, KS
Winland, John Pvt. Co. D
    Antietam, MD: National Cem.
Yoho, Rueben Pvt. Co. H
    Winchester, VA: National Cem.
Zimmerly, Jacob Pvt. Co. A
    Staunton, VA: National Cem.

SUPPLEMENT

Belt, William Sgt. Co. D
    Monroe Co, OH
Larrick, Benjamin Pvt. Co. H
    Antietam, MD: National Cem.
Matchett, George Pvt. Co. C
    Winchester, VA: National Cem.
Morris, Andrew Pvt. Co. C
    Hartshorn, OH: Church Cem.
Okey, Levin Pvt. Co. D
    Graysville, OH: Church Cem.

JOSEPH
VAN MATRE

MEDAL OF HONOR
PVT CO G
116 OHIO INF
OCT 9 1923

NOTES
PREFACE

1 James M. Dalzell, *Private Dalzell* (Cincinnati: Robert Clarke & Co., 1888), p. 174.
2 Thomas F. Wildes, Record *of the One Hundred and Sixteenth Regiment Ohio Infantry Volunteers in the War of the Rebellion* (Sandusky, Ohio: I. F. Mack & Bro., Printers, 1884), Author's Preface.

NOTES
CHAPTER 1

1 Benson J. Lossing, *Mathew Brady's Illustrated History of the Civil War* (New York: Gramercy Books), p. 512.
2 Frederick Phisterer, *Statistical Record of the Armies of the United States* (New York: Jack Brussel, Publisher), p 5.
3 Frederick H. Dyer, *A Compendium of the War of the Rebellion* (Des Moines, Iowa: The Dyer Publishing Company, 1908), Volume III.
4 Wildes, p. 5.
5 Ibid.
6 Phisterer, p. 5.
7 Ibid.
8 Warren Wilkinson, *Mother May You Never See the Sights I Have Seen* (New York: Harper & Row, 1990), p. 6.
9 Dalzell, p. 13.
10 Wildes, p. 7.
11 Robert Hunt Rhodes, ed. *All for the Union The Civil War Diary and Letters of Elisha Hunt Rhodes* (New York: Orion Books, 1985), p. 13.
12 Dyer, Volume III.
13 Wildes, p. 9.
14 Ibid. p. 12.

NOTES
CHAPTER 2

1 Dalzell, pp. 16-17.
2 Charles Wetzel, "The 116th Was There," Installment Two. From files of Monroe County Historical Society, Woodsfield, Ohio.
3 Wildes, p. 14.
4 Ibid., pp. 15-16.
5 Ibid., p. 17.
6 Wilkinson, p. 10.

7 Wildes, p. 20.
8 Ibid., pp. 5-6.
9 Wilkinson, pp. 20-21.
10 Wildes, pp. 20-21.
11 Ibid., p. 21.
12 Charles M. Walker, *History of Athens County Ohio* (Cincinnati: Robert Clarke & Co., 1869), p. 303 and p. 308.
13 Carl Sandburg, *Abraham Lincoln The Prairie Years and The War Years One Volume Edition* (New York: Galahad Books, 1993), p, 345.
14 Paul M. Angle and Earl Schenck Miers, ed. *The Living Lincoln* (New York: Barnes & Noble, 1992), p. 381.
15 James McPherson, *What They Fought For* (Baton Rouge & London: Louisiana State University Press, 1994), p. 56.
16 Ibid., p. 60.
17 Kevin Phillips, *The Cousins Wars Religion, Politics and the Triumph of Anglo-America* (New York: Basic Books, 1999), P. 419.
18 Ibid., p. 413.
19 Walker, *Athens County*, p. 172.
20 Phillips, p. 420.
21 Ibid., p. 422.
22 Wildes, p. 24.
23 Karen Romick, List of Underground Railroad Conductors from Stafford, Ohio; Monroe County Historical Society, Woodsfield, Ohio.

NOTES
CHAPTER 3

1 Wildes, p. 25.
2 Ibid.
3 Charles S. Grunder and Brandon H. Beck, *The Second Battle of Winchester June 12-15, 1863* (Lynchburg, Va.: H. E. Howard Inc., 1989), p. 14.
4 Ibid., pp. 10-11.
5 Wildes, p. 26.
6 Ibid.
7 Ibid., p. 27.
8 Dalzell, p. 94.
9 Wildes, p. 27.
10 Mark D. Okey, *The Justice of Our Cause* (Okey, 1999), p. 112.
11 Wildes, p. 28.
12 Dalzell, p. 22.
13 Wildes, pp. 28-29.
14 Ibid., p. 29.

15 Ibid.
16 Ibid., pp. 29-30.
17 Ibid., p. 31.
18 St. Clair Mulholland, *116th Pennsylvania Volunteers In the War of the Rebellion* (Philadelphia: F. McMannus, Jr. & Co. 1903), p. 13.
19 John J. Pullen, *The Twentieth Maine A Volunteer Regiment in the Civil War* (Philadelphia and New York: J. B. Lippincott Company, 1957), p. 38.
20 Ibid., p. 39.
21 Ibid., p. 38.
22 Dyer, Volume III, p. 1546.
23 Wildes, p. 31.

NOTES
CHAPTER 4

1 Wildes, p. 31. Champ Clark, *Decoying the Yanks* (Alexandria, Va.:
2 Time-Life Books, 1984), p. 33 and p. 46.
3 Wildes, p. 33.
4 Ibid.
5 U. S. War Departments, *The War of the Rebellion: A Compilation of the Official Records of the Union and Confederate Armies* (Washington, D.C.: U.S. Government Printing Office, 1880-1901), XXXI, p. 747; hereafter cited as OR, all references are to Series I unless otherwise noted.
6 Thomas A. Lewis, *The Shenandoah in Flames* (Alexandria, Va.: Time-Life Books, 1987), p. 43.
7 Scott C. Patchan, *The Forgotten Fury: The Battle of Piedmont* (Fredricksburg, Va.: Sergeant
Kirkland's Museum and Historical Society, Inc., 1996), pp. 25-26.
8 Ibid., p. 26.
9 OR, XXI, p. 747.
10 Okey, p. 164.
11 Wildes, p. 34.
12 OR, XXI, p. 747.
13 Wildes, p. 35.
14 OR, XXI, p. 747.
15 Wildes, p. 36.
16 OR, XXI, p. 747.
17 Ibid., p. 748.
18 Wildes, p. 37.
19 OR, XXI, p. 749.

NOTES
CHAPTER 5

1 Wildes, p. 41.
2 Ibid., p. 42.
3 James R. Furqueron, "The 'Best Hated Man' in the Army: Part II," *North & South*, June 2001, pp. 75-76.
4 Wildes, pp. 42-43.
5 Ibid., p. 45.
6 Ibid., p. 43.
7 Ibid., p. 44.
8 United States Census, 1860: Monroe County, Ohio.
9 "Army Correspondence," *Spirit of Democracy*, 25 February 1863, p.2.
10 Stephen B. Oates, "The Man at the White House Window," *Civil War Times*, November/December 1995, p. 59.
11 James Street, *The Struggle for Tennessee (Alexandria, Va.: Time-Life Books, 1985)*, p. 142.
12 Oates, p. 59.
13 McPherson, *What They Fought For*, p. 57.
14 Wildes, p. 47.
15 Ibid., p. 44.
16 OR, XXV/2, p. 606.
17 Wildes, p. 46.
18 Ibid., p. 48.
19 Elam J. Dye to His Mother and Brother, August 23, 1862, Letter.
20 Wildes, p. 49.

NOTES
CHAPTER 6

1 Wildes, p. 53.
2 Henry Woodhead, ed. *Echoes of Glory* (Alexandria, Va.: Time-Life Books, 1991), p. 40.
3 Wildes, p. 51.
4 Champ Clark, *Gettysburg the Confederate High Time* (Alexandria, Va.: Time-Life Books, 1985), p. 23.
5 Grunder and Beck, p. 16.
6 Jubal Anderson Early, *Narrative of the War Between the States*, 2nd ed. (1912; New York: Da Capo, 1989), p. 243.
7 Ibid.
8 OR, XXVII/2, p. 67.
9 Angle and Miers, p. 556.
10 Wildes, p. 58.

11 Early, p. 244.
12 Charles C. Osborne, *Jubal, The Life and Times of General Jubal A. Early, C.S.A.* (Chapel Hill, N.C.; Algonquin Books, 1992), p. 170.
13 Early, p. 247.
14 OR, XXXVII/2, p. 478.
15 Ibid., p. 60.
16 Ibid., 61.
17 Wildes, p. 57.
18 OR, XXVII/2, p. 66.
19 Clark, *Gettysburg*, pp. 24-25.
20 OR, XXVII/2, p. 53.
21 Ibid., p. 336.
22 Wildes, p. 65.
23 Ibid.
24 "Army Correspondence," *Spirit of Democracy*, 1 July 1863, p.2.
25 Wildes, p. 60.
26 Ibid., p. 61.
27 Ibid.
28 Ibid., p. 62.
29 Angle and Miers, p. 564.
30 Wildes, p. 66.
31 Ibid., p. 71.
32 Angle and Miers, p. 559.
33 OR, XXVII/2, p. 177.
34 Gregory Jaynes, *The Killing Ground* (Alexandria, Va.: Time-Life Books, 1986), 81.

NOTES
CHAPTER 7

1 OR, XXVII/2, pp. 182-183.
2 Benjamin F. Dye to His Wife, November 30, 1863, Letter.
3 Wildes, p. 75.
4 Ibid., p. 77.
5 Benjamin F. Dye to His Wife, January 10, 1864, Letter.
6 Benjamin F. Dye to His Brother, February 8, 1864, Letter.
7 Wildes, p. 79.

NOTES
CHAPTER 8

1 Jaynes, p. 26.

2 Ulysses S. Grant, *Memoirs and Selected Letters* (New York: Literary Classics, 1990), p. 26.
3 William Shea and Earl J. Hess, *Pea Ridge Civil War Campaign in the West* (Chapel Hill, N.C.: University of North Carolina Press, 1992), p. 230.
    4 Ibid., p. 278.
    5 Lewis, *Shenandoah*, p. 136.
    6 Wildes, p. 80.
    7 Ibid., p. 81.
    8 Ibid., p. 82.
    9 Ibid., p. 84.
    10 Ibid., pp. 84-85.
    11 Ibid., p. 85.
    12 Ibid., p. 86.
    13 Lewis, *Shenandoah*, p. 136.
    14 OR, XXXVII/1, p. 79.
    15 Wildes, p. 87.
    16 Lewis, *Shenandoah*, p. 36.
    17 Patchan, p. 98.
    18 OR, XXXVII/1, p. 80.
    19 Ibid.
    20 Lewis, *Shenandoah*, p. 33.
    21 Wildes, p. 87.
    22 Dalzell, pp. 72-75.
    23 Ibid., p. 73.
    24 Ibid., p. 76.
    25 Grant, p. 489.

NOTES
CHAPTER 9

    1 Grant, p. 796.
    2 Lewis, *Shenandoah*, p. 40.
    3 Ezra J. Warner, *Generals in Blue* (Baton Rouge: Louisiana State University Press, 1964), p. 244.
    4 Angle and Miers, p. 358.
    5 Patchan, p. 6.
    6 Wildes, p. 90.
    7 Dyer, III p. 1552.
    8 Patchan, p. 24.
    9 Wildes, p. 91.
    10 Lewis, *Shenandoah*, p. 42.
    11 Patchan, p. 51.

12 Wildes, pp. 91-92.
13 Patchan, p. 27.
14 Ibid., 30.
15 William C. Davis, *The Battle of New Market* (Garden City, N. Y.: Doubleday & Company, Inc., 1975), p. 24.
16 Patchan, p. 224, Note 548.
17 Ibid., p. 98.
18 Wildes, p. 93.
19 Gottlieb Sheifley, "The Battle of Piedmont," *National Tribune*, 14 March 1889.
20 Patchan, p. 103..
21 Ibid., p. 107.
22 OR, XXXVII/1, p. 117.
23 Patchan, p. 109.
24 Sheifley.
25 Ibid.
26 Patchan, p. 115.
27 Ibid., p. 109.
28 Ibid., p. 108.
29 Sheifley.
30 Patchan, p. 126.
30 Wildes, p. 93.
32 Patchan, p. 126.
33 OR, XXXVII/1, p. 117.
34 Wildes, p. 94.
35 Ibid., p. 100.
36 Wildes, pp. 97-98.
37 Ibid., p.96.
38 Sheifley.
39 Patchan, p. 154.
40 Wildes, p. 99.
41 Samuel Tschappat, "Who Shot Gen. Jones," *National Tribune*, 21 January 1909.
42 Wildes, p. 100.
43 Lewis, *Shenandoah*, p. 49.
44 Patchan, p. 225.
45 William F. Fox, *Regimental Losses In The American Civil War 1861-1865* (Albany, N.Y.: Albany Publishing Company, 1889) p. 450.
46 B. C. Drake, "Sketch of the Lynchburg Raid," *National Tribune*, 01 June 1916.
47 Joseph W. A. Whitehorne, "Piedmont," *The Civil War Battlefield Guide* ed. Frances H. Kennedy (Boston: Houghton Mifflin Company, 1990), p. 234.

48 Wildes, p. 94.
49 Fox, p. 450.
50. Colonel James Washburn to B. R. Cowen, June 9, 1864, Letter.
51 *Official Roster of the Soldiers of the State of Ohio in the War of the Rebellion Vol. VIII* (Cincinnati: The Ohio Valley Press, 1888), pp. 181-214; hereafter cited as Roster.
52 Washburn.
53 Wildes, p. 98.
54 Ibid.

NOTES
CHAPTER 10

1 Gary Walker, Hunter's *Fiery Raid Through Virginia Valleys* (Roanoke, Va.: A&W Enterprise, 1989), p. 133.
2 Ibid.
3 OR, XXXVII/1, p. 536.
4 Lewis, *Shenandoah*, p. 50.
5 Ibid.
6 Wildes, p. 101.
7 OR, XXXVII/1, p. 598.
8 Wildes, p. 103.
9 Ibid.
10 Ibid., pp. 104-105.
11 Lewis, *Shenandoah*, p. 58.
12 Wildes, p. 105.
13 Ibid., p. 106.
14 Osborne, p. 257.
15 Wildes, p. 107.
16 Early, p. xviii.
17 Jeffery D. Wert, *From Winchester to Cedar Creek*, 2nd ed. (1987; rpt. Mechanicsburg, Pa.: Stackpole Books, 1997), p. 23.
18 Lewis, *Shenandoah*, p. 53.
19 Osborne, p. 257, and Walker, *Raid*, p. 295.
20 Lewis, *Shenandoah*, p. 60.
21 Wildes, p. 107.
22 Early, p. 375.
23 Wildes, p. 108.
24 Ibid.
25 Ibid., p. 111.
26 OR, XXXVII/1, p. 124.
27 Walker, *Raid*, p. 325.
28 Wildes, p. 108.

29 Walker, *Raid*, p. 323.
30 Wildes, p. 109.
31 Walker, *Raid*, p. 326.
32 OR, XXXVII/1, p. 100.
33 Wildes, p. 112.
34 OR, XXXVII/1, p. 103.
35 Wildes, p. 110.
36 Ibid., p. 112.
37 Ibid., pp. 113-114.
38 Frank E. Vandiver, *Jubal's Raid* (New York: McGraw-Hill Book Company, Inc., 1960), p. 51.
39 Early, p. 376.
40 Wildes, p. 112.
41 Ibid., p. 114.
42 Osborne, p. 259.
43 Wildes, p. 113.
44 Quartermaster Sergeant Ezra Walker, Diary of July-September 1864, USAMHI, Entry of July 1, 1864.
45 Ibid., Entry of July 2, 1864.
46 Wildes, p. 124.
47 Ibid., p. 122.
48 OR, XXXVII/1, p. 507.
49 Grant, p. 797.
50 Early, p. 379.

NOTES
CHAPTER 11

1 OR, XXXVII/2, p. 315.
2 Wildes, p. 127.
3 OR, XXXVII/2, p. 341.
4 Wildes, p. 128.
5 OR, XXXVII/2, p. 365.
6 Wildes, p. 128.
7 OR, XXXVII/2, p. 366.
8 OR, XXXVII/1, p. 287.
9 Wildes, p. 129.
10 Ibid.
11 Ibid., p. 130.
12 OR, XXXVII/1, p. 292.
13 Wildes, p. 131.
14 Ibid., p. 133.
15 Ibid., p. 134.

16 Ibid., p. 131.
17 Ibid.
18 Rhodes, p. 172.
19 Ibid.
20 OR, XXXVII/1, p. 287.
21 Wildes, p. 131.
22 OR, XXXVII/1, p. 292.
23 Ibid.
24 Ibid.
25 Wildes, p. 133.
26 Ibid., p. 136.
27 Ibid., p. 135.
28 Ibid., p. 136.
29 Ibid., p. 138.
30 Warner, p. 196.
31 James B. McPherson, "Tried by War," *Civil War Times*, November/December 1995, p. 71.
32 Clark, *Decoying the Yanks*, p. 43.

NOTES
CHAPTER 12

1 Warner, p. 103.
2 OR, XXXVII/2, p. 423.
3 Ibid.
4 Hiller B. Zobel, "Enlisted For Life," *American Heritage Civil War Chronicles*, Winter 1993, p. 21.
5 Osborne, p. 57.
6 Early, p. 398.
7 Walker, Diary, Entry of July 24, 1864.
8 Lewis, *Shenandoah*, p. 91.
9 OR, XXXVII/1, p. 296.
10 Ibid, p. 293.
11 Wildes, pp. 141-142.
12 Walker, Diary, Entry of July 24, 1864.
13 Wildes, p. 143.
14 OR, XXXVII/1, p. 294.
15 Wildes, pp. 145-146.
16 Walker, Diary, Entry of July 27, 1864.
17 Wildes, p. 146.
18 Ibid.
19 Early, p. 401.
20 Lewis, *Shenandoah*, p. 100.

21 Wildes, p. 140.
22 Angle and Miers, p. 612.
23 Lewis, *Shenandoah*, p. 103.
24 Edward J. Stackpole, *Sheridan in the Shenandoah Jubal Early's Nemesis* (Harrisburg, Pa.: The Telegraph Press, 1961), p. 106.
25 Ibid., p. 141.
26 Walker, Diary, Entry of August 5, 1864.
27 Ibid., Entry of August 6, 1864.
28 Wert, pp. 12-13.
29 OR, XXXVII/2, p. 436.
30 Wildes, pp. 136-137.
31 Walker, Diary, Entry of August 11, 1864.
32 Ibid.
33 Ibid., Entry of August 12, 1864.
34 Lewis, *Shenandoah*, p. 122.
35 Phillip Sheridan, *Personal Memoirs of P. H. Sheridan/ Civil War Memoirs*, ed. Paul Andrew Hutton, (1888; rpt. New York: Bantam Books, 1991), p. 227.
36 Walker, Diary, Entry of August 17, 1864.
37 Ibid., Entry of August 19, 1864.
38 Osborne, p. 327.
39 Walker, Diary, Entry of August 22, 1864.
40 Osborne, p. 319.
41 Ibid., p. 326.
42 Walker, Diary, Entry of August 24, 1864.
43 Ibid., Entry of August 25, 1864.
44 OR, XLIII/1, p. 360.
45 Ibid., p. 375.
46 Ibid.
47 Ibid.
48 Ibid.
49 Wildes, p. 161.
50 Ibid., pp. 160-161.
51 Ibid., pp. 158-159.
52 Ibid., p. 157.
53 Walker, Diary, Entry of August 26, 1864.
54 Commissary Sergeant William T. Patterson, Diary July-October 1864, Ohio Historical Society, Entry of August 26, 1864.
55 Sheridan, p. 234.
56 Wildes, p. 161.
57 Patterson, Entry of September 3, 1864.
58 Sheridan, p. 235.
59 Wildes, p. 162.

60 OR, XLIII/1, p. 367.
61 Wildes, p. 163.
62 Patterson, Entry of September 3, 1864.
63 Jerry Korn, *Pursuit to Appomattox* (Alexandria, Va.: Time-Life Books, 1987), p. 31.

NOTES
CHAPTER 13

1 Walker, Diary, Entry of September 6, 1864.
2 Ibid., Entry of September 7, 1864.
3 Ibid.
4 Ibid., Entry of September 8, 1864.
5 John S. Bowman, ed. *The Civil War Almanac* (New York: World Almanac Publications, Bison Books, 1983), p. 227.
6 Wildes, p. 168.
7 Wert, p. 42.
8 OR, XLIII/2, p. 83.
9 Wildes, p. 169.
10 Patterson, Entry of September 17, 1864.
11 Lewis, *Shenandoah*, p. 109.
12 Ibid.
13 Wert, p. 44.
14 Stackpole, pp. 192-193.
15 Early, p. 419.
16 Wert, p. 53.
17 Lewis, *Shenandoah*, p. 116.
18 Patterson, Entry of September 19, 1864.
19 Wildes, p. 169.
20 Ibid.
21 Patterson, Entry of September 19, 1864.
22 Wildes, p. 170.
23 OR, XLIII/1, p. 376.
24 Wildes, p. 172.
25 OR, XLIII/1, p. 376.
26 Dalzell, p. 96.
27 Wildes, p. 171.
28 Patterson, Entry of September 27, 1864.
29 Dalzell, p. 97.
30 Wert, p. 92.
31 Wildes, p. 172.
32 OR, XLVIII/1, pp. 376-377.
33 Patterson, Entry of September 19, 1864.

34 OR, XLIII/1, p. 377.
35 Wildes, p. 172.
36 Ibid., pp. 172-173.
37 OR, XLIII/1, p. 377.
38 Rhodes, p. 189.
39 Lewis, *Shenandoah*, p. 122.
40 OR, XLIII/1, p. 118.
41 Lewis, *Shenandoah*, p. 122.
42 Wildes, p. 173.
43 Angle and Miers, p. 621.
44 Patterson, Entry of September 19, 1864.

NOTES
CHAPTER 14

1 Early, p. 428.
2 OR, XLIII/1, p. 555.
3 Early, p. 429.
4 Stackpole, p. 245.
5 Wert, p. 111.
6 Sheridan, pp. 252-253.
7 Wert, pp. 115-118, and Stackpole, p. 248.
8 Wert, p. 119.
9 Wildes, p. 181.
10 Wildes, p. 181, and Wert, p. 120.
11 Wert, pp. 120-121.
12 Wildes, p. 181.
13 Ibid.
14 Ibid., 182.
15 Wert, p. 121.
16 Wert, p. 121, and Wildes, p. 182.
17 OR, XLIII/1, p. 378.
18 Wert, p. 124.
19 Wildes, p. 182.
20 OR, XLIII/1, p. 378.
21 Patterson, Entry of September 22, 1864 and September 28, 1864.
22 Ibid., Entry of September 28, 1864.
23 Wert, p. 122.
24 Wildes, p. 182.
25 Wert, p. 124.
26 Ibid., p. 125.
27 Ibid.
28 OR, XLIII/1, p. 379.

29 Stackpole, p. 253.
30 OR, XLIII/1, p. 364.
31 Ibid.
32 Ibid., p. 124.
33 Ibid., p. 371.
34 Ibid., p. 556.
35 Patterson, Entry of September 22, 1864.
36 Wildes, p. 184.
37 Ibid.

NOTES
CHAPTER 15

1 Stackpole, p. 262.
2 Wildes, p. 186.
3 Wert, pp. 142-143.
4 Wildes, p. 188.
5 Sheridan, p. 264.
6 OR, XLIII/2, p. 196.
7 Wert, p. 143.
8 Ibid., pp. 143-144.
9 Wildes, p. 190.
10 Patterson, Entry of October 3, 1864.
11 Wildes, p. 190.
12 Sheridan, p. 262.
13 Lewis, *Shenandoah*, p. 135.
14 Patterson, Entry of October 4, 1864.
15 Ibid.
16 Wildes, p. 191.
17 Ibid.
18 Patterson, Entry of October 6, 1964.
19 Wildes, p. 192.
20 Ibid.
21 Wetzel, Installment One.

NOTES
CHAPTER 16

1 Sheridan, p. 264.
2 Patterson, Entry of October 6, 1864.
3 Sheridan, p. 265.
4 Wildes, p. 194.
5 Early, p. 436.

6 Lewis, *Shenandoah*, p. 139.
7 Wildes, p. 197.
8 Patterson, Entry of October 11, 1864.
9 Wert, p. 167.
10 Thomas Lewis, *The Guns of Cedar Creek* (New York: Dell Publishing, 1988), p. 119.
11 Wildes, p. 197.
12 Lewis, *The Guns*, p. 119.
13 Ibid., p. 120. (Early claimed that Conner was hit by artillery fire), Early, p. 437.
14 OR, XLIII/1, p. 371.
15 Lewis, *The Guns*, p. 121.
16 Wildes, p. 198.
17 Patterson, Entry of October 13, 1864.
18 Wildes, p. 198.
19 Lewis, *The Guns*, p. 122.
20 Wildes, p. 200.
21 Lewis, *The Guns*, p. 119.
22 Wildes, p. 198.
23 OR, LXIII/1, p. 372.
24 Wert, p. 169.
25 Wildes, p. 198.
26 William Henry Mobberly, Diary, *Genealogical Notes and Civil War Diary of William Henry Mobberly*, Transcribed by Wilma McCurdy McIntyre, Monroe County, Ohio Historical Society, Woodsfield, Ohio, p.77.
27 Wildes, p. 199.
28 Sheridan, p. 270.

NOTES
CHAPTER 17

1 Early, pp. 437-438.
2 Osborne, p. 360.
3 Early, p. 438.
4 Wert, p. 173.
5 Mobberly, Entry of October 17, 1864, p. 78.
6 Wildes, p. 201.
7 Stackpole, p. 280.
8 Early, pp. 440-441, and Wert, p. 175.
9 Wildes, p. 202.
10 Wert, p. 178.
11 Okey, pp. 183-184.

12 Ransom Griffin, "Sheridan At Cedar Creek," *National Tribune*, 9 September 1909.
13 Wert, p. 178.
14 Patterson, Entry of October 19, 1864.
15 Lewis, *The Guns*, p. 208.
16 Okey, p. 184.
17 OR, XLIII/1, p. 373.
18 Ibid.
19 Wildes, p. 203.
20 Ibid.
21 Lewis, *The Guns*, p. 209.
22 Ibid., p. 211.
23 Wildes, p. 204.
24 Lewis, *Shenandoah*, p. 147.
25 Wert, p. 191.
26 Lewis, *The Guns*, p. 216.
27 Wert, p. 183.
28 Wildes, p. 205.
29 Ibid.
30 Ibid.
31 Ibid., p. 206.
32 Return of the 116th Ohio Infantry Volunteers, September 1864, Ohio Historical Society, Columbus, Ohio; and OR, XLIII/1, pp. 373-374.
33 Wildes, p. 206.
34 Wert, p. 188.
35 Wildes, p. 207. Bill Kelble believes it was Gordon's and Ramseur's troops fighting here.
36 Wert, p. 188.
37 Patterson, Entry of October 19, 1864.
38 OR, XLIII/1, p. 374.
39 Patterson, Entry of October 19, 1864.
40 Lewis, *The Guns*, p. 265.
41 Ibid.
42 Osborne, p. 367.
43 OR, XLIII/1, pp. 373-374 and p. 380.
44 Wildes, p. 207.
45 Wert, pp. 216-219, and Wildes, p. 208.
46 Moses Edgar, "Sheridan At Cedar Creek," *National Tribune*, 2 December 1909.
47 Griffin, "Sheridan," and Okey, p. 185.
48 J.C. Iverson, "Says Sheridan Arrived At 9:45 A.M.," *National Tribune*, 2 December 1909, and Lewis, *Shenandoah*, p. 152.
49 Wildes, p. 209.

50 Wert, p. 219.
51 Wildes, p. 211.
52 Lewis, *The Guns*, p. 298.
53 Wildes, p. 212.
54 Lewis, *The Guns*, p. 228.
55 Wildes, pp. 212-213.
56 Ibid., p.199.
57 Ibid., p. 206.
58 Wert, p. 246.
59 Ibid.
60 Wildes, p. 215.
61 Ibid., p. 213.
62 Ibid., p. 219.
63 Patterson, Entry of October 21, 1864.
64 Mobberly, Entry of October 24, 1864, p. 80.
65 Wildes, pp. 219-220.
66 OR, XLIII/2, p. 436.
67 Wildes, p. 221.
68 Edgar Ervin, *Pioneer History of Meigs County to 1949* (Meigs County, Ohio: Meigs County Historical Society), p. 189.

NOTES
CHAPTER 18

1 Bowman, p. 233.
2 Mobberly, Entries of November 11 and 12, 1864, pp. 81-82.
3 Early, p. 454.
4 Lewis, *The Guns*, p. 318.
5 Wildes, p. 222.
6 Ibid., p. 223.
7 Ervin, p. 192.
8 Wildes, p. 223.
9 Ibid., pp. 223-224.
10 Ibid., p. 226.
11 Ibid., p. 227.
12 Corporal Louis Sulsberger, Diary, Entry of January 17, 1865, Monroe County Library, Woodsfield, Ohio.
13 Wildes, p. 228.
14 Ibid., p. 230.
15 McPherson, *What They Fought For*, pp. 41 and 60.
16 Wildes, p. 231.
17 Sergeant James Stafford to Corporal Benjamin F. Dye, October 10, 1863, Letter.

18 Korn, p. 33.

NOTES
CHAPTER 19

1 Sheridan, p. 293.
2 Ibid., p. 299.
3 OR, XLVI/3, p. 32.
4 Korn, p. 79.
5 Wildes, p. 236.
6 OR, XLVI/1, p. 1173.
7 Korn, p. 79.
8 OR, XLVI/1, pp. 674-677.
9 Ibid., p. 1214.
10 OR, XLVI/3, p. 377.
11 Ibid.
12 Ibid., p. 393.
13 Wildes, p. 237.
14 OR, XLVI/3, pp. 378-379.
15 Wildes, p. 239.
16 OR, XLVI/3, p. 430.
17 Ibid.
18 Ibid., p. 393.
19 Ibid., p. 433.
20 Korn, p. 91.
21 Ibid., 92.
22 A. Wilson Greene, *Breaking the Backbone of the Rebellion: The Final Battles of the Petersburg Campaign* (Mason City, IA: Savas Publishing Company, 2000), p. 361.
23 OR, XLVI/3, p. 431.
24 Ibid., p. 434.
25 Korn, p. 92.
26 Ibid.
27 Greene, p.362.
28 Ibid.
29 OR, XLVI/1, p. 1214.
30 Ibid., p. 1217.
31 Ibid., p. 1174.
32 Greene, p. 380.
33 Ibid., pp. 380-385.
34 Noah Andre Trudeau, *Out of the Storm The End of the Civil War, April-June 1865* (Boston: Little, Brown and Company, 1994), p. 61.
35 Greene, p. 386.

36 Ibid., pp. 386-387.
37 Ibid., p. 390.
38 Ibid., p. 391 and OR, XLVI/1, p. 1174.
39 Korn, p. 99.
40 OR, XLVI/1, P. 1179.
41 Ibid., p. 1195.
42 Ibid., p. 1189.
43 Greene, p. 397.
44 OR, XLVI/1, p. 1195.
45 Greene, p. 404.
46 Ibid., p. 399.
47 OR, XLVI/1, p. 1217.
48 Ransom Griffin, "The 116th Ohio at Fort Gregg," *National Tribune*, 22 August 1912.
49 Wildes, p. 244.
50 Griffin, "Fort Gregg."
51 OR, XLVI/1, p. 12
52 Wildes, p. 241.
53 Griffin, "Fort Gregg."
54 Wildes, p. 242.
55 Dalzell, p. 121.
56 *Medal of Honor Recepients 1863-1978* (Washington, D.C.: U.S. Government Printing Office, 1979), pp. 238 and 246.
57 Griffin, "Fort Gregg."
58 Ibid.
59 G. K. Campbell, "Capture of Fort Gregg," *National Tribune*, 6 March 1902.
60 Wildes, p. 242.
61 Greene, p. 401.
62 Korn, p. 78.
63 Greene, pp. 404-405.
64 Wildes, pp. 242-243.
65 OR, XLVI/1, p. 1195.
66 Greene, p. 403.
67 Griffin, "Fort Gregg."
68 OR, XLVI/1, p. 1174.
69 Ibid., p. 1217.
70 Greene, p. 406.
71 Wildes, p. 245 and Griffin, "Fort Gregg."
72 Wildes, p. 245.
73 Korn, p. 99.
74 OR, XLVI/1, p. 1217 and Wildes, p. 248.

NOTES
CHAPTER 20

1 OR, XLVI/3, p. 1378.
2 Trudeau, p. 70.
3 Ibid., p. 90.
4 Korn, p. 111.
5 Trudeau, p. 72.
6 OR, XLVI/1, p. 1174.
7 Sulsberger, Entry of April 4, 1865.
8 Wildes, p. 249.
9 Trudeau, p. 97.
10 Ibid., p. 98.
11 Wildes, p. 250.
12 Korn, p. 118.
13 C. M. Keyes, ed. *The Military History of the 123rd Ohio Volunteer Infantry* (Sandusky, Ohio: Register Steam Press, 1874), p. 111.
14 Christopher M. Calkins, *Thirty-Six Hours Before Appomattox: The Battles of Sayler's Creek, High Bridge, Farmville and Cumberland Church* (Farmville, VA.: The Farmville Herald, 1980).
15 Ibid.
16 OR, XLVI/3, p. 611.
17 Trudeau, pp. 115-116.
18 Ibid., p. 104.
19 Wildes, p. 251.
20 Trudeau, pp. 120-122.
21 Chris M. Calkins, *The Battles of Appomattox Station and Appomattox Court House April 8-9, 1865* (Lynchburg, VA.: H.E. Howard, Inc., 1987), p. 19.
22 Korn, p. 78.
23 Calkins, *Battles of Appomattox*, p. 25.
24 Ransom Griffin, "Rushing After Lee's Army," *National Tribune*, 15 August 1912.
25 Wildes, p. 251.
26 Ibid., p. 252.
27 Calkins, *Battles of Appomattox*, p. 26.
28 Ibid., p. 27.
29 Ibid., p. 48.
30 Wildes, p. 252.
31 Ibid., p. 257.
32 Ibid., p. 263.
33 Ibid., p. 264.
34 Calkins, *Battles of Appomattox*, p. 80.

35 Griffin, "Rushing."
36 Korn, p. 136.
37 Ibid., p. 138.
38 Ibid., p. 139.
39 Calkins, *Battles of Appomattox*, p. 80.
40 Ibid., 90.
41 Griffin, "Rushing."
42 Wildes, p. 255.
43 Francis A. Bartley, "Fighting With The 116th Ohio," *National Tribune*, 26 June 1924.
44 Wildes, p. 253.
45 Ibid., p. 255.
46 T. C. Smith, "The 116th Ohio in the War," *National Tribune*, 3 March 1927.
47 Wildes, pp. 253-254.
48 Smith.
49 Wildes, p. 254.
50 Ibid.

NOTES
EPILOGUE

1 Griffin, "Rushing."
2 Korn, p. 153.
3 OR, XLVI/1, p. 1175.
4 Wildes, p. 264.
5 Leroy D. Brown, *Address of Hon. L. D. Brown at the Reunion of the 116th Ohio Volunteers, Held at Caldwell, Ohio, September 17, 1884* (Caldwell, Ohio: Press Steam Print, 1884), p. 7.
6 Wildes, p. 269.
7 Ibid. p. 270.
8 Sulsberger, Entry of June 21, 1865.
9 "The 116th O.V.I. Arrived at Camp Dennison," *Spirit of Democracy*, 28 June 1865, p.2.
10 Wildes, p. 271.
11 Bowman, p. 206.
12 Brown, p. 8.
13 Wildes, p. 136.
14 Ibid. p. 266.
15 Dalzell, p. 175.
16 Wetzel, Installment Fourteen.
17 Jonathan Eig, "A Small Ohio Town, Hurt Deeply by War, Still Produces Soldiers," *The Wall Street Journal*, 19 March 2003, p. 1.

18 Wildes, Note Page.

BIBLIOGRAPHY

Angle, Paul M., and Miers, Earl Schenck, ed. *The Living Lincoln*. New York: Barnes & Noble, 1992.

"Army Correspondence." *Spirit of Democracy*, 25 Feb. 1863, p.2.

Bartley, Francis A. "Fighting With the 116th Ohio." *National Tribune*, 26 June 1924.

Bowman, John S., ed. *The Civil War Almanac*. New York: World Almanac Publications, Bison Books, 1983.

Brown, Leroy D. *Address of Hon. L. D. Brown at the Reunion of the 116th Ohio Volunteers, Held at Caldwell, Ohio, September 17, 1884*, Caldwell, Ohio: Press Steam Press, 1884.

Calkins, Chris M. *The Battles of Appomattox Station and Appomattox Court House April 8-9, 1865*, Lynchburg, Va.: H. E. Howard, Inc., 1987.

Calkins, Christopher M. *Thirty-Six Hours Before Appomattox: The Battles of Sayler's Creek, High Bridge, Farmville and Cumberland Church*, Farmville, Va.: The Farmville Herald, 1980.

Campbell, G. K. "Capture of Fort Gregg." *National Tribune*, 6 March 1902.

Clark, Champ. *Decoying the Yanks*, Alexandria, Va.: Time-Life Books, 1984.

Clark, Champ. *Gettysburg the Confederate High Tide*, Alexandria, Va.: Time-Life Books, 1985.

Dalzell, James M. *Private Dalzell*, Cincinnati: Robert Clarke & Co., 1888.

Davis, William C. *The Battle of New Market*, Garden City, N.Y.: Doubleday & Company, Inc., 1975.

Drake, B. C. "Sketch of the Lynchburg Raid." *National Tribune*, 01 June 1916.

Dye, Benjamin F. Letter to His wife, November 30, 1863.

Dye, Benjamin F. Letter to His wife, January 10, 1863.

Dye, Benjamin F. Letter to His Brother, February 8, 1864.

Dye, Elam J. Letter to Mother and Brother, August 23, 1862.

Dyer, Frederick H. *A Compendium of the War of the Rebellion*. 3 vols. Des Moines, Iowa: The Dyer Publishing Company, 1908.

Early, Jubal Anderson. *Narrative of the War of the Between the States*. 2nd ed. 1912; New York: Da Capo, 1989.

Edgar, Moses. "Sheridan At Cedar Creek." *National Tribune*, 2 December 1909.

Eig, Jonathan. "A Small Ohio Town, Deeply Hurt by War, Still Produces Soldiers." *The Wall Street Journal*, 19 March 2003, p.1.

Ervin, Edgar. *Pioneer History of Meigs County to 1949*, Meigs County, Ohio: Meigs County Historical Society.

Fox, William F. *Regimental Losses In The American Civil War 1861-1865*, Albany, N.Y.: Albany Publishing Company, 1889.

Furqueron, James R. "The 'Best Hated Man' in the Army: Part II." *North & South*, June 2001, pp. 75-76.

Grant, Ulysses S. *Memoirs and Selected Letters*, New York: Literary Classics, 1990.

Greene, A. Wilson. *Breaking the Backbone of the Rebellion: The Final Battles of the Petersburg Campaign*, Mason City, Iowa: Savas Publishing Company, 2000.

Griffin, Ransom. "The 116th Ohio at Fort Gregg." *National Tribune*, 22 August 1912.

Griffin, Ransom. "Rushing After Lee's Army." *National Tribune*, 15 August 1912.

Griffin, Ransom. "Sheridan At Cedar Creek." *National Tribune*, 9 September 1909.

Grunder, Charles S., and Beck, Brandon H. *The Second Battle of Winchester June 12-15, 1863*, Lynchburg, Va.: H. E. Howard Inc., 1989.

Iverson, J. C. "Says Sheridan Arrived At 9:45 A.M." *National Tribune*, 2 December 1909.

Jaynes, Gregory. *The Killing Ground*, Alexandria, Va.: Time-Life Books, 1986.

Keyes, C. M., ed. *The Military History of the 123rd Ohio Volunteer Infantry*, Sandusky, Ohio: Register Steam Press, 1874.

Korn, Jerry. *Pursuit to Appomattox*, Alexandria, Va.: Time-Life Books, 1987.

Lewis, Thomas A. *The Shenandoah In Flames*, Alexandria Va.: Time-Life Books, 1987.

Lewis, Thomas. *The Guns of Cedar Creek*, New York: Dell Publishing, 1988.

Lossing, Benson J. *Mathew Brady's Illustrated History of the Civil War*, New York: Gramercy Books.

McPherson, James M. *What They Fought For*, Baton Rouge & London: Louisiana State University Press, 1994.

McPherson, James. "Tried By War." *Civil War Times*, November/December 1995, p.71.

Medal of Honor Recipients 1863-1978, Washington D.C.: U.S. Government Printing Office, 1979.

Mobberly, William Henry. Civil War Diary Transcribed by Wilma McCurdy McIntyre.

Mulholland, St. Clair. *116th Pennsylvania Volunteers In the War of the*

Rebellion, Philadelphia: F. McManus, Jr. & Co., 1903.

Oates, Stephen B. "The Man at the White House Window." *Civil War Times*, November / December 1995, p. 59.

Official Roster of the Soldiers of the State of Ohio in the War of the Rebellion. Vol. VIII. Cincinnati: The Ohio *Valley Press, 1888*.

Okey, Mark D. *The Justice of Our Cause*, Okey, 1999.

Osborne, Charles C. *Jubal. The Life and Times of General Jubal A. Early, C.S.A.*, Chapel Hill, N.C.: Algonquin Books, 1992.

Patchan, Scott C. *The Forgotten Fury: The Battle of Piedmont*, Fredericksburg, Va.: Sergeant Kirkland's Museum and Historical Society, Inc. 1996.

Patterson, William T. Civil War Diary.

Phillips, Kevin. *The Cousins Wars Religion, Politics and the Triumph of Anglo-America*, New York: Basic Books, 1999.

Phisterer, Frederick. *Statistical Record of the Armies of the United States*. New York: Jack Brussel.

Pullen, John J. *The Twentieth Maine A Volunteer Regiment in the Civil War*, Philadelphia: J. B. Lippincott Company, 1957.

Return of the 116th Ohio Infantry Volunteers, September 1864.

Rhodes, Robert Hunt, ed. *All for the Union The Civil War Diary and Letters of Elisha Hunt Rhodes*. New York: Orion Books, 1985.

Sandburg, Carl. *Abraham Lincoln The Prairie Years and The War Years One Volume Edition*. New York: Galahad Books, 1993.

Shea, William and Hess, Earl J. *Pea Ridge Civil War Campaign in the West*, Chapel Hill, N.C.: University of North Carolina Press, 1992.

Sheifley, Gottlieb. "The Battle of Piedmont." *National Tribune*, 14 March 1889.

Sheridan, Phillip. *Personal Memoirs of P. H. Sheridan/Civil War Memoirs*. Ed. Paul Andrew Hutton. 1888; rpt. New York: Bantam Books, 1991.

Smith, T. C. "The 116th Ohio in the War." *National Tribune*, 3 March 1927.

Stackpole, Edward J. *Sheridan in the Shenandoah Jubal Early's Nemesis*, Harrisburg, Pa.: The Telegraph Press, 1961.

Stafford, James. Letter to Corporal Benjamin F. Dye, October 10, 1863.

Street, James. *The Struggle For Tennessee*, Alexandria, Va.: Time-Life Books, 1985.

Sulsberger, Louis. Civil War Diary.

"The 116th O.V.I. Arrived at Camp Dennison." *Spirit of Democracy*, 28 June 1865.

Trudeau, Noah Andre. *Out of the Storm The End of the Civil War, April-June 1865*, Boston: Little, Brown And Company, 1994.

Tschappat, Samuel. "Who Shot Gen. Jones." *National Tribune*, 21

January 1909.
United States Census, 1860: Monroe County, Ohio.
U.S. War Department. *The War of the Rebellion: A Compilation of the Official Records of the Union And Confederate Armies.* 128 Vols. Washington, D.C.: U.S. Government Printing Office, 1880-1901.
Vandiver, Frank E. *Jubal's Raid*, New York: McGraw-Hill Book Company, Inc., 1960.
Walker, Charles M. *History of Athens County, Ohio*, Cincinnati: Robert Clarke & Co., 1869.
Walker, Ezra. Civil War Diary.
Walker, Gary. *Hunters Fiery Raid Through Virginia Valleys*, Roanoke, Va.: A&W Enterprise, 1989.
Warner, Ezra J. *Generals in Blue*, Baton Rouge: Louisiana State University Press, 1964,
Washburn, James. Letter to B. R. Cowen, June 9, 1864.
Way, George A. "Army Correspondence." *Spirit of Democracy*, 2 July 1863, p.2.
Wert, Jeffery D. *From Winchester to Cedar Creek.* 2nd ed. 1987: rpt. Mechanicsburg, Pa.: Stackpole Books, 1997.
Wetzel, Charles. "The 116th Was There." Installments in newspaper, Woodsfield, Ohio: Monroe County Historical Society.
Whitchorne, Joseph W. A. "Piedmont," in *The Civil War Battlefield Guide.* ed. Frances H. Kennedy. Boston: Houghton Mifflin Company, 1990
Wildes, Thomas F. *Record of the One Hundred and Sixteenth Ohio Infantry Volunteers in the War of the Rebellion*, Sandusky, Ohio: I. F. Mack & Bro., Printers, 1884.
Wilkinson, Warren. *Mother May You Never See the Sights I Have Seen*, New York: Harper & Row, 1990.
Woodhead, Henry, ed. *Echoes of Glory.* Alexandria, Va.: Time-Life Books, 1991.
Zobel, Hiller B. "Enlisted for Life." *American Heritage Civil War Chronicles*, Winter 1993, p. 21.

SOURCES

Cedar Creek Battlefield Center, Middletown, Virginia (troops position maps for the Battle of Cedar Creek, locations for the 116th Ohio during the Battle of Cedar Creek and Battle of Stickley's Farm; general information about the Battle of Cedar Creek and Middletown).

Department of the Army, U. S. Army Military History Institute, Carlisle

Barracks, Pennsylvania, (photographs, *National Tribune* articles, Walker diary).

Monroe County Historical Society, Woodsfield, Ohio (regimental history and newspaper article).

Monroe County Public Library, Woodsfield, Ohio (Mobberly Diary and Sulsberger Diary, general information).

National Park Service, United States Department of the Interior, Appomattox National Historical Park, Appomattox, Virginia (troop location information, general information).

National Park Service, United States Department of the Interior, Petersburg National Battlefield, Petersburg, Virginia (troop movement and location maps for the Battle of Fort Gregg, Battle of Appomattox Court House, Battle of Rice's Station and fighting at Hatcher's Run, general information).

National Park Service, United States Department of the Interior, Wilson's Creek National Battlefield, Republic, Missouri (list of research resources, soldier roster).

National Archives, Washington, D.C. (personal service records, pension records).

Noble County Public Library, Caldwell, Ohio (cemetery information and grave locations).

Ohio Historical Society, Columbus, Ohio (descriptive and muster rolls, illustration and photograph of the 116th O.V.I. regimental flag, newspaper microfilm, Patterson Diary, regimental histories, regimental return, research information).

Wichita Public Library, Wichita, Kansas (interlibrary loans).

Note: Private sources are listed in the acknowledgements.

INDEX

Adams, Clarkson, 50.
Ady, Nathaniel, 129.
Again, James, 198.
Alford, Samuel, 90, 228.
Allen, Jesse, 51, 60, 228.
Allen, William, 33, 103.
Allison, Carmi, 30, 51, 103.
Allison, Charles, 30, 182, 194.
Amos, David, 210.
Anderson, John, 90.
Andrews, Charles, 210.
Andrews, Hiram, 228.
Annon, Jesse, 91.
Archer, Dickerson, 167, 228.
Arckenoe, Frederick, 31, 45-46, 49, 228.
Armstrong, Elmer, 2, 5, 27, 50, 62.
Armstrong, Robert, 50, 89.
Arnold, Henry, 91.
Arnold, William, 135.
Athney, Jacob, 49.
Athney, John, 49.
Atkinson, John, 91.
Atkinson, Mathew, 148.
Ayers, Craven, 51.
Bailey, (Balley) John, 49, 214.
Baker, Elias, 49.
Baker, Caleb, 49.
Baker, Hiram L., 19, 26.
Baker, John, 90, 214.
Baker, Stephen, 228.
Ballard, Fredrick, 5, 15, 39, 192.
Barcus, David, 90.
Barcus, Lewis, 91.
Barnes, Abel, 182.
Barnes, Franklin, 90.
Barnes, William, 90.
Barnhouse, Sheppard, 33.
Barret, Samuel, 210.

Barrett, David, 84, 90.
Barrett, Isaac, 90.
Barrett, John, 90.
Barrows, Bradley, 49, 91.
Bartley, Francis, 220.
Bassett, William, 214.
Bates, Dighton, 91.
Bates, George, 51, 138.
Battin, Byron, 27.
Beach, George, 198.
Beach, John, 90.
Bean, George, 210.
Bean, John, 49.
Beardmore, Emon, 50, 90, 148.
Beaver, Peter, 148.
Bell, William, 50.
Belt, William, 210, 232.
Bennett, Charles, 228.
Bennett, Daniel, 90, 183.
Bennett, Elijah, 90.
Berry, Thomas, 214.
Beyers, Amos, 37.
Biddenharn, William, 116, 191.
Blair, George, 102.
Blowers, C. M., 90.
Bonam, William, 49.
Booth, Miller, 50.
Bougher, John, 210.
Bowman, John, 49.
Boyd, Belle, 62.
Boyd, James, 102.
Brady, Ebenezer, W., 5, 31, 50, 187.
Brister, William, 63.
Brock, Addy, 89.
Brock, Daniel, 51.
Brock, David, 91.
Brock, Elias, 89.
Brock, Joseph, 49.
Brock, William, 49, 89.
Brown, Dr. Josiah, 41, 50.

Brown, John, 49.
Brown, Leroy D., 156, 167.
Brown, Matthew, 5, 21, 31-33, 92, 116-117, 128, 161, 192.
Brown, Stephen, 91.
Brown, William H., 27.
Bruny, David, 182.
Bryan, Washington, 90.
Buchwald, John, 90.
Buckley, Asher, 51.
Bullock, James E., 167.
Bunting, Elijah, 91.
Burch, George W., 49.
Burnside, Maj. Gen. Ambrose, 34, 63.
Burton, Jesse, 49, 135.
Bush, William, 50, 90, 192, 209.
Butler, Nathaniel, 91, 210.
Butt, Jacob, 50.
Butterworth, Abraham, 27, 51.
Butts, Jacob, 41.
Byers, Emanuel, 198, 228.
Byers, Francis, 115.
Cackley, John, 91.
Cagg, Andrew, 91.
Cain, William, 91.
Caldwell, Francis, 182.
Campbell, James, 49.
Campbell, John, 50.
Carlton, Abner, 134, 198, 228.
Carlton, Alvah, 51.
Carpenter, Jacob, 183.
Carpenter, Reason, 33.
Carpenter, Robert, 33, 182.
Carson, James, 91.
Cayton, (Cayson) Luther, 51, 91, 228.
Chambers, Elwood, 90.
Chambers, Robert, 50.
Chaney, Richard, 31, 90, 92, 182, 192, 229.
Chase, William, 206.

Chick, John, 91.
Clark, William, 51, 123, 229.
Clegg, Joseph, 229.
Clemets, Nelson, 91.
Cline, Charles A., 167, 192.
Clithero, E., 115.
Cobb, John, 51, 182, 191.
Cochran, Alexander, 18, 21, 39, 43, 49, 192, 196.
Cochran, Harrison, 27, 90.
Cole, John, 208.
Coleman, Marion, 90.
Comstock, Josephus, 229.
Conger, Daniel, 229.
Conger, David, 90.
Connor, Joseph, 103.
Cooley, Leonard, 50.
Coulter, Abraham, 49.
Coulter, George, 102.
Coulter, Jesse, 49.
Cox, Jackson, 50.
Craig, Leonard, 137.
Cramblett, Samuel, 49, 155.
Crook, Maj. Gen. George, 67-68, 70, 76, 98-100, 104, 107, 110-112, 114, 119-124, 133, 136-137, 151-152, 155, 163, 165, 176, 179, 181, 220.
Cullison, Joseph, 27.
Cummins, Joel, 115.
Curtis, Andrew, 210.
Custer, Brig. Gen. George A., 129, 147, 159, 218.
Daines, Royal, 103.
Dally, James, 103.
Dalzell, James, iv, 2, 5, 6, 15, 17, 37, 39, 64, 72-73, 106, 206-207, 226.
Danford, Milton, 141.
Danford, William, 49.
Davies, William, 51.
Davis, Charles, 102, 229.
Davis, James, 51, 220.

Davis, Miles, 90, 134, 229.
Davis, Pres. Jefferson, vi, 40-41, 57, 63, 75, 211, 217.
Dennis, John, 49, 193, 229.
Derwiler, John, 89.
Devore, John, 102.
Dillon, Henry, 33, 210.
Dillon, Jacob, 33, 91.
Dillon, John, 33.
Dillon, Capt. Peter, 192, 229.
Dinsmore, Samuel, 225, 229.
Dirkes, Charles, 134, 229.
Dix, Scott, 90.
Dobbins, Samuel, 50, 115, 229.
Doland, John, 90.
Drake, Benjamin, 88, 91.
Drake, John, 148.
Drum, James, 90, 134, 155.
Dudley, Jacob, 214.
Dudley, Joseph, 51.
Dumm, John, 229.
DuPont, Capt. Henry A., 71, 83.
Dye, Benjamin, 37, 49, 58-61, 63-64, 89, 193, 229.
Dye, Bazil, 123.
Dyer, Robert, 89.
Dyer, William, 49.
Earley, Alfred M., 229.
Earley, James, 20, 50-51, 59, 123-124, 182, 199, 229.
Early, Lt. Gen. Jubal A., 42, 44-46, 96, 98-102, 104-105, 108-112, 115, 118-121, 123-127, 129-133, 136-137, 139, 142-144, 150-151, 154-158, 162-164, 166-168, 170-171, 177-180, 183-184, 186, 194.
Eberle, Charles, 50.
Eddy, Leander, 50, 115, 229.
Edge, Frederick, 49.
Edgar, Moses, 178-179.
Efaw, Lienjenius, 91, 135.
Egger, John, 50, 103.

Elliot, Brig. Gen. Washington, 39, 46.
Ellis, Milton, 69.
Eoff, Leander, 229.
Evans, Eli, 50.
Ewers, John, 214.
Farley, Joshua, 31, 115-116, 229.
Feiger, Phillip, 103, 210.
Fenton, S. 51.
Ferrell, William, 50, 167.
Ferrill, James, 134.
Finley, James, 135.
Fisher, Jacob, 51.
Fisher, William, 33, 90, 102.
Fleak, Samuel, 49, 91.
Fleishman, Henry, 50.
Flowers, William, 90.
Forsythe, Samuel, 90, 206, 208, 210.
Frame, A.B., 31, 43.
Frazer, Jesse, 167.
Frost, Consider, 91, 229.
Frost, Ephraim, 49, 91.
Fuller, Edwin, 91.
Fulton, Charles, 142-143, 229.
Furguson, Edward, 230.
Gannon, George, 50, 90, 230.
Gardiner, Perry, 103, 214.
Gates, Albert, 49, 89.
Gates, Samuel, 49.
Gatten, Jefferson, 102.
Gerlds, Joseph, 51, 123-124, 208.
Gibbon, Maj. Gen. John, 190-191, 196, 198-199, 201, 203-204, 207, 209, 212, 214, 218, 222.
Gibson, Arthur, 124.
Gilbert, Harley, 51.
Gilbert, J., 91.
Gilchrist, James, 49, 91.
Gilkey, Dr. Walter, 5, 31, 41,

- 263 -

51.
Gillmore, Dallas, 148.
Gillmore, Stephen, 206.
Glashier, James, 51.
Golden, W. R., 5.
Gordon, Maj. Gen. John B., 44, 121, 143, 157, 165, 170-172, 177-178, 186, 194-195, 215, 218-220, 222.
Gowdy, John, 50-51.
Gowdy, Micajah, 103.
Graham, Jehiel, 167.
Grandon, Mathew, 51, 230.
Grant, Lt. Gen. Ulysses S., 57-58, 60, 63-68, 70, 72-76, 94-95, 97, 104, 107-108, 111, 118, 120, 125-127, 130, 132, 140, 142, 144, 147, 156-158, 162, 164, 168, 171, 184-185, 187-188, 190-191, 194-197, 199-202, 209, 211-213, 215-216, 220-222.
Gratton, Jefferson, 49.
Gray, Alford, 90.
Gregg, Jacob, 91.
Griffin, Ransom, 69, 140, 173, 179, 191, 205-207, 209, 216-217, 219-220, 222.
Griffith, Orlando, 182.
Groce, David, 209.
Groves, John, 91, 230.
Grubb, Wells, 90, 103.
Hall, Abel, 49.
Hall, Jacob, 90.
Hall, James, 77, 89.
Hall, John W., 90, 167.
Hall, Joseph, 91, 167.
Hall, William, 209.
Halleck, Maj. Gen. Henry W., 41, 52, 54, 64, 66, 74, 76, 110, 118-119, 128, 158, 168, 171.
Halliday, Samuel, 148, 182.

Halpine, Col. Charles, 76, 107.
Hamilton, Evander, 102, 230.
Hamilton, Israel, 148.
Hanning, D.J., 30.
Harbin, John, 230.
Hardesty, Oliver, 50.
Harman, Henry, 49, 102.
Harman, John, 89, 134, 138, 148.
Harris, Col. (C.S.) Nathaniel, 202, 204, 208.
Harris, Col. Thomas, 165-166, 171, 173, 178-179, 181, 191, 201, 204, 208.
Harrison, James, 91.
Hartley, James, 155, 209.
Hartley, John, 51.
Hatch, Nathan, 91.
Hathaway, Robert J., 27.
Hay, John, 148.
Hayden, Nathaniel, 89.
Hayes, Col. Rutherford B., 13, 120, 122, 151, 174.
Hayes, Samuel, 115-116.
Hazen, Maj. Gen. William, 31.
Headly, James, 90.
Heald, John, 90, 192.
Heck, Oswald, 45, 49, 230.
Henderson, Citizen, 50.
Hendry, Isaac, 230.
Henry, Otis, 210.
Henshaw, Edward, 91.
Henthorn, Andrew, 27.
Henthorn, Ephraim, 90.
Hetzer, Orville, 148.
Heuthorn, John, 194.
Hewett, Pardon, 182.
Hickman, Peter, 90.
Hill, Elza, 134, 230.
Hill, Hezekiah, 230.
Hitchcock, Myron, 209.
Hixenbaugh, H. B., 90.
Hogue, Stephen, 34, 63.

Holmes, Wendell, iv, 121.
Hooker, Maj. Gen. Joseph, 40, 56.
Howell, Levi, 210.
Hoydt, Uriah, 90.
Hoyt, Royal, 103, 230.
Hubbard, Daniel, 49, 102, 230.
Hudson, Dr. John, 5.
Hughes, James, 89.
Hull, John, 31,175.
Hull, Lucious, 51.
Hull, Samuel, 230.
Humphrey, Edgar, 113, 115-116.
Humphrey, Fred, 100, 103, 141, 209.
Humphrey, John, 51.
Humphrey, Morris, 51.
Hunnel, Thomas, 230.
Hunter, Maj. Gen. David, 74-78, 83, 85, 94-99, 102, 104-106-108, 110-111, 118-121, 125, 127-128, 144, 158.
Hunter, James, 115.
Hunter, William, 103.
Hurd, Daniel, 49, 90.
Hurd, Jacob, 50, 210.
Hutchinson, Robert, 50, 209
Hysell, Eben, 51.
Hysell, George, 51.
Hysell, Martin, 209.
Jackson, A.G., 134.
Jackson, Maj. Gen. Thomas J., 14, 18, 21, 23, 40, 62, 98.
James, Wesley, 91.
Jefferies, Abram, 230.
Jennings, Henry, 50.
Johnson, Armstrong, 210.
Johnson, Dr. James, 5, 18.
Johnson, George, 89, 91.
Johnson, Henry, 37, 145-146, 148.
Johnson, Joseph, 198, 230.
Jones, Amos, 33, 135.
Jones, Brig. Gen. William E., 22-29, 35, 78-79, 81, 83, 86-87.
Kalb, Abraham, 230.
Karr, Hamilton, 21, 31, 116, 166, 172-173, 179, 207.
Kershaw, Maj. Gen. Joseph B., 171-172, 174, 177, 214.
Kestner, George, 90.
Keyes, Edwin, 31, 76, 101-104, 141, 230.
Keyes, George, 90.
Keyler, Jacob, 89.
Keylor, Emanuel, 134.
Keyser, James, 210.
Keyser, Jesse, 49.
Keyser, John, 91.
Kibble, John, 210.
Kimpton, James, 89.
King, Edward, 34, 206, 210.
King, Henry, 33.
King, Samuel, 167.
King, Silas, 63, 113, 116, 133-135, 230.
King, William, 33, 89.
Kirkbride, Eli, 91.
Knowles, Richmond, 51, 196.
Koons, John, 51.
Krouse, Morris, 33, 89.
Kulow, John, 91.
Ladd, Asa, 27, 51.
Lafaver, (Lafavor), William E., 103, 117.
Lafevere, James, 49, 214.
Lamp, George, 115-116, 230.
Lang, John, 50.
Larrick, Benjamin, 138, 232.
Larrick, John, 91.
Latch, Charles, 50.
Latchaw, John, 50, 89.
Lee, Gen. Robert E., 1, 28, 34-

35, 40-42, 52, 57, 73, 96, 98-99, 121, 132, 139, 142, 144, 170, 186, 194-197, 199-200, 202, 208-213, 215-218, 220-222.
Lee, William J., 15, 19, 37, 50, 104, 134, 194.
Light, Mathias, 230.
Lincoln, Pres. Abraham, 1, 10, 34, 43, 52, 54, 66, 75-76, 94, 107, 110-111, 119-121, 125-127, 141, 148-149, 163, 184, 186, 199, 226.
Lindsay, James, 209.
Littleton, Isaac, 214.
Logan, James, 187, 217.
Longstreth, David, 210.
Lowry, Edward, 155, 210.
Lupton, Levi, 31, 45, 50, 59.
Luthey, Samuel, 27, 49.
Lyon, George, 91.
Mahl, Valentine, 210, 230.
Mahoney, John, 50.
Mahoney, Richard, 90, 231.
Mallory, Capt. Thornton, 31, 113, 116, 191.
Mann, Capt. James, 31, 46, 84, 86, 92, 198-199, 217.
Mann, David, 50.
Mann, Wilson, 50.
Manning, John, 49, 194.
Manning, Mike, 87, 136.
Marias, Mathew, 90.
Marsh, James, 50.
Martin, Henry, 33.
Martin, Jacob, 103.
Martin, John, 34.
Martin, Robert, 33, 91.
Martin, Wilson, 31-33, 92, 116, 128, 156, 192, 231.
Matchett, George W., 50, 134, 232.
Matheny, Isaiah, 27.

Mathews, E. J., 51.
Mathews, Henry C., 206, 210.
Mathews, Samuel, 51.
Mathias, Theodore, 49.
Matz, Jacob, 33.
McAfee, Mark, 91.
McBride, William, 91.
McCain, John, 231.
McCammon, Robert, 90.
McCausland, Brig. Gen. John, 97, 125.
McClellan, Maj. Gen. George, 1, 34, 141, 144, 184, 186.
McCollock, Samuel, 91.
McCollough, Moses, 90.
McConnell, Samuel, 214.
McCoy, Gilbert, 209, 231.
McCoy, Stephen, 51, 89.
McCulloch, Samuel, 49.
McDonald, George, 51.
McElroy, James, 115.
McElroy, John, 155.
McFarland, Alex, 91.
McFarland, William, 214.
McGee, Wesley, 91.
McHugh, Samuel, 49.
McIlwee, John, 148.
McKenzie, James, 231.
McKnight, Levi, 123.
McLane, Benjamin, 50, 210.
McLean, Wilmer, 220.
McMillan, William, 49, 231.
McNeal, Horace, 103.
McNeil, William, 148.
McNeill, Capt. (C.S.) J.H., 22, 32-33, 70.
McVeigh, Jerome, 134, 148.
Meade, Maj. Gen. George, 52-53, 57, 144, 200, 212.
Meek, Newton, 49, 89.
Meigs, Lt. John R., 158-159, 161.
Mercer, Joshua, 148.

Metz, William, 90.
Meyers, Adam, 92.
Mickel, Leonard, 49.
Mickle, Wisley, 51.
Miers, Lt., 8.
Miller, Christian, 134.
Miller, James, 103.
Miller, Madison, 90, 231.
Miller, Richard, 89.
Milroy, Maj. Gen. Robert, 14, 15, 16, 21, 28-29, 35, 38-39, 41-48, 52, 54-56, 64-65, 69, 201.
Miracle, Garrison, 89.
Mishack, Jacob, 148.
Mobberly, James, 90, 231.
Mobberly, William, 209, 231.
Moffett, Eldridge, 90.
Montgomery, John, 90.
Montgomery, William, 50, 148, 231.
Moor, Col. Augustus, 68, 70-71, 79-81, 83, 95.
Moore, David, 103.
Moore, Lafayette, 51.
Moore, Mathew, 148.
Moore, Michael, 51.
Morris, Andrew, 198, 232.
Morris, John, 33.
Morris, Maj. William T., 5, 7, 18, 43, 62, 135, 163.
Morris, Rep. James R., 2, 61, 163-164.
Morris, William, 134.
Morrison, Joseph, 49, 91.
Morrow, John, 50.
Mosley, William H., 116, 148, 194.
Mott, John, 91.
Mowder, Henry, 50, 90.
Mozena, Isaiah, 103.
Mozena, Lewis, 148, 209, 231.
Mozena, Milton, 148, 182.

Muhlenberg, Frank, 8.
Mulligan, Col. James, 7, 19, 26, 111, 121-122.
Myers, William, 31.
Neptune, Frederick, 89.
Newton, Emory, 51.
Nixon, Joshua, 90.
Norris, John, 148.
Norris, Josiah, 90.
Okey, Emanuel, 91, 225.
Okey, Gardener, 231.
Okey, Henry, 23, 26-27.
Oliver, James, 49.
Ollam, Adam, 27.
Ord, Maj. Gen. Edward, 195-201, 210, 212-213, 216, 218.
Paith, Joseph, 49.
Palmer, Charles, 90.
Parker, Sheldon, 49.
Parrish, Joseph, 51.
Parrott, William, 51, 182-183.
Patterson, Benjamin, 123-124.
Patterson, Sampson, 50, 231.
Patterson, William T., 135, 138, 142, 144, 149, 156, 159, 164, 226.
Patton, Elijah, 91.
Paugh, Fayette, 91.
Perkey, Joseph, 91.
Peterson, Thomas, 33, 91.
Pfiefer, Henry, 90.
Phelps, I., 148.
Phelps, Richard, 89.
Phelps, Royal, 167.
Piggot, James, 91.
Pitcock, Hiram, 51.
Powell, Andrew, 91, 155, 231.
Powell, Lemuel, 231.
Preshaw, James, 50, 90.
Price, Isaac, 50, 134.
Purkey, Joseph, 85, 194.
Putnam, Col., 6.
Railing, Solomon, 34.

Ray, George, 33, 210.
Reddin, Uriah, 214.
Rhimes, Christian, 155.
Rhmer, Christian, 50.
Rhodes, Elisha H., 3, 114.
Rich, Solomon, 91, 231.
Ridgeway, Benjamin, 50.
Ridgeway, C., 31.
Ring, Benjamin, 49.
Ring, Jacob, 49.
Risley, Reason, 51.
Robbins, Alexander, 50.
Robinette, William, 27, 51.
Rodecker, Adam, 90.
Rogers, Erwin, 231.
Rogers, James, 209.
Rose, Daniel, 50.
Rose, Frederick, 89.
Rowley, Thomas,
Rucker, Mathias, 33, 135.
Rufener, Samuel, 209, 231.
Rush, John, 167.
Russel, Isaac, 103.
Ruthmiller, (Reithmiller,) John, 103, 206, 209.
Rutter, William, 51.
Sammons, Benjamin, 135, 210.
Sampsell, Dr. James, 191.
Sampson, George, 50, 210.
Saxton, James, 115.
Schafer, Charles, 123.
Schappat, (Tschappat), John, 210.
Schoupe, Phillip, 90.
Schultz, Peter, 90.
Scott, William, 25, 49, 103.
Sears, D., 148.
Sechrist, Joseph, 155.
Secoy, Lewis, 148, 187.
Secoy, Matilda, 187.
Shafer, Hiram, 49.
Shafer, Hugh, 51.
Shafer, Solomon, 49.

Shahan, Leander, 34, 134.
Shannon, Dr. Thomas, 41, 143, 177, 182.
Shayhan, (Shahan) Abalard, 33.
Sheffield, Benjamin, 27.
Sheifley, Gottlieb, 80, 82, 84, 86, 91, 141.
Sheppard, Dave, 72-73.
Sheridan, Maj. Gen. Phillip H., 65, 118, 120, 125-127, 130 – 132, 136, 139, 142-144, 147-148, 150-151, 155, 157-164, 166, 168, 170-171, 177-181, 183-184, 186-187, 195, 199-200, 212, 215, 218, 220.
Sherman, Hopson, 49, 214.
Sherman, Maj. Gen. William T. 65-66, 120, 125, 157, 160, 186, 190, 194-195.
Shumway, Sylvester, 89, 231.
Sibley, Hiram, 18, 31, 39, 50-51, 192.
Sidders, Jacob, 134.
Sigel, Maj. Gen. Franz, 65-76, 79.
Sigler, George, 27, 148, 231.
Simmons, James, 50.
Simmons, Thomas, 34.
Sinclair, James, 90.
Skiles, Joseph, 90.
Smith, Dr. Thomas, 41, 50-51, 220.
Smith, James, 51.
Smith, John, (A) 89.
Smith, John, (E) 50, 198.
Smith, Joseph, 206, 210.
Smith, Mann, 49, 89.
Smith, Robert, 33, 89.
Smith, Samuel, 51, 231.
Smith, Simpson, 49.
Smith, Thomas, 155.
South, Thomas, 232.
Spear, Thomas, 91.

Spencer, Samuel, 91.
Sprague, Cyrus, 90.
Spriggs, Cyrus, 49.
Spriggs, William, 61.
Springer, James, 232.
Stanley, Rufus, 51, 91.
Starkey, Minor, 198.
Starr, Moses, 103.
Steed, Jonas, 33.
Steel, Samuel, 49, 232.
Steen, James, 33.
Stephens, (Stevens), Henry, 87.
Stephens, Frederick, 210.
Stephens, Samuel, 91.
Steuber, Lewis, 50.
Stevens, Andrew, 33.
Stewart, James, 148, 155, 183.
Stine, James, 90.
Stoneking, James A., 15, 232.
Stoneman, William, 115-116, 232.
Stout, James, 191-192, 206.
Straight, Alexander, 103, 182.
Straub, Reinhard, 50.
Strong, James, 198.
Sulsberger, Louis, 212, 224.
Summons, Joseph, 89.
Sutton, William, 33, 91, 232.
Swain, Jeremiah, 210.
Swartz, Francis, 89.
Swett, Isaac, 51.
Tacker, Walter, 103.
Tasker, George, 91.
Taylor, Enoch, 51.
Teters, Lt. Col. Wilbert B., 9, 17, 20, 21, 24, 86, 91, 153, 168, 175, 182, 190, 192, 210, 213, 217, 223-224.
Thoburn, Col. Joseph, 85, 112-115, 122, 124, 137, 151, 165-166, 177, 181, 183-184.
Thomas, Maj. Gen. George, 65, 125.

Thompson, Freeman, 12, 206-207-208, 232.
Thompson, Hugh, 50, 89.
Thoner, Martin, 134.
Thornberry, Riley, 90.
Tidd, Samuel, 49, 90.
Tiffany, Edmond, 50, 155-156.
Tillett, Edward, 49.
Tilton, Benjamin, 91,
Tisher, William, 91.
Tribby, Isaiah, 148.
Truax, John, 210.
Tschappat, Samuel, 87.
Tucker, George, 49.
Vallandigham, Clement, 60-61, 164.
Van Horn, Gilbert, 102.
Van Meter, (Matre) Joseph, 206-208, 232.
Van Vorhes, Col. Nelson, 10.
Varley, John, 31, 161.
Vickers, Albert, 90.
Vickers, Albin, 103.
Vickers, John, 103.
Walker, Ezra, 18, 37, 76-78, 104, 106-107, 121-124, 127-129, 132-133, 135, 157, 192.
Walter, Jacob, 50.
Walter, John, 27, 50.
Walters, John J., 214.
Walton, Jacob, 50.
Wannhas, Jacob, 51.
Warren, Alex, 103.
Warren, Frederick, 91,
Washburn, Col. James, 5, 7, 11, 13, 15, 16, 22-23, 26, 30-33, 35, 39, 47-48, 52, 62, 71, 81-82, 84, 87-89, 100, 112-113, 115, 117-118, 128, 184, 225-226.
Waterman, Charles, 51.
Watson, Charles, 50, 135.
Watson, Davis, 90.

115, 117-118, 128, 184, 225-226.
Waterman, Charles, 51.
Watson, Charles, 50, 135.
Watson, Davis, 90.
Watson, Nelson, 103.
Watson, Yoho, 148.
Way, George, 51.
Weakly, (Weekly) Aaron, 49, 182.
Webster, Gilbert, 105.
Webster, Orderly, 157.
Weddle, Daniel, 27, 148.
Welch, John, 49.
Welch, John F., 69, 98,
Wells, Col. George, 67, 95, 112, 122, 133-134, 145-147, 153-154, 165-166.
Wells, Robert, 30.
Wheaton, William, 50, 148.
White, Erastus, 198.
Whitlach, Eli, 210.
Whitman, James, 183.
Wildes, Lt. Col. Thomas F., iv, 3-6, 9-11, 13-18, 21-25, 28-33, 35-37, 40-42, 46-48, 51-58, 60-62, 64-65, 67-70, 72, 84-88, 92, 96-97, 99, 101-102, 104, 106-107, 109-110, 112-118, 122-125, 128-130, 134-138, 140, 142, 144-147, 152-154, 156-163, 166, 168, 172-183, 188-193, 199, 225-227, 232.
Wiley, Aurellius, 50.
Wiley, George, 167.
Wilkinson, John, 27.
Williams, A. W., 5.
Williams, Ephraim, 206, 208.
Williams, John, 148.
Williams, Reese, 84, 86, 91, 192.
Williamson, George, 49.

Wilson, Joseph C., 91, 232.
Wilson, James, 182.
Wilson, Richard, 33, 232.
Wilson, Robert, 15.
Wilson, Samuel, 33.
Winland, John, 90, 232.
Witham, Thomas, 91.
Wood, Ira, 51.
Worder, James, 49.
Wright, Maj. Gen. Horatio G., 110-111, 118-119, 121, 136, 151, 168, 174-175, 178, 181, 198, 200-202.
Yockey, Edward, 90.
Yoho, Isaac, 210.
Yoho, Peter, 33, 148.
Yoho, Ruben, 232.
Young, John, 103.
Zimmerly, Jacob, 49, 90, 232.
Zimmerly, Samuel, 49, 90.

ABOUT THE AUTHOR

Gerald L. Earley was born into a family with a strong Civil War heritage-three of his great-grandfathers served in the Federal Army during the Civil War. Motivated by the stories told by his grandmothers about their Civil War veteran fathers, he began studying the Civil War at an early age. He is a graduate of Wichita State University with a major in Political Science and a minor in History and is a veteran who served in the emergency evacuation of South Vietnam at the close of the Vietnam War.

www.ingramcontent.com/pod-product-compliance
Lightning Source LLC
Chambersburg PA
CBHW060110170426
43198CB00010B/832